T0357847

TOTAL DEFENSE

TOTAL DEFENSE

THE NEW DEAL AND THE INVENTION
OF NATIONAL SECURITY

ANDREW PRESTON

THE BELKNAP PRESS OF HARVARD UNIVERSITY PRESS

Cambridge, Massachusetts & London, England

2025

First printing

Library of Congress Cataloging-in-Publication Data

Names: Preston, Andrew, 1973– author.
Title: Total defense : the New Deal and the invention of national security / Andrew Preston.
Description: Cambridge, Massachusetts : The Belknap Press
of Harvard University Press, 2025. | Includes bibliographical references and index.
Identifiers: LCCN 2024042060 (print) | LCCN 2024042061 (ebook) |
ISBN 9780674737389 (cloth) | ISBN 9780674300484 (pdf) |
ISBN 9780674300491 (epub)
Subjects: LCSH: National security—United States—History—20th century. |
New Deal, 1933–1939. | Cold War. | United States—Politics and
government—1945–1953. | United States—Military policy.
Classification: LCC E806 .P764 2025 (print) | LCC E806 (ebook) |
DDC 973.917—dc23/eng/20241029
LC record available at https://lccn.loc.gov/2024042060
LC ebook record available at https://lccn.loc.gov/2024042061

To John: scholar, mentor, friend

CONTENTS

TOTAL DEFENSE

INTRODUCTION

OVER THE PAST CENTURY, one of the great transformations in world history has been the emergence of the United States as a world power. Economically, politically, militarily, or culturally, few places on earth have remained untouched by the extension of American influence. Since at least World War II, moreover, the United States has transformed the international system itself. To be sure, since its inception as an independent nation-state in the late eighteenth century, it had interacted with countries all around the world. But those interactions became deeper, less sporadic, and more systemic from the early twentieth century. Since then, the nation has operated decisively, often definitively, in virtually every facet of global affairs. For better or worse, this development has been transformational not just for the United States, but for the entire world.

The emergence of the United States as a world power in the first half of the twentieth century triggered an equally revolutionary change in American strategic thought: the invention of "national security." Under this new concept, the basic idea of national defense shifted radically, from a narrow definition of territorial self-defense to a much more expansive one based on a heightened awareness that distant threats could eventually harm the basic safety of the United States in a variety of ways, ideologically and economically as well as physically. As this book illustrates, before World War II Americans thought of national defense as the protection of their borders and the territory within them from direct physical attack. This was not unusual: it was how other countries viewed national defense, and it's how international law recognized the only legal use of state violence, in the right to repel a direct attack as a matter of national self-defense. The new doctrine of national security changed all that.

This fundamental change in US strategic thought was a product of the modern world. In the late nineteenth and early twentieth centuries, breathtaking advances in communications and transportation and a sharp rise in transnational trade and migration ushered in the first era of globalization. The resultant sense of interconnectedness led American leaders to believe that US security had become tied to developments beyond the traditional confines of the North American continent, beyond even the western hemisphere. As a result, pushed by President Franklin Roosevelt and the internationalists who supported him, from the late 1930s Americans began to envision national defense as the protection of their general place in the world—and ultimately their way of life—from any plausible threat, no matter how theoretically remote or geographically distant. Security became ideological as well as territorial, normative as well as physical, global and not just continental. It became, as it still is today, all-encompassing.

The changes to the modern condition that produced global interdependence also fostered the rise of domestic social insurance programs and the welfare state. Just as unprecedented technological innovations added to the complexity of international relations, so did they accelerate the pace of industrial relations and intensify the complexity of social life at home. In late nineteenth-century America, the spread of a wide range of socioeconomic problems stimulated the rise of the progressive movement and soon prompted the federal government to begin regulating the economy and controlling social conditions. These efforts, while novel for their time, remained limited until the implementation of Franklin Roosevelt's liberal New Deal programs in the 1930s. Reaching its apogee in the Social Security Act of 1935, the New Deal forged a new social contract between the federal government and the American people. Socioeconomic security, historians have shown, was not only the New Deal's overriding concern but also its signature political and policy innovation.[1]

Previously in American political culture, liberalism sought the protection of individual rights against the encroachments of the state. But in the decades before the New Deal, the unprecedented challenges of global interdependence and the power of industry posed new and more complex challenges to individual rights. Liberalism thus had to be recalibrated, now with the state as the guarantor of individual rights—indeed, as the only institution large and powerful enough to protect the individual from the forces of technology, capital, industry, and global interdependence. Through politics and policy, Roosevelt and the New Deal were in the vanguard of this recalibration of liberalism.[2]

It was no coincidence that the invention of national security closely followed the creation of social security; as Chapter 4 demonstrates, the causal arrow flowed very much from the welfare state to the warfare state.[3] The modern condition offered people countless rewards: vast riches, labor-saving devices, easy transcontinental and even transoceanic travel, and effective medicine. But it also threw people into the depths of new perils: mass urban poverty, social dislocation, totalitarian ideologies, and mechanized warfare. The modern condition thus created opportunities, but at the cost of social stability. In other words, modernity amplified the problem of insecurity. But the new social contract of the New Deal seemed to stop the economic crisis of the Depression from spiraling out of control and, in the process, save American democracy itself. And when a new world crisis escalated in 1936–1937, posing unprecedented and bewildering challenges to the United States in the world, Roosevelt expanded the social democratic contract to include government protections against possible international threats. This expansion of the government's protective role created a holistic, indivisible program that Roosevelt often referred to as "total defense." By definition, this was not a limited program: "partial defense is inadequate defense. If the United States is to have any defense, it must have total defense. . . . Our plans for national security, therefore, should cover total defense."[4] In so doing, he broadened the basis of national defense beyond all recognition, so much so that the very phrase "national security" meant something different in 1937 than it had only a few years before.

Since then, it's been difficult to think of American national defense in any other way. The phrase "national security" is flexible enough to include almost any manner of international relations, including many that may seem mostly domestic in origin, but is precise enough to convey meanings of safety and defense. Protecting the national security means protecting all aspects of the nation against all manner of threats, however loosely defined. And it can be defined very loosely indeed. "What does national security cover?" asked John M. Deutch, formerly Bill Clinton's director of central intelligence and deputy secretary of defense. His answer was maddeningly vague in terms of theory yet uncannily accurate in terms of actual practice: "a good definition of national security covers all affairs that affect men and women and all affairs that affect international and domestic issues."[5] Deutch's imprecision isn't all that different from how Lyndon Johnson described the 1964 Gulf of Tonkin Resolution, a nebulous national security document that committed America to a disastrous national security war in Vietnam: the resolution, LBJ boasted, was like "grandma's nightshirt—it covered everything."[6]

―――――

SCHOLARS HAVE BEEN more precise. In the late 1930s and early 1940s, various academics and writers, most notably political scientist Edward Mead Earle and journalist Walter Lippmann, attempted to define the new term, as we'll see in Chapters 4 and 5. Their most important innovation was to define national security in ways capacious enough to include protection of the nation's cultural values, ideals, and norms alongside protection from physical attack and invasion, thus making everything both a means and an end of defense. In the decades after World War II, others would go on to endow the term with greater rigor, but without moving much beyond the meaning of these original definitions laid down during the war.

Strangely, the federal government itself never explained what it meant by "national security," and none of the canonical American texts of the early Cold War—the Truman Doctrine, the National Security Act, NSC-68—actually defined the term. That task fell mainly to intellectuals who came after Earle and Lippmann. "Discussions about semantics are singularly futile things which I would prefer to avoid," Earle tartly noted, and after his exertions during World War II he left the codification of terminology to others. His only later attempt to come up with a definition for national security, in 1950—"This must not be defined in crudely military or strategic [terms], although there is, of course a military factor. . . . The security goal is much more far-reaching and much more subtle in character. It is in fact a compound of all the other factors involved"—remained in rough draft and was never published. And in any event, it didn't advance much beyond his wartime formulations.[7]

After Earle and Lippmann, whose writings were wartime political acts meant to justify US intervention against the Axis powers, the first to codify national security in an ostensibly neutral sense were political scientists Harold Lasswell, Arnold Wolfers, and Robert E. Osgood in the early 1950s, and they all converged on the principles that threats to American security were distant and remote, social and ideological, and not necessarily territorial or physical. For Lasswell, whom we will encounter at several points in this book, the "distinctive meaning of national security is *freedom from foreign dictation*. National security policy implies a state of readiness to use force if necessary to maintain national independence."[8] The "quest for security," Wolfers wrote in 1951, "points beyond mere maintenance and defense."[9] Exactly what "national security" pointed to, he argued elsewhere, was "ambiguous" because it was determined by culture, politics, and changing context. Nonetheless, its essential meaning was clear enough. At a minimum, ensuring national security meant protection from "external dangers" and "external violence," but it was more than that: it was "normative in character," with its aim "to protect and preserve . . . the minimum national core values, national independence and territorial integrity."[10] This holy trinity of ideology, sovereignty, and physical safety defined the parameters of American national security. If the United States could engage freely with the rest of the world on terms that didn't encroach upon the holy trinity, then the nation was considered secure. Osgood agreed that the benchmarks for "national survival" were the preservation of "territorial integrity, political independence, and fundamental government institutions," but there was an even higher plane than this. "National security," he argued in 1953, "is a related but broader end, since it embraces not only survival but the nation's ability to survive."[11] A dozen years later, political scientists Morton Berkowitz and P. G. Bock emphasized ideological factors almost to the exclusion of territory. "National security," they wrote in their influential 1965 textbook, "can be most fruitfully defined as *the ability of a nation to protect its internal values from external threats*."[12]

A more recent analyst of national security is historian Melvyn Leffler. For Leffler, too, American national security is extra-territorial, defined by its protection of a way of life in the modern world "more than defending territory."[13] National security, he writes in a classic essay, is "defined as the protection of core values from external threats. . . . Certainly, it involves more than national survival." As a term, "core values" can be as ambiguous as "national security" itself, but Leffler is specific: "core values are the objectives that merge ideological precepts and cultural symbols such as democracy, self-determination, honor, and race consciousness with concrete interests such as access to markets and raw materials." They are "the goals worth fighting for," because they are what keep Americans secure in an interdependent world.[14] In 1992, around the time Leffler was developing his theory of national security, political scientists similarly defined it as "preserving the United States as a free nation with

5

its fundamental institutions and values intact."[15] Dwight Eisenhower, who not only thought about the meaning of national security but also practiced it, put it more vividly, if less rigorously: "Spiritual force, multiplied by economic force, multiplied by military force, is roughly equal to security. If one of these factors falls to zero, or near zero, the resulting product does likewise."[16] Methodologically, Leffler concludes, by "integrating core values, power, and foreign threats, the national security approach forces historians to study geopolitical and strategic issues in relation to political economy, ideology, and culture."[17]

This book, by contrast, makes no attempt to provide a theory of national security. Instead of defining the term, I trace how others have defined it in the past, how some of those definitions became the basis of policy, and how national security came to have its current meaning. And it's that broader meaning that's important. "National security" is just a signifier of a much broader worldview—political, cultural, economic, strategic—and this book charts the evolution of that broader worldview through the usage of a particular term. It follows Quentin Skinner's advice that "when a word changes its meaning" we must be prepared to examine not only the word (or phrase) itself but, more importantly, its "role in upholding complete social philosophies."[18] In the case of national security, it's not that a catchy new term emerged in the 1930s to describe existing policies of national defense; rather, the new term emerged at that moment because Americans needed one to describe a totally new way of thinking about national defense. The shift was radical, not just nominally but conceptually, as well.

To be sure, the phrase "national security" matters, not least because of its emotive, ideological, and political power, and this book pays a great deal of attention to it. Put together, those two simple words pack an incredible punch. In exploring the sources of that power, this book emulates other interesting histories of "keywords" that have not only described or defined but actually shaped political culture and international relations. These accounts trace how the meanings of important words and phrases have changed substantially over time, and especially drastically at certain historical moments, and this book takes a similar approach. It is therefore not just an intellectual policy history of American national security, but a critical genealogy of American national defense and threat perception.[19]

The broader definition of national defense known as national security coalesced politically and ideationally in the years of 1937 to 1942 and has been normalized ever since. Because it was a cultural construct from the outset, national security was politicized from birth. My approach here owes much to the international relations theories of securitization positing that security is not objective or natural but socially and culturally constructed by "discourses of security." What matter aren't just "struggles over security among *nations,* but also struggles over security among *notions.*"[20] But national security was also a political construct, highly contingent on the currents of domestic politics within the United States. My approach also owes much to the "intermestic" interpretation in diplomatic history, in which domestic politics does much to shape America's international relations (and vice versa).[21]

Countless scholars have written countless books and articles on particular aspects of US national security policy and strategy, but critical analysis of the concept itself is rare. Thus the Wolfers, Osgood, and Leffler definitions are important to how we think about the nature of threat perception before we begin to evaluate the policy responses to those threats. Yet, while their definitions are indispensable, it's important to note that they're not timeless. The definitions are themselves products of their particular time, both in terms of the period in which they were written and the period they examined—namely, the early Cold War.[22]

This Cold War time stamp is found on other typologies of national security that have proliferated since Lasswell, Wolfers, and Osgood first published their programmatic work in the early 1950s. But, almost always without realizing or recognizing it, such self-referential, self-reinforcing definitions unwittingly describe, and as a result naturalize, what national security came to mean in the era of World War II and the early Cold War and has meant ever since.[23] Wolfers assumed that "We know roughly what people have in mind if they complain that their government is neglecting national security or demanding excessive sacrifices for the sake of enhancing it," and while that was true when he wrote those words in 1952, and while it remains true today, it wouldn't have been true before the late 1930s.[24] Before then, "national defense" was construed very narrowly; the very term "national security" was used infrequently, and when it was, it often did not refer to the defense of the United States and its way of life against global and ideological threats.[25] On one hand, then, accounts that portray a national security tradition stretching back to the founding of the republic are clearly anachronistic.[26] On the other, accounts that locate the origins of American national security in the early Cold War, perhaps even with the passage of the National Security Act in 1947, are right to historicize it but are late by about ten years.[27]

What does a decade matter—especially if the meaning of national security established between 1937 and 1942 changed little through the Cold War and beyond? A lot, it turns out. While historically small, especially when considering the grand sweep of over 250 years of US diplomatic history, that ten-year difference has largely concealed the social-welfare origins of national security. A small group of historians, including most notably Daniel Yergin and John A. Thompson, have historicized national security as an invention of the years before US intervention in World War II, and this book builds on their important work.[28] Yet they too neglect the causal influence of New Deal liberalism.[29] Other historians have done a thorough job tracing a lineage from warfare to welfare; this book, by contrast, draws a line from welfare to warfare.[30] Locating the sources of national security as a coherent doctrine of strategic thought in the era of the New Deal and the world crisis of the late 1930s reveals its surprising origins in welfare liberalism rather than in reactionary anti-communism or conservatism. It allows us, for example, to resolve the apparent paradox that a liberal Democrat, Harry Truman, established the national security state and a Republican, Dwight Eisenhower, was the one to lament it.

This time stamp is one of the ways in which "national security" differs from "the national interest," a parallel and sometimes overlapping but distinct term that was ultimately supplanted by it. By contrast, the national interest was, and still is, timeless, in that American leaders have invoked it in the same fashion since the late eighteenth century, even if the particular national interest at any given time changed with context and circumstance. When it first became common parlance to speak of "national security" in the late 1930s, the phrase served as an expansive alternative to narrower references to the national interest. This is almost certainly why Roosevelt and other internationalists turned to the more alarming word "security" instead of the more deliberative "interest": it was debatable whether it was in the national interest to resist Nazi Germany, but the debate was over when Roosevelt convinced Americans that resisting the Germans was a matter of basic safety. He referred to the war virtually never as a matter of national interest, but often as a matter of national security.

The understanding of the national interest was narrower, more in keeping with the American diplomatic tradition, and aligned with traditional security imperatives for protecting territorial sovereignty.[31] For this reason, it was favored by advocates of restraint. In 1934, Charles Beard called the national interest "the supreme, ultimate motive," contrasting it with the lesser economic and material interests that often deflected policymakers from pursuing the true "public interest" or "general welfare" of the nation and its people.[32] Just over a decade later, Hans Morgenthau, one of the founders of the Realist school of international relations theory, portrayed moral values and the national interest as polar opposites: one bore a sentimentality that Americans were supposedly fond of but that only clouded their judgment and led them astray in pointless foreign crusades; the other offered a clear-eyed view of what Americans should truly prioritize, maximizing power in an anarchical world.[33] Later scholars emulated Beard in perceiving the national interest as inherently economic in nature.[34] Historian H. W. Brands has provided perhaps the most commonsensical definition: the national interest is "a conception of an overriding common good transcending the specific interests of parties, factions, and other entities smaller than the nation as a whole."[35]

The basic difference between *interest* and *security* is one of necessity. At the heart of any prognosis of national security is the protection of the United States from harm. The national interest seeks something more discretionary: an advantageous position, improvements in conditions that facilitate basic security, a greater level of prosperity, or the promotion of values and norms. The national interest highlights what Americans *want* to do; national security mandates what they *must* do. National security is about survival and is therefore nonnegotiable, for without survival there is no national interest to pursue.[36] In the eyes of its early theorists, this made national security "a far less subjective concept than the national interest."[37] As a result, over the course of the Cold War and through the "war on terror," national security overtook the national interest by absorbing most of its concerns and including them within the requirements of defense. "The term 'national interest,'" one observer noted in 1979, "has almost completely dropped out of the vocabulary of students of international politics."[38]

––––––

IF NOTHING ELSE, perceptions of insecurity are grounded in, and conditioned by, fear.[39] When Roosevelt surveyed the United States in 1938, he saw a nation "perplexed by doubt and fear and uncertainty," and he believed that his main role was to lessen those anxieties through the power and legitimacy of the federal government.[40] To be insecure is to be afraid, and usually when people are afraid it is due to their uncertainties about the future, so the main goal of any pursuit of security is to reduce uncertainty and fear. A history of national security will therefore also be a history of fear, as this book certainly is.

But any history of American fears of the external world must rest on a contradiction. When the United States was a minor actor on the world stage, its fears were almost entirely internal—of slave rebellions, of racial impurity, of moral deviance, of religious nonconformity; for African Americans, Indigenous Americans, and many immigrant and religious groups, fear conditioned much of their daily existence. But as the United States became more powerful, eventually the most powerful state in the international system, its fears of the outside world actually increased, even as its internal fears showed little sign of dissipating. With great power, it seems, comes great fear.[41] Empires throughout history have strengthened their sense of security by expanding their territory, interests, and reach, but the opposite was true for the twentieth-century United States.[42] This was largely due to the rise of one of the main sources of fear: uncertainty. Before World War II and the Cold War, as Chapter 1 demonstrates, Americans were more certain of their place in the world, and especially of their security from external attack. Americans benefited from "the tremendous good fortune that surrounds their international position," Calvin Coolidge said in surveying the state of the nation in 1926. "We fear no one; no one fears us."[43] But that would cease to be the case only a decade after Coolidge left office.

Once again, the presidency of Franklin Roosevelt marked the critical disjuncture. Despite his sunny confidence and optimism, Roosevelt's most powerful political weapon was fear, which he skillfully wielded even as he promised the American people that they would overcome their fears together. He soothed anxieties in one moment, aggravated them in another.[44] Judith Shklar famously pointed to "the liberalism of fear" as the political philosophy best suited to eliminating cruelty and other forms of punitive, arbitrary punishment. In seeking to quell their fears of cruelty and violence, people would rally to the liberal state as the only entity designed to protect the rights of the individual—after all, the motivational power of fear is one of the oldest principles of politics.[45] And although Shklar didn't explicitly mention "security" as the ultimate goal of the liberalism of fear, in essence she argued that personal security, from cruelty as well as from the encroachments of the state, was liberalism's proper objective.[46] Roosevelt's approach to national security enabled the rise of what Brett Gary rightly calls "national security liberalism," which by straddling the seeming divide between security and liberty managed to connect the individualist, reformist, and rights-based strands of the liberal tradition.[47] Where Shklar highlighted a liberalism of fear, Roosevelt practiced what could be termed a liberalism of war. The New Deal's reconfiguration of risk in matters of political economy, and revelations of how to turn unknowable uncertainty into knowable calculations of manageable risk, had important, applicable lessons for foreign and defense policy.

Yet this leads to a further paradox: because the continental United States was realistically immune to physical attack and invasion—a very real threat faced by all other major powers of the time—Roosevelt and other internationalists had to stoke fears about America's place in the world. Anthropologist Mary Douglas once noted that carefully scientific calculations of risk are "transformed" into something more emotive, and therefore pliably potent, when they enter the political realm.[48] Roosevelt, with his acute political intuition, knew this full well. He had to exaggerate American vulnerability, as Thompson memorably puts it, to convince Americans that their nation must intervene in the world crisis.[49] Roosevelt raised risks for the United States by elevating uncertainty, and the doctrine of national security was born from this exaggeration of vulnerability through the elevation of uncertainty. He thus embraced a kind of liberalism of fear even if it wasn't at all well-suited to a politics of progressivism; the liberalism of fear is reactive, not progressive, which made it perfectly suited to national security but not at all suited to social security.[50] Roosevelt was renowned for his internal contradictions and hypocrisies, the artful management of which made him one of the most successful politicians in American history.[51] But this was one contradiction that even he couldn't master, and the end result, only just beginning to emerge when he died, was that national security eclipsed social security. Just as we should locate the origins of the national security state in the late 1930s and early 1940s, we should also locate the origins of what would come to be called Cold War liberalism in the era of the New Deal.[52]

Security, of course, is a topic hardly exclusive to America, and nor is it exclusively a product of modernity. Sociologist Charles Tilly once referred to the state as a "protection racket," and while Hobbes, Locke, and Jefferson might well have raised an eyebrow at the social contract's being compared to organized crime, they would surely have recognized the basic principle: the state provides a basic level of internal and external security and, in return, citizens give their allegiance. Tilly had the formation of the modern state in mind, but James C. Scott has adopted the concept and taken it back several millennia, to the formation of the earliest states.[53] Lauren Benton and other scholars have extended its application to territorial empires, which could provide security—as well as opportunity—to those who bow to their dominion.[54] This dynamic was certainly true for the formation of the United States itself in the eighteenth century.[55] But there was something unusual about the modern American case, and not just because it caused the now-ubiquitous term "national security" to be coined. In the societies Tilly and Benton study, security and protection were immediate concerns, and it's telling that Scott sees state formation as a defense against raiders looking to plunder food. Virtually worldwide, people have had to face the constant probability of physical violence imposed from the outside in ways the modern United States has almost never experienced. "For one thing is quite certain," advised Frederick William, the ruler (or "Great Elector") of Brandenburg: "if You simply sit still, in the belief that the fire is still far from Your borders: then Your lands will become the theatre on which the tragedy is played out."[56] This was eminently sensible for a ruler of a German state located in tightly packed, perennially violent, and constantly competitive seventeenth-century Europe. It made less sense for the twentieth-century United States, until American leaders also turned to the metaphor of fire as they crafted a new doctrine that altered the strategic calculus and geopolitical landscape from continental and regional to global.

A last word about this book's objective, and the methods it uses to fulfill it. It does not set out to provide a detailed history of US foreign and military policies; instead, it selects only certain of these policies for close examination, guided by a motive to uncover the deeper undercurrents of the ideas that shaped policy. Nor does it assess the validity or success of specific policies; it investigates the source of the threat perception behind military policies, as well as changes to these perceptions over time. Much of the evidence, however, does come from military policy: one of the best ways to measure the rise and fall of external fear, uncertainty, and risk is to measure the rise and fall of military personnel and expenditures, because they are likely an accurate barometer of American fears of the outside world. And as its focus on warfare indicates, this book examines security in its most elemental sense: the basic safety of the nation in the world. In this analysis, other types of security—economic, cultural, and so forth—are important but subordinate to military security. Yet, as this book demonstrates, these other types of security became as integral to national security as military defense from attack and invasion. By World War II and the early Cold War—but not before—all types of security had become inseparable and indivisible.

Finally, because my main target is a general idea of security, based on changing perceptions of threat, uncertainty, risk, fear, and the role of the state in addressing them, I turn primarily to the sources of that idea: the people who thought about it and shaped the national response to it. As a result, the book's cast of historical characters is eclectic, including not only politicians and policymakers but also the producers of culture, from historians, political scientists, and economists to activists, writers, painters, and (especially) filmmakers—and in particular, those who had a foot in both camps, policymaking and cultural. Many of these characters appear recurrently in these pages, making their entrances and exits in various arguments about the nature of American security and insecurity in a constantly changing international environment. But because national security was, from the very outset, an elite-driven project rather than a popular cause, I also pay extensive attention to what elites said and did.

In essence, this book aims to find the source of the idea, now axiomatic, that the security of the United States often had little to do with the immediate safety of the continental United States itself. In making the case for going to war in Europe in January 1918, Theodore Roosevelt set forth a novel idea that is now as basic a truism in American political culture as any: if we don't fight them there, we'll have to fight them here. "And never forget that this fight is primarily America's fight," he declared. "Our troops fight abroad beside the Allies now so that at some future time they may not have to fight without allies beside their own ruined homes."[57] Once unthinkable, his justification for intervention overseas is now boilerplate. The easy, technologically deterministic explanation is that the growth of global interdependence started Theodore Roosevelt's logic chain. But there was much more to it than that, and the process was much more contingent. The surprising story of how and why it happened is the subject of this book.

[1]

THE BLESSINGS OF FREE SECURITY

ON HIS 1831 tour of the United States, Alexis de Tocqueville identified a wide variety of features of American public life. Democracy, of course, was the most important. Religion and voluntarism were unusually prevalent in American society, and both helped give shape to a peculiarly populist strain of democratic politics, but republicanism remained influential as well. Yet Tocqueville also singled out an enormously powerful structural condition, "a peculiar and accidental situation in which Providence has placed the Americans," that has been mostly overlooked ever since. "The Americans have no neighbors and consequently no great wars, financial crises, invasions, or conquests to fear," he noted; "they need neither heavy taxes nor a numerous army nor great generals; they have also hardly anything to fear from something else which is a greater scourge for democratic republics than all these others put together, namely, military glory."[1]

Tocqueville was on to something. Though he did not use the term, he had identified a geopolitical condition that was later called "free security." The concept itself is straightforward: due to geographical good fortune, the United States faced no major external threats. From the end of the War of 1812 until the Japanese attack on Pearl Harbor, no single power was strong enough to threaten the country, and no combination of hostile powers formed that could do so, either. With vast oceans insulating the continent and only weak neighbors to the north and south, Americans remained free not simply from invasion, but from even a plausible threat of invasion. Only the British had the potential to do some harm, and they were, for the most part, sympathetic to American dominance in the western hemisphere, especially after the Civil War. There are some limitations to the concept of free security, discussed below, but for most of the nineteenth century and well into the twentieth, Americans could generally take for granted their nation's safety in the world.[2]

The geopolitical freedom the United States enjoyed between 1815 and 1941 was unprecedented in modern world history. For centuries, no other state, let alone an emerging great power whose ambitions threatened to unsettle the international status quo, had been able to take its security almost entirely for granted. "A half-century ago," George F. Kennan marveled in 1951, "people in this country had a sense of security vis-à-vis their world environment such as I suppose no people had ever had since the days of the Roman Empire."[3] For most other states, even the greatest of great powers, foreign policy was determined to some extent by what other states were doing. The foreign policy of the most powerful state in the international system, Great Britain, was made not only in London, but also in Paris, Berlin, Moscow, and other world capitals. For many states that were less powerful, foreign policy was made entirely elsewhere; Poland's, for example, was completely conditioned by what Berlin and Moscow were planning. Foreign policy was thus an aspect of national defense, even national survival. But US foreign policy was made entirely in Washington because American officials did not have to worry about their vulnerability to invasion or attack. This meant that American policymakers had unusual freedom in crafting foreign policy: thanks to free security, fear was almost entirely absent from their considerations, or indeed from American thinking about the wider world. The United States had a foreign policy, of course—every nation does—but it was one of almost total choice rather than necessity.

Neglected by historians, free security in fact possesses tremendous potential to explain the history of the United States in the world. It can help us understand, for instance, why domestic politics played an inordinate role in the crafting of US foreign policy. As free security lessened fear and necessity from American considerations of the wider world, it created space for other factors—cultural, spiritual, ideological, economic, political—to apply pressure and carry influence.[4] Indeed, if US foreign policy was made in cities other than Washington, they were not London and Moscow, but New York, Boston, New Orleans, Chicago, and San Francisco. By allowing for a small defense budget and freeing Americans from the fear of attack and invasion, free security also provided space for what Samuel Huntington once called the "business pacifism" that created the unmatched industrial boom between the Civil War and World War I.[5] Carl Schurz, once a German revolutionary and later a US senator and thus someone with an intuition for comparison, believed that the uniquely small US fiscal-military state enabled by free security was in fact the very basis of national development. Americans "have over all the great nations of the world one advantage of incalculable value," he said in 1893. "We are the only ones not under any necessity of keeping up a large armament either on land or water for the security of its possessions, the only one that can turn all the energies of its population to productive employment, and the only one that has an entirely free hand."[6] Free security also helps explain why Americans could heed warnings by George Washington and Thomas Jefferson to avoid permanent and entangling alliances: they simply didn't need any, and it's no coincidence that a new era of multilateralism dawned when free security disappeared with the coming of World War II and the onset of the Cold War. Free security made Americans more than simply dominant on the North American continent. It made them masters of their own fate.

———

FROM THE MOMENT of its inception, however, the new nation struggled to master its own domestic integrity, let alone its fate in an anarchic international environment. In its first decades, the United States could hardly take its security for granted. Threats from European empires and Indigenous nations—real, potential, and imagined—abounded from all directions. Not only was free security a fantasy in the early republic, the nation faced a constant struggle simply to survive with its sovereignty and territory intact, not least from countless threats of disunion from within. The new American states were jealous of their autonomy and the national government had to face down perpetual secessionist plots in its early decades.[7] There were, Alexander Hamilton observed (echoing the text of the new constitution), two unceasing security threats to national existence: "insurrection or invasion."[8]

Insecurity was thus the new nation's greatest vulnerability. The authors of the *Federalist Papers* recognized the severity of the problem and spent a good deal of their efforts theorizing ways to address the chronic "Dangers from Foreign Force and Influence" to the immediate "SAFETY of the people," as John Jay put it in *Federalist* 3, that threatened to destabilize their project. Such "Dangers" emanated not from remote, anti-republican ideologies in distant lands, but from European intrigue on the Mississippi and the Saint Lawrence.[9] National defense thus meant the actual self-defense of US borders and territorial claims.

At this early stage, geography was not an advantage but a weakness. "Though a wide ocean separates the United States from Europe," Hamilton argued in *Federalist* 24, "there are various considerations that warn us against an excess of confidence or security. On one side of us and stretching far into our rear are growing settlements subject to the dominion of Britain. On the other side and extending to meet the British settlements are colonies and establishments subject to the dominion of Spain." Hamilton's analysis of Indigenous peoples was brutally candid: "The savage tribes on our Western frontier ought to be regarded as our natural enemies [and the Europeans'] natural allies; because they have most to fear from us and most to hope from them." Showing a prescience about the dynamics of what would later be called globalization, Hamilton explained why Americans couldn't take for granted the safety of their remoteness. "The improvements in the art of navigation have, as to the facility of communication, rendered distant nations in a great measure neighbours."[10] In a follow-up, he made the point even clearer: "The territories of Britain, Spain and of the Indian nations in our neighbourhood, do not border on particular States; but incircle the Union from MAINE to GEORGIA."[11] National security—a phrase used only twice in the *Federalist Papers*—thus meant something very particular to the founding generation, akin to national self-defense against direct, physical attacks. According to James Madison, the national government's most important task was to provide "security against foreign danger" in the most literal meaning.[12]

In such a dangerously anarchic world, Jay, Hamilton, and Madison made the case that only a national union—a strong union, with a strong military—could provide Americans with adequate security. The unheeded warning Benjamin Franklin had issued to the colonies in 1754—"Join, or Die"—was even more urgent now that the United States no longer had royal protection but was actually Britain's adversary.[13] But perhaps the European powers were the least of the Americans' concerns, for disunion would mean anarchy among the many newly independent states, which would lead in turn to competition and inevitably to war.[14] Madison made the case with unusual bravado: "America, united with a handful of troops, or without a single soldier, exhibits a more forbidding posture to foreign ambition, than America disunited, with an hundred thousand veterans ready for combat."[15]

Yet, Madison's rhetorical flourish aside, if the United States was to be a properly functioning nation, the need for a proper national army and navy that could repel a foreign invasion was urgent. The catch, Madison acknowledged in *Federalist* 41, was the deep-seated fear that a standing army was a threat to republican liberty. But with real threats massing on the borders of the United States, the fear of a theoretical risk from within struck him as perversely self-defeating. Was the raising of an army a price worth paying? "The answer," Madison replied to his own rhetorical question, "seems to be so obvious and conclusive as scarcely to justify such a discussion in any place," because it was simply "in vain to oppose constitutional barriers to the impulse of self-preservation." Whether the United States would have to fight wars was out of Americans' hands and instead dependent on the actions of other nations, European or Indigenous. Under such conditions, it would be suicidal not to raise sufficient national armed forces. "A standing force therefore is a dangerous, at the same time that it may be a necessary provision." And in any event, the new plan for a government under the new federal Constitution would act as the ultimate safeguard: "The Union itself . . . destroys every pretext for a military establishment which could be dangerous."[16] Hamilton, unsurprisingly, pressed this argument even further than Madison. He called for permanent readiness for war—and thus for a strong standing army—on the grounds that it "contains in it nothing offensive" but was instead "a mere precaution for self defence."[17] This logic naturally also drew him to endow the president with strong commander-in-chief powers, as the president could react more quickly than Congress or the states to sudden threats to the nation. "In the conduct of war," he wrote in a strikingly modern tone, "the energy of the executive is the bulwark of the national security."[18]

Of perceived foreign dangers, the revolution in the French colony of Saint-Domingue (Haiti) stands out as an important threshold in the prehistory of "national security." The Haitian Revolution was the largest and most successful slave rebellion in modern history, and whites in the US South feared that revolution would spread across the sea to their own enslaved population. This was, as we shall see, similar to how Americans constructed later fears of an external adversary (whether alleged Russian-Jewish Bolsheviks, Japanese saboteurs, or Muslim terrorists) that sought to export a fifth column to attack the United States from within. There to help speed the revolt of the enslaved were the British and Spanish, who had been encouraging anti-US resistance since the American Revolution.[19] With the Haitians leading by example and inspiration, said one Kentucky politician, "I fear our slaves in the south will produce another St. Domingo."[20] The most direct way for this to happen, Southern whites reasoned, would be through US plantations continuing to import enslaved labor, especially from Saint-Domingue but also from elsewhere in the Caribbean. Aroused with the spirit of freedom and "their hands still reddened with the blood" of the French, declared a petition from New Orleans, the enslaved "are arriving daily in great number in our midst," and "perhaps tomorrow their smoking torches will be lighted again to set fire to our peaceful homes."[21] The short-term solution to this particular source of insecurity was to close off the overseas slave trade, first from the western hemisphere and shortly later from Africa. Thomas Jefferson even proposed the creation of a combined British-French-US force to "confine this disease to its island."[22]

Soon after, the United States marked its gravest moment of insecurity in the War of 1812. After years of Great Britain's seizing US seamen on the high seas and regularly occupying sovereign US territory, war broke out pitting the United States against an allied force of the British and a large confederacy of Native Americans, culminating in what stood for nearly two centuries as the most serious violation of national security in US history: the burning of Washington, DC. Because Americans perceived the conflict with Britain as an existential struggle for the survival of republicanism in the new world, the War of 1812 also incorporated the protection of core values into the cause of national self-defense.[23] Yet this was still a very different notion of self-defense from the modern doctrine of national security, for the need to defend core values arose from the immediate need to defend the actual integrity of the nation's territorial sovereignty. Tellingly, the end of the war diminished the British threat, which in turn put an end to anxieties about the survival of the United States and its core values in the face of foreign dangers. By 1817, at the inauguration of James Monroe, a New York newspaper exulted that security threats to the United States "have all, or nearly all, vanished." Monroe "has the world before him."[24]

Yet even before then, amidst the chronic insecurity of the era, Americans remained confident of their place in the world. From its moment of creation, the United States saw itself as a peer to the imperial powers of

Europe, and the Americans viewed their task as not just safeguarding their security but also compelling others to accept them as sovereign equals.[25] Sometimes these attempts at peer recognition came through diplomacy, but often they were expressed through aggressive saber-rattling.[26] A key source of this remarkable self-confidence was the latent potential of the very geographical position that, for the time being, elevated America's geopolitical risk but, over the long term, raised the prospect of the endless opportunity that would result from national safety. Even as its pages justified a strong central government by emphasizing US vulnerability, the *Federalist Papers* also acknowledged that the "great extent of the country is a further security," and that the "distance of the United States from the powerful nations of the world, gives them the same happy security. . . . In this respect our situation bears another likeness to the insular advantage of Great-Britain."[27]

Americans soon had reason to feel even more confident as the nation's "great extent" underwent a relentless process of territorial expansion, and their vulnerable western flank was "converted from a perilous frontier into a land of security and peace" with the acquisition of Louisiana.[28] The reality may have been different—the United States in fact laid shaky claim to a vast stretch of land that was hardly empty—but the principle of ensuring security through expansion was now firmly established. The circular logic of this process reinforced what were presumed to be the authentic bases of national identity—race (whiteness), gender (masculinity), and religion (Protestantism)—and in turn strengthened this nationalism to justify the expansion of the nation itself.[29]

The architect of the Louisiana policy—who became president shortly after the United States fought a naval war with France and saw relations with Britain deteriorate nearly to the point of war, and so had the security of the nation foremost in mind—recognized that, in the long term, the geographical advantages the United States enjoyed would be enhanced with the strengthening of its geopolitical position. In his prescient but, at the time, outrageously overconfident first inaugural address, Thomas Jefferson pointed to the "blessings" of free security that would "make us a happy and a prosperous people." Tocqueville would later point to many of the same traits Jefferson lauded, including the widespread belief in an "enlightened" religion and the egalitarian spirit that motivated American industry as well as democracy. But underpinning it all was the geographical stroke of luck on which the United States was founded. "Kindly separated by nature and a wide ocean from the exterminating havoc of one quarter of the globe," Jefferson boasted, Americans could enjoy "possessing a chosen country, with room enough for our descendants to the thousandth and thousandth generation." Not coincidentally, this was also the occasion on which Jefferson warned Americans away from "entangling alliances," for a country blessed with such a good position in the world would hardly need to be burdened with commitments to others.[30]

THE TERM "FREE SECURITY" itself was unknown in the nineteenth century. Instead, it was coined in 1960, over a century after Tocqueville's tour of antebellum America, in an article by the historian C. Vann Woodward. "Throughout most of its history the United States has enjoyed a remarkable degree of military security, physical security from hostile attack and invasion," Woodward observed. "This security was not only remarkably effective, but it was relatively free" because Americans benefited from it without needing to invest in its conditions. It simply existed, "enjoyed as a bounty of nature" and independent of anything the United States did. Free security vanished in the 1940s, when the resort to total war, the advent of airpower, the rise of hostile ideologies, and the emergence of an interconnected world meant that the United States could no longer assume its own security in foreign affairs. The disappearance of America's free security in the Cold War, Woodward argued, was one of three revolutionary transformations then shaping the modern world (the other two were the invention of nuclear power and the end of the Eurocentric world brought about by decolonization), and the one to which he gave greatest priority.[31]

Since then, while nuclear weapons and decolonization have attracted enormous amounts of attention, free security has been more or less ignored, even by historians of nineteenth-century America and US foreign relations.[32] According to Fareed Zakaria, free security is intellectually vacuous and analytically useless because it implies that the United States was uninvolved and uninterested in world affairs before World War II, and therefore akin to "isolationism," another label that is out of scholarly fashion (because the United States has always been highly active in world affairs). Even worse, Zakaria argues, free security rests uncomfortably on assumptions of American exceptionalism, especially the notion that Americans were somehow uniquely benevolent in their foreign and military policies.[33]

It's a mystery, however, why free security should be thought of as inherently exceptionalist or isolationist, even if some historians have erroneously portrayed "the young republic Tocqueville visited" as living "in happy isolation from world power struggles."[34] Nothing could be more misleading. Not only was the United States never isolated from the rest of the world, free security actually enabled the United States to be unusually aggressive and acquisitive. The US republic may have been secure, but it was hardly peaceful. Free security did not result from Woodward's "bounty of nature" but was won through perpetual warfare pushing outward against Indigenous nations, Mexicans, Canadians, and others. It did not arise from anything virtuous that inhered in American politics or culture, but rather from a fluke of geography and a temporary set of unusual geopolitical circumstances. Free security did not make Americans any more or less virtuous than other people. But it did have a profound effect on US foreign relations.

Tocqueville wasn't the only one to notice the blessings of free security. "We find ourselves in the peaceful possession, of the fairest portion of the earth, as regards extent of territory, fertility of soil, and salubrity of climate," declared a young Abraham Lincoln in an 1838 speech. Even more, Lincoln assured his audience they could feel utterly secure against foreign enemies. "Shall we expect some transatlantic military giant, to step the Ocean, and crush us at a blow?" he asked. "Never! All the armies of Europe, Asia and Africa combined, with all the treasure of the earth (our own excepted) in their military chest; with a Buonaparte for a commander, could not by force, take a drink from the Ohio, or make a track on the Blue Ridge, in a trial of a thousand years."[35] Hyperbole, to be sure, but underneath the bravado lay a foundation of geopolitical truth.

The existence of free security was in part geographical, but it was also due to favorable prevailing geopolitical conditions, such as the relative military weakness of Mexico and Canada. But perhaps even more important was British acceptance of US sovereignty, interests, and power, initially on the North American continent and then, after the Civil War, throughout the western hemisphere. While this sounds like the natural order of things today, there was no Anglo-American "special relationship" in the nineteenth century. The United States had fought two major wars in the first fifty years of its existence, both times against the British, and in the decade between 1835 and 1845 animosity ran high between Washington and London along what would become the border with Canada, from New Brunswick–Maine and Ontario–New York all the way west to the Oregon Country. Tensions then resurfaced during the Civil War. Thirty years after that, the US and British governments exported their differences to South America. Across the nineteenth century, several Anglo-American disputes had the potential to spark conflict, perhaps even war.

Yet none of these disputes actually led to war. In fact, all were settled amicably, and major treaties established lasting bonds of international cooperation. There were no further "cousins' wars" after 1815.[36] Canada, the site of so much Anglo-American competition, became a model of international stability after Canadian Confederation in 1867.[37] As historians have pointed out, the Monroe Doctrine, pronounced by the upstart United States in 1823 as a unilateral declaration of international independence, existed as a working principle only because Britain tolerated it and the Royal Navy protected it.[38] Having invested a great deal of capital in American industry and westward settlement, and not wanting a war in which Canada would be a strategic hostage, the British were willing to let the United States be the dominant power in the Americas. The Anglo-American peace that prevailed after 1815 provided the bedrock for America's place in the world. As Thomas Jefferson put it in the 1820s, long after he had sparred with London, Britain was the "nation which can do us the most harm of any one, or all on earth"—but "with her on our side we need not fear the whole world."[39]

———

BY THE 1820S, the fate of geography and the quirks of geopolitics had effectively removed all serious threats to the United States. But did that mean that Americans enjoyed an antebellum peace dividend? If free security was real and apparent, and Americans did not have to worry about their nation's physical safety in a dangerous world, this should have been reflected in a small military and correspondingly low levels of defense spending. But was this the case? In other words, just how "free" was free security?

Interestingly, this was a question on which both Tocqueville and Woodward agreed. With the requirements of defense minimal, budgetary pressures related to the military were also minimal. As Tocqueville had put it, Americans needed "neither heavy taxes nor a numerous army nor great generals," and (with apologies to Andrew Jackson and William Henry Harrison) he was largely correct. Woodward also pointed to the advantage free security gave to the American fiscal regime. "The security thus provided," he concluded, "was free in the sense" that it made unnecessary "the elaborate and costly chains of fortifications and even more expensive armies and navies that took a heavy toll of the treasuries of less fortunate countries and placed severe tax burdens upon the backs of their people." Woodward rested his case on an arresting fact: as late as 1861, the United States had the second-largest merchant marine in the world, after Great Britain's, yet possessed a naval force that was less than a tenth the size of the Royal Navy.[40]

It's true that America's free security was not literally cost-free. When measured in terms of total expenditures on armed forces, diplomats, territorial acquisition (such as the Louisiana Purchase), and especially the waging of war—all of which required raising the national debt, which itself created additional rolling costs in terms of interest payments and refinancing charges—foreign and military affairs accounted for up to four-fifths of the federal budget between 1789 and 1860. In 1861, of course, the outbreak of the Civil War led to unprecedented levels of military spending and federal debt. Americans also spent relatively more than other great powers on military and foreign affairs. Overall government expenditures were seven times higher in Britain and five times higher in France— yet, adjusted proportionately, Washington spent twice as much on defense spending as London or Paris did.[41]

This did not, however, mean that military and foreign affairs imposed a heavy fiscal burden on the antebellum United States. Close to 80 percent of the federal budget may have gone toward such costs, but this stemmed more from the fact that the federal budget was not very large—certainly not by twentieth-century standards of the American welfare state, but also not by comparison with European states in the nineteenth century. Spending on the military was thus correspondingly low in absolute terms, at most about one-third the amount Britain and France appropriated for military expenditure.[42]

As a result, tax revenues were also small—as was, not coincidentally, the direct tax burden on the American people. Standing armies were thought to represent a threat to republican liberty not simply because the presence of a large military could allow a potential dictator to seize power, but because of the large fiscal burdens, and growth of coercive state power, they would inevitably create. By 1860, after the United States had fought three major wars and spent eight decades expanding from the Atlantic to the Pacific and from the Great Lakes to the Rio Grande, tax revenues still accounted for only 1.1 percent of American GDP. The government instead raised most of its income from tariffs. This was not coincidental: the founders had deliberately placed the customs house at the heart of the fiscal-military state they created.[43] That federal revenues nonetheless increased over thirtyfold between 1790 and 1860 points to the final reason the fiscal burden of military and foreign affairs was relatively light: as the size and population of the United States grew, the national economy grew as well; and as the national economy grew, overseas trade grew with it, stimulating additional revenues from customs and duties. The nation could thus raise and spend larger amounts of money even as the strain of bearing those costs actually decreased. If security wasn't actually free, it was incredibly cheap and easily affordable.[44]

Free security, then, helped keep the size of the federal government small. This doesn't mean that the United States had a "weak" state in the nineteenth century. Historians have thoroughly debunked "the myth of a weak state," and rightly so. The federal government was active, indeed activist, in matters such as economic development and territorial expansion, and its involvements in the national economy and in creating a continental republic were neither incidental nor minor. Moreover, when one takes governmental power in the aggregate—in terms of governments at all levels (municipal, state, federal) and the many overlapping sources of federal power—it's clear that the American government was anything but weak.[45] Yet the state was nonetheless small, very small, when it came to one of its biggest roles: military affairs and foreign policy. The purpose of the military, Secretary of State Daniel Webster declared in a Fourth of July address in 1851, was to defend the security of the nation from direct foreign attack. "To do this, it need not be large." And if an unexpected emergency arose, the military had "the means of great and sudden expansion" that could be "brought to any point where a hostile attack shall at any time be made or threatened."[46]

One way of measuring this small military state is by the size of its departments charged with maintaining security. For a nation of America's burgeoning power, international ambitions, and overseas economic interests, its foreign service was peculiarly tiny and amateurish. In 1890, the State Department employed only sixty-seven officials in Washington, most of them clerks who divided their tasks alphabetically by country rather than by regional expertise. The United States did have 238 consular offices abroad, but more than a fifth of these were concentrated in Canada and Mexico. The rank of ambassador did not even exist until 1893.[47] A slightly different problem afflicted the Interior Department. Created in

1849 to oversee the development of the west, Interior was much bigger in size and budget than State but even more disorganized and fragmented, and constrained by a mandate to work with private interests—this at a time when the United States still assuredly faced decades of conflict with Indigenous nations and possible future conflict with Mexico and Britain. The Bureau of Indian Affairs was similarly disjointed and unprepared.[48]

Just as telling was the poor quality of the foreign service, which until 1906 was the last bastion of the notorious spoils system and thus a dumping ground for unqualified political appointees. With the White House frequently alternating parties in the 1880s and 1890s, turnover of personnel was high. When Democrat Grover Cleveland came into office in 1893, for example, he replaced 90 percent of foreign service officers, who had been appointed by his Republican predecessor. In 1897, Cleveland's Republican successor, William McKinley, was more judicious, but still replaced over 40 percent.[49] The Pendleton Act of 1883, which brought in sweeping reforms to depoliticize the civil service and reward merit instead of party loyalty, did not apply to the State Department until 1888; even after that, until 1906, consuls and diplomats based overseas lay beyond its reach.[50] The result was "a constant succession of temporary amateurs," according to the British diplomat Sir Harold Nicolson, and a foreign service of poor quality and widespread ridicule.[51] "The American people ought to understand," admonished the *Atlantic Monthly* in 1878, "how and why their consular system is the shabbiest in the whole world."[52] As the historian Robert Beisner puts it, the nineteenth-century foreign service "consisted largely of time-serving functionaries, party hacks, bumptious fools, and petty corruptionists."[53] In an era when the transatlantic cable and the spoils system seemed to make face-to-face diplomacy an anachronism, the editors of *The Nation* even suggested that Congress could abolish the foreign service altogether.[54]

Only a country without an acute sense of threat would have taken its diplomacy so lightly, and it's telling that the eventual push for foreign service reform came not from a greater awareness of strategic danger but from industrialists and chambers of commerce who worried that their economic interests were not being adequately represented abroad.[55] Similarly, the US government did not require the use of passports to enter the country until American entry into World War I; before then, the gradual professionalization of passport and citizenship services was driven by immigration, not security concerns.[56] And when the US Border Patrol was established to police the southern border, in 1924, its objective was to control the flow of migrant labor, not to contribute to national defense.[57]

With a low level of external threat, the responsibilities of citizenship were correspondingly light and relatively few Americans were pressed into military service.[58] In 1845, on the eve of the Mexican War, the US Army had only 826 officers and 7,683 enlisted men; in 1869, after the expansion years of the Civil War and at the height of Reconstruction, it counted an overall force of just 36,953, barely three percent of its wartime peak of over a million men in the Union Army.[59] The comparison with Great Britain, a great power with a much smaller land army than its European rivals, is stark. In the final quarter of the nineteenth century, US armed forces averaged 52,260 in total personnel per year; the high point came in 1898, during war with Spain in the Caribbean and the Pacific, when 235,785 men were under arms. Over the same period, Britain's armed forces averaged 279,231, with a peak near 490,000 coming in 1900 during the Boer War. Thus the *average* size of Britain's military was still tens of thousands of men greater than the single-year *peak* strength of the US military.[60] Given the land mass and length of borders the US Army theoretically had to defend, the discrepancy is astonishing—all the more so considering that, by 1815, Britain's privately held East India Company possessed an army of 230,000 men, nearly equal to the US peak-strength force, just to protect its commercial stake in a territory less than half the size of the contiguous United States.[61]

Just as startling was the size of the nineteenth-century naval fleet. Depending on how naval strength is measured, as late as 1889 the United States had between the twelfth- and seventeenth-largest navy in the world—yet this was a country with a larger merchant marine, greater volume of overseas trade, and longer domestic coastlines to defend (in theory) than any other great power (with the possible exception of Russia, whose coasts were blocked mostly by thick, permanent ice).[62] Throughout the century, the US Navy's primary task was to protect overseas commerce from pirates and privateers rather than to guard against invasion by another power.[63] The building of coastal fortifications, deemed an urgent national priority after the harrowing experience of the War of 1812, proceeded slowly from the 1820s onward as Congress hesitated in the face of spiraling costs. By the end of the century, America's coastlines remained as unguarded as they had been a hundred years before.[64]

The smallness of the American armed forces (except during times of war) marked a sharp contrast between the United States and Europe.

Compared to some of the other great powers of the time—Britain, France, Prussia/Germany, and Austria-Hungary—Americans got off lightly when it came to serving in the military. Consider the number of military personnel as a proportion of the total population (with figures taken every ten years between 1800 and 1900). The peak figure for the United States was 0.13 percent in 1870, right after the Civil War and during Reconstruction. By comparison, the peak figures for the European powers (all of which are from 1810, at the height of Napoleonic Wars) were 2.38 percent for Austria-Hungary, 3.66 percent for France, 3.88 percent for Prussia/Germany, and 5.30 percent for Great Britain. Perhaps this is to be expected. Yet even the *lowest* figures for the other powers were much greater than the *highest* US figure of 0.13 percent: 0.73 percent for Austria-Hungary (1880); 0.82 percent for Prussia/Germany (1860); 0.96 percent for Great Britain (1880, 1890); and 1.02 percent for France (1840). In other words, Europe's low points were still five to eight times higher than America's peak during the Civil War era; and depending on the specific country, high points in Europe were eighteen to forty-one times greater than America's.[65]

Thus, if the Americans really did have an "unexceptional state" that was more similar to than different from its European counterparts, the military remained stubbornly exceptional.[66] People at the time noticed this discrepancy, even if most historians since have not. Indeed, it was a source of pride for nineteenth-century Americans, who equated a powerful permanent military with European monarchy and tyranny. "The cost of fortifying all the important points of our coast, as well as upon the whole Atlantic as the Gulf of Mexico," Webster boasted in his July 4 speech, "will not exceed the amount expended on the fortifications of Paris."[67] Europeans felt likewise. The Americans, French President Adolphe Thiers noted in 1872 with a mix of admiration and envy, "know how to create, in an instant and with extraordinary effort . . . the necessary force to respond to any eventuality."[68] Max Weber, whose typology of bureaucratic state power did much to establish the myth of the weak state, also noticed this discrepancy on his travels in America in 1904. Part of what made the United States different from the modern states of Europe, he remarked, was the absence of a powerful military and permanent conscription.[69]

While European powers built large standing armies and navies to protect themselves against attack—not merely a theoretical prospect in the nineteenth century, given that every major European state often faced the threat of imminent invasion and only one (Britain) escaped it—the United States had the luxury of devoting its armed forces to other tasks. The military accounted for the majority of US federal spending because many of its duties were in fact domestic in nature. The federal government's main tasks throughout the nineteenth century—aside from the obvious need to keep the country intact—had to do with absorbing and developing new territories. Thus, while the majority of public spending may have gone toward military affairs, the funds were not always to be used for national self-defense. A significant amount went to the Army Corps of Engineers, which expended its efforts a great deal more on domestic expansion and development than on preparing to repel a potential foreign invasion. Funds were put toward building dams, levees, canals, and roads for internal improvement more than toward military necessity, and after the passage of the General Survey Act of 1824, the Corps of Engineers took on the task of mapping the endlessly varying contours of a rapidly expanding nation.[70] It also became a key broker between private interests and the federal government on settlement issues involving water usage.[71] Revealingly, the Engineers were largely insulated against the cuts the rest of the Army endured in the wakes of wars and recessions.[72]

Frequent conflicts with Indigenous nations, before and especially after the Civil War, were also domestic in nature, given that fighting with Native Americans occurred as US settlers spread westward. The federal government devoted large resources to fighting its Indian Wars, and to attendant projects of removal, settlement, and enforcement, particularly in the 1830s–1840s and 1870s–1880s.[73] Even then, conflict with Indians posed a financial burden that was easily carried. In the two decades after the Civil War, when perennial fighting with Native Americans was at its peak, the annual cost was just under $1 million—at a time when the Treasury was running a surplus of over $100 million.[74]

In fact, the truly remarkable thing about the American military state in the nineteenth century was its latent potential, or as Ira Katznelson has aptly called it, its "flexible capacity."[75] In 1820–1821, as part of an effort to balance the need for reform of the armed services in the aftermath of the War of 1812 with the need to save money in the aftermath of the Panic of 1819, Secretary of War John C. Calhoun conceived of an "expansible Army," with a small but highly skilled and professional body of regulars in peacetime that would be able to grow exponentially upon the outbreak of war.[76] True to Calhoun's vision, the US military showed an incredible—some would say unmatched—ability to expand when circumstances required, almost on a moment's notice. At the start of a war, the US Army and Navy always found themselves wholly undermanned and underequipped—unprepared, in other words, to wage a major war. Yet each time, in 1812, 1846, 1861, and 1898, they were able to raise sufficient manpower and materiel, suddenly and effectively. The military went from a peak force total of 11,631 in 1812 to 46,858 in 1814 (or 402 percent growth); from 20,726 in 1845 to 60,308 in 1848 (291 percent); from 27,958 in 1860 to 1,062,848 in 1865 (3,801 percent); and from 43,656 in 1897 to 235,785 in 1898 (540 percent).[77]

Just as incredible was the subsequent demobilization: after each of these wars, the peak total of military personnel fell precipitously. By 1816, the military was down to 16,743 personnel; by 1822, it could count only 9,863 men in its ranks. The drawdown after the Mexican War was equally sharp, to 20,699 by 1851. This, too, was unprecedented: a small peacetime military that became a mighty leviathan when called upon and then shrank back to a puny, peacetime size once the fighting was over. To be sure, the Civil War began a ratcheting effect in which the military did not quite fall back to prewar levels and the overall size of the armed forces grew, slowly but steadily, over time. But while the post–Civil War military was larger than its antebellum predecessor, it was nowhere close to the heights it achieved during the war: in 1866, only a year after the war had ended, a military that once had over a million men fell to 76,749; by the end of Reconstruction in 1877, it had only 34,094 in service, still larger than the antebellum figures but not by much. A similar pattern followed the Spanish-American War. For the nineteenth-century US military, mobilization and demobilization were short and sudden; long-term growth was long and gradual.[78]

To pay for these sudden military exigencies and targets of opportunity—such as nearly half of Mexico in 1848—the federal government had an uncanny ability to raise enough money for wartime expenditures and territorial purchases through borrowing instead of higher taxation. The source of much of this income was domestic, but the government found it pretty straightforward to raise the rest by selling bonds to international creditors, mostly in London; either way, though, US debt was denominated in US dollars, keeping the fiscal-military state as protected as possible from the turbulence of financial markets.[79] Just as remarkable was the government's ability to pay off those debts relatively quickly. Previous great powers had run into problems with war debts, which afterward led to the destabilization of empires and even home nations—Britain, for example, faced this crippling problem after the Seven Years' War and both world wars. But the United States avoided this fate every time it went to war, even when it had to raise unprecedented sums through borrowing. Debts from the Revolutionary War and the War of 1812 were paid back by the mid-1820s, and by 1835 the government had retired all of its debt. The Mexican War led to further borrowing ($49 million), but that was mostly paid off by the time the Civil War broke out in 1861. War with the Confederacy forced the Union into deeper levels of debt than had previously been thought possible—a total of $2.7 billion—but by the 1880s much of that had been paid down.[80]

But although the nineteenth-century military state was unusually small, it was anything but weak. The military was in fact precisely fit for purpose, only as large as it needed to be and highly effective when called upon.[81] The latent capacity of an expansible military allowed a small-government, anti-statist republic to have its cake (a small standing military) and eat it, too (waging war to expand territory). This was the founders' very intention: a state that was powerful enough to ensure the nation's stability and prosperity, yet small enough to allay fears of concentrated power.[82] Underpinning everything was free security. Without the needs of self-defense pressing down upon the country's politics, not to mention its finances, the military could remain an oddly minor appendage to a rapidly growing colossus of a nation.

———

TO AMERICANS OF THE early republic, security meant something direct and physical—there was nothing abstract about the American sense of threat before 1815. Yet, even as the European (and especially British) threat gradually ebbed following the War of 1812, American threat perception remained narrow. The boundaries of national self-defense extended only as far as the borders of the continental United States. This didn't mean that the United States lacked interests overseas, even important ones. But it did mean that Americans perceived foreign threats only if they were immediate and direct.

In his first stint as secretary of state, Daniel Webster codified just how direct the premises of national defense really were—and what caused him to do so was, ironically enough, a now-rare direct attack on the United States. In December 1837, a rebellion erupted in Upper Canada (present-day Ontario) in protest at the corruption of colonial rule and, more generally, at the principle of monarchical government. Canadian republicans received support from their American cousins, mostly moral but also in the form of supplies and some weapons. Colonial authorities suppressed the rebellion quickly enough, but not before British troops burned a US ship, the *Caroline,* that was anchored on the American side of the Niagara River and aiding the Canadian rebels. A member of the British raiding party even shot and killed an American citizen, Amos Durfee, who was aboard the *Caroline.*[83]

The resulting controversy raged for several years, sustained by the prospect that the state of New York would try Durfee's killer, a British subject named Alexander McLeod, and hang him. Protestations on both sides were vigorous: the British argued that an individual participating in an act of war sanctioned by a sovereign state could not be held accountable under the terms of domestic law; the Americans countered that the attack on the *Caroline* was hardly a legal act of war. In 1841, Webster settled the issue and soothed Anglo-American tensions by acknowledging the point that soldiers should not be held legally accountable—otherwise, how could states wage war?—but insisting that the British had overstepped the bounds of legitimate self-defense. In pressing this point, he defined the scope of national defense as narrowly and as rigidly as possible. The "necessity of self-defence," he informed the British, must be "instant, overwhelming, leaving no choice of means, and no moment for deliberation." This stricture did not rule out all preemptive military action, but it drastically narrowed the range of possibilities. The United States "is jealous of its rights," first and foremost "the right of the absolute immunity of its territory, against aggression from abroad; and these rights it is the duty and determination of this Government fully and at all times to maintain."[84]

Webster's *Caroline* standard not only prohibited aggressive wars of conquest (albeit more in theory than in practice for the expansionist United States) but also made it difficult to launch preemptive and preventive attacks on potential enemies. It was used in international law well into the twentieth century: in 1945, in San Francisco, the architects of the United Nations invoked it while drafting the organization's first charter; a year later, in Nuremberg, it offered a precedent for the British and American lawyers who prosecuted Nazi war criminals.[85] But more immediately, it meant that antebellum America did not envision self-defense as anything more than fending off attacks against the United States itself.

FREE SECURITY WAS a prevailing condition between the War of 1812 and the end of the Civil War, but it was neither absolute nor perfect. Both ideological ambition and territorial expansionism raised the possibility of conflict with European powers that still had ambitions of their own in the western hemisphere. Americans were not alone in the world, and threats to the United States existed.

Spain, Portugal, and France had once been imperial powers in the new world, but beginning with the Haitian Revolution a wave of anti-colonial national movements swept them almost entirely from the hemisphere. Paraguay and Venezuela won their independence in 1811, followed by Argentina in 1816, Mexico in 1821, Brazil in 1825, and Chile in 1826. Just as it took the United States eight years of fighting to secure its independence from Britain, none of the Latin American revolutions proceeded smoothly or quickly. Fighting sometimes lasted a decade or more, and Spain, which had the most to lose from new-world decolonization, sought to recapture its colonial prizes even after the nationalists had won the war.

Further north, many saw recolonization as a threat to the basic security to the United States. It wasn't clear why the reassertion of Spanish colonialism would be any more threatening than the initial colonial regimes that had coexisted with the United States since 1783. The reason was in fact as much ideological as military: once European monarchy and empire had been banished, few Americans wanted to see their return. Eventually, they hoped, the entire hemisphere would be comprised of self-governing republics, which would trade peacefully with each other and avoid the fate of war-torn Europe. The risk of recolonization seemed particularly severe in the early 1820s, when the reactionary Holy Alliance—the conservative monarchies of France, Austria, Russia, and Prussia—intervened in Spain to prop up the reactionary monarchy. Only Britain now stood for the forces of liberalism in Europe. After the events in Spain, John C. Calhoun, President James Monroe's secretary of war, feared that conservative interventionism would extend to the western hemisphere. Members of the Holy Alliance could now help Spain retake its lost possessions, and probably grab some land for themselves along the way. "The next step of the allies," warned Calhoun, "would be against ourselves—to put down . . . the first example of successful democratic rebellion." The result would be an imperial scramble for America.[86]

The one member of Monroe's cabinet who recognized the sheer implausibility of this worst-case scenario was the secretary of state, John Quincy Adams, probably the most skilled diplomat and visionary strategist in American history. Adams agreed that the European powers should be prevented from reconquering lost territory, but he didn't fear something so unlikely. Instead, he realized that the retreat of Spain and Portugal from Latin America presented an opportunity to separate the old world from the new and enable the United States to be the preeminent power in the western hemisphere.[87] When British foreign secretary George Canning approached the United States in 1823 with the offer of an alliance to prevent the Spanish reconquest of Latin America or the establishment of new European colonies, Adams demurred. Monroe and Calhoun were eager to accept Britain's offer, but Adams instead wanted to issue a unilateral declaration that the United States would keep to its hemisphere and expect the Europeans to keep to theirs. He convinced the president, who conveyed Adams's strictures in his 1823 Annual Message to Congress, a state paper that later became better known as the Monroe Doctrine: the United States would not allow any new-world state that had thrown off the shackles of colonialism to be recolonized; nor would it permit the transfer of any colonies from one European power to another. If the sovereignty of a colony changed, it would have to be in favor of national independence.[88]

Adams's strategy was based on both confidence and caution. He was an ardent believer in manifest destiny before the term had been coined and was certain that the United States would come to rule the entire continent. He himself helped speed the process along by negotiating an 1819 treaty with Spain that gave Florida to the United States and secured Spanish recognition that the southern border of the United States extended all the way to the Pacific. But he was also cautious of his nation's potential to expand beyond the continent and provoke distant threats to gather on American shores. The United States was supremely secure and free of threat so long as it remained in the western hemisphere. When it ventured further, it invited trouble. "The cause of your independence is no longer upon trial," he reminded his fellow Americans in a memorable Fourth of July speech in 1821. "The final sentence upon it has long since been passed upon earth and ratified in heaven." The old world was stuck in the ways of despotism and ignorance, and America would tarnish itself if it joined

Europe's sordid struggles, even on the side of right against wrong. The United States, he declared in what has become one of the most quoted passages in American diplomatic history,

> has abstained from interference in the concerns of others, even when the conflict has been for principles to which she clings, as to the last vital drop that visits the heart. . . . Wherever the standard of freedom and independence has been or shall be unfurled, there will her heart, her benedictions and her prayers be. But she goes not abroad in search of monsters to destroy. She is the well-wisher to the freedom and independence of all. She is the champion and vindicator only of her own.[89]

The specter of the Holy Alliance quickly vanished. It briefly returned when France invaded Mexico in 1862 under the pretext of ensuring that the Mexican government did not default on its debts to European creditors. Napoleon III proclaimed the birth of the Second Mexican Empire and installed an Austrian, Maximillian, as Mexico's new imperial ruler. Normally, Washington would not have allowed such a clear violation of the Monroe Doctrine, but with the outbreak of the Civil War these were not normal times. A restoration of monarchy in Mexico, under French auspices no less, could have been seen as a threat to US security, but Mexico was still militarily weak—much weaker, even, than it had been in 1846—and nobody in America felt alarmed. Ironically, the main reason the French were even there was not as a spur to French or Mexican expansionism into the United States but as a buffer against American manifest destiny. Napoleon's "Grand Design" actually conceded the security requirements of a "powerful and prosperous" United States, just not one that would "grasp the whole Gulf of Mexico." In this effort at defensive diplomacy, he was supported by his fellow Europeans who marveled but also trembled at the geopolitical and industrial giant the United States had the potential to become. The Belgians encouraged Napoleon to "raise a barrier" to the Americans, while British Prime Minister Lord Palmerston hoped the French would "stop the North Americans . . . in their absorption of Mexico." French meddling in Mexico complicated some of the Union's plans to invade Texas, but claims that France and Mexico represented a threat to either the Confederacy or the Union were rare. Maximillian was an irritant, and definitely an insult, but not a security risk. After 1865, with the Civil War over, Washington pressed France to leave. Mexican independence was restored, and Maximillian faced a firing squad in 1867.[90]

The French were easily disposed, but the British would not go away. Canning's approach to the Monroe administration in 1823 marked a détente of sorts, especially after the war a decade before, but Anglo-American tensions persisted and periodic crises burst forth. The clash along the Ontario-New York border that resulted in the sinking of the *Caroline* provoked a war scare in Britain and the United States, yet it was merely one instance of several in a century of Anglo-American tension. Anglophobia was one of the main popular political ideologies of the day, reinforced time and again by frequent diplomatic and occasional military skirmishes.[91] Britain was also perceived to be an obstacle to manifest destiny. One of the motivating factors for war with Mexico in 1846 was President James Polk's fear that if he didn't move to seize the California coastline, the British would.[92] Tensions increased again during the Civil War with the *Trent* and *Alabama* affairs, in which the British seemed to be aiding the Confederacy. After the war, Washington demanded and won compensation from London for selling warships to a hostile power despite official British neutrality.[93]

Fears of British power became particularly strong in the South after London abolished slavery throughout its empire in 1833 and vowed to use the Royal Navy to enforce the abolition of the international slave trade. Some Southerners even panicked that the British would lead a crusade to drive slavery from the United States itself or provoke an uprising of the South's large enslaved population. With such a small US military on hand, one Southern observer warned, Britain will take advantage of "our own utterly defenceless condition" to "*Cripple* this country for several years to come" and "parallize us in our slave labour institutions; and thus dry up the main source of our wealth and power as a Nation."[94] Such fears underpinned Southern desires to annex Texas, an ideal outlet for the region's burgeoning and restless enslaved population—the Haitian Revolution and Nat Turner's bloody 1831 uprising in Virginia, among other revolts, were still fresh in white Southern minds—and also thought to be a target of British designs. The acquisition of Texas, Calhoun argued on the Senate floor, was actually an instance of preemptive self-defense against British aggression.[95] Ironically, the fear of Britain's potential as an abolitionist power led many Southerners, usually staunch defenders of states' rights and a small central government, to call for a vast expansion of the US Navy. In the 1840s Secretary of the Navy Abel Parker Upshur, a Virginian who also briefly served as secretary of state, wedded Southern navalism to westward expansionism that helped fuel Southern support for the Mexican War.[96]

Yet the extent to which any of these episodes involving the British were actual threats to American security is questionable. They were, for the most part, contests over US interests, honor, and ambition, not security. Southerners did have much to fear from abolitionism, but their fellow citizens to the north were much more of a threat than the Royal Navy (exaggerating the British threat did, however, justify the acquisition of additional territory for slavery). When Polk negotiated for half the Oregon Country and preempted British designs on California, moreover, he was advancing an American dream to be a continental power, not protecting US security—whether Britain held California or Oregon had no bearing on the safety of the United States as it was then constituted. In any event, despite Britain's power, by the 1840s there was an imbalance of power on the North American continent that decidedly favored the United States. In garrisoning Canada, the British tried to maintain parity with the size of the US Army, but the policy was hostage to imperial fortunes elsewhere, and the vast and sudden expansion of the US military in the Civil War made it impossible for London to uphold a credible security guarantee.[97]

The United States did face a perennial threat to its sovereignty and territorial integrity, indeed to its very existence, but it came from within. In the antebellum era, no foreign power could put the safety of the United States at risk quite like Americans themselves. Recall Lincoln's Lyceum speech of 1838, in which he declared that no foreign power, or combination of powers, could threaten the United States. "At what point then is the approach of danger to be expected?" he asked. "I answer, if it ever reach us, it must spring up amongst us. It cannot come from abroad. If destruction be our lot, we must ourselves be its author and finisher."[98] Lincoln believed that slavery was the only force powerful enough to kill off the United States, and he was by no means alone.

Every nation, no matter how secure, faces some level of foreign threat, and the nineteenth-century United States was no different. However implausible its war scares may now seem—with Peru in 1852, for example, or with Chile in 1891—they felt real at the time.[99] Yet there are degrees of security and insecurity; they are not absolute conditions. Instead of assuming that states are either totally secure or totally insecure, it is instead better to think of security as a sliding scale. And on the spectrum of security/insecurity, the threats the United States faced between

1815 and the end of the century were at the very end of the minor side of the scale—after all, that war scare with Peru was over control of the Pacific guano trade.[100] This was an insignificant level of threat to compared to the relentless interstate competition found not just in conflict-prone Europe, but also in post-independence South America, where states of relatively equal strength jockeyed for position, resources, and territory and fought two regional wars amidst perennial border skirmishes.[101] By contrast, the only direct threats to the United States came from Britain, which in fact was more cooperative than confrontational in the 1800s, and after the Civil War the British challenge to US hegemony in North America faded entirely. Other threats were theoretical, based on American suppositions rather than European intentions. Indeed, if there was a source of insecurity in the western hemisphere, it was the United States itself.

JOHN QUINCY ADAMS once referred to the United States as a "dangerous" nation, a fitting if ironic description.[102] American settler colonialism was an inexorable and irresistible process that moved steadily west, south, and north from the original thirteen colonies. By the early nineteenth century, the federal government in Washington was discovering what the imperial government in London had encountered when it tried to limit white settlement in the mid-eighteenth century: try as it might, authorities could do little to block the flow of people westward. In 1763, following the Seven Years' War, London issued the Proclamation Line along the Appalachian Mountains to placate its Indigenous allies; settlement beyond that line was prohibited, which incensed the colonists and became a key stimulant to revolutionary anger. In the antebellum era, the new nation expanded cautiously at first, fearful of provoking insoluble questions about slavery, and it rejected several opportunities to annex new territories, such as Texas and Cuba, that would also expand Southern slave power. But still the people pushed westward, supported by banks and developers back east and (ironically) in Britain, dragging the federal government along with them. The Civil War slowed but did not stanch the flow of settlers, and after fighting ended in 1865 westward settlement expanded again. By this time, with the issue of slavery removed and the continental borders of the nation fixed, the federal government had lost all its ambivalence.[103]

Adams, himself a passionate expansionist, didn't believe that the United States itself was "dangerous," simply that other nations—principally the

European powers—found the inexorable spread of its ideology and territory threatening to the future of monarchy and colonialism.[104] Adams's phrase was also true in a more literal sense that he didn't want to acknowledge: it wasn't just the spread of America's values that was dangerous, but the spread of its people, often through violence. The Spanish foresaw the expansionist danger posed by this new "irresistible colossus" right after US independence, and within a few decades American traders were already taking advantage of the collapse of the Spanish empire to push into Colorado and New Mexico, with destabilizing consequences.[105] By the time the US Civil War broke out, the irresistible colossus had crossed the entire continent. To do so, Americans had to seize land and displace people and states who stood in their way. Obstacles to manifest destiny stood little chance. This was one area in which Tocqueville's analytical powers failed him: free security did not create a peaceful republic but instead removed constraints from US territorial ambition and made Americans dangerous to all those who stood in their way.

In 1845, the publisher of the of the *Democratic Review*, John L. O'Sullivan, gave this expansionist impulse a name, manifest destiny, though in practice such providential assumptions about America's future had existed since the first years of European transplantation two centuries before. Westward expansion, O'Sullivan claimed, was not simply America's divine right but its responsibility to the world, a mandate from heaven to spread democracy, Christianity, and civilization across a continent long benighted by heathenism and anarchy. O'Sullivan and other expansionists feared that rival forces, perhaps the British or French, possibly the Russians, would steal Americans' destiny from them. But on the whole, expansionism was an internal force, domestic in origin and execution and made possible by the absence of a serious foreign threat to the United States. With the pace of settler colonialism quickening on the ground, the ideology of manifest destiny provided a powerful justification for the creation of a continental republic.[106]

O'Sullivan's vision was widely held, and providential assumptions saturated the ideology and rhetoric of expansion. A typical example was the worldview of Jedidiah Morse, a Congregationalist minister, founding member of the American Board of Commissioners for Foreign Missions, and father of the man who invented the telegraph. He was also one of the nation's foremost geographers who literally wrote the book on *American Geography*, a standard textbook used up to the Civil War, and was commissioned by the War Department to survey the Great Lakes region for the potential of future settlement. Morse's work blended divine inspiration with geographical expertise. The first edition of *American Geography*, published in 1789 when the states of the union were still only loosely united, argued that historically "empire has been travelling from east to west. Probably her last and broadest seat will be America." The people of the United States "cannot but anticipate the period, as not far distant, when the AMERICAN EMPIRE will comprehend millions of souls, west of the Mississippi."[107] The Civil War did nothing to diminish American providentialism—quite the opposite, in fact, as America's trial by fire only seemed to confirm that it was destined for greater things. In Lincoln's eyes, the United States was the "last best hope of earth," and the Almighty had spared it from disunion for a reason.[108] Optimism about America's future world role even flourished amidst the ruins of the devastated South. "The powers of Europe may now recognize in the United States a colossal rival, vast in territory, in population, and in ambition" and "fearing nothing which the world can offer in competition or in conflict," claimed a Southern writer in the winter of 1866. "The monarchies of Europe combined would present but a feeble barrier to the future advance of this now giant power!"[109]

There was an argument, albeit a highly self-serving one, that territorial expansionism itself was a matter of national self-defense.[110] The antebellum United States was a rapidly growing country, with a surging population and a booming market economy; it simply couldn't be held back. While debating Abraham Lincoln during the 1858 Senate election, Stephen Douglas put it this way: if the choice was between growth or death, who wouldn't chose growth? Especially if growth was naturally occurring and inevitable? Americans had enough land for the moment, he told the audience at his second debate with Lincoln, "but this is a young and a growing nation. It swarms as often as a hive of bees, and as new swarms are turned out each year, there must be hives in which they can gather and make their honey." If the population continued to swell at current rates, Americans would soon fill the entire continent. Who was to tell them they could not? "I tell you," Douglas urged his listeners, "increase, and multiply, and expand, is the law of this nation's existence. You cannot limit this great republic by mere boundary lines, saying, 'this far shalt thou go, and no further.'" What, he asked, would happen if a father tried to stop a boy's growth by fitting a hoop around his waist? "Either the hoop must burst and be rent asunder, or the child must die.

So it would be with this great nation." The message, not all that different to Benjamin Franklin's admonition of 1754, was clear: expand or die.[111]

America's neighbors, who often claimed or even occupied the same land Americans coveted, had good reason to be concerned. While the nineteenth-century United States was moving constantly like a swarm of bees, or growing relentlessly like a twelve-year-old boy, Mexico and Canada were falling further and further behind, and though their growth could sometimes be impressive, it wasn't nearly on the same geographic, demographic, or economic scale as their colossal neighbor. In his next debate with Lincoln, Douglas proclaimed that the United States "will extend and expand until it covers the whole continent" and become "one grand ocean-bound republic." Americans "can go on and extend indefinitely, just as fast and as far as we need the territory." To shouts of approval, he declared that Cuba was in America's sights. And "when it be comes necessary to acquire any portion of Mexico or Canada, or of this continent or the adjoining islands, we must take them as we find them."[112] Not everyone agreed with Douglas—Lincoln certainly didn't—but his view that the best defense was a good offense had been the basis for US foreign policy since at least 1803.

Native Americans were most at risk from US expansion. As historians have pointed out, North America remained overwhelmingly Indigenous for centuries after European arrival and settlement, indeed, long after even the American Revolution.[113] Violent conflict between Native Americans and US Americans occurred frequently and Indigenous forces inflicted crushing blows in battle after battle, often with the US Army suffering greater casualties. But the violence inflicted by US Americans, and the inexorable force of their westward settlement, proved an even greater force, and as the US republic grew through the nineteenth century the overall trendline did not favor Indigenous people. The United States could call on a widening array of forms of power—military, political, and economic—that grew exponentially as the nineteenth century went on, and though Native Americans had developed highly effective military tactics for warfare against the United States, the Americans' advantages in technology and demographics were ultimately determining. As powerful and autonomous as Indigenous nations were, they had to contend with the constantly growing power of a constantly growing industrial giant.

For Indigenous nations, accustomed to their own senses of place and security on the continent, this development was not only startling but ominous. With their frequent raiding in Mexico's northern states in the 1830s and '40s, the Comanches had prevented Mexicans from gaining a permanent settlement foothold. In fact, Comanche raiding had made Mexico so weak in its far north that it inadvertently created the conditions for the US rout of Mexico in 1846–1848. When Washington imposed its peace terms on Mexico City, the scale of US military superiority was obvious: by Article 11 in the Treaty of Guadalupe Hidalgo, the United States agreed to guarantee Mexican security against future Indian raiding. Not coincidentally, 1848 marked the zenith of Comanche power, which receded dramatically in the ensuing decades and was finally extinguished by a US military offensive in 1874. The Lakotas, who commanded a similarly powerful empire to the north of the Comanches, also mounted a long-running campaign against the continual encroachment of the United States. Their triumph in Red Cloud's War, in 1868, resulted in Lakota dominance of much of the Great Plains, but the US Army—and just as importantly, US settlers—kept coming. A decade later, despite the Lakotas winning a famous victory at the Battle of Little Bighorn, the United States prevailed in the Great Sioux War and the Lakota empire came to a similar fate as the Comanche.[114]

It's important to stress that Native Americans were not simply passive victims or that their eventual military defeat was inevitable.[115] The near-constant warfare between the United States and various Indigenous nations was not a one-sided conquest of American victories interspersed with rare Indigenous victories such as Little Bighorn. But it's equally important to recognize these nineteenth-century wars for what they were: US Americans on the offensive, Native Americans on the defensive, in a struggle for control of the continent. Seen in this light, America's Indian Wars were a means to push US expansion, not a defensive reaction to threats to US sovereignty or security. White settlers and soldiers on the frontlines may have felt fearful, and they experienced horrific violence, but the conditions that gave rise to such fear and violence were entirely their own creation. Moreover, there was never any question that the United States itself was at risk of being invaded and occupied. The battlefront of the Indian Wars was continually pushed further and further west, as the United States kept moving into what had effectively been the sovereign domain of Native Americans. The results—massacre, displacement, and destruction of communities—were catastrophic.[116] Stephen Douglas may have justified this kind of warfare as simply a matter of protecting American security, but it hardly qualifies as an act of self-defense.

Mexico, a much weaker military power than the Indigenous nations and empires that held vast territories coveted by the United States, also had plenty of reason to worry. Even so, the US invasion of 1846 blindsided Mexican leaders, who hadn't quite believed a sister republic would act so aggressively, as well as many Americans who opposed launching what Ulysses Grant later called "a wicked war" of outright conquest. Despite equally fierce Mexican resistance and American dissent, the conflict was as a total mismatch. "Strictly speaking," one Mexican official noted shortly before the war began, "the army does not exist. What today bears that name is only a mass of men without training and without weapons." The course of battle did little to allay these concerns. After the Battle of Cerro Gordo, a Mexican observer concluded that "the Yankees are invincible" and that the Mexican Army was no match for the superior technology and firepower of the United States. US troops campaigned deep into the heart of Mexico and eventually occupied the capital, and the only uncertainty of the final peace settlement was during the congressional debate over just how much Mexican territory the United States should take.[117]

Having twice been invaded by the United States, in 1775 and 1812, the people of British North America had every reason to worry they would share Mexico's fate. American talk of a manifest destiny to establish a republic across the entire continent, including north of the Great Lakes and Saint Lawrence River, exacerbated such fears, as did the sporadic fighting that broke out between the United States and the Canadian colonies. Before the Civil War, expansionists like Douglas sometimes hinted that Canada would one day be absorbed, inevitably but peacefully, into the United States, and right after the war Secretary of State William Seward tried to purchase British Columbia along with Alaska.[118] More menacingly, after the Civil War Irish nationalists based in New England and New York, known as the Fenians, invaded eastern Canada, while the more serious power of the Union Army seemed poised to turn north and take by force what Webster and Douglas had assumed would eventually happen anyway, peacefully.[119]

The responsibility of maintaining Canadian defense in the face of a constant threat of American invasion, peaceful or otherwise, took a heavy toll on the British, which in turn spurred Canadians to plan for a future on their own. In the debates over independence, nationalists argued that only a united Canada could deter the Americans. Thomas D'Arcy McGee, the poet-politician from Montreal who was always alert to "the American warning," reminded his hesitant colleagues that "our neighbor to the south of us has always been aggressive" because of the constant "desire among them for the acquisition of new territory." The entire short history of the United States proved his point:

> They coveted Florida, and seized it; they coveted Louisiana and purchased it; they coveted Texas, and stole it; and then they picked a quarrel with Mexico, which ended by their getting California. . . . The acquisition of Canada was the first ambition of the American [nation], and never ceased to be so, when her troops were a handful and her navy scarce a squadron. Is it likely to be stopped now, when she counts her guns afloat by thousands and her troops by hundreds of thousands?[120]

Such fears didn't disappear until the problems of Reconstruction and military demobilization cooled American expansionist fervor. Canadian Confederation happened in 1867, strengthening the north and stabilizing continental relations, and in the end ushering in a permanent "North American democratic peace."[121]

The Civil War not only marked a victory of the Union over the Confederacy, it also signaled a collapse of the European presence in North America and the beginning of the United States' clear dominance in the western hemisphere. The North's victory eliminated the only genuine threat to the security of the United States—the slaveholding South—and after 1865 the growth of America's industrial and economic power was no longer shackled to the uncertainties of sectional divisions. While other great powers worried constantly about being attacked and invaded, the US government—and its people—could now focus almost exclusively on building their economy and consolidating their nation. As foreign threats disappeared following the Civil War, the United States entered a golden age of economic growth and unsurpassed industrial innovation. Free security across an entire continent meant that Americans had unfettered access to almost all strategic raw materials. It also meant they could plan for the future without risk of being occupied, divided, plundered, or forcibly deindustrialized. As the historian Paul Kennedy has put it, by the end of the nineteenth century the United States had "*all* the economic advantages which *some* of the other powers possessed *in part*, but *none* of their disadvantages."[122] At a time when the European powers eyed each other suspiciously across common borders and narrow strips of water, the foundation for America's strategic edge was unrivalled geopolitical safety. Later, it would serve as a platform for an ambitious projection of American power around the world.

———

IF ANYONE FORGOT the hemispheric dominance of the United States, Richard Olney was quick to remind them. Olney was a pugnacious, Harvard-trained lawyer from Boston—Henry James once wrote euphemistically of his "passion for disposing of a difficulty promptly"—who made his fortune as a railroad lawyer in the Gilded Age before becoming President Grover Cleveland's attorney general in 1893.[123] In an era when the United States had more industrial strife than any other country, Olney took a dim view of organized labor. In response to a wave of worker unrest that culminated in the 1894 Pullman strike and brought the country right up to what he called "the ragged edge of anarchy," he devised a constitutional argument that permitted the use of federal troops as strike-breakers. Thirty people died in the confrontation, the union leader Eugene Debs was arrested and later imprisoned, and the strike ended. Yet as a lawyer, Olney also believed that binding arbitration was the best way forward, and hoped it would prevent further violent conflict between capital, industry, and government on one side against unions and workers on the other.[124]

Olney was also a nationalist, and part of his distrust of labor was that it was too foreign, too captive to foreign influences, too corrosive of the national purpose. Thus he already had a firm belief in America's place in the world when Cleveland moved him from Justice to become secretary of state in 1895. He immediately stepped into the Venezuela crisis with Britain, which at that point was threatening to become something more than a diplomatic standoff. The immediate issue was defining the border between Venezuela and British Guyana, but for the United States the larger issue was whether it should continue to tolerate Europe's presence in the western hemisphere. To Olney, the British government was behaving no better than American unions, and he treated London with the same brusque authority as he had Debs and the Pullman strikers. London had to agree to binding international arbitration of the boundary dispute, he told the government of Lord Salisbury, or else. "To-day," Olney declared, "the United States is practically sovereign on this continent, and its fiat is law upon the subjects to which it confines its interposition." Why was the United States so powerful in the hemisphere? It was not thanks to the "pure friendship or good will" felt by the Latin American republics; nor was it due to America's "high character as a civilized state." It was instead a basic matter of power. "It is because," Olney bluntly explained in the most basic realist terms, "its infinite resources combined with its isolated position render it master of the situation and practically invulnerable as against any or all other powers."[125]

The directness with which Olney addressed the British government—then the most powerful state in the international system, the head of one of the world's largest economies, the center of global finance, and the master of the largest empire in world history—was astonishing. Most astonished was Lord Salisbury himself, by all accounts livid at the impertinence of the upstart Americans. But Olney was right—in the western hemisphere, the United States was virtually immune from attack and thus held the balance of regional power. If Britain wanted to settle the dispute peacefully, it would have to do so on American terms. Salisbury and his cabinet realized this once they had calmed down, and Britain submitted to arbitration. The result was a boundary settlement that satisfied all of America's interests, most of Britain's, and little of Venezuela's.[126]

We began with Alexis de Tocqueville, and so perhaps the last word should go to another French visitor to America. For over twenty years, from the presidency of Theodore Roosevelt to the presidency of Calvin Coolidge, Jules Jusserand served as the French ambassador to Washington. Like Tocqueville, Jusserand took readily to American life: he formed a close, personal relationship with Roosevelt and his inner circle, and he married an American citizen. Despite his familiarity with America, Jusserand still marveled at its emergence as a world power and economic hegemon, and he agreed with the conclusion his compatriot had reached seventy years earlier. What made it all possible was the uniquely fortunate position in which Americans found themselves. The United States, Jusserand observed, "was blessed among nations. . . . On the north she had a weak neighbor; on the south, another weak neighbor; on the east, fish, and on the west, fish."[127]

[2]

THE BATTLE OF PLEASANT VALLEY

T WAS 1909, and America was under attack. After crushing the US Navy in the Pacific and landing armies in Panama and Mexico, Japan invaded the United States and swiftly occupied California. Alarmed by the sudden shift in the global balance of power, Britain rushed to America's aid. The Royal Navy sank the Japanese fleet and then moved its troops to the continental United States to link up with what remained of the humbled US Army. Together, in a massive combined force, British and American troops defeated the Japanese at the decisive Battle of Pleasant Valley, Idaho, just as a joint Anglo-American fleet steamed toward the Japanese home islands. Japan sued for peace, the English-speaking nations of the world joined in confederation, the other nations agreed to form an international parliament with British and Americans at the helm, and a perpetual peace of worldwide democracy and liberal commerce reigned supreme.

This account isn't actual history, of course, but a piece of speculative fiction that sprang from the imagination of an obscure American writer, Ernest Hugh Fitzpatrick. Fitzpatrick's novel, *The Coming Conflict of Nations*—which carried the ominous subtitle *The Japanese-American War*—told of a utopian future rising from the ashes of a dystopian world war in which the United States was at first invaded, occupied, and humiliated, but then redeemed through an Anglo-American commonwealth and the dawn of a liberal international order. His account may have been fiction, but Fitzpatrick had been inspired by a very real clash of civilizations in California two years before, when white Americans rioted at the prospect of their children being taught in the same classrooms as young

Japanese Americans. The government in Tokyo responded with an angry protest to Washington, and a war scare gripped both countries.[1]

Fitzpatrick found little fame as a writer, but his fevered dreams were hardly unusual at the time, and the ideas on which his book was based—everything from hopes of an Anglosphere confederation to fears of Japanese power—were fairly common.[2] That same year, 1909, saw other accounts of a war scare with Japan, many of them written by sober-minded analysts rather than writers of fictional future war.[3] Fearmongering invasion literature was hardly unique to the United States; British writers had been speculating about a German invasion since the 1880s. But there was a key difference: British fears of a German invasion were all too plausible, whereas American fears of a Japanese invasion were so unrealistic as to be entirely fictive.[4]

Nonetheless, in the first decades of the twentieth century, American strategists furiously churned out warnings about Japanese conquest. Most notable among them was Homer Lea, a self-made military expert who, despite the lack of any formal training, wrote *The Valor of Ignorance,* an influential polemic about American unpreparedness and naiveté in world affairs. The intelligent, irrepressible Lea was physically unfit to join the military, on account of his diminutive stature and chronic health problems, but there was nothing to stop him volunteering his services as an analyst of world affairs and military matters. After attending Stanford, he became an adviser to Chinese elites, at first for the emperor's circle and then, correctly sensing a change in political fortunes, for Sun Yat-sen and his burgeoning Republican China movement.[5]

These experiences in China gave Lea an authoritative worldliness, which in turn lent his ideas a veneer of reasonable legitimacy. In *The Valor of Ignorance,* he argued that Americans had too long assumed they were invulnerable to attack. As a result, they lived in an "excessively opulent" haze of willful ignorance that gave them a false sense of security. Rather than being secure in its continental sanctuary, the United States was actually acutely vulnerable to invasion—not from a European power, but from Japan. America's defenses were useless, wrote Lea, its military small and decrepit, and the first lines of America's Pacific defense—the Philippines, Hawai'i, and Alaska—were soft targets that Japan could easily occupy. After that, with the bulk of the US Navy stationed in the Atlantic, there was nothing deterring Japan from invading California and Washington. Lea even drew up detailed tactical maps of how Japan would likely conquer the west. Once they were ensconced in the western states, with control of the strategic redoubt of San Francisco Bay, Japanese forces would be almost impossible to dislodge, especially as US troops coming from points east would have to cross mountains and deserts before they could even engage the Japanese in battle—and especially with a self-indulgent America itself laid low by peace movements and "the crumbling diseases of feminism, commercialism, and socialism."[6]

The Japanese, by contrast, were battle-tested from their victory over Russia in 1905, and they did not suffer any delusions that the international order was naturally liberal or peaceful. Their goal was the goal of all aspiring powers in history: regional supremacy. "There now remains but one power for Japan to put aside in order to make her supreme in the Pacific," Lea warned. "That nation is the United States." But the threat went deeper still, beyond the geopolitical to the cultural and the social, because the two countries represented completely different ways of life. Lea didn't begrudge the Japanese pride in their island nation, a "race-rock" that provided the durable foundation for Japanese culture, but he did begrudge their claims to equality with Americans. "No national ideals could be more antithetic than are the ethical and civic ideals of Japan to those existent in this Republic," Lea wrote. With their "sword-girded gods and militant bonzes," the Japanese "are heathen in the eyes of this Republic, heathen in all the contemptuous, naked inferiority that that term in a Christian nation implies." Most ominously, the Japanese had been infiltrating the United States and its territories with seemingly innocent migrants, so that by 1909 Hawai'i, California, Oregon, and Washington were all prone to a hostile takeover from within.[7]

Lea's account may have seemed factual, but it was no less fanciful than Fitzgerald's novel (as David Starr Jordan, president of his alma mater, took pains to point out).[8] Yet unlike Fitzgerald's book, *The Valor of Ignorance* wasn't an obscure curiosity but a widely read expert analysis. Lea's book was dedicated to his one of mentors, Secretary of War Elihu Root, and carried not one but two prefaces by recently retired US Army generals. In the first, Adna R. Chaffee exclaimed that the "popular belief that the United States is free of opportunities for invasion is all 'tommy rot,'" partly because the size of the army "is so ridiculously small."[9] In the second, J. P. Story warned that the "richer a nation may be in material resources, the more likely it has been to fall a prize to a more militant people." Japan's territorial ambitions, combined with "the menace of the 'Yellow Peril,'" meant that Americans needed to wake up to the imminent danger they were in. Above all, concluded General Story, "Mr. Lea shows clearly that we are confronted by conditions which may imperil our national security, peace, and welfare."[10]

Homer Lea's polemic perfectly captured the forces at work that would eventually produce the modern doctrine of national security: a distant, global threat that could one day reach American shores, coupled with an ideological and cultural threat that wasn't merely territorial but was linked to a military threat from abroad that could destroy the American way of life. *The Valor of Ignorance* was a prophecy of a still-undefined concept of self-defense, right down to Story's rare invocation of "national security," a term that still wasn't yet in common usage. Lea's warnings weren't heeded at the time, but by making these false starts toward "national security" he and a small but growing number of others like him laid the foundations for the next revolution in US foreign policy.

———

THE DECADES BETWEEN the Civil War and the Great War saw increased global interdependence and the advent of new, deadlier military technologies, yet America's place in the international system changed very little. The United States did begin projecting its power beyond the western hemisphere, especially in East Asia, but it still remained a secondary player in world politics even as war broke out in Europe in 1914. Tellingly, even though American ambitions grew with the turn of the century, the size of the army did not. The reason was simple: there was little need. As one congressman, Theodore Burton of Ohio, declared during a heated debate over the 1908 Naval Appropriation bill, "Our country has enjoyed an unprecedented growth and has attained a position in the very fore front among nations, not by the strength or armies or navies, but by our unique position." Large armed forces in peacetime ran contrary to the principles of republican democracy, and, with its expansible army, the nation was more than capable of fending for itself in an emergency: "whenever the Republic is in peril tens of thousands will rise up ready to defend our country with the last drop of blood."[11]

Burton lost the debate, and Congress appropriated funds for the construction of more ships. Yet even this increase was modest by international standards (especially compared to the naval arms race Britain and Germany were waging) and saw the construction of only three battleships.[12] As Congressman Burton recognized, the United States still enjoyed the blessings of free security. To be sure, the acquisition of overseas colonies in 1898—the Philippines, Hawai'i, and elsewhere—exposed the United States to a new kind of geopolitical vulnerability. But these were matters of imperial security, not national self-defense. The empire was certainly in harm's way; the metropole manifestly was not.

In fact, the likes of Burton—those who were wary of a large, permanent military establishment and US interventionism abroad—positively reveled in the detachment free security provided them. So pervasive was the nation's self-confidence in its self-defense that even military men acknowledged it. "The idea of a hostile force landing on our coast is simply preposterous," General William Tecumseh Sherman conceded in 1880. Alfred Thayer Mahan felt likewise more than twenty years later, despite the European powers' naval buildup. "In considering possible wars with the great nations of the world," he observed in 1903, "it seems to me inconceivable that any one of them should expect seriously to modify or weaken our position in this hemisphere."[13]

Yet for military men like Sherman and Mahan, free security wasn't a blessing but a curse, the source of popular complacency and official apathy that, in turn, were the chief causes of what Mahan called "a confessed unpreparedness for war."[14] Its most eloquent critic was military strategist—and Sherman protégé—Emory Upton. After graduating from West Point shortly before the outbreak of the Civil War, Upton fought in the conflict almost continuously, from the First Battle of Bull Run right through to the last few battles in Georgia that continued even after Robert E. Lee surrendered at Appomattox. Upton returned to West Point after the war, this time as an instructor. He lamented the state of the US Army, now a fraction of its wartime strength, and longed for the United States to emulate the great military states of Europe, with their large standing armies and permanent, professional general staffs.

Upton's moment came when General Sherman commissioned him to travel to Europe and report on any lessons American commanders could learn to reform the US Army. Having harbored strong views for a long time, Upton held little back. In a cascade of technical publications on armaments and military operations, he drafted a blueprint for a larger, more technologically advanced US Army that could lead the United States in a global, imperial age. Few people beyond West Point, however, read his work. When Upton, the victim of unrelenting, agonizing headaches that doctors found difficult to explain and impossible to treat, took his own life in 1881, he left behind a nearly finished manuscript, *The Military Policy of the United States*. His manuscript could have been lost forever. Instead, it found a cult following among uniformed officers, spending years making the rounds and growing in stature as a lost voice of radical wisdom. In 1904, Upton's manuscript came to the attention of a kindred spirit, Secretary of War Elihu Root, who liked it so much that he had it published at government expense.

Upton's and Root's visions were separated by a quarter-century, but their reformist impulse was the same. The United States, Upton wrote in *The Military Policy of the United States,* needed a bigger, better-equipped, and professionally trained army, but popular ignorance and congressional penny-pinching stood in the way. Victory against Britain in 1815, in Mexico in 1848, and in successive Indian Wars had "so blinded the popular mind . . . as to induce the belief that as a nation we are invincible." In thrall to the same delusion, lawmakers "make a merit of neglecting the national defense"—a failing that led Upton and his "brother officers" to despair that "We have no military policy." Even though transportation and communications technologies were advancing at a rate faster than at any point in human history, bringing nations and empires closer than ever before, Upton worried that "our remoteness from powerful nations has led to another delusion—that we shall forever be free from foreign invasion."[15]

Root made some progress in fulfilling Upton's expansive vision while he was at the War Department—but not much.[16] "In reality," an army officer lamented in 1895, "the Army is now a gendarmerie—a national police." He wasn't wrong. By this time, having pacified the west, the army saw more action breaking labor strikes at home than defending the nation against foreign enemies. In 1897, in a global survey of military power, the German General Staff simply ignored the US Army.[17] This wasn't just foreign chauvinism: Secretary of State John Hay himself privately acknowledged that the United States lacked the military strength to enforce the famous Open Door Notes he drafted in 1899–1900. Still, within a few years of becoming Secretary of War, Root had managed to boost spending on the army more than threefold, to an average of approximately $150 million per year, and the War Department spent more under the five years of Root's watch than it had in the previous nineteen. While spending for the Spanish-American War and its aftermath certainly bloated the average annual spending under Root, it remained high, and at roughly triple the rate, even after the end of major hostilities in Cuba and the Philippines.[18] Yet even this breakneck expansion still left the army well short of even the smallest armies in Europe.[19]

The turn of the century saw more overseas action for US forces, but it mostly came in the forms of intervention in and occupation of small countries in Central America and the Caribbean. Not coincidentally, this was when President Theodore Roosevelt, formerly police commissioner of the city of New York, reconceived the army's gendarmerie duties as extending outward, beyond the contiguous United States, in response to "flagrant cases" of "wrongdoing or impotence" by other sovereign states. With that, in his famous 1904 corollary to the Monroe Doctrine, Roosevelt bestowed upon the US armed forces the authority of "an international police power."[20] As he explained on another occasion, "wars with uncivilized powers are largely mere matters of international police duty, essential for the welfare of the world."[21] Duty was the operative word, for while Americans saw their self-appointed policing role as a responsibility, even an act of generosity, it was also a thankless task. "Whatever the American people might think or say about it," wrote Henry Adams, "they would sooner or later have to police those islands, not against Europe, but for Europe, and America too."[22]

The best way to think of this new role for America, as an international police power, was like an insurance policy, a notion that would later provide much of the glue holding together the disparate parts of "national security." As Secretary of State Philander Knox explained in 1912, while defending the new, interventionist mission of the Monroe Doctrine, "Like an insurance risk, our risk decreases as the conditions to which it pertains are improved."[23] This type of international police action didn't require a large army, so if it was a kind of insurance policy its premiums were low, and over the next century much of the actual policing on the ground was done in partnership with highly repressive US-trained local forces.[24]

In the absence of a clear and present danger to the continental United States, there just seemed no need to build a large standing army. When it came to policing the world, for instance, most of the action was hunting down financial criminals who got rich from conning Americans out of their money before fleeing to safe havens abroad.[25] By contrast, there was an obvious need for a robust Navy, which prevented foreign approaches to American coastlines and protected merchant US shipping, while also policing the seas and promoting American interests in regions as far away as East Asia. In the event of an invasion, a strong army would be absolutely vital, but the unlikelihood of invasion meant that a strong army was a luxury Americans could live without. General John M. Schofield appreciated the irony he and other army men found themselves in. "The situation of the United States is directly the opposite of that of the continental powers of Europe," he lamented to the Secretary of War in 1894. "Here there exists no necessity for great armies in the field." With coastal defenses bolstered in the 1880s–1890s, the Navy could project American power outward. "The purpose of the Navy," Schofield recognized, "is for operation beyond the reach of the guns of American fortification."[26] Or, as Roosevelt explained in 1906 when the army was still languishing and the navy rapidly growing, "We are so fortunate that in this country we can get along with a very small army; an army, which, relative to the population of the country, is smaller than the police force of any one of our great cities." He added, however, that between the Panama Canal then under construction and the need to enforce the Monroe Doctrine, "With the navy the case is different."[27]

Roosevelt framed the ability to project military power internationally as a matter of necessity, but in fact it was vital to national ambition rather than national survival. As he put it in justifying his call for naval expansion, "We have not the choice . . . as to whether this country will play a great part in the world; we cannot help playing a great part."[28] This wasn't a new theme for Roosevelt. "We cannot, if we would, play the part of China, and be content to rot by inches in ignoble ease within our borders," he said in 1899. If "isolated" in this way, the United States was "bound, in the end, to go down before other nations which have not lost the manly and adventurous qualities. If we are to be a really great people, we must strive in good faith to play a great part in the world."[29] It was a strange analysis: unlike China, which was surrounded by aggressive imperialist powers, the United States enjoyed hegemonic dominance over its region and wasn't remotely at risk of having its major cities carved up into foreign-run entrepôts. Such dreams bore a strong resemblance to Stephen Douglas's pre–Civil War justification of westward expansion as a matter of basic security rather than what it actually was: a bid for national greatness. However desirable the greatness, it was not an example of self-defense.

Navalists like Mahan likewise admitted that while the United States did not need a big navy to defend itself, it did need greater naval power to advance its growing international interests, especially economic interests.[30] In making a version of Mahan's argument during the debate over a big navy in 1908, Admiral George Dewey, hero of the naval victory over Spain in Manila Bay, turned geography on its head, arguing to Congressman Burton and other anti-navalists that America's long coastlines and far-flung insular possessions helped ensure US continental security but also meant that American interests were almost uniquely vulnerable.[31] In the twenty years between the war with Spain and US intervention in World War I, the army's budget shrank by a fifth, while naval expenditures more than doubled, and the rapidly modernizing navy joined the front rank of the world's maritime powers.[32]

Even these increases, however, still left the US Navy far short of the powerful, technologically advanced navies found in Europe.[33] It's true that the spurt of shipbuilding that began in the 1880s and culminated in 1908–1909 with the round-the-world journey of Teddy Roosevelt's Great White Fleet greatly increased the size and stature of the US Navy. But beyond the gleaming hulls of some new battleships, American military power, even naval power, was less than it seemed. As Katherine Epstein has pointed out, the Great White Fleet couldn't even run on its own steam because it had to refuel at ports in the British Empire. Similarly, when Admiral George Dewey defeated the Spanish fleet in Manila Bay, in 1898, he received his orders over British telegraph cables and then sailed to the Philippines from a makeshift base in Hong Kong, courtesy of the Royal Navy. By the outbreak of World War I, the US Navy was behind only Britain and Germany in the number of battleships, but its fleet was way out of balance: many big ships, but very little else to support them in terms of the support vessels, overseas ports with dry docks, and communications networks that drew no headlines but were absolutely vital for a navy to function. "Reports of the United States' rise to a lead role on the global stage in the early twentieth century," Epstein observes, "have been greatly exaggerated."[34]

———

THIS STATE OF BENIGN neglect began to change around the time war broke out in Europe, which unquestionably heightened Americans' foreign-threat perception. And for good reason, too: 1914 saw not only the outbreak of war in Europe, but also the escalation of an ideological "war at home": anarchists and leftist radicals escalated subversion activities, culminating in the bombing of a preparedness parade in San Francisco that killed ten people, while German agents operating undercover in the United States mounted a sabotage campaign.[35] This wave of domestic violence followed the sudden spike in political and industrial unrest of the late nineteenth century, punctuated by events like the 1886 Haymarket affair in Chicago and the 1901 assassination of William McKinley in Buffalo. In this febrile atmosphere, with many Americans already feeling under siege in their own country even before they entered the Great War, foreign powers seemed to pose novel, heightened dangers from abroad. In this new era, Americans faced potential danger from three foreign sources—Japan, Mexico, and Germany—though none of them, not even Germany, was in fact a direct threat to American security. For precisely that reason, though, advocates of stronger defense elevated these threats beyond all reasonable proportion.

The threat from Japan was geographically the most remote and so on one level the least likely, though not because of Japanese weakness. Japan had only recently proven itself in lopsided victories against China (1894–1895) and Russia (1904–1905), which made it the strongest military power in the western Pacific. Ever since John Hay had issued his Open Door Notes, Americans worried that the colonization of China by other powers would threaten US interests by closing off the Pacific.[36] The Japanese military worried Americans a great deal, especially in comparison with the pallid state of their own armed forces. If war broke out, "Japan would hand the United States a dose of humiliation that would make it hang its head in shame for its ignorance for decades to come," warned one observer in 1910. "Japan is a first-class war power. We are not."[37] While the US Navy was probably superior in strength, and certainly in tonnage, Japan's naval forces were already concentrated in the western Pacific, where much of the action would initially happen in an interimperial war: the northern tip of the Philippines, an American colony, was little more than two hundred miles south of Taiwan, a Japanese colony, and should Japan successfully occupy the Philippines, or at least the main island of Luzon, then Hawai'i would become much more vulnerable. Meanwhile, US security services monitored Japanese support for Filipino and Hawaiian nationalists agitating against US colonial rule, often from a base in Japan itself.[38] At the dawn of the American overseas empire, amidst an eruption of imperialist fervor, McKinley had quietly worried that the Philippines would soon prove to be an Achilles heel, stretching the requirements of American defenses beyond their capabilities. He was right: the Philippines would be extremely difficult to defend, so the Hawaiian Islands, particularly Pearl Harbor on Oahu, became the main forward defense post that would come to the Philippines' rescue and prevent Japan from dominating the Pacific world.[39]

But as Homer Lea had laid out in his lacerating critique of American strategy in the Pacific, fears of Japan extended further still, all the way to the west coast of the United States. Should Japan seize control of the Philippines, and then Hawai'i, there would be little to stop it from invading California, Oregon, and Washington. Thanks to a well-placed leak in Washington, the *New York American* reported that the Japanese ambassador warned US diplomats, "We know every detail of your defenses on land and sea, every bay, inlet, and sounding on your coast from Seattle to San Diego and down to Mexico. We know the weak spots in your five great transcontinental railways between the Pacific and the Rocky Mountains. We know the defendable passes, the destructible bridges." With such knowledge, the ambassador boasted, "we could undoubtedly occupy the State of California and your entire Pacific coast and hold it against all comers for a year or more."[40] The accuracy of the report is doubtful, but even if it was embellished, or made up—like Fitzgerald's future history— it still provided a good reflection of the anxiety Japan provoked in the years before World War I.

Californians certainly didn't see the vulnerability of the west coast as fictional.[41] Yet such fears stemmed, as they often do, not from foreigners' intentions or capabilities, but from internal fears about American society that were then projected outward. In the case of Japan, the supposed threat to American security originated with Japanese immigration and the nativist response to it. In California, schools segregated Japanese and white students, which in turn encouraged wider anti-Japanese protests that quickly turned violent. (This was the unrest that had originally spurred Homer Lea to write *The Valor of Ignorance*.) The unrest prompted Tokyo to lodge an official diplomatic protest with Washington. Theodore Roosevelt may have been unsympathetic to the nativist rebellion out west, but there was no way he could openly side with the government of Japan against the people of California. Trapped between equally intractable domestic and international pressures, he resorted to a classic political fudge that solved the immediate crisis without resolving the fundamental problem. In the so-called Gentlemen's Agreement of 1907, an unofficial political compromise that had no force in law, Japan promised to stem the flow of migrants to America while the United States promised not to pass an immigration exclusion act aimed at the Japanese.[42]

The crisis passed, but Americans now worried even more about the supposed Japanese fifth-column threat from within that could potentially link up with the growing power of the Japanese military. Shortly after the Gentlemen's Agreement, the Army war-gamed a possible conflict with Japan; the result was a fairly swift Japanese occupation of the Philippines, Hawai'i, and California.[43] Roosevelt then ordered the War and Navy Departments to draw up contingency plans, known by the codename War Plan Orange, in case of conflict with Japan. In 1910, the specter of Japan even prompted one lawmaker to draft legislation for the establishment of a "council of national defense" that would coordinate grand-strategic planning for waging the type of industrial, transoceanic warfare that promised to become more frequent. This long-term forerunner to the National Security Council didn't receive much support at the time, but it hinted at the turn toward securitization that US defense planning would take a few decades later.[44]

Still, while breathless fears of a coming war with Japan grabbed headlines and sold books, most American strategists doubted there was any imminent danger to the United States. While Japan was a strategic competitor, and while the Philippines and Hawai'i were certainly at risk of attack, there was nothing to suggest that Japan posed a direct threat to the United States. The most authoritative historian of War Plan Orange dismisses the periodic invasion scares as "detached from political reality," the products of "paranoia" rather than serious threat assessment.[45] As an Army war gamer put it in 1911, a Japanese invasion of California was "too fantastic to be seriously contemplated," and by this time military strategists—including no less a figure than Alfred Thayer Mahan—doubted that Japan could even occupy Hawai'i let alone the western states.[46]

———

THE THREAT FROM MEXICO, much closer to home but limited in scale and scope, was a regional problem, not a national threat. There were certainly reasons for the United States to be concerned: revolutionaries had been active in the borderlands for decades; nationalists issued the Plan of San Diego, which called for the return of Texas, New Mexico, Arizona, and California, in 1915; and Germany's infamous Zimmermann Telegram promised to assist Mexico in reclaiming this "lost territory" in 1917. It's also true that Pancho Villa and his forces in northern Mexico attacked border towns in the southwest, most infamously Columbus, New Mexico, in March 1916, where seventeen Americans died in the first foreign conflict on US soil since 1815.[47]

With the exception of the Columbus raid, though, these attacks, while serious for the border towns involved, were little more than pinpricks that the US government perceived as a matter of personal safety and local order rather than a crisis of national sovereignty.[48] With millions of soldiers tied down in Europe, the prospect of a German incursion via Mexico was wholly unrealistic, and German rhetoric was overblown far beyond their intentions and capabilities.[49] While some Americans living in boundary-line towns were understandably nervous, tensions along the southern border did not set off panic in Washington about an impending Mexican conquest of the United States. Small detachments of US troops were stationed to keep watch along the border, but they took for granted the security of the nation and their ability to inflict disproportionate harm on anyone who attacked it. Much as they had been doing since 1911, when fighting during the Mexican Revolution barreled right up to the US border, American civilians gathered on their side of the border atop train cars and hotel rooftops to watch the "spectacle" of battle, vicariously thrilling to the sound of bullets whizzing past rather than fearing their towns would be occupied.[50]

Nor, despite pervasive racial contempt for their southern neighbors, did Americans worry about a fifth column that would allow Mexico to erode American security or social cohesion from within. Washington introduced new enforcement measures to tighten its control of the border and reduce immigration, slowing but not ending the fluidity of the borderland areas between northern Mexico and the US southwest, but this was only partially due to security concerns. It was instead Mexicans who fretted that the transborder violence would lead to occupation and even loss of sovereign territory—not an idle worry given Mexico's loss of territory only 65 years before, US annexations in the Pacific and the Caribbean only two decades before, and constant US military interventions in the region that were still ongoing. Congress even drew up plans for making Mexico City an offer it couldn't refuse—the purchase of Baja California—only to be dissuaded by more cautious diplomats.[51]

Thus while US-Mexico relations were fraught, and occasionally violent, the imbalance of power between, as Woodrow Wilson put it, "a powerful nation like this against a weak and distracted neighbor" was simply too great to cause Americans to reconsider their traditional notions of territorial self-defense.[52] Americans felt contempt for Mexico, not fear. In 1914, for example, a US naval commander felt that his Mexican counterpart had dishonored American sailors by refusing to apologize for a minor misunderstanding with a full military salute. His response to this slight was to land US Marines at Veracruz and occupy the city for seven months, at the cost of over 300 Mexican lives. Or consider that when Pancho Villa's irregulars raided American border towns in sporadic hit-and-run operations, the US Army responded by invading northern Mexico with 10,000 troops, with impunity and without fear of reprisal, in what was billed as the Punitive Expedition. In fact, Wilson felt so secure about the Mexican threat that he allowed other forces in the civil war to cross US territory in their own bid to hunt down Pancho Villa.[53] Pershing's mission for "retribution," recalled Columbus resident Mary Means Scott, was "the culminating show" in a local drama, the expedition's departure "a thrilling sight to us."[54] When the American delegation at a 1923 inter-American women's conference proposed a pacifist resolution, the Mexican delegates surprised their northern neighbors by objecting: Mexico, they said, had to preserve its right to use armed force because of the constant need for self-defense against the United States. As one shocked American delegate reported afterward, "all fear the United States, and were not at all reserved in telling me so."[55]

———

BECAUSE IT CAME in many forms, the threat from Germany was clearly of a different magnitude. Like the purported threat from Japan, it stemmed from fears of an overseas competitor that could feasibly project military power far beyond its own borders. But more directly, fears of Germany were also rooted in actual sabotage German agents committed on US soil even before Americans entered the war. If Germany was to defeat Britain, it had to break the supply chain of food, clothing, munitions, weapons, and other war supplies that an ostensibly neutral America shipped to Britain and France. To do that, the German army's Sektion Politik trained saboteurs to live undercover and secretly blow up supply depots and docks. The port of Baltimore was a hotbed of German activity, but the biggest single act of sabotage was the 1916 detonation of an ammunition storage facility at Black Tom Island in New York City's harbor, which caused a massive explosion that damaged buildings six miles away in midtown Manhattan. Even though the term wouldn't be coined for another 85 years, the federal government's "homeland security" response, combined with US entry into the war, brought German sabotage to an end.[56]

Germany also had potential allies, such as Mexico, to join it in under-mining US power in its own backyard. One reason why Roosevelt, Wilson, and Lansing wanted to expand the terms of the Monroe Doctrine was that instability in the hemisphere promised the Germans all sorts of op-portunities to cause trouble. Suspicion that Germany would use Venezu-elan or Dominican indebtedness as leverage to bring them under its con-trol had prompted Roosevelt to issue his corollary in the first place.[57] A decade later, a similar geopolitical vision produced a two-decade US military occupation of Haiti. Goaded by longstanding suspicions of Ger-many and France, and heeding the Navy's fears that a foreign power could easily take over the strategic harbor at Môle Saint-Nicolas, Wilson au-thorized the occupation of Haiti in 1915.[58] And while the Zimmermann Telegram revealed how the United States could be exposed to German en-croachment on its southern flank, the Wilson administration had already been concerned that Mexico was susceptible to hostile foreign manipula-tion.[59] In response, Congress regulated border crossings for the first time with the Passport Control Act of 1918.[60]

But the prospect of a German threat elsewhere loomed much larger than sabotage at home or possible interference in America's neighbors. It was war on the high seas of the North Atlantic and on the battlefields of Europe that led to a more widespread and systematic reevaluation of the tenets of American security.[61] The fighting that broke out in Europe in the summer of 1914 was far away and unlikely to reach US shores, but it still made Americans start to rethink the terms of their self-defense and what it meant in a fully globalized world. The US Navy, which had been exaggerating the German threat for years to justify greater military spend-ing, made this case particularly forcefully.[62] Even if these efforts were false starts, and remained incomplete until the outbreak of the next world war, they laid the groundwork for more radical revisions to come.

Partly this reconsideration was, like Homer Lea's hothouse strategic thinking that foresaw a Japanese invasion of North America, based on the assumptions that German aggression in Europe would inevitably ex-pand to the western hemisphere, and that Germany would quickly seize Caribbean islands as a way to box the United States in and confine it to continental North America. "Germany has the keenest land-hunger of any nation," the journalist and judicial reformer Stuart H. Perry wrote shortly after the outbreak of war. "In ambition she is unsurpassed by any." Pos-sessing "little racial vigor," the peoples south of the Rio Grande would easily fall to "the Teuton," who in turn would transform the Caribbean into a German lake "into which we could enter only by sufferance."[63] Stuart's alarmism was far-fetched, however. After all, Germany had swiftly abandoned an attempt to gain a foothold in Venezuela, in 1903, when confronted with the combined swagger of the US Navy and the Monroe Doctrine, and it's difficult to see why it was in a better position to expand in the western hemisphere while it was waging war on two fronts in Europe.[64]

Despite their implausibility, though, these extreme fears weren't unusual—in fact, they weren't even all that extreme. Others went further, warning not just about German incursions into the Caribbean or that US ports were undefended all the way from Maine to Virginia, but, as one *Harper's Weekly* contributor put it in 1914, that Germany was planning an "Attack on New York."[65] Because "we do not hear the sounds from the guns," a government spokesman told an audience in Pittsburgh, Americans mistakenly "believe that distance protects us and that danger is a myth." Such delusions were as dangerous as a German invasion itself, for they left America unprotected against "a sword of cruelty, oppression, and slavery . . . at the dictates of German commanders."[66] The possibility of a German victory, with Britain removed as a blocking force in Europe and a guarantor of the Monroe Doctrine in the Atlantic, was the worst possible outcome of all, and it gave rise to an alarmist literature about Germany along the lines of what Lea had done for Japan. "You realize," a *New York Times* columnist wrote in addressing Wilson directly, "that if the Germans should by any chance destroy the British fleet New York would be the first objective after London."[67] Americans, another alarmed strategist predicted, would then see "the towns all along the Hudson River—Albany, Poughkeepsie, and others—laid in ruins" if Germany invaded Canada through the soft underbelly of upstate New York.[68] Unsurprisingly, Homer Lea contributed to the genre by detailing a future war with Germany in his 1912 book *The Day of the Saxon*.[69]

More sophisticated perceptions of threat focused on what a German victory, with "military autocracy astride the ruins of Europe and dominant on the seas," would mean for world order even without an outright invasion of the United States.[70] In a pair of influential articles, the US diplomat Lewis Einstein pointed out that German hegemony would be hostile to the United States and would therefore deny Americans the open access to overseas markets they had come to rely on. Britain, Einstein observed, had acted as a shield for the American republic for over a century, but a German victory would remove that shield forever.[71] Much of this worry stemmed from the technological advances that had made global-ization both prosperous (in communications, such as undersea telegraph cables) and dangerous (in military force, such as submarines and torpe-does) and that had extended US interests while also making them more vulnerable. For this reason, shortly before the war Henry Cabot Lodge proposed legislation to expand the Monroe Doctrine so that it explicitly included the safeguarding of far-flung communications installations under the terms of "national safety."[72] "If Germany had deliberately sought an issue that would array the world against her, she could hardly have found one more certain to accomplish this result" than submarine warfare, wrote the Columbia political scientist Munroe Smith, for it "is not only illegal and barbarous, it not only shocks the sense of right and the conscience of humanity, but it also menaces the welfare of the world because of the ex-tent to which civilization rests upon ocean carriage."[73]

For the first time since the early nineteenth century, Americans per-ceived distant, global threats to the United States through an ideological framework and not just as a direct military danger. Germany appeared to present a challenge that could transcend the territorial sovereignty of the United States. "Why are we fighting Germany?" asked Secretary of the Interior Franklin K. Lane. "The brief answer is that ours is a war of self-defense." On closer inspection, however, Lane's war of self-defense "to save America" rested on the goals "to preserve self-respect, to justify our right to live as we have lived, not as some one else wishes us to live"— goals, in other words, that had little to do with "self-defense" as tradi-tionally conceived.[74]

By these more expansive terms of self-defense, security transcended the needs of any one country anywhere. It wasn't merely US security that was vulnerable, another member of Wilson's cabinet argued during the debate over intervention: "Civilization is at stake."[75] The war was a contest for the fate of the world and how the world's people would be governed and interact with each other, a war of ideas and values and not just for terri-tory. It was also a war of laws: even though both the British and Germans violated international laws that protected neutrals like the United States, American lawyers sided almost unanimously with Britain, not by the strict letter of the law but in the spirit of the civilized rule of law.[76] From London, even before the United States entered the war, ambassador Walter Hines Page warned that Germany had launched an "assault on democratic civili-zation" that had in turn triggered a "world-wide conflict between military monarchy and free government." The outcome would "change the course of history for a century," whether the United States became a belligerent or not.[77] "If sheer brute force is to rule the world," he wrote on another occasion, "it will not be worth living in."[78] Page's apocalyptic outlook was widely shared. After Wilson asked Americans to enter the war to make the world safe for democracy, Progressives, Christian pacifists, and others who had opposed intervention embraced the war with its goal of protecting liberty and ending tyranny. As the Progressive editor Hamilton Holt put it in his newspaper, *The Independent,* in 1918, "Woodrow Wilson is today the acknowledged leader of the forces of democracy engaged in the overthrow of absolutism, and the great champion of liberalism on earth."[79] The reformer Ray Stannard Baker's conversion was just as dramatic: "the Germans and all they stood for," he vowed, "had to be defeated."[80]

The prospect of a German victory also amplified the notion that the future of world politics would be a contest between peace-through-liberty and militarism-through-tyranny—and, most novel of all, the notion that tyranny was determined to snuff out liberty wherever it flourished, most notably in what would be the last bastion of liberty, the United States. In this global struggle, Americans wouldn't be defending liberty just from the outside, but also from within. Edward House, perhaps Wilson's closest foreign-policy adviser, believed that "if Germany wins, it means the unspeakable tyranny of militarism for generations to come." Even more ominously, House warned that a German victory would "ultimately mean trouble for us" not simply for the external threat it would pose but because of the undemocratic changes it would force upon the United States. To protect against such a threat that having conquered Europe would presumably be on the march worldwide, the United States would have to "abandon . . . permanent peace" and instead "build up a military machine of vast proportions."[81] Liberty was unlikely to survive the transformation of America into a military fortress, or as Harold Lasswell would later call it, a "garrison state." Wilson agreed, telling House that "if Germany won it would change the course of our civilization and make the United States a military nation."[82]

———

THE GREAT WAR was a battle for civilization in another way, too, one that spoke to racial insecurities that ran deeper than the honor of modern nation-states or the freedom of overseas commerce. The civilization Wilson and others wanted to save was derived from Europe, not Latin America, Asia, or Africa.

White Americans had already long harbored an anxiety that the intensifying global circulation of people, compounded by the white man's burden in places like the Philippines, would endanger their place in the world.[83] Overseas imperialism, for instance, could uplift Filipinos to the extent that they rebelled and eventually, as Texas Congressman James Slayden put it, "imperiled Caucasian civilization at home and the integrity of the white race" everywhere.[84] Empire could also inadvertently open America's door to its conquered subjects, leading many American whites, especially in the South, to become unlikely anti-imperialists.[85] Unrestricted immigration, warned the Asiatic Exclusion League in 1907, could let in anticolonial radicals from India as well as "trained soldiers [and] armed fanatics" from Japan who were bent on destroying American democracy from within.[86] Even if immigrants weren't determined to foment a revolution from within, their sheer numbers could prove overwhelming. Without immigration controls, warned the editors of the *El Paso Times* in 1911, the "Latin will overcome the Anglo-Saxon in this country in a few years—unless you wake up."[87]

In fact, national self-defense had already been invoked to justify immigration restrictions. In 1888, port authorities in San Francisco denied permission for Chae Chan Ping, a Chinese man legally resident in the United States, to return after a visit to China. In a decision the following year, the Supreme Court upheld the exclusion and did so partially on grounds that would later be considered national security. Congress, the court maintained, had been well within its rights to pass an 1882 law banning Chinese immigration that was "approaching the character of an Oriental invasion, and was a menace to our civilization," and although Chae Chan Ping had a permit allowing him reentry when he left San Francisco in 1887, Congress was also within its rights to pass a law while he was away that barred reentry permits. The government, the court pronounced in its decision upholding the extended ban, had not only the right to safeguard its borders, but also a responsibility to preserve the nation's "absolute independence and security throughout its entire territory." As the court went on to explain,

we are but one people, one nation, one power. To preserve its independence, and give security against foreign aggression and encroachment, is the highest duty of every nation, and to attain these ends nearly all other considerations are to be subordinated. It matters not in what form such aggression and encroachment come, whether from the foreign nation acting in its national character, or from vast hordes of its people crowding in upon us. The government, possessing the powers which are to be exercised for protection and security, is clothed with authority to determine the occasion on which the powers shall be called forth.

It was entirely at the government's discretion whether Chae Chan Ping was "dangerous to its peace and security" even though "there are no actual hostilities with the nation of which the foreigners are subjects. The existence of war would render the necessity of the proceeding only more obvious and pressing."[88] In a similar case three years later, this time involving a Japanese immigrant sailing from Yokohama on the very same ship, the *Belgic*, Chae Chan Ping had taken from Hong Kong, the court affirmed its rationale that immigration controls were "inherent in sovereignty, and essential to self-preservation," even though there was no law at that time prohibiting Japanese from entering the country.[89]

The intensity of racialized fears about the Great War in Europe, however, were on a different register. As W. E. B. Du Bois pointed out, for many white Americans "it is not war that alarms them; but the fact that those whites who should fight blacks are fighting each other."[90] Du Bois was right to point out that the racial anxieties of empire were dwarfed by those generated by the Great War. It was not just a contest between Britain and Germany, wrote an alarmed Lothrop Stoddard, but "the first White Civil War" within European Christendom in which the mass slaughter of Anglo-Saxon Britons and Teutonic Germans would leave the white race prone to "migrations which would swamp whole populations and turn countries now white into colored man's lands irretrievably lost to the white world." The main demographic threat, as Stoddard saw it, came from Asia, not Africa, "and the logical end of the White Civil War is racial bankruptcy and the collapse of civilization."[91] Combined with unrestricted immigration, the war amounted to what one critic, deliberately echoing the sociologist Edward Alsworth Ross, called "race suicide" that would eventually mean the subservience of white Americans.[92] "As in all wars since Roman times," lamented Madison Grant, Stoddard's occasional collaborator and perhaps the most widely recognized eugenicist of the day, "the little dark man is the final winner."[93] The renowned naturalist and eugenicist Henry Fairfield Osborn harbored similar fears that the Great War was "dysgenic rather than eugenic."[94] Thomas Dixon, who authored the pro-Confederacy, pro-Klan book that filmmaker D. W. Griffith made famous in the movie *Birth of a Nation,* wrote the script for a short preparedness film called *The Fall of a Nation.*[95] In a February 1917 cabinet meeting, Wilson himself even briefly contemplated staying out of the war "to keep the white race or part of it strong to meet the yellow race" in a future conflict.[96]

As one of those in attendance recalled, "This was a novel and unexpected angle."[97] He shouldn't have been surprised, though, for such views were fairly mainstream among white Americans at the time. Stoddard may have been a Klansman, but this was at a time when Klan membership was hardly unusual. He, Grant, and Osborn were widely respected, Ivy League–educated public intellectuals, while Slayden was an original trustee of the Carnegie Endowment for International Peace as well as a president of the pacifist American Peace Society. And while Wilson was no Klansman, he was both a white Southerner who comfortably accepted Jim Crow segregation as the natural ordering of American society and a Progressive who believed that orderly hierarchies would create the political stability on which social progress could be built.[98] When political elites in Europe and the United States planned for the world that would emerge after the Great War, they did so on the basis that people of color worldwide would not receive any further rights or sovereignty than they already had (which is to say, virtually none).[99] In the years leading up to the Great War, Congress even debated passing an outright ban on African Americans serving in the military.[100]

Thus for all of Wilson's wartime declarations about democracy and national self-determination, it became immediately clear after the war that he wasn't referring to the non-white or extra-European worlds. The international system of the interwar period was in fact based squarely on the expansion of empires, not their retrenchment. If civilization was to be saved, it was white civilization—from itself, certainly, but also from others the world over who were seeking the same rights white Americans and Europeans enjoyed.[101] By this view, the already civilized if wayward Germans didn't pose much of a threat at all. If the Germans actually managed to invade the United States, Andrew Carnegie predicted, "They would make themselves at home and, learning the advantages of staying with us, would become applicants for citizenship, rather than our opponents in warfare."[102] It was a view shared from the Hall of Mirrors at Versailles all the way to the pages of one of Lothrop Stoddard's books on the need for a racial and imperial world order.[103] Nobody said anything similar about the Mexicans or Japanese.

Needless to say, African Americans did not share this view of racialized international security.[104] For them, Germany wasn't as much of a threat to democracy as the United States. As the National Association for the Advancement of Colored People put it in a wartime call to "Enlist!"—not in the segregated Army, where opportunities for Blacks were limited, but in the NAACP—"we know that the fight for humanity and democracy abroad is not more important than the fight for humanity and democracy at home."[105] Du Bois agreed with white supremacists like Stoddard and Grant that the war was a civil war among Europeans, whose "despising of the darker races" led them to fight for colonial advantage in Africa, yet Du Bois did not foresee the end of white dominance as an inevitable result of the war. Thus he drew up an eight-point plan for how US entry into the war should lead to the improvement of conditions for African Americans; he also called for the end of colonialism in Africa. "These are not minor matters," he cautioned. "They are not matters that can wait." If Americans were "to realize world peace and self-government, let us insist that neither the world nor America can be happy and democratic so long as twelve million Americans are lynched, disfranchised, and insulted—so long as millions of other darker folk are exploited and killed."[106]

And if reform didn't come? Then there would be trouble. "There must be a change soon in the attitude of the white men toward the black, else there will be a revolution," predicted one African American writer.[107] Despite fleeting moments of optimism that the war would somehow galvanize racial cooperation at home, Du Bois agreed with this pessimistic radicalism. As part of his famous "Credo," republished in the wake of the war, he professed Peace and Patience but also confidence that "the wicked conquest of weaker and darker nations by nations whiter and stronger but foreshadows the death of that strength."[108] That death, however, would have to wait, and the postwar settlement negotiated in Paris, where Wilson rejected a Japanese-sponsored racial-equality clause and acquiesced in the spread of British and French colonialism in East Asia, Africa, and the Middle East, didn't augur well for the future of international race relations.[109] For now, the editors of *The*

Crisis bitterly noted, the war had merely succeeded in "making the world safe for the white race."[110]

―――――

WHAT WERE AMERICANS fighting for anyway? Was the Great War an existential struggle for the survival of the United States as a sovereign nation-state? Was it a battle to protect ever-expanding US interests in a global age? Its national honor? Its racial purity? Or was it to help create a better world order, not just for Americans but for all people? These were tricky questions, not least because the answer to the most basic question about national survival was clearly "no." "We run no danger of invasion," a peace group led by Randolph Bourne pointed out, and nothing Wilson or preparedness advocates said could alter this geopolitical reality.[111] In fact, Wilson himself concurred behind closed doors, and even Roosevelt had to concede that Americans still enjoyed an "immunity from danger."[112] As the historian Daniel Larsen has demonstrated, American officials thought of vital national defense in very precise, limited terms that did not much venture beyond the nation's borders and coastlines.[113]

Many of the modern developments that frightened Americans into thinking their security was now compromised actually made it easier to provide for national defense. To take one example, the "sea wasps"—submarines—that menaced transatlantic convoys could also "practically insure us against invasion on either the Atlantic or Pacific seaboards," one defense expert noted at the height of the *Lusitania* crisis in 1915.[114] To take another, the completion of the Panama Canal in August 1914—the same month that war broke out in Europe—produced what one military analyst called "a radical change in the strategical situation."[115] With it, the US Navy could now fend off any hostile advance, on either coast, "in shorter time, by weeks, than can be done by any other nation."[116] Mahan had pointed out this geopolitical benefit as early as 1890, and it was Roosevelt's original rationale for building the canal in the first place.[117]

With such clear advantages, the persistence of the free security of the continental United States, even amidst a world at war, remained self-evident despite the domestic fulminations of military preparedness campaigners. Writing after the United States had joined the war, *The New Republic*'s Walter Weyl, an ardent supporter of fighting a war to end all wars, conceded that, because the conflict in Europe lacked "immediacy and proximateness" for the average American, its underlying causes "could not possibly appeal to the Iowa farmer . . . as they appealed to the Norman peasant." Unlike the Frenchman, the "Iowa farmer was not afraid for himself or his country, and would hardly have believed in a German invasion had it occurred."[118]

By the winter of 1917, then, Woodrow Wilson was caught in a difficult bind between war and peace. His solution to this dilemma resulted in the launch of a truly revolutionary change in US foreign policy—a global vision, known ever since as Wilsonianism, that fueled America's rise as an activist, interventionist world power—with the periods "before" and "after" 1917 signifying totally different eras. Rarely has a single individual loomed as large over US foreign policy as when Woodrow Wilson took the United States into the Great War.

We can date the beginning of this revolution with some precision. On April 2, 1917, Wilson traveled the short distance from the White House to the Capitol to deliver his famous call for a war to make the world "safe for democracy." Why he did so, and why at that particular moment, is still a matter of conjecture.[119] By contrast, it's clear what Wilson did *not* do: he didn't say that the United States was under attack, or that it was likely to come under attack, and in asking Congress to issue a declaration of war he didn't portray Germany as a threat to US security. Unlike every war president who followed him, Wilson did not say that the United States needed to fight for self-defense. Even the infamous Zimmermann telegram received only a vague, passing mention. The decision for war, he told the hushed congressional audience, was not an unavoidable necessity but instead a matter of "choices of policy to be made."[120]

To be sure, there were many justifiable reasons for Wilson to seek a declaration of war. On January 31, Germany announced it would resume unrestricted submarine warfare in the Atlantic, making US ships—and American citizens traveling on other vessels—vulnerable to sudden attack; that was Wilson's initial reason to break diplomatic relations with Berlin. Then on February 28 came the Zimmermann telegram. But while there were risks to American life on the high seas, and in theory to US territorial sovereignty in the southwest, Wilson chose not to make entry into the Great War a matter of national self-defense. The reason was simple: there was no clear and present danger to the security of the United States. Even "if Germany won," he told an advisor, "she would not be in a condition to menace our country for many years to come"—and that was only if Germany won, hardly a sure thing.[121] Elsewhere, he candidly admitted of

America's world position that "the fortunes of its own people are not involved" in the European war.[122] As his secretary of state, Robert Lansing, observed at the time, it would have been politically difficult if not impossible to take the United States into a European war over a relatively small number of deaths on the high seas.[123] Wilson agreed, having already signaled earlier in the year that the world's "fundamental human rights" and "the principles of a liberated mankind," not US self-defense, were at stake.[124] In his war address, Wilson didn't use any of the words that would become staples of later national security rhetoric, such as "threat" and "danger," and even indirectly he didn't portray the conflict with Germany as a matter of protecting US sovereignty or territorial integrity.

After framing intervention as a matter of choice in the opening sentence of the speech (a theme he returned to at various points), Wilson laid out the reasons for war. First, by blocking "the free highways of the world" on the high seas, Germany was not just in violation of international law: it had launched "a war against all nations." While the loss of American lives "has stirred us very deeply," Wilson was quick to point out that the ships of other countries had also come under attack. "The challenge is to all mankind," he said, not just to the United States. Curiously, he focused more on how Germany threatened values and principles than human life or territorial integrity: if Germany presented a challenge, it was to the smooth functioning of global society rather than the United States itself. He called on Americans to fight for "the vindication of right, of human right, of which we are only a single champion." America's purpose, he said, "is to vindicate the principles of peace and justice in the life of the world as against selfish and autocratic power." In the speech's stirring final paragraph, Wilson told Americans

> we shall fight for the things which we have always carried nearest our hearts—for democracy, for the right of those who submit to authority to have a voice in their own Governments, for the rights and liberties of small nations, for a universal dominion of right by such a concert of free peoples as shall bring peace and safety to all nations and make the world itself at last free.[125]

All worthy causes, to be sure, but conspicuously absent was the oldest cause for war: self-defense.

"The world must be made safe for democracy." Even the speech's most well-known clarion call was more ambiguous—and ambivalent—than we've appreciated. As a wordsmith, few presidents have been as talented as Wilson, in large part because of the painstaking care with which he drafted his own speeches. We can safely assume that he recognized the unusual emotive power this particular turn of phrase would carry with audiences around the world. We can also assume, then, that this masterful stylist's use of the passive voice was deliberate, and that he left deliberately vague what would make the world "safe for democracy". Unsurprisingly, few of the legislators that day who were voting on Wilson's request for a declaration of war expected US troops would be sent to the fighting in Europe.[126]

We shouldn't be too hard on Wilson's stylistic lapse, for it was almost certainly unavoidable. Wanting to take the nation into the war, but also aware that his reasons for doing so went well beyond the normal dictates of American statecraft, Wilson was caught in a difficult bind. The easiest case to make for war is always self-defense, preferably in defense of territorial sovereignty, but Wilson couldn't realistically make that case in 1917. In this sense, his war address had more in common with McKinley's call for a war to defend the nation's honor and ideals in 1898 than it did with presidential doctrines during the Cold War and the War on Terror. The Wilsonian revolution in American national security was thus something of a false start, casting Americans in the lead role on the world stage, but for abstract principles rather than clear and present dangers. Wilson had conceded as much more than a year before his war address, in a 1916 speech to an annual gathering of railroad barons in New York. After reassuring them that he was a man of peace who had no intention of taking the United States to war, he admitted that sometimes a nation did have to go to war, "because if there is one thing that the individual ought to fight for, and that the Nation ought to fight for, it is the integrity of its own convictions. We can not surrender our convictions. I would rather surrender territory than surrender those ideals which are the staff of life of the soul itself."[127]

In his war address Wilson did, however, make two new and important gestures to what would later become the modern doctrine of American national security. First, he conflated the defense of American lives with the defense of American values; it now mattered greatly to the American interest whether foreign people could practice democratic self-governance or pursue open commerce. Second, although he didn't use the term, Wilson argued that globalization had exposed the United States to new threats, making them less distant and more menacing. Yet for precisely the same reason, it was now America's duty to protect the "scruples of humanity . . . that were supposed to underlie the intercourse of the world." Globalization, and international "outlaws" like Germany that would put it at risk, made it necessary for the United States to enforce law and order in the world community. This took Roosevelt's concept of foreign-policy-as-policing and gave it a global beat. As the international theorist and peace activist Norman Angell told Wilson at the time, insecurity to one member of the community inherently made all members insecure.[128] On this basis, Wilson thus began the process of elasticizing the terms of American national defense away from the narrow protection of territorial sovereignty. He could not complete the process, though, and it faded with the downfall of his vision for a new world order following the end of the war. These false starts toward a new way of thinking about America's position in the world couldn't survive the world order that followed the Great War, yet they laid important groundwork for the national security revolution that was soon to come.

———

IN MILITARY TERMS, the United States had a very good war. The War and Navy departments rose to meet immense logistical and strategic challenges and American servicemen played an important role in beating back the Germans in 1918. With US economic might now mobilized, and with the influx of millions of fresh recruits only just beginning to be felt, Germany sued for peace on Wilson's terms. But this moment of triumph for Wilson ironically marked the beginning of the end of Wilsonianism. The Senate rejected the League of Nations and Americans quietly retreated from their assigned mission to make the world safe for democracy. Perhaps this turn away from a new global order was a lost opportunity, but it was to be expected. The new and seemingly enduring threats posed by the war turned out to be transient, and they quickly disappeared with the advent of peace. Because the nature of these new threats underwrote Wilson's new world order, their disappearance undermined the order's very foundations.

The war hadn't brought a permanent end to America's free security; in fact, the Allied victory not only reinstated but strengthened it immeasurably. The journalist Walter Weyl had noticed this even while the war raged. The United States, he observed in early 1918, still possessed an "unexcelled strategic position" stemming from several factors, "the greatest of which is our relative security" which made the United States uniquely "immune from serious German attack." If Germany could be defeated, Americans would no longer have anything to fear in the world. Despite the new conditions of a global age, Americans retained their structural geopolitical advantages. "We still preserve a remnant of our former physical and moral isolation," Weyl concluded. "We have the freedom of wanting nothing."[129]

Weyl was prescient, his theory given hard supporting evidence after the war ended. Germany was defeated, Europe was exhausted, Mexico was exposed, Russia was convulsed with civil war, Japan hadn't gained much, and Britain's Royal Navy, which had long informally upheld the integrity of the Monroe Doctrine for Americans, remained the world's dominant sea power. Surveying a world map in 1919, Americans would have liked what they saw: all their geopolitical advantages remained intact and all their strategic vulnerabilities had vanished. Moreover, US economic power had grown: after the British blockade and German submarines caused a slowdown in 1914–1915, American exports and bank loans, mainly to the Allies, surged to meet wartime demand, allowing Wall Street to supplant the City of London as the world's financial hub by 1916.[130] Thus while the war had changed everything in much of the world, US foreign policy could resume its usual course as if the Great War had never happened.

Even Wilson had to acknowledge the blissful geopolitical condition in which the country he led into war now found itself. "Who has an arm long enough, who has an audacity great enough," he told an audience in Spokane, Washington, in the fall of 1919—inexplicably so, given that he was barnstorming the country to build support for League membership— "to try to take a single inch of American territory or to seek to interfere for one moment with the political independence of the United States?" When he promised Americans that investing in the League would offer them "98 per cent insurance" against international risk—a critical idea in the development of national security, as we'll see in the next two chapters—it still seemed a bad deal next to the 100 percent guarantee they seemed to get from a return to a traditional foreign policy.[131]

To be sure, the United States did not retreat into a mythical state of "isolationism." Throughout the decade after the war, Americans constantly worked with their partners to stabilize the economic and political situation in Europe. But, without a clear and present danger, the United States refused to join the League, and even denied a French request for an Anglo-

American security guarantee against future German aggression.[132] After the war, officials dismissed the relevance of faraway places in Asia and Europe to US security, and as the historian Daniel Immerwahr rightly notes, it's impossible to conceive of their successors having the same care-free attitude twenty-five years later.[133] Even ardent Wilsonians who carried a torch for US membership in the League recognized the structural difficulty of their task. "Will that disturb us? Can we not keep on reading the Farewell Address under our own vines and fig trees?" asked the distinguished political scientist Albert Bushnell Hart about the revival of hostile powers in Europe or Asia. "Certainly we can." But that wasn't the issue for Hart—not if democracy was to be saved around the world and not if petty conflicts were to be brought to an end before they could spread into something larger. If Americans wanted safe passage in the world, and if they wanted an open international society to thrive, then they needed to act as the primary guarantor of a new world order.[134] For an internationalist like Hart, whether the United States was in direct danger was beside the point, for something much grander and much more precious was at stake. Yet for most other Americans, it was precisely the point.

It's therefore too easy to overestimate the Great War's impact on American conceptions of security. The changes to the requirements of American national defense were neither sudden nor permanent, and they weren't among the war's many consequences. The Great War was globally epochal in many ways, but its impact on American perceptions of threat was remarkably fleeting. This shouldn't be surprising: without a sense of urgency or necessity—and, especially, without a sense of dread—Americans saw little need to play the postwar role Wilson had assigned them. American free security was still alive and well after the Great War had ended, and while the United States remained a great power it had for now given up trying to remake the world in its image. With Pleasant Valley, Idaho, still safe for now, calls to make the rest of the world secure fell flat. To Warren Harding, who promised "To safeguard America first" while campaigning for the presidency in 1920, the fatigue with crusading Wilsonianism was palpable.[135]

This left the United States free to pursue, as it had always done, a foreign policy of almost total choice, driven by ideals as much as interests. Americans benefited from a "peculiarly fortunate situation," Secretary of State Frank Kellogg explained in a 1926 speech. The United States was able to reduce the size of its armed forces drastically after the Great War because of its unique "geographical isolation from those areas of the world where conflicting territorial or political issues" created permanent tension, insecurity, and large standing armies.[136] Two years later, a full decade after the war's end, Kellogg crowned his long career in public service by convincing fourteen other governments to sign a utopian document, the 1928 General Treaty for Renunciation of War as an Instrument of National Policy, that vowed to end war as the world knew it.

The next year, Kellogg won the Nobel Peace Prize as a visionary for a new kind of international relations. But two of the treaty's original fifteen signatories took different paths and returned the world to a very old kind of international relations: Japan invaded Manchuria in 1931 and the rest of China in 1937, then Germany invaded Poland in 1939, plunging the world into a war even more brutal and destructive than the Great War. For a time, the United States was able to stay out of the fighting that convulsed the rest of the world. And when it finally did join the war, as the last of the great powers to do so, it fought on terms that would change US foreign policy and military strategy forever.

[3]

MORAL INSURANCE

WOODROW WILSON NEVER IMAGINED he'd be a war president, and he certainly didn't want to be one. When war broke out in Europe in 1914, he did everything he could to keep the United States out of the conflict. At first this wasn't all that difficult a task, as most Americans weren't keen to enter the fighting either. And why should they be? The United States had no clear security interests at stake, and the only significant movement to push for intervention—coming from preparedness campaigners in the Plattsburgh movement, the National Security League, and the American Defense Society—consisted mainly of Republicans devoted to Wilson's nemesis, Theodore Roosevelt.

In this first phase of the war, Wilson adamantly opposed preparedness as unwise, unnecessary, and counterproductive. Without a clear and present danger threatening the United States, an enlarged military made up of peacetime conscripts would only undermine, not protect, American democracy. He explained his position in his second annual message to Congress, in December 1914. "From the first," he reminded his audience, "we have had a clear and settled policy with regard to military establishments. We never have had, and while we retain our present principles and ideals we never shall have, a large standing army." Germany simply did not pose a risk that should lead Americans to abandon this tradition; and if Germany did end up posing a greater risk, Americans would turn to their expansible army, as they always had. "If asked, Are you ready to defend yourselves? we reply, Most assuredly, to the utmost; and yet we shall not turn America into a military camp. We will not ask our young men to spend the best years of their lives making soldiers of themselves." American

77

military power would "make itself effective should occasion arise," but that occasion was not yet on the horizon. Most important was Wilson's justification: "when half the world is on fire we shall be careful to make our moral insurance against the spread of the conflagration very definite and certain and adequate indeed."[1]

What exactly was "moral insurance"? For Wilson in 1914, it meant devising foreign policies—in this case neutrality—that would allow the United States to mitigate against the uncertainty of risk in a way that would preserve the cherished traditions of American democracy. The greatest danger was not from Germany. Instead, it came from the abuse of power and infringement of liberty that would result from building a large standing army.

When Wilson reversed his policy on preparedness a year later, and urged Americans to gird for war, he also changed his mind on the metaphorical risk of fire and the nature of insurance. "I want you to realize just what is happening," he cautioned an audience in Pittsburgh not long after his conversion to preparedness, in January 1916. "The world is on fire, and there is tinder everywhere. The sparks are liable to drop anywhere, and somewhere there may be material which we can not prevent from bursting into flame." Because Americans had been effectively fireproof in the world system for a century, they had failed to do what was necessary to manage risk. Thanks to global interdependence and the rise of German militarism, that risk was now threatening to become unmanageable. "It amazes me to hear men speak as if America stood alone in the world and could follow her own life as she pleased," he said, even though he himself had spoken along those very lines only a year before. "I must tell you that the dangers are infinite and constant," making it "absolutely necessary that this country should prepare herself, not for war, not for anything that smacks in the least of aggression, but for adequate national defence." The truth was now straightforward: "America can not afford to be weak."[2] He sharpened the point two nights later before an audience in Milwaukee: "the rest of the world is on fire and our own house is not fireproof. Everywhere the atmosphere of the world is thrilling with the passion of a disturbance such as the world has never seen before, and it is wise ... that we should see that our own house is set in order and that everything is done to make certain that we shall not suffer by the general conflagration."[3]

It was no coincidence that Wilson used fire as an analogy to explain the new state of things to American audiences. The comparison of warfare to fire is natural: both can quickly spread out of control in unpredictable ways, the damage caused by war is often from the burning of buildings and even people, and metaphors linking them—firefights, the firing of guns, in the line of fire, and so forth—are commonplace. But even more specifically, the social and cultural fabric of Wilson's America had been shaped inordinately by fire. The Southern cause in the Civil War, which did much to shape Wilson's worldview, was finally consumed when advancing Union soldiers burned Atlanta in 1864 and retreating Confederate soldiers burned Richmond in 1865. Between then and the Great War, the harnessing of heat, through steam engines and blast furnaces, fueled the second great industrial revolution in history that made the United States the richest country in the world. Yet it was also an era when fire could be unimaginably destructive: rapidly growing, poorly planned cities still consisted mainly of wooden buildings; brick buildings were held together by flammable mortar; and new, increasingly common fuels like coal, oil, and gas were stored in hazardous conditions in densely populated cities. Chicago burned in 1871, as did much of Boston the next year, with Baltimore following suit in 1904 and San Francisco in 1906. Countless smaller towns and cities suffered similar fates.[4]

Nor was it strange that Wilson alluded to the necessity of insurance, specifically fire insurance. During his lifetime, when holding other types of insurance policies wasn't all that common, taking out fire insurance had become much more widespread: when Wilson was an adolescent, insurance covered approximately half of burn-damaged buildings; by the time he was president, that coverage had grown to over three-quarters.[5] In telling Americans they had to get "our own house . . . in order" and do whatever it took "to make certain that we shall not suffer by the general conflagration," Wilson was drawing on this increasingly common practice of paying for coverage to hedge against the costs of uncertainty—to turn, as Frank Knight argued, uncertainty into risk—especially when those uncertainties could start in one particular place but then spread to devastate an entire city.

Yet individuals, even in the aggregate, could never afford policies that would cover the entire community. As an expert in fire insurance noted in 1916, the same year Wilson gave his warning that the world was burning, "little thought has been given to the communal aspects of the economic system of fire insurance" because most people assumed it was a matter of individual responsibility. Yet it was obvious that the entire community, not simply one or two homeowners, would likely suffer from the outbreak of a fire. This was the problem of what Berkeley mathematician A. W. Whitney called "the conflagration hazard," an apt metaphor that Wilson had used to explain the dangers posed by the Great War.[6] "Fireproof construction of single buildings does not make them safe, if they are surrounded by burnable buildings," noted another fire insurance specialist, which meant that the wider community had to act in concert to prevent a fire from spreading in the first place, before the damage had been done.[7] Thus the issuance of such policies had to come from a large, powerful, centralized source. As economists pointed out, businesses might be tempted to save money by using smaller companies offering cheaper premiums, or even foregoing insurance altogether, but doing so would backfire by not providing adequate coverage to cover major losses. Ultimately, despite their problems, only the largest insurance brokers were a safe bet. Managing risk by collectivizing damage and pooling costs—what Knight called "consolidation," with groups easier to manage than the individual—made much more sense than every family or business acting alone for themselves.[8] Another solution, spearheaded by progressive states like Wisconsin and New York in the years before the Great War, was to regulate fire insurance so that coverage was guaranteed and premiums remained affordable.[9]

These approaches to fire insurance formed the conceptual basis of Wilson's turn to preparedness. The analogy to international security was easy to draw: as preparedness groups demonstrated in 1915–1916, it was impossible for smaller groups to organize large-scale military force on a voluntarist basis; only the federal government could provide adequate protection in a hostile world. Large private brokers could provide local insurance against fires, but for adequate coverage against potential international risks, of the kind posed by empires like Germany and Japan, only the federal government would do. This is what Wilson meant when he told his listeners in Milwaukee that it was time to "fireproof" their country in a world at war. "Constant vigilance is the price of security," intoned the Wilson administration's Committee on Public Information during a public-education campaign on fire prevention that also provided a moral of the story of the Great War.[10]

The widespread use of the fire metaphor reflected a much broader trend in the evolution of national security—a trend just as important as the change in military threat perception explored in the previous chapter. For a theory of national self-defense as comprehensive as national security to work in practice, it would need not only to identify more complex and distant threats to the continental United States but also to establish a much more robust system of meeting those threats. For Americans confronting the problem of the Great War, this meant developing a comprehensive warfare state that included a broader social safety net alongside a larger military establishment. Because the war occurred during the Progressive era, when the complexities of industrial democracy and global interdependence forced policymakers to become much more interventionist in managing national and international affairs, and when the foundations of free security came into question for the first time in a century, the innovators of national security found it much easier to create a modern warfare-welfare state than ever before.[11] And while this new state receded in the interwar period, it never went away entirely, instead remaining ready to be revived and expanded when the next crisis came.

———

NOT ALL AMERICANS shared Wilson's hesitant dread at the prospect of the United States becoming a readily prepared "military nation."[12] The outbreak of war in Europe gave a significant boost to advocates of a larger US military, bringing to a head the crusade that Emory Upton and Elihu Root had launched decades before. In 1914–1915, the heirs to this crusade—led by Root's close friend, Army Chief of Staff General Leonard Wood—organized a campaign for military "preparedness," arguing that the parlous state of the US Army left the nation in a vulnerable defensive position in case of attack and too weak to be able to play a decisive role in world affairs. In the event of an attack or other national emergency, cautioned one military strategist, all the nation could do was stage a holding action so that the armed services could mobilize and expand to sufficient strength.[13] At the outbreak of war in Europe, the United States could call on just over a hundred thousand soldiers—fewer, notes the historian Michael Neiberg, than the casualties the French army suffered in just the first two weeks of the war.[14] The preparedness movement therefore called for a much larger military, enhanced coastal defense, and a greater emphasis on strategic planning to ensure the protection of the United States in a world at war. Preparedness campaigners also called for more focus on national cohesion, a tighter linkage between domestic security and national defense, and greater awareness of

the opportunities a diluted national identity presented to foreign enemies. Preparedness, in other words, captured the essence of an emerging
national security ideology like nothing before.

In fact, the most prominent and influential of these preparedness
groups was the first in American history to bear the name of this emerging but still-unformed doctrine of defense: the National Security League
(NSL). The brainchild of two passionate preparedness campaigners—
Republican Congressman Augustus Gardner, a conservative progressive
from Massachusetts, and Stanwood Menken, a well-connected Wall Street
lawyer—the NSL's mission was to mount a nationwide "patriotic education" campaign in favor of enhanced military training and enlarged armed
forces through peacetime conscription. Based in New York and counting
250 branches nationwide at its height in early 1917, the NSL featured an
impressive array of elites from industry, banking, law, and government—
or, most commonly, people who moved effortlessly between the private
and public sectors—including two recent Secretaries of War (Elihu Root
and Henry L. Stimson) and several titans of industry (Cornelius Vanderbilt,
Bernard Baruch, Henry Frick, Simon Guggenheim).[15] One of their fellow
founding members, US Army Colonel Frederic Louis Huidekoper, had
already been warning about the lack of an adequate force for a decade.
After touring the Western Front in 1915, Huidekoper published, under
NSL auspices and with an introduction from General Wood, a revised and
updated edition of Emory Upton's classic history of America's small armed
forces under a new and more direct title: *The Military Unpreparedness of
the United States*.[16]

Gardner set the idea for the NSL in motion when he took to the floor
of the House of Representatives, in October 1914, to propose the establishment of a bipartisan "National Security Commission" to investigate
the state of America's military readiness. Using an allusion to the new
technology of moving images, which of course traded in the selling of
fantasies, he cast doubt on the hallowed American tradition of an expansible military to address sudden emergencies. "The theory in this country
that we can create an army and a navy right off the reel," he said when
introducing his National Security Commission resolution, "is totally and
entirely wrong."[17] As a former National Guardsman who had fought the
Spanish in Cuba, Gardner spoke from the kind of experience that was
hard for others to dismiss. Neither could anyone doubt the sincerity of
his convictions: when the United States entered the Great War in 1917,
Gardner resigned from Congress and reenlisted in the army, at the age of

fifty-two. And as the son-in-law of Henry Cabot Lodge, he also had clout. A short time later, Lodge himself introduced the same resolution in the Senate, arguing that while the expansible army had been appropriate for its time, the nation now faced a war that posed challenges "far beyond anything which the framers of the Constitution could have imagined." In such an unprecedented world crisis, the "organic law" allowed for the growth of a much larger permanent army and navy, and the means to pay for them. A new, enlarged army wasn't necessary if the current one was fit for purpose, but, Lodge lamented, "Ours is not." And, unlike in years past, American weakness would simply be "a standing invitation to aggression and attack."[18]

The National Security League wasn't the only preparedness group; others also based their mission on the safeguarding of American shores from foreign invaders. Despite its sharp edges, the NSL was actually considered too soft by many in the preparedness movement, and they broke away to form a new outfit, the American Defense Society (ADS), which allied itself to Theodore Roosevelt.[19] Shortly after the founding of the ADS, Roosevelt's first cousin, Philip Roosevelt, started publishing *American Defense,* a magazine dedicated to promoting the twin causes of preparedness and Americanism. The first issue, in January 1916, featured articles with titles such as "America's History of Unpreparedness," "The Navy We Have Not," and "The Bloodthirsty Pacifists," the last of which argued that peace crusaders brought on violence by enabling aggressors to launch wars.[20] Roosevelt castigated Wilson's fitful moves toward preparedness by making a now-common combustible analogy: "To prepare a little but not much, stands on a par with a city developing a fire department which, after a fire occurs, can put it out a little, but not much."[21]

Wilson initially rejected the call for preparedness by publicly rebuking, among others, Congressman Gardner.[22] "It is said in some quarters that we are not prepared for war," Wilson declared in his 1914 annual message to Congress on the state of the nation. "What is meant by being prepared? Is it meant that we are not ready upon brief notice to put a nation in the field, a nation of men trained to arms?" To Wilson, the question was absurd because the idea of preparedness was absurd: "Of course we are not ready to do that; and we shall never be in time of peace so long as we retain our present political principles and institutions." And the more he thought about preparedness, the more absurd it seemed. "What is it that it is suggested we should be prepared to do?" he asked the members of Congress. "To defend ourselves against attack? We have always found means to do that, and shall find them whenever it is necessary without calling our people away from their necessary tasks to render compulsory military service in times of peace." This seemed a certainty to Wilson not simply because of the sanctity of American tradition but the impossibility of a foreign attack on US soil. "We are at peace with all the world. No one who speaks counsel based on fact or drawn from a just and candid interpretation of realities can say that there is reason to fear that from any quarter our independence or the integrity of our territory is threatened."[23]

To Wilson, preparedness represented an almost total break with the terms of American democracy. In every conflict since the War of 1812, including the Civil War, Americans rose to challenges as they arose. Preparedness, by contrast, "carries with it a reversal of the whole history and character of our polity." Bowing to its demands "would mean merely that we had lost our self-possession, that we had been thrown off our balance by a war with which we have nothing to do" and "whose causes can not touch us." Wilson could not have been any clearer as he tried to bring the matter to what he hoped was a close: "Let there be no misconception. The country has been misinformed. We have not been negligent of national defense."[24]

But of course, that was not the last word on the subject. The preparedness movement instead increased in size and activity in 1915–1916, and German attacks on US shipping increased as the war ground on. And as the course of the war—and just as importantly, the domestic politics of war—changed, so did Wilson's stance. In the winter of 1916, he traveled to places where intervention was a tough sell, such as Chicago, Cleveland, and Topeka, to give a series of stump speeches on the need for a larger army. Although he didn't dwell on the remote prospect of a direct enemy attack, he admonished Americans not to think of themselves as a nation apart. "This is the last war . . . of its kind or of any kind that involves the world that the United States can keep out of," he said in a campaign speech that promised to stay out of the war even as it hinted that was becoming increasingly untenable. "I say that because I believe that the business of neutrality is over; not because I want it to be over, but I mean this, that war now has such a scale that the position of neutrals sooner or later becomes intolerable."[25] On another occasion that year, in announcing US support for the creation of a new international organization to regulate world affairs—what would become the League of Nations—he warned Americans: "We are participants, whether we would or not, in the life of the world. The interests of all nations are our own also. We are partners with the rest. What affects mankind is inevitably our affair as well as the affair of the nations of Europe and of Asia."[26] Upholding the principles of humanity didn't exactly amount to a call for national defense, let alone national security, but it was a crucial start.

Preparedness groups welcomed Wilson's about-face even if they couldn't abide his holistic globalism. Their common denominator was an insular nationalism that easily translated into a prejudicial nativism widely embraced as "100% Americanism." As the NSL and ADS continually demonstrated, fear of an enemy within came easily to preparedness advocates; militarism and nativism proved to be a natural pairing.[27] Even before American entry into the war intensified nationalistic fervor, both Roosevelt and Wilson had come out against "hyphenated" Americans who might harbor dual loyalties. Americans were "a composite and cosmopolitan people," Wilson said in calling for patriotism while also cautioning against a nationalistic overreaction. "We are of the blood of all the nations that are at war."[28] Before 1917, Wilson actually introduced a previously obscure but ultimately enduring catchphrase to political discourse— "America First"—to stress upon all Americans the need not to ally with the causes of the old country over the needs of American neutrality. But the views of many other Americans, not least those who had marched for preparedness, had already slipped beyond such subtleties into an ideology of 100% Americanism, and in 1917 the intensification of American patriotism brought the rest of the country with them.[29]

Ultimately, the key objective for the preparedness movement was keeping America safe from foreign invaders, be they German armies or Jewish immigrants. Many of those who called for a larger military establishment were nationalists, not globalists or Wilsonians. The NSL and other like-minded preparedness groups failed to provide answers to the challenges of globalism, or even those facing US foreign policy in an interconnected world, because they didn't really care about those sorts of questions in the first place. Their real goal was to keep America pure, strong, and, in the words of the NSL president, "a manly Nation."[30] Their cause embodied much older ideas, about protecting America's continental sovereignty and keeping the nation free from foreign attack and pure from foreign influence, rather than new visions of global interdependence.[31] In its vision of US foreign policy for the new era, the NSL promised a stalwart

"Defense not offense" as it stood "guard at the door"—hardly a liberal internationalist blueprint for remaking the world in America's image.[32]

———

FOR PREPAREDNESS CAMPAIGNERS, whether they were nationalists or internationalists, insurance proved to be an irresistible metaphor. Insurance and military efficiency sprouted from the same conceptual ground as progressivism: a desire for improvement by modernizing and rationalizing society in ways that preserved what were thought to be the core elements of American identity, democracy, and sovereignty. It wasn't a stretch, then, for advocates of a larger military to locate their position within broader trends that propelled a progressive state in the pursuit of a better society. "What else can there be but insurance to property, life, and happiness to the body politic in the maintenance of a well-disciplined army of liberty-loving and patriotic citizens?" asked an army major in 1915.[33] Another preparedness campaigner proposed that the 3.5 percent of income the average American spent on insurance become the benchmark for national defense spending.[34] One naval strategist of the era even portrayed the stockpiling of oil reserves at strategic points around the world as "an important part of the national insurance."[35]

At the time, however, insurance was mostly still a private affair. Risk and uncertainty are the lifeblood of capitalism, and few societies were more capitalist than the United States. Americans simply accepted risk as part of the natural economic order of things. Until the New Deal, they considered risk personal, not social. If they wanted to pool their resources to hedge against risk, that was literally their business, not the government's. From its halting origins in colonial maritime insurance, and later in the Philadelphia and Boston financial markets of the early nineteenth century, private insurance coverage grew exponentially. The value of life insurance policies, for example, grew ten thousandfold between 1825 and 1875, and, as we've seen, fire insurance coverage also expanded at a similarly stunning rate. Around the time of World War I, large insurers such as Equitable and Met Life innovated "group insurance" policies to provide blanket coverage to employees of private companies. Aside from workplace accident compensation, which began to proliferate in the states in the early twentieth century, however, government played little role in this emerging industry's bonanza, and the main competitors to private insurance companies were fraternal orders and church denominations car-ing for the widows of deceased ministers. Most government proposals to mitigate the crippling effects of a downturn—such as the Populist "subtreasury plan" of the 1880s–1890s, which would use government funds and infrastructure to enable farmers to hedge against wild fluctuations in commodities prices—went nowhere. By the onset of the Great War, government-provided social insurance of almost any kind was nonexistent in voluntarist America, even as it spread in Europe.[36]

Yet even though government social insurance was still but a dream in the mind of progressive planners like I. M. Rubinow, the problem-solving allure of the insurance principle was strong enough to inspire even greater plans that went beyond mere local or even national protection.[37] Taking advantage of the increasing commonality of insurance, Josiah Royce proposed it as the basis of a new world order that would guarantee perpetual world peace. Royce, a philosopher at Harvard and leading intellectual of religion and morality, unveiled his plan at the singularly inauspicious moment of August 1914. Undeterred, he argued that the outbreak of the Great War—already on its way to becoming the most destructive war in European history—made plans like his more timely than ever. Once novel, the "insurance principle . . . tends more and more both to pervade and to transform our modern social order." Royce's plan never caught on because it was literal, not metaphorical: he actually envisioned world politics could be tamed by a common fund into which nations paid and which independent trustees (more honest and scrupulous than politicians) managed "with no political power or obligations whatever." Because by its very nature insurance "very largely takes the form of mutual insurance," it was superior to other forms of social protection: "It contributes to peace, to loyalty, to social unity, to active charity, as no other community of interpretation has ever done."[38]

With its rejection of politics, lack of enforcement, and inattention to power differentials in the international system, Royce's insurance plan died a quick death; unlike other peace initiatives of the time, it wasn't even all that helpful in building a foundation for the League of Nations. But it did help popularize the notion that political sovereignty could best be protected not through military might alone, but in conjunction with social cohesion fostered by the state. This was the formula Franklin Roosevelt later perfected with his social security/national security dyad and that has remained potent ever since. Moreover, Royce also identified one of the key problems that has bedeviled national security up to the present: moral hazard. As Royce admitted, "the very success of the plan . . . would tend to render individual nations careless," for just as "the man whose house is insured may thereby be rendered less rather than more careful with regard to the risk of fire," a nation with insurance—or military preparedness—could well be more inclined to settle its disputes with force. Rather than preventing conflict, insurance could actually encourage the resort to war.[39]

The risk of moral hazard wasn't much of a concern for preparedness advocates, many of whom were in fact eager to justify preparedness in progressive terms. Some, such as the Harvard pragmatist philosopher Ralph Barton Perry, argued that preparedness would enable the state to provide wayward young men with purpose and structure while also bringing all Americans into closer communion with the nation and its cause in the world.[40] Others, such as Theodore Roosevelt, argued that "our ultimate aim" was a comprehensive national policy of "military and industrial preparedness," with one "as vital as the other" so that Americans could "guarantee future peaceful and just development at home and future immunity from attacks by outside nations."[41] Roosevelt particularly believed that military service would acculturate immigrants to the basic civic duties of American citizenship.[42]

Still others offered an even more systematic conception of the state's social-welfare obligations to its citizens in an increasingly complex world. Building on the growth of the social-welfare state in a progressive age, and foreshadowing many of the ideas later implemented by the New Deal's social/national security state, the Yale economist Henry Crosby Emery argued that military preparedness could provide a simple and affordable hedge against the risks of the modern world system, thereby protecting US citizens from the perils of uncertainty. As the dangers of random unpredictability increased, the state's protective capacities against these uncertain risks must expand, too. This was a marked departure for Emery, who made his reputation in the 1890s theorizing that financial speculators were entitled to amass large fortunes because they assumed risks on behalf of others in society—indeed, for the benefit of others—while generating broad economic growth if they were successful (but taking on the risk of financial ruin by themselves alone). Emery lived a fascinating life—as the first non-Yalie to become a professor at the university, an eyewitness to the Bolshevik Revolution, a prisoner of war after being captured by the Germans while fleeing Russia for Sweden, and an American banker in China—but he was best known for his theories of managing risk in financial speculation. By the era of the Great

War, however, he had dramatically changed his view and come to accept that the least the federal government could do for its people was to take on much of the burden of risk management in the modern world. Domestic political economy was as good a place as any to begin.[43]

In 1913, General Wood invited Emery to address the officer corps at the Army War College on the relationship between economics and warfare. The traditional American aversion to a large standing army that cost money and threatened liberty was woefully outdated, Emery argued to a receptive audience. Whereas America had long been "exempt by our geographical position" from the problems of the world, modernity had made that increasingly untenable: "Our isolation to-day . . . is by no means so complete as we had formerly thought." Pacifism was no longer realistic, he argued; nor was disarmament, for the reach of modern weapons meant that even a relatively isolated country like the United States was at risk. To those who argued that war was destructive, Emery countered that war was the foundation of modern capitalism, and that capitalist societies could mobilize for war in ways that actually ensured prosperity and enhanced productivity. In fact, by not properly preparing for war, the United States was taking a massive economic risk by not being ready for the day war came—and according to Emery, that day was inevitable in an ever-closer, interdependent world.

But even more, Emery argued, preparedness would provide a social-welfare benefit that would ensure domestic security as well as defense against foreign enemies. Given the technical skills required of the modern soldier, "compulsory army service is nothing more than compulsory education" and not the infringement of individual liberty people often assumed. Smart businessmen who had once shunned insurance as an unnecessary expense were now spending money to protect themselves against unexpected risks, and preparedness, Emery assured, was merely "in the nature of business insurance." This was a worthy kind of government expense because of the double security it provided citizens, from both external and internal dangers. Not only were Americans "living in a fool's paradise to assume so readily this absence of risk for ourselves," they were also foolish to think they couldn't "afford insurance much better than other nations." Emery conceded that his knowledge of military tactics was limited, but given global conditions he felt confident that the United States had to start taking out national insurance through preparedness. And on subjects he knew well, he was emphatic. "Despite the fact that we all grumble about taxes"—the 16th Amendment legalizing a national direct income tax had only just been ratified—"the fact remains that we have as yet only scratched the surface of the taxing capacity of the American people for Federal needs." Coming from a gold-standard Republican economist, this was a remarkable assessment, but Wood and his fellow army officers would have appreciated it all the same.[44]

By linking together political economy, social welfare, and national defense, economists like Emery turned out to be just as critical innovators of national security as Homer Lea or Elihu Root. The idea that war could be a guarantor of personal welfare in an industrial democracy was not just new, but revolutionary. Previously, the concept of insurance had done metaphorical work for *opponents* of a larger military—recall, for example, Wilson's 1914 speech to Congress in which he channeled hallowed tradition to claim that a small standing military provided the nation with "moral insurance" against domestic militarism. But by 1916, metaphor was becoming reality, and even Wilson changed his mind to accept that if the nation needed "moral insurance," it would have to come in the form of a larger standing army and universal military training.

Sure enough, when he reversed his position on preparedness Wilson also inverted his insurance metaphor. But he went even further than that, unexpectedly so given that it came in a speech to railroad tycoons in New York. "America is always going to use her Army in two ways," he told the assembled captains of industry. One was in pursuit of national defense, or what Wilson euphemistically called "the purposes of peace." But the second had nothing to do with war, or even peace for that matter: "she is going to use it as a nucleus for expansion into those things which she does believe in, namely, the preparation of her citizens to take care of themselves." This was a modern, two-dimensional version of national defense: "there is not merely the military side, there is the industrial side." Preparedness would enable the federal government to train a generation of young men in vocational skills to protect their social security while at the same time building up forces to protect America's national security. Wilson vowed that his plan "will make these same men at one and the same time industrially efficient and immediately serviceable for national defense," which was very much in keeping with other plans floating around. But Wilson was even more ambitious, for military defense was but a means to an end. "Men will think first of their families and their daily work, of their service in the economic ranks of the country," he explained, "and only last of all of their serviceability to the Nation as soldiers and men at arms." Two years before Wilson had found such an idea anathema, contrary to everything in the American political tradition. Now, he assured people that it was "the ideal of America."[45]

———

PROPELLED BY THIS ideological fuel from preparedness and progressivism at home, and Wilsonianism abroad, US entry into World War I gave rise to an enormous American warfare state. Until then, American wars had been fought on an ad hoc, emergency basis as a series of one-offs that didn't require a large, permanent military establishment. The army may have grown thanks to the modernizing efforts of military reformers such as Upton, Root, and Wood, but by 1917 it remained small, especially when compared to Europe's armies even before their expansion after 1914. The navy was in better shape yet still in the same overall position.

The Wilson administration's first task was to ensure it had enough of a military to be able to fight the nation's first land war in Europe. The United States had fought a major campaign in the Philippines, but that was very small scale compared to what it would take to help defeat Germany; it certainly couldn't expect to do so with an army roughly the size of Mexico's or Belgium's.[46] Mobilizing for the Great War posed a greater logistical, fiscal, and political challenge than Americans had ever faced, or than traditional notions of voluntarism and an expansible army were used to handling, and so the size and coercive power of the state grew as a result. Congress increased defense spending by 2,400 percent in just two years, from 300 million in 1916 to 7.1 billion in 1918; it would nearly double again, reaching a peak of 13.5 billion, for the 1919 fiscal year.[47] (Even those increases only raised a military that was the world's seventh largest.)[48] Congress also approved conscription, only the second time Americans had been subjected to the draft.[49] The Navy had already been steadily increasing in the decades before the war, but the challenge of expanding the army to fight a ground war on another continent was particularly daunting: not only would the US Army have to enlist millions of new soldiers, it would have to equip, train, house, feed, and transport them across the Atlantic under enemy fire.

The result, exulted one observer, was an army that had "expand[ed] from a Mexican border column into a steel-hard machine capable of cracking the shining armor of Germany."[50] This may have been nationalistic wartime hyperbole, but as an assessment of US military effectiveness in Europe it wasn't far off the mark: after overcoming an inevitably steep learning curve and an initially haphazard mobilization effort, US forces made a vital contribution to the defeat of Germany in 1918.[51] That this unprecedented American mobilization was successful owed everything to a vast increase in government power, with two major pieces of legislation paving the way in 1916. First, the National Defense Act brought forth a near-doubling of the Army, a quadrupling of the National Guard and the granting to the president authority to federalize it in times of emergency, the creation of the ROTC, and the establishment of an aerial service branch that would later become the air force. Second, the Naval Act significantly expanded the size of America's forces at sea, not just in capital ships but also in the kind of support vessels and infrastructure in which the country was sorely lacking.[52] The only thing missing for now was the proper development of aviation (especially bombers), which lagged behind the air corps of the European powers.[53]

Naturally, with such a massive and sudden increase in the size of the armed forces and the scale of their mission, there was a correspondingly massive and sudden increase in demand for wartime materiel, which in turn stimulated a new era of innovation in American industry. Much of this was stoked by security fears. Now cut off from the world's leading petrochemicals industry, in Germany, and fearful that this would put the United States at a strategic disadvantage, US companies like Du Pont, aided by the appropriation of German trade secrets, ramped up their own petrochemicals development and production, not only helping the US war effort but also laying some of the seeds for the economic boom of the postwar decade.[54] Auto manufacturers, fast becoming the dominant sector of the new industrial economy, similarly transitioned their production lines to make vehicles and other materiel for the war effort. Despite the very strong antiwar views of its visionary founder, who launched a "peace ship" to Europe in 1915, the Ford Motor Company worked overtime to churn out not just trucks and cars for the military, but also steel helmets, Eagle-class anti-submarine surface ships, and even aircraft engines.[55] Thus, despite Henry Ford's pronounced anti-statism, widely shared among his peers, industry worked closely with government. As the president of the recently established United States Chamber of Commerce observed in 1918, "War is the stern teacher that is driving home the lessons of cooperative effort."[56]

Private industry wasn't the only beneficiary of US intervention, as the welfare side of the warfare state also received a significant boost. Once the nation entered the war, Congress passed the Military and Naval Insurance Act, thereby creating the first comprehensive social-welfare system for servicemen and their families—including the provision of life insurance, described by Treasury Secretary William McAdoo as a "right" for citizens serving their country.[57] The 1914 War Risk Insurance Act, amended in 1917 to broaden coverage in such a way that prompted one expert to call it "probably the greatest single step that has ever been made in the history of insurance, not only in this country, but in the world," established a unit within the Treasury Department to widen access to life insurance for servicemen.[58] As Children's Bureau director Julia Lathrop, one of the architects of the expanded bill, put it to skeptical lawmakers, "The least a democratic nation can do, which sends men into war, is to give a solemn assurance that their families will be cared for—not kept from starvation, but kept on a wholesome level of comfort."[59] The military also created a fairly broad state-provided healthcare system for wounded soldiers and sailors that became the forerunner to the Department of Veterans Affairs (although, ironically, these healthcare plans were motivated by a desire to reduce the costs of postwar pensions for disabled veterans).[60] The federal government also used the war to set up new programs, and work with private organizations like the YMCA, to compel improvements in the moral character and standard of living of millions of American men.[61]

To pay for all this, Congress passed the War Revenue Act of 1917, which tripled—and, for some of the higher brackets, quadrupled—income tax rates which had only just been made constitutional a few years before. This built on the Revenue Act of 1916, which raised taxes to pay for Wilson's preparedness program.[62] And to ensure the running of a smooth wartime economy, Wilson established the National War Labor Board and the War Labor Policies Board, with representatives from both workers and management sitting on both bodies, and the War Industries Board to ensure rational purchasing by the War and Navy departments.[63]

Such measures pulled at the seams of the voluntarist constraints that had prevented the emergence of a full-blown welfare state. The seams wouldn't actually break until later, under the combined pressures of the New Deal and World War II, but the wartime measures of 1918 were nonetheless unprecedentedly strong, especially in promoting the idea that the federal government was the only entity that could ensure security of all kinds for all Americans. According to the Treasury department, they reflected "a national government enterprise with the authority and financial strength of the greatest and most democratic government in the world."

For the security of the American people, the government entered "a business undertaking that it alone could afford to enter and one which no combination of private capital would have dared risk." This was nothing less than "Uncle Sam's great and growing civilian army engaged in national service."[64] Economists concurred. Wartime conditions made most risks uninsurable for private companies, so wartime necessity compelled the government to step in. The effect was to raise the standard of living for servicemen and their families, a large enough cohort of the population to have a major impact on national social welfare. In particular, the 1917 expansion of the War Risk Insurance Act marked the advent of a "state-socialistic program that is being adopted in America under the stress of war conditions."[65]

FREE SECURITY HAD ALLOWED for the United States to have such a small military until 1917, but traditional fears of a large, standing army and a federal government with strong taxing powers were key factors, too. The reactionary character of many of the preparedness groups, such as the National Security League, not only reinforced these longstanding anxieties about republican political liberties but also stoked the progressives' growing fears about Republican political intrigues. None of this bode well for democracy in America. Wilson spoke for many when he worried that once they went to war Americans would "forget there was ever such a thing as tolerance." No doubt he had the NSL in mind. "To fight you must be brutal and ruthless," he said as he agonized over the decision for war, "and the spirit of ruthless brutality will enter into the very fibre of our national life, infecting Congress, the courts, the policeman on the beat, the man on the street."[66] As he confided to one of his officials, "War is autocratic."[67]

These were prescient words. As Wilson pointed out, war made it impossible to maintain a neutral stance, let alone a dissenting one. This is true for any society at war, at any point in history, but in 1917 there was a unique American twist to this truism. Because the United States itself was more or less immune from foreign attack, the federal government had to explain the stakes of the war in no uncertain terms to the American people; and because those stakes were mostly conceptual—to safeguard civilization and build a new world order, not to defend life and property in the continental United States—the architects of war had to exaggerate the gains and losses at stake in America's war to an almost eschatological scale. This task fell mainly to a new government body that, in true bureaucratic fashion, had a deceptively anodyne name—the Committee on Public Information, or CPI—that hid the scope of its powers. Headed by George Creel, a progressive journalist who promised Wilson that he'd whip American opinion "into one white-hot mass instinct with fraternity, devotion, courage, and deathless determination," the CPI demonized Germany and apotheosized the United States.[68]

Wilson himself certainly lived up to his words. Once at war, motivated by Wilson's warning to the "hyphenated Americans" of immigrant stock that "If there should be disloyalty, it will be dealt with a firm hand of stern repression," the federal government ruthlessly cracked down on any lingering antiwar opposition.[69] The protection of secret information, a relatively new phenomenon in US statecraft that wasn't codified until the 1911 Defense Secrets Act, drastically tightened during the war. The Army expanded its Military Intelligence Division to root out anyone suspected of infringing the war effort, which quickly came to include not just German saboteurs but Japanese communists and members of the Universal Negro Improvement Association. Military and police forces were already tackling the problems of domestic sabotage and terrorism, but two months after joining the war Congress passed the Espionage Act, which aimed to prevent interference with military preparations and operations but also effectively criminalized dissent. A year later Congress passed the even more restrictive and punitive Sedition Act; when the socialist leader Eugene Debs continued giving antiwar speeches, he was charged with sedition and received a ten-year prison sentence. Despite broad claims that the war would make the world safe for democracy, Wilson himself never really squared the circle between war and individual liberty—quite the opposite, in fact, as the widespread repression at home illustrated.[70]

In a classically American fit of civic voluntarism, public-private partnerships sprang up to help protect American security and ensure prowar unity, often through the suppression of dissent, with non-state organizations effectively acting as an auxiliary force to service the Wilson administration's homefront needs. Needing little encouragement to do its part to enforce national discipline, the NSL took it upon itself to help police the war effort in both thought and deed. But even its zealous patrolling of the domestic front lines was surpassed by the American Protective League (APL), a Bureau of Investigation offshoot made up of private citizens who offered to monitor immigrants, socialists, union members, and especially

German American communities in the hunt to root out "slackers" who dodged the draft. APL volunteers—as many as 250,000 by early 1918—were private citizens, but they carried federal badges and coordinated their operations, or "slacker raids," with law enforcement at all levels of government. While they caught very few actual slackers trying to evade the new Selective Service system, tens of thousands of young American men were swept up in the APL's dragnet.[71]

Civic voluntarism was quintessentially American; so too was federalism. Groups like the NSL and APL therefore weren't the only ones ready to augment Washington's efforts to root out any potential threat to the nation—so too were the states. In 1916, Congress created the Council of National Defense to coordinate the nation's economic and resourcing needs in waging a new kind of war, but its functions were soon eclipsed by existing departments and agencies once the war broke out. In truth, CND had little to do with national defense from external enemies. Its duties included bolstering public morale, educating the public on the objectives of the war, and sharpening public perceptions of the enemy—in other words, it was also a propaganda ministry not unlike the Committee on Public Information—and these operations soon constituted most of its wartime role. Perhaps inevitably, the CND's ministering to the psychological imperatives of the home front could be every bit as socially invasive as the efforts of the National Security League and American Protective League. Moreover, the CND created a branch council of defense in each of the states, and many of these coercive propagandistic tasks fell to the state councils—many of which were more activist and wielded more authority than the federal CND. The Nebraska Council of Defense, to take one representative example of many, targeted German Americans by successfully pushing for a ban on foreign-language teaching and religious services (not coincidentally, German was the state's predominant foreign language).[72] Minnesota established its own Commission on Public Safety and gave it "almost dictatorial powers."[73]

WITH WILSON FOCUSED on victory, it fell to his allies in the progressive movement to reconcile domestic liberalism with foreign war. Progressives feared the antidemocratic effects of war, but many of them couldn't shake the nagging suspicion that war might actually help create a more egalitarian democracy. John Dewey, whose views influenced many progressives, overcame his wariness of war to embrace Wilsonian intervention as an opportunity to achieve a truly progressive society through a truly enlightened, more efficient state. Dewey's optimism was grounded in his certainty that the United States would embrace its role in the new world order that was in formation. "In actuality we are part of the same world as that in which Europe exists and into which Asia is coming," he explained even before the United States had entered the war. "Industry and commerce have interwoven our destinies. To maintain our older state of mind is to cultivate a danger."[74] Central to this moderately prowar, progressive vision was a stronger federal government that would centralize many of the powers of the state in the interests of taming private industry, regulating the economy, and providing Americans with greater social equality and a shared patriotic identity. (Not coincidentally, Creel's CPI and General Wood's army were both thoroughly progressive institutions.) But also central was the notion that the United States was now enmeshed in global networks, of ideas and especially trade, that in turn presented Americans with new challenges to their place in the world. Only stronger government could meet the new challenges of a global age.[75]

For these progressives, chief among them the editors of *The New Republic*, a new magazine for the well-connected liberal intelligentsia, the entire basis of this new world order turned on what Dewey had diagnosed as a crisis of interdependence. Modern industrial society as an increasingly transnational phenomenon meant that the long period of America's free security was coming to an end. The "isolation which has meant so much to the United States, and still means so much," Herbert Croly presciently noted in his 1909 bible for progressivism, *The Promise of American Life*, "cannot persist in its present form."[76] It was probably Croly—the magazine's editorials were unsigned—who declared "The End of Isolation" in *The New Republic*'s inaugural November 1914 issue and compared the impact the war would have on the United States to the transformative impact European contact had on Native Americans centuries before.[77] Walter Lippmann, who used his position at the magazine to become the most celebrated of the progressive intellectuals, put a similar argument more bluntly in 1916: "isolation is out of the question because it postulates an impossibility. . . . Those who talk of isolation merely reveal their indifference. They simply refuse to face the stern realities which a change in world conditions has revealed to the imagination."[78]

In itself, with a growing number of American commentators identifying 1914 as a new era, this wasn't a particularly original insight. But the

New Republic progressives went further, by making connections between the security of the United States in a new world order with the security of the American people in a new industrial democracy. They weren't the only progressives to see the war as a chance to centralize governmental authority and thereby facilitate a more democratic society, but they were unusual in arguing that security was indivisible, be it foreign or domestic.[79] In 1909, Croly had argued that the "Atlantic Ocean will, in the long run, fail to offer the United States any security from the application of the same searching standards. Its democratic institutions must be justified, not merely by the prosperity which they bestow upon its own citizens, but by its ability to meet the standards of efficiency imposed by other nations. Its standing as a nation is determined precisely by its ability to conquer and to hold a dignified and important place in the society of nations."[80] Once that moment of truth arrived in 1914, Croly called on Wilson to build "a political and economic organization better able to redeem its obligations . . . to its own citizens," which in turn would allow Americans to return peace and stability to Europe.[81] Lippmann drew a similar link between what would later come to be called social security and national security. Many of his fellow progressives, he acknowledged, worried "that the war against Prussian militarism would result the other way, that instead of liberalizing Prussia the outcome would be a prussianization of the democracies." That was a possibility, but only as "the result of a German victory. And that," Lippmann added, "is why we who are the most peaceful of democracies are at war."[82]

It was Croly and Lippmann's collaborator at *The New Republic,* the political economist Walter Weyl, who provided the fullest expression of an emerging liberal welfare-warfare state. Weyl saw the state as a kind of benevolent protection racket, much as social scientists would in later decades, in which the people exchanged loyalty to the state for reforms that would improve both the quality and equality of daily life and enhance citizens' security in American society. Only the federal government could curb the ever-growing, overbearing political power of corporations and tame the "wild excesses of individualism." The "democratic ideal," Weyl explained in *The New Democracy,* his 1912 blueprint for a better society, "is not only to maintain, but vastly to increase and improve, the life, health, intellect, character, and social qualities of the citizenry." In this compact, the "democratic control of government" was essential, for only it could provide the "peace, social security, and general well-being" that all Americans of all classes desired, within the bounds of political accountability.[83]

Initially, with the outbreak of war, Weyl feared that America's steady if uneven march of progress had run into a wall. "Our isolation is gone," he declared in 1916, "and with it our sense of security and self-direction." The war in Europe conclusively demonstrated "that we were in a military sense vulnerable," that "mere distance" no longer provided "complete safety," and that "unarmed neutrality and a mere lack of hostile intention does not always save a nation from invasion." The United States was no longer "a remote island in a blue sea."[84] For these reasons, Weyl was an enthusiastic supporter of intervention, and he anticipated Wilsonian ambitions to make the world safe for democracy by drawing a Rooseveltian analogy to the dictates of domestic order. Just as "anarchistic" forces eroded domestic security, and just as the state uses "compulsion . . . over the individual citizen" to ensure order so as to make political justice and social progress possible, so must the United States and other like-minded democracies enforce international order. The "future of international concord lies . . . not in a purely *laissez-faire* policy, but in applying force to uphold a growing body of international ethics."[85] Ever since its founding, the American state had provided its citizens democracy through the security of self-government and the rule of law; that, too, could be the solution for international order, through the establishment of a league of nations. Weyl called this "internationalism," and he hoped it could be an effective antidote to nationalism everywhere. But the end goal wasn't simply for the altruistic benefit of others. "We are going abroad," he explained, "to protect our own American democracy." The reformation of world order would lead to international peace and, in turn, ensure the security of the United States. Weyl was no starry-eyed idealist. "However much we desire internationalism," he wrote in 1918, "we can accept it only on the condition of security. Safety comes first."[86]

Not all progressives fell in line with Wilson's war. Randolph Bourne, Weyl's erstwhile colleague at *The New Republic* and a Dewey protégé at Columbia who bitterly fell out with his mentor over American intervention, didn't believe that anything good could come from war. Bourne was deeply skeptical that war could be protective of the people's welfare or could provide for their social insurance. Instead, the state had a will of its own, a pure will to power for the sake of power, and only those who wielded it stood to benefit. Military intervention was therefore antidemocratic, for all it did was enhance the power of those already in power. The reason for this was straightforward, Bourne wrote: "War is the health of the State." It was true, he acknowledged, that the people looked to the state for protection when frightened for their safety, but such threats only existed because of the state's obsession with maximizing its power in the first place. And during the Great War, the United States itself wasn't even under threat. America's cause in 1917 was thus one of "offensive self-defense, undertaken to support a difficult cause to the slogan of 'democracy.'" While it instilled a "Consciousness of collectivity," it was not the kind of collectivist mindset progressives should welcome. Feeling insecure, the people would coalesce to "produce concerted action for defense, but also to produce identity of opinion." It was impossible for the war to be progressive, Bourne argued; it couldn't help but be reactionary and repressive, and it was an inevitable outcome of the wartime emergency that ordinary Americans would suffer simply for expressing peaceful opinions that were harmless, indeed commonplace, before the onset of war. "The State," he warned, "is a jealous God and will brook no rivals."[87]

————

RANDOLPH BOURNE and Walter Weyl didn't live to see how their clashing visions of national security fared. A month after the war ended, Bourne died in the influenza pandemic at the age of 32; a year later, Weyl passed away from cancer at the age of 46. But it's likely that both would have been surprised at how suddenly the holistic ideology of national security disappeared from the political scene. Despite the manic state-building efforts of the Great War, the American warfare state remained embryonic compared to what had happened in Europe and what would later happen in the United States during World War II and the Cold War. Partly this was because Weyl's plan for how the state would provide for Americans' security, both at home and abroad, was actually rather limited and lacked a broad base of support. But mostly it was due to the ebbing of the international crisis that allowed for the growth of a warfare state in the first place.

When the war ended, preparedness groups strove to maintain their mission despite losing their reason for being. Both the National Security League and the American Defense Society tossed aside their call for permanent universal military training and instead dedicated themselves to a countersubversion crusade against "various disturbing elements generally masquerading under the guise of socialism."[88] These "elements" often being Russian and Jewish, the remaining hardcore of preparedness became a wholeheartedly nativist movement. The NSL urged the American people to "wake up" to a gathering storm of a "social revolution downward" that planned for "the overthrow of American institutions and ideals just as surely as if a Bolshevist army was marching on Washington."[89] Anti-communism, which easily slipped into anti-Semitism, became the NSL's new crusade, while the ADS went on the offensive against immigration. Following a series of bomb attacks in New York and Washington in 1919, the Department of Justice joined in, targeting domestic anarchists and communists, mostly Russian Jewish immigrants who heeded Vladimir Lenin's call from Moscow for world revolution.[90] So did the War Department, which drafted Special Plan White to combat political threats of internal subversion.[91] By 1924, the year Congress effectively slammed the door on further immigration, the American Defense Society published Madison Grant's white-supremacist fantasy of an "America for the Americans."[92] Without a great power to fight, the only remaining enemy seemed to lurk within.

The effective repression of leftists and radicals, combined with the tightening of anti-immigration restrictions and the receding of any semblance of threat in the international arena, brought Americans back into an era of free security. This was not due to the sudden disappearance of many of the things that supposedly made Americans feel vulnerable—quite the opposite, in fact, as military technologies at sea, on the ground, and in the air continued to advance. Neither did the international conditions that Croly, Lippmann, and Weyl had observed during the war disappear: the world remained deeply interconnected, Americans traveled widely in the interwar years, and US companies did booming business in Europe, Latin America, and Asia. But America's potential enemies were in ruin, either defeated (Germany), weakened from revolution and civil war (Mexico and the Soviet Union), or contained (Japan, for now), while domestic subversives on the left actually went into decline because the newly established Soviet Union shunted them aside in its claim for the undisputed leadership of world revolution.[93] Thus while the United States wasn't exactly isolated in the world—indeed, it never had been—the continuation of global interdependence did not automatically translate into heightened threat perception for US foreign policy. And with the expensive turbulence of the war years behind them, Americans were happy to stop paying the premiums for moral insurance that Wilson had started when he embraced preparedness in 1915. The Great War's moment of insecurity turned out to be just that—a moment—and it vanished almost as quickly as it emerged.

[4]

THE BRIDGE IN CHICAGO

I N THE FALL OF 1937, the state of the nation and the state of the world appeared to be moving in opposite directions. At home, despite a sharp downturn that began earlier that year, the New Deal had seemed to tame the Depression, and though the economy hadn't yet fully recovered there was a sense that the worst of the crisis was over. Overseas, however, conditions were deteriorating. In Europe, Nazi Germany was rearming, Italy had conquered Ethiopia, and Spain's democracy was under siege, while in Asia the Japanese army had invaded China that very summer.

The escalation of the world crisis troubled Franklin Roosevelt, but as much as he would have liked to do something about it he was constrained by public opinion at home. Few Americans sympathized with Germany or Japan, but fewer still wanted the United States to intervene to stop them. But Japan's assault on China spurred FDR into action. In August 1937, Japanese tactics in the Battle of Shanghai—the deliberate targeting of Chinese civilians and little impunity for the city's European and American imperial enclaves—shocked Americans. The Japanese faced determined resistance, and their siege dragged on through September and into October. At that point, Roosevelt was on a national speaking tour, and he used a stop in Chicago to address the crisis in China.

In unusually strong terms, using language he normally reserved for domestic opponents of the New Deal, Roosevelt condemned the "reign of terror" that was plaguing the world. In an interdependent age of transcontinental military technologies and mass totalitarian movements, "let no one imagine that America will escape, that America may expect mercy, that this Western Hemisphere will not be attacked and that it will continue tranquilly and peacefully to carry on the ethics and the arts of civilization." The world was now in "a state of international anarchy and instability from which there is no escape through mere isolation or neutrality." In the speech's most memorable passage, Roosevelt compared war to a virus and warned that an "epidemic of world lawlessness is spreading." When disease raged out of control, the normal government response was to impose a "quarantine of the patients in order to protect the health of the community against the spread of the disease." It was now time, FDR concluded, to quarantine aggressive states such as Japan before they spread the virus of war and conquest to the international community itself.[1] During a previous global conflict, Wilson's analogy to the uncontrollable forces of war had been fire. Roosevelt's was disease.

Thus did Franklin Roosevelt deliver one of the most memorable foreign-policy speeches in American history. Yet he hadn't planned to use his time in Chicago to talk about the world crisis. He was actually there to dedicate the opening of a new bridge over the Chicago River that connected the northern and southern halves of Outer Drive (later known as Lake Shore Drive) for the first time. And for the people of Chicago, the opening of the Outer Link Bridge was a much bigger deal than the war in China. Up to a million people turned out to hear Roosevelt, and over two thousand police—one-third of the entire force—were there to keep order not only for the president's speech but for the "music, pageantry, and a parade." FDR was ceremonially "driven twice through the loop" and showered with "cheers and festoons of ticker tape . . . streaming down from office windows." Thirty-six thousand cars—more than would normally use the other city bridges in an entire day—crossed in the first hour of operation, a figure that would have been even higher had so many drivers not stopped to collect souvenir windshield stickers to commemorate the special occasion. The *Chicago Defender* declared the celebrations "by far the greatest civic demonstration in the city's history."[2] Harry Hansen, a prominent local historian, called the opening of the bridge "the realization of a dream" that began a century before.[3] Urban planner H. Evert Kincaid judged the bridge a centerpiece in "the most important of all the dreams for civic betterment."[4] The *Chicago Daily Tribune* declared the construction of the bridge "undoubtedly one of the greatest achievements—if not the greatest—that any city has ever accomplished."[5]

This hometown boosterism was exaggerated, perhaps, but understandable. 1937 marked the centenary of Chicago's incorporation as a city, and the double-decked Outer Link Bridge—the world's largest bascule bridge, which could be raised to allow for the passage of river traffic—signaled ambitious plans for the city's growth in the automobile age.[6] Solving the puzzle of the Chicago River had been at the heart of these ambitions for decades. Before the opening of the bridge, links between the North Side and the South Side of Chicago had been snarled by the "strangling traffic burdens" of bridges on local city streets.[7] As the authors of a 1929 City Council study put it, the two halves of Chicago effectively operated as separate municipalities, and "the Chicago River forms the dividing line." A bridge that would connect an expressway between the two halves was "vitally necessary" for the smooth functioning of the rapidly expanding city. Once built, it would create "one of the most important thoroughfares in the country."[8]

Everyone agreed on the need to bridge the gap in the city's main transportation artery, but nobody could agree on how to fund it. Several proposals came before Congress in the 1920s, but none was successful.[9] The onset of the Depression, which in turn led to Herbert Hoover's fiscal retrenchment of an already-tight public purse, made the likelihood of an Outer Link Bridge all the more remote. The city and state governments began initial work on the bridge anyway, funding it with bond issuances, but the gap between ambition and feasibility—financial, but also engineering—was too great, and by the time Roosevelt entered the White House in 1933 the bridge project was stalling along with most of the city's other locally funded infrastructure projects.[10] But Roosevelt's election, and the coming of the New Deal, changed things. The Public Works Administration (PWA), headed by Secretary of the Interior Harold Ickes, himself a Chicagoan, filled the funding gap and ensured that the bridge would be completed.[11]

The Outer Link Bridge was one of the many PWA projects that completely transformed America's urban landscape.[12] For the throngs of people to see it opened, the bridge captured the very essence of Roosevelt's promise to the American people: the New Deal didn't simply use countercyclical measures to prime the pump and revive the old economy, it did so in ways that improved the daily lives of ordinary Americans. In fact, the reason Roosevelt was on a speaking tour of western states that autumn, beginning in Wyoming and ending in Chicago, was to celebrate the planning achievements of the New Deal. He had taken a similar tour in 1934, when the New Deal was facing its first serious bout of criticism. With the recent recession putting the country once again in a similar frame of mind, it was natural for him to return to some of those New Deal works projects that were "doing a national good"—such as the massive hydroelectric dams at Bonneville, Oregon, and Grand Coulee, Washington—and whose construction he had inaugurated only a few years earlier. As Roosevelt made his way east to Chicago in late September 1937, over a grueling ten days of rallies, speeches, and meetings in every northern state from Washington to Minnesota, he gave an impassioned, sometimes defiant, defense of the New Deal.[13]

The liberalism that sat at the heart of social democracy provided Roosevelt with the opening to his Chicago speech as well as his segue to the world crisis. On his western swing, he had "seen the happiness and security and peace which covers our wide land," and while he took pride in the New Deal's part in bringing security to the American people he also couldn't help but contrast it with other parts of the world. In earlier eras, Americans could observe foreign crises with detachment, but "under modern conditions" they "must, for the sake of their own future, give thought to the rest of the world." This was not only because the United States was in the world, but because crisis conditions everywhere were fundamentally the same. "There is a solidarity and interdependence about the modern world," he told the crowds in Chicago, which made it "impossible for any nation completely to isolate itself from . . . upheavals in the rest of the world."[14] Contrary to the judgment of historians, then, the speech's foreign-policy topic was hardly "ostensible" or "unrelated" to the dedication of the bridge, and nor had Roosevelt "abruptly changed the subject."[15] It was precisely on point.

If Roosevelt's speech was supposed to prompt Americans to "give thought" to world affairs, he chose what was probably the most challenging location imaginable. Chicago was a politically combustible city, home to polar opposite views on economics and foreign affairs. The New Deal had passionate support in Chicago, which had been transformed by public works projects of the kind that had brought Roosevelt to the city that autumn day.[16] Moreover, much of the theory behind the New Deal came from the progressive social planners at the University of Chicago, such as Charles Merriam. But the city was also home to some of the New Deal's fiercest critics, ranging from *Tribune* publisher Robert McCormick to the neoclassical economists at the university.[17] Yet the choice of Chicago was deliberate. Secretary of State Cordell Hull, who was "increasingly worried over the growth of isolationist sentiment," urged the president to "make a speech on international cooperation in the course of his journey" to the western states, "particularly in a large city where isolation was entrenched."[18] Chicago was perfect.

Other domestic concerns animated what appeared to be a foreign policy speech. In seeking peace for the international community, Roosevelt drew on the metaphor of policing. Maintaining order was necessary for security to exist, yet the interwar era was marked by a crime wave fueled by Prohibition and the Depression. In response, the New Deal offered not just a program for social welfare but also a war on crime, and these two expansions of state power were supposed to work in tandem to preserve domestic order by maintaining a broad state of security. Roosevelt turned to the concept of policing as he was drafting his Chicago remarks, telling Ickes that he wanted to keep the "bandit nations" in line, and the fear of world "lawlessness" featured prominently throughout the quarantine speech.[19] Two weeks later, in a letter to Woodrow Wilson's old advisor Colonel Edward House, Roosevelt said Americans had to use "our influence to curb the riot" raging around the world rather than hiding in their houses behind locked doors. The metaphor may have been different, but the law-and-order sentiment was the same.[20]

Fittingly, the speech's Foucauldian "quarantine" metaphor, which drew on the use of the government's emergency powers at their most extreme, came from Ickes, who, as secretary of the interior and head of the PWA, operated at the very center of the New Deal's most statist interventions in American society. There was no mention of a quarantine in the version of the speech the State Department drafted, and the first a "startled" Hull knew about it was when he and his aides gathered to listen to it on the radio with "vexation and misgiving."[21] Nor, moreover, was the notion of imposing a quarantine to control "dangerous and loathsome contagious disease" purely metaphorical.[22] Roosevelt himself, afflicted with polio, knew this all too well. Congress had already passed two Quarantine Acts (1878 and 1893) establishing procedures for the outbreak of infectious diseases among people, and public health officials aggressively—and unusually, at least compared to Britain—resorted to imposing quarantines to curtail local outbreaks of disease, as well as during the influenza epidemic of 1919–1920, and in 1937 polio outbreaks were still controlled by imposing a local quarantine of the infected.[23] And for decades, US agricultural officials had successfully used quarantines to reduce contagious diseases among livestock.[24] In fact, many listening to Roosevelt's speech would likely have encountered a serious contagious disease—and government efforts to control it—in their own lives.

But perhaps most crucially for Roosevelt's audience, the quarantine was also a key tool in the increasingly strict immigration controls for arrivals from East Asia. The notion that Asians—more precisely Japanese, for whom the epithet was originally coined—constituted an unstoppable "yellow peril" social virus had been fixed in the western imaginary for decades by the time Roosevelt went to Chicago. On Angel Island in San Francisco Bay, as well as at ports in Hawai'i, highly invasive medical examinations often further led to the enforced quarantine of immigrants. A medical regime of inspection and quarantine existed on Ellis Island for European immigrants, too, but because Americans pathologized Asian diseases as more virulent and lethal than those from Europe (even if they were the same diseases), the resort to quarantining was more frequent on Angel Island. In invoking a quarantine against Japanese aggression, FDR's extension of biopolitics to international relations was not just a stylistic flourish.[25]

Whatever its cultural and ideological origins, in October 1937 the quarantine speech met with a mixed reception, and did little to change the existing foreign policy of strict neutrality; some Congressmen even called the speech an impeachable offense, and neither the Germans nor the Japanese took it seriously.[26] But it did lay down the political and ideological foundations on which Roosevelt only a few years later launched a revolution in American war and diplomacy that would expand the first line of US defense geographically, conceptually, and politically. The ideological basis of that revolution was already on display in Chicago in October 1937, when Roosevelt started to weave its two main strands—social economic welfare and national self-defense—together into the new doctrine that would soon be known as "national security."

This vision of government, expressed at an actual bridge in Chicago, marked a metaphorical bridge between an old order and the new: from old concepts of limited state intervention in national economics and international relations to new concepts of an activist, often unrestrained role for the state in managing the domestic economy and world order. In national security terms, the New Deal was the forerunner to the Cold War consensus, while quarantine was the forerunner to containment.

And what of the Outer Link Bridge? During World War II, which proved to be the making of "national security," Chicagoans stood on it to watch the "ships of war, built in the many shipyards of the Great Lakes, enter the Chicago [River] for passage down the Mississippi to the Gulf" before sailing to do battle in the Atlantic or the Pacific.[27] Later, during the Cold War, city leaders in Chicago officially rechristened it with an entirely appropriate name: the Franklin Delano Roosevelt Memorial Bridge.[28]

————

THE WALL STREET Crash of 1929 ushered in a period of chronic instability and crisis in which the futures of capitalism, democracy, and world peace were suddenly in jeopardy. One of this era's defining characteristics was perpetual uncertainty. As Ira Katznelson has argued, uncertainty breeds fear because it is grounded in ignorance about the future: people are uncertain because they have no way of knowing when the crisis they're in will end, or even by what means it could end. Uncertainty is immeasurable because it is based upon an infinite number of unpredictable variables, and thus upon imperfect knowledge. In the 1930s, when serious planning about future probabilities was still in formation, understandings of both the past (the sources of the crisis) and the future (the ways out) were little more than conjectures. The prevalence of uncertainty was, in turn, the cause of pervasive fear. The New Deal was therefore designed to alleviate uncertainty and overcome fear.[29] The same would soon be true of one of the New Deal's most consequential products, national security.

As the University of Chicago economist Frank Knight theorized in his landmark 1921 book *Risk, Uncertainty and Profit,* uncertainty was a different conceptual state than risk. Unlike uncertainty, risk could be calculated based on a wide array of sources of information. Because it was based on information, risk could be managed through individual choice or policy prescription. A "*measurable* uncertainty, or 'risk' proper," Knight argued, "is so far different from an *unmeasurable* one that it is not in effect an uncertainty at all." There was a "crucial . . . distinction between measurable risk and unmeasurable uncertainty" as to make them almost totally different phenomena.[30] Turning anarchic uncertainty into manageable risk, Katznelson argues, was the New Deal's prime objective, because from there New Dealers could build a system to ensure security.[31] This new liberalism prioritized security as much as it did liberty, because without security there could never be any liberty.

There was, however, considerable irony in Knight's position as a lodestar for the New Deal. For one thing, he hated the New Deal, which represented "a fundamental historical drift of western civilization toward bureaucratic tyranny" and sent him into his own psychological depression. "This to me is the meaning of the 'New Deal,'" he wrote to Friedrich Hayek in 1934: "it is just a detail in the general movement of west European civilization away from liberalism to authoritarianism."[32] For another, when Knight theorized about uncertainty and risk, he actually did it to praise uncertainty and warn about excessive attempts at risk management. Managing risk was a natural instinct for individuals but, theoretically, if broadly adopted as government policy, it could neutralize the fluctuating dynamics of capitalism and render it inert. "It is a question of how far to go," he surmised, and he worried about an innate tendency of the state to go too far.[33] Capitalism required profit derived from individual choice, and without uncertainty there could be no profit. If this meant somebody, somewhere, would incur loss, so be it; that was capitalism. By contrast, government management of risk, even for the benefit of society, would only make the economy unprofitable at the expense of individual liberty.[34] Thus the reformers' assumptions that Americans needed "security to progress," he wrote (directing his comment specifically to the New Deal economist Alvin Hansen), "smack of naiveté."[35] Tellingly, Knight's antonym for "security" was not uncertainty, risk, fear, or even insecurity—it was "adventure."[36]

Knight was especially critical of the new macroeconomic vision of John Maynard Keynes, the Cambridge economist whose landmark 1936 book *The General Theory of Employment, Interest and Money* provided sophisticated justification for a mildly statist response to the Depression. In a lacerating review of Keynes's "unsubstantiated" theory, he lamented that it "requires extensive re-interpretation . . . before it can be accepted as sound or useful." Sounding very much like the formidably exacting teacher he was renowned to be, Knight chided Keynes for relying on so many "caricatures which are typically set up as straw men" and "abstractions" that made the book hard to read and even harder to understand. It provided no real theory at all.[37] He was even more scathing in private. Knight vented to his Chicago colleague Jacob Viner that Keynes was just pandering to the "anti-intellectual" crowd with comforting but simplistic theories; instead of devising useful theory, Keynes was instead merely "passing the keys of the citadel out of the window to the Philistines hammering at the gates."[38]

But in Knight's critique of Keynes, there was further irony still, because the differences between their views, while great, were not as great as they appeared.[39] As Angus Burgin has pointed out, the first, interwar generation of Chicago School economists was more intellectually ecumenical and

ideologically inconsistent than the more famous swashbuckling economists who followed in the 1960s and 1970s. Knight's own views were
flexibly eclectic enough to have something for everyone (although perhaps
not Keynes). He may have hated the New Deal, but he also didn't have
much faith in laissez-faire capitalism—which, if left unchecked, would de-
vour itself, and the societies it purported to serve along with it—and he
saw more statist interventions in economic life as an inevitable if regret-
table response to the Depression. "We cannot go back to laissez faire in
economics even in this country," he wrote in 1933.[40] Keynes couldn't have
put it better himself.

The same year that Knight published *Risk, Uncertainty, and Profit*,
Keynes published his *Treatise on Probability*. While Keynes's concerns
were different than Knight's, he also perceived the calculation of risk as a
sliding scale and implied the unknowability of uncertainty. Probability
could therefore be intuited, but never known definitively.[41] *A Treatise on
Probability* marked a significant moment in Keynes's evolution as an economist who used theory to encourage social reform.[42] The key difference
between Knight and Keynes was that the Knightian entrepreneurial
spirit recoiled from Keynesian macroeconomics and Rooseveltian social
security as misguided quests for an equilibrium that would manage risk
to the point of total stability—which could ultimately pose an existential threat to capitalism itself. For Knight, uncertainty was the essence
of capitalism; for Keynes and Roosevelt, managing risk would be its
salvation.

From 1933 onward, Roosevelt and his advisers often turned to Keynesian solutions as they grappled fitfully with the crisis of the Depression.
The fit was an easy one, as Roosevelt and Keynes shared a temperamental
and philosophical communion: they were both moderates, reformers
rather than revolutionaries, who feared communism as much as laissez-
faire. Roosevelt was "the trustee for those in every country who seek to
mend the evils of our condition," Keynes notified readers of *The Times* of
London at the start of 1934. "If he fails," then all hope of "rational change"
will fail with him, "leaving orthodoxy and revolution to fight it out."[43]
Keynes was a lifelong admirer of Edmund Burke, a cautious reformer often mistaken for a doctrinaire conservative, and his own disposition in
the face of emergency was rooted in a Burkean wariness of radicalism and
a "doctrine of least risk."[44] While Roosevelt was no intellectual, and was
probably more familiar with Edward Burke (an anti–New Deal congress-

man from Nebraska) than he was with the philosopher, moderation was also his operating principle.

In his *General Theory,* Keynes hoped that his ideas would lead to "gradually getting rid of many of the objectionable features of capitalism."[45] This was also the spirit of the New Deal. One of the most objectionable of those features was uncertainty—or, as a different group of progressive economists was beginning to call it, insecurity. The basic rule of Keynesianism, Keynes himself explained to the nonacademic readership of *Redbook* magazine, was that in times of economic emergency "it is for the government, the collective representative of all the individuals in the nation, to fill the gap" left by struggling private industry and capital. "If private individuals refuse to spend, then the government must do it for them."[46] Uncertainty, and with it fear, reigned during a crisis. Keynes proposed to rescue the people by providing them with certainty and assurances that they would be secure, even in a time of emergency governed by a crisis of rapidly changing and difficult-to-comprehend developments. In fact, having just used his inaugural address to reassure the American people that "the only thing we have to fear is fear itself—nameless, unreasoning, unjustified terror which paralyzes needed efforts to convert retreat into advance"—Roosevelt the politician was already well ahead of Keynes the theorist.[47]

———

AS THE HISTORIANS David Kennedy and Jennifer Klein have shown, the concept of security—what Klein actually calls, with good reason, "an ideology of security"—sat at the heart of the New Deal and defined its very purpose and essence.[48] This quest for security has led Jonathan Levy to frame the New Deal as the onset of "The Age of Control" that used government regulatory power to "de-volatize capitalism"—that is, to move the underlying dynamics of economic activity from fearful uncertainty to manageable risk.[49] This basic idea of security is now commonplace to the economic activity of the contemporary United States, but at the time it was launched the New Deal was a massive experiment in both democratic politics and capitalist economics.

Just as US foreign policy has never been truly isolationist, American capitalism has never been truly laissez-faire; government has always played a role in economic life. But under Franklin Roosevelt, the balance of power shifted, so that government held more of it at the expense of private interests and operated, as Charles Merriam, a University of Chicago political scientist and social planner, put it, under the principle of "guidance by the common will."[50] Thus the ultimate economic imperative for the state was no longer to passively facilitate prosperity, but, as a group of New Deal economists put it, to actively guarantee "the greatest possible security of livelihood."[51] Roosevelt put it in more accessible language. Before the industrial age, an American's "security, then as now, was bound to that of his friends and his neighbors." But in the modern world, where previously "men had turned to neighbors for help and advice, they now turned to the Government." The reason was simple: "Our Government [is] fulfilling an obvious obligation to the citizens of the country . . . because the citizens require action."[52]

Even though it was in some ways an odd value for a progressive to hold, as it could come at the expense of justice or liberty, this basic principle—security—was thus Roosevelt's watchword. "Among our objectives I place the security of the men, women and children of the Nation first," he explained to Congress in 1934, and it was the government's overriding duty to give the people "security against the hazards and vicissitudes of life."[53] In announcing his intention to work with Congress to pass a comprehensive social insurance bill, he repeated these words and emphasized that attaining security "remains our first and continuing task; and in a very real sense every major legislative enactment of this Congress should be a component part of it."[54]

Rexford Tugwell, a key advisor on such issues, knew that Roosevelt was asking the American people to "yield him their trust as a protector."[55] This was a significant demand, but it was one with which Tugwell—and a clear majority of Americans—were comfortable. Yet for Knight and others already suspicious of government authority, this new political contract had an ominously Hobbesian, even Cromwellian, ring to it. Still reeling from his defeat to Roosevelt in 1932, Herbert Hoover warned that the New Deal's offer of security would not only go unfulfilled, but would curtail American freedom and result in different types of insecurity.[56] When Social Security started operations, Hoover refused to participate lest he be "numberified" by anonymous bureaucrats.[57] Ira Jewell, a Philadelphia corporate lawyer and prominent critic of the New Deal, similarly declaimed that "promised material security would lead mankind into the morasses of despotism" characterized by "a false security, a false efficiency, and a false economy."[58]

The early prophets of neoliberalism made related arguments. Lionel Robbins warned that it was "not a question of bartering the prospects of greater wealth for greater security; security goes as well."[59] Later, in a famous chapter on "Freedom and Security" in *The Road to Serfdom*, Friedrich Hayek drew a similar conclusion. Writing from his wartime refuge in England, the Austrian economist singled out the quest for security, and the state's duty to find it, as one of the most significant social changes of the era. Although Hayek was no friend of big government, he recognized there were two types of security, one more pernicious than the other: the more benign form of state-sponsored security such as conventional pension and national insurance plans, as well as funding to recover from the "hazards of life" that individuals could not possibly protect themselves against, such as accident, disease, fire, or flood. Even these benign forms of social assistance, however, could slide into the second, more dangerous type of security: the imposition of total security in all aspects of life, especially the vagaries of a capitalist economy, which inevitably led to socialist controls and eventually a police state. Under such conditions, "the demand for security may become a danger to liberty." Total security required planning, and systemic planning inevitably led to a planned economy. The bewildering newness of modern life created complex problems that in turn led to popular demands for security. "Some security is essential if freedom is to be preserved," Hayek conceded, but not when taken to extremes, and he had New Dealers such as Merriam in mind when he warned that "nothing is more fatal than the present fashion among intellectual leaders of extolling security at the expense of freedom."[60]

Tugwell countered that the New Deal's critics were missing the point. Rooseveltian security promised order, but not at the expense of justice or liberty. While the economic crisis had also led communists and fascists to offer "order and security," Tugwell reasoned, the difference was that "the accompanying regimentation was omitted" in the New Deal.[61] More than liberty, property, or prosperity, even more than democracy itself: security was the very foundation of the New Deal order because, in an unprecedented, existential crisis, everything else rested on it. Or, in Merriam's formula, "the democratic agenda" depended upon the attainment of "security, order, justice"—in that order.[62]

To undertake such a domestic mobilization effort, the New Deal needed a systematic capacity for systemic planning. This would solve "the basic dilemma of capitalism," the economist and *New Republic* contributor George Soule wrote in 1934. "Either it must surrender to social planning or else repeat the mistakes and perpetuate the rigidities" that led "society into crisis" in the first place.[63] Even though Roosevelt is justly remembered as a pragmatic extemporizer, and the New Deal as a big process of trial and error, even to mount speculative policies required careful planning of how various parts of society would interact with one another in constructive ways. This meant planning not only to provide relief and recovery from the economic crisis, but also, through reform, to help avert future crises. It's crucial to remember that the New Deal didn't simply respond to the Great Depression, but to Herbert Hoover's half-heartedly voluntarist response to the Great Depression. And that meant preparing for future threats. As Merriam put it in a critical review of Hoover's first post-presidential book, "The truth is that our American choice is not one between planning on the one side or no planning on the other, but between planning in advance and planning after the event." The former was "deliberate and mature" and "based on careful analysis," the latter "hasty and inevitably defective." One was a sensible way to deal with unknown but plausible future risks, the other a relic of a bygone age of laissez-faire.[64]

Part of the problem was the impossibility of ever accurately predicting the future. One of Keynes's criticisms of neoclassical economics was that it possessed an unwarranted confidence in its abilities to predict complex, long-term developments. Drawing on Burke, he had similar misgivings about communist revolutionaries' promises of a distant utopia they couldn't possibly foresee. Yet that didn't absolve people from planning for future contingencies even if they were "fluctuating, vague and uncertain." The right response wasn't blithe confidence or revolutionary hope, but prudence in planning for, and guarding against, realistic future contingencies knowing that they would need constant adjustment or might not ever actually happen. The weather, he argued, "is only moderately uncertain." Real uncertainty was instead both truly unknowable but also feasible—in this sense, "the prospect of a European war is uncertain," a poignant example given that he was writing in 1937.[65] It wasn't just "actual hardships" that caused the crisis, Tugwell noted, but the "uncertainties" that hardship created.[66]

This was where insurance came in. Keynes himself chaired the National Mutual Life Assurance Company's board of directors and helped manage its assets, and during the war he expressed "wild enthusiasm" for the Beveridge Report that established national insurance in Britain.[67] Even though it could fall victim to the paradox of thrift—a core Keynesian problem in which excessive saving leads to widespread underconsumption and inadvertently causes or deepens an economic crisis—insuring against plausible threats was the best way to turn unmeasurable uncertainty into manageable risk and prevent a wider social breakdown. On this basic point, economists as divergent as Keynes and Knight agreed on the diagnosis, even if they disagreed on the ultimate cure.[68]

KEYNES AND KNIGHT, however, were not the ones who would make social insurance a reality in the United States. Those efforts were instead led by a loosely connected group of economists and social planners, including Tugwell, who for decades had been unsuccessfully preaching a gospel of security but now, thanks to the New Deal, found themselves thrust into the limelight of public policy.

Foremost among them was Isaac Rubinow, "the outstanding American theoretician of social insurance." Fleeing antisemitic persecution, Rubinow left Russia in 1893, at the age of eighteen, and settled in New York. After studying economics and political science at Columbia, he received his M.D. at New York University; eventually he moved west, to Cincinnati. His training in both the social and medical sciences afforded him an especially acute insight into the conditions of the industrial working class. He also studied the insurance systems then emerging in Europe, a comparative framework that enabled him to propose seemingly new solutions to problems in American society.[69] His book *Social Insurance,* published in 1913, instantly became the standard work on the subject in the United States and shaped much of the discussion on social security two decades later. Insurance was "essentially a social function" because it provided for the "substitution of social effort for individual effort" and, under a sufficiently expansive program, "the subsequent elimination of risk." This was essential for American society in the industrial boom of the Machine Age, beset as it was by chronic social and economic insecurity. If "the measure of security of life is the measure of the progress of civilization," Rubinow believed, then American civilization still had a long way to go.[70]

The culmination of Rubinow's life's work, and his definitive contribution to the debate on social insurance in America, was his 1934 book *The Quest for Security.* His skills as both a social scientist and a public advocate were on full display across the more than six hundred pages of detailed economic evidence, often livened with Rooseveltian analogies and parables. Rubinow made his case in terms Knight would have recognized even while disagreeing with their application. Security meant stability, but the "Four Horsemen of the Apocalypse"—accident, illness, old age, unemployment—threatened "to disturb this equilibrium. Anything may happen—and many things do happen." Rubinow proposed that these four horsemen posed uncertainty, and the fear it bred, only because there was little protection from them for most Americans. But a program of social insurance could provide that protection. This way, "individual misfortune" could be mitigated through collective social action, and naturally enough Rubinow turned to fire by way of example: "when San Francisco or Baltimore burns the sum total of individual misfortunes becomes a mass catastrophe." Smart public policy could handle the four horsemen, because while their arrival was always a shock when it happened, the probability they would one day arrive was not a surprise. Armed with evidence and backed by the power of government—individual action was "futile"—the social planner could overcome fear through foresight. This would complete America's quest for security.[71]

Abraham Epstein was the other leading theorist of social security—indeed, he made the phrase common currency in interwar social planning. Epstein's background was strikingly similar to Rubinow's: he too was a Jewish refugee from the pogroms of czarist Russia, and after emigrating to New York, he too moved inland, settling in Pittsburgh.[72] This shared experience of personal insecurity (as a Jew in Russia and an immigrant in New York) followed by a settled, respected life in the Midwest, gave Rubinow and Epstein a profound insight into the needs for, the requirements to achieve, and the essential value of a baseline level of security in everyday life. In his 1933 book *Insecurity, a Challenge to America,* Epstein made an impassioned case for social security, like Rubinow touching on many of the same themes about uncertainty, probability, and risk, and arguing that the "struggle of human progress has been a battle for security." And of course, he too invoked the threat of fire and the now-obvious need to insure against it.[73]

But Epstein also argued that economic insecurity was a modern phenomenon, and that preindustrial societies worldwide had never known it. The Industrial Revolution removed laborers from the land, and made them dependent on earning a wage, thereby putting them under the control of a personal boss as well as the impersonal whims of the market. The Depression wasn't unusual, or unexpected, but merely the ultimate crisis of this utterly modern capitalist dynamic. Earlier societies had the luxury of taking their economic security for granted. Modern America did not.[74] It's unlikely he read Epstein on social planning, but T.S. Eliot made a similar point about modernity as the source of social insecurity. Earlier eras, wrote the poet in 1941, flourished because of a "sense of freedom and adventurousness" and "an unconscious confidence." But the wasteland of the modern global order had instead produced "the recklessness of disinheritance and despair. Now the fear of insecurity may be something which strikingly distinguishes our time from the past."[75]

As a groundswell of popular support for government-run pensions grew nationwide, Roosevelt began exploring ways to make it government policy. In June 1934, three weeks after he told Congress that security was his leading objective, he set up the Committee on Economic Security under the leadership of a fellow New Yorker and the first-ever woman to hold a Cabinet appointment, Secretary of Labor Frances Perkins.[76] Before moving to Washington, Perkins had built a career advocating for the security of working-class Americans, particularly women. As head of the New York chapter of the National Consumers League, she witnessed firsthand the devastation a fire at the Triangle Shirtwaist Company had inflicted upon lower Manhattan. The inferno, caused by a disregard for basic safety, killed 146 workers, most of them women, because they couldn't escape a burning building that lacked proper means of escape. The Triangle fire galvanized the Progressive movement and had a long-term inspirational effect on Perkins along with other major figures in New York's Democratic Party such as future Senator Robert Wagner and future Governor Al Smith. In response to the tragedy, Perkins helped build a coalition in the state assembly to pass laws improving workplace conditions and safety protocols.[77] Security was therefore Perkins's watchword, too. To overcome the "fear of what the future might bring," her committee recommended that Congress pass a capacious program of social insurance.[78] This, she said, needed planning beyond the current crisis; it required government to be "foresighted about future problems."[79]

Advocates for a program of national social insurance had to make the case not only that there was a need for it, but also that the power, authority, and resources of the federal government alone could meet such a need. If they could demonstrate need, the government would have to be the provider, given how great the scale of the task was.[80] This fit with Roosevelt's basic view, which he attributed to Abraham Lincoln, that the main purpose for the existence of government was to do what citizens could not do for themselves.[81] Rubinow wrote incessantly on this point.[82] So did Epstein. "Only through federal legislation," he cautioned, was social security realistic. The crisis was national, and the shortcomings of the states, and of private corporations, were such that "the federal government must definitely lead." Having investigated the haphazard, often insoluble condition of private pensions for the state of Pennsylvania in the 1920s—which itself was indicative of the flaws of private pensions nationwide—he had good reason to doubt the power of anything below the federal government.[83]

Epstein's logic was irresistible—even, ironically, to private interests. There was, after all, a role in Adam Smith's classical economics for the power of government to violate individual liberty if it meant safeguarding the security of "the whole society"—his example was "in order to prevent the communication of fire."[84] In the depths of the Depression, some economists underwent a needs-must, security-first conversion from orthodox economic theory to welfare liberalism.[85] And even some business leaders conceded the point that insecurity for some would soon mean insecurity for all. "Security for workers must be sought" because without it "security for capital is impossible," the dean of Harvard Business School warned the industrialists of America in 1931. The plain truth was that in a complex, integrated society, "security for capital cannot long exist apart . . . from security for labor."[86] As the New Deal launched, Henry Harriman, president of the usually conservative US Chamber of Commerce, likewise expressed support for "the philosophy of planned national economy."[87] When personal health insurance was dropped from the proposed social-security legislation, when Roosevelt pushed for old-age pensions to be funded through contributions rather than redistributive taxation, and when it became clear that Democrats, holding massive majorities in Congress as well as the White House, were determined to pass a social security bill that largely left African Americans out in the cold, private insurance companies realized that resistance was futile. Not coincidentally, they also realized that a government pension would stimulate even greater demand, and that they could make a lot of money by building on a public program whose scale would necessarily impose a limit on benefits. Thus from the outset, social security would be coopted, and for many Americans surpassed, by private corporations as they invested in what Jennifer Klein calls the "security business."[88] And business would prove to be good. At his company's exhibit at the 1939 New York World's Fair, which was a massive statue in the center of a tranquil "Garden of Security," the president of the insurance company Equitable could barely contain his excitement in declaring: "Security! The modern world is in constant search of security."[89]

Still, despite such limitations—Epstein himself was so disillusioned that he angrily disowned the Social Security Act and denounced its racial exclusivity, while other social theorists derided its "timidity"—the move toward a program of publicly funded social security was profound and consequential.[90] In drawing on his frequent use of metaphors about tyranny and warfare, Roosevelt justified the expansion of the American welfare state as a revival of the foundational relationship between government and the people. Until the New Deal, he told a deliriously supportive crowd as he kicked off his reelection campaign in 1936, private industry and capital had grown so powerful that they were trampling on the rights of Americans. Much in the way the Founders had done more than 150 years before, the people had a right to fight back—but they couldn't do it alone. "Against economic tyranny such as this, the American citizen could appeal only to the organized power of Government" to "protect the citizen in his right to work and his right to live." Fighting back against tyranny was a hallowed part of the American political tradition, Roosevelt proclaimed, and it was needed once again because of the newness of the modern condition. "Government in a modern civilization has certain inescapable obligations to its citizens," chief among them the provision of a basic level of "protection" for the people.[91]

The Social Security Act, passed in 1935, was the culmination of all these efforts and the centerpiece of the New Deal. Based on the fundamental principle of providing Americans not just with economic stability but with security from the fear of uncertainty, it created the nation's first-ever broad, publicly funded safety net. Despite its many compromises to racial and gender orders that privileged heterosexual white men over all others, and despite its limitations of coverage, it marked the fulfillment of a dream social reformers had pursued for decades. As the Social Security Board declared in its first annual report, "The security of a people is a great cooperative enterprise," a sentiment which embodied the spirit of the New Deal itself.[92] Always the bedrock of Roosevelt's political philosophy, security had come to define the policies of his presidency, too.

————

UNCERTAINTY, FEAR, and attempts to insure against the calculable risks of modernity's crises weren't solely confined to the domestic realm. Historians aptly note that the "emergence of an ideology of security in the 1930s would have major ramifications for public policy, industrial relations, and corporate decisions," but this new ideology also had equally profound, long-lasting consequences for the conduct of foreign policy that historians have yet to explore.[93] In fact, it was New Deal liberalism's entrenchment of social security at the heart of American society that created the conditions for a doctrine of national security to emerge as well.

Until the late 1930s, the phrase "national security" had a dual meaning. It did sometimes refer to foreign threats in the international system, although these threats were narrowly construed as direct threats to US territorial sovereignty and usually referred to the coastal defense of the continental United States.[94] Such references literally meant "the security of the nation" and were invariably premised on repelling a physical attack against U.S borders; this literal meaning was still in use in the late 1930s.[95] Occasionally, in the middle of the nineteenth century, Americans used national security to refer to the problem of sectional division. This is what Charles Sumner meant when he said, only a few months after the Civil War, that "justice to the freedman is now intimately linked with the national security. Be just, and the Republic will be strong. Be just, and you will erect a barrier against the Rebellion."[96] Yet here again, the meaning of national security was simply about the preservation of the nation's political integrity, and thus narrowly reduced to a direct threat to territorial sovereignty.

Yet until the later stages of the New Deal, "national security" also had a second meaning that was essentially the same as "social security" or "economic security" and could refer to pensions, consumer standards, workplace conditions, or insurance. For instance, to Orin Judson Field, chief clerk at the Department of Justice, "our national security and prosperity" were dependent upon "the maintenance of our legal and civic rights" through "the zealous prosecution and the vigorous and impartial enforcement of the statutes enacted by Congress for our common welfare"; his examples of such "national security" policies were the Pure Food and Drug Act, the Railroad Safety Appliance Act, the Sherman Antitrust Act, and various interstate commerce laws.[97] Samuel Crowther, a prominent reporter covering finance and industry, offered a similar term to describe the New Deal: "nation-saving."[98] National security often referred more specifically to the financial sector, especially the solvency of banks but also the operations of investment firms and stock markets. "National Security Bank" was a common name nationwide, and the phrase fronted other private corporations as well—the National Security and Improvement Company, the National Security Life and Accident Company, and so on—to refer to assets, holdings, insurance, or collateral.[99] To the noted Wall Street investor John F. Hume, "The national security" was grounded in the elemental fact that "our Government owes its life to the credit of its bonds."[100]

Revealingly, even those with a political horizon that stretched across the oceans perceived "national security" through a domestic socioeconomic lens. In 1935, William Yandell Elliott, a longtime political science professor at Harvard, proposed a program of constitutional reform that would strengthen the president's authority to tackle systemic threats to "the national security" of the United States. This should be unsurprising— Elliott is remembered today as a Cold Warrior and National Security Council analyst who at one point commuted weekly between Cambridge and Washington as he balanced his teaching at Harvard with his duties as a consultant to the House Foreign Affairs Committee. He was also Henry Kissinger's mentor and, in 1951, sponsored Kissinger's founding of the legendary Harvard International Seminar. For Elliott, America's postwar hegemony was paramount, the only way that civilization could be victorious in its Cold War "struggle for national survival" with communism. But this expansive global vision was still to come. In 1935, while he was a member of the New Deal–friendly Business Advisory Council, the "need for constitutional reform" that Elliott felt was vital to a program for "national security" stemmed from the economic crisis of the Depression, not the challenge posed by revisionist powers in Europe and Asia. Roosevelt deserved to be invested with greater executive powers because he "promised, and so far delivered, economic security." Elliott's plan for national security gave foreign affairs cursory treatment, with various powers posing manageable challenges to US interests but not a direct threat to US security.[101]

The Depression presidents also perceived the economic crisis in these terms. To them, national security meant the stability and integrity of the country, which in turn meant that it was economically sound and free of social division. Hoover wasn't normally fond of Keynesian theory, but he inadvertently invoked Keynes's paradox of thrift in warning the American people that "the enemy of our national security" was what "we vaguely call 'hoarding.' It strangles our daily life, increases unemployment, and sorely afflicts our farmers."[102] During the 1932 campaign, Hoover railed against Roosevelt's promise to use government power to solve the

Depression by arguing that deficit spending would undermine the economy: "In periods of emergency and stress, steadfast adherence to sound principles of government is indispensable to national security and a prerequisite to recovery in business, agriculture and employment."[103] Yet after Roosevelt had defeated him in the election, Hoover responded to accusations he had been too hands-off by pointing to his policies to stimulate exports and industrial output. These "unprecedented emergency measures," he said, "undoubtedly saved the country from economic disaster" and served "to defend the national security."[104] Wrestling with the verdict of the voters, and in all likelihood history, Hoover tried to have it both ways, but either way his main perception of national security was the relationship between socioeconomic conditions and the stability of the country overall.

In his first term, Roosevelt's conceptual approach was in fact little different, and the basic premise that "national security" was a socioeconomic matter was one of the few things he and Hoover shared. In his second Fireside Chat, Roosevelt explained that the launch of the New Deal was meant to ward off any further loss of income, jobs, savings, and homes, which caused "not only economic effects of a very serious nature, but social results that might bring incalculable harm." Appeals for calm and attempts to rally the spirit of the people could only go so far—what was needed instead was a plan for government policies to intervene in the economy that was "not only justified but imperative to our national security." Roosevelt's own economic philosophy was normally one of caution, but "the methods of normal times had to be replaced in the emergency" or else the very future of the United States would be in doubt.[105]

Because of its importance to social tranquility, this domestic version of "national security" also included law and order as one of its key objectives. Policing at home represented the front line of national security every bit as much as the projection of military power overseas. Domestic policing was changing in the period, modernizing along bipartisan progressive notions of applying efficiency, bureaucracy, and the scientific method to social problems of the day. And with bootleggers, gangsters, and bank robbers, the social problems of the day were acute. In 1932, Republicans campaigned on the principle of "enforcement of the law as the very foundation of orderly government and civilization. There can be no national security otherwise." But policing didn't really attain its modern guise until the New Deal, when Franklin Roosevelt launched a "War on Crime" to offset any turbulence caused by either the Depression or his redistributive economic policies. According to J. Edgar Hoover's leading biographer, "Only with the New Deal . . . did the FBI begin to resemble the agency we know today," and only "the tools of New Deal liberalism" could make this happen. Congress bestowed upon Hoover's force a sweeping new set of law-enforcement and surveillance powers, and funding, and in 1935 the existing bureau was rechristened as the Federal Bureau of Investigation.[106] Roosevelt supported the FBI's prosecution of tougher law enforcement because "the control of crime," he told the National Parole Conference, "will promote our national security."[107] In May 1941, with war approaching, Roosevelt augmented existing law enforcement by creating the Office of Civilian Defense (OCD).[108]

Roosevelt also leaned heavily on another trope that would define national security: emergency. The reasons he did so were obvious: with the Depression, the United States was clearly in the grip of a genuine, and seemingly indefinite, state of emergency, and the entire shape of the New Deal was molded to alleviate it. Many of the first pieces of New Deal legislation bore the imprint of emergency—the Emergency Banking Act, the Federal Emergency Relief Administration, the Emergency Farm Mortgage Act—and the legal basis of the Economy Act, which provided the basis for a new era of government intervention into the national economy and passed only eleven days after Roosevelt took office, was entirely premised on the distinction between normal times and an emergency. The National Industrial Recovery Act, which regulated wages and prices and established the Public Works Administration, declared that a "national emergency . . . is hereby declared to exist."[109] It was the basic duty of a democratically elected government to "meet the problems of an emergency," Roosevelt said. "Unless those problems are met, uncertainty and fear on the part of the people are likely to result."[110] This was the economic emergency that gave the executive a wide range of new powers, and it was this emergency that had created a threat to national security—literally, the security of the nation, its integrity threatened from within by an unimaginable social and economic crisis.

———

THE EMERGENCY ALSO LED Roosevelt to deploy another metaphor of nearly uncontainable ideological power: war. In his inaugural address, he repeated a message he had campaigned on the year before: new measures, even "by the Government itself," were needed to correct the imbalances in the economy because the insecurity was so great it warranted "treating the task as we would treat the emergency of a war." He revealed that he planned to "ask the Congress for the one remaining instrument to meet the crisis—broad Executive power to wage a war against the emergency, as great as the power that would be given to me if we were in fact invaded by a foreign foe."[111]

As the historian William Leuchtenburg once argued, the analogy to war was fitting not only because of the existential threat of the Depression, but because the New Deal itself was grounded in a philosophy of war. World War I provided the model of efficient, centralized planning in a crisis environment that Roosevelt and the New Dealers countlessly invoked for legitimacy and continually followed for results. Herbert Hoover had also referenced the Depression as a crisis similar to war, but Roosevelt sharpened the analogy, mentioned it more frequently, and made it the basis of actual policy. And as Democrats returned to power for the first time since the days of Woodrow Wilson, they fell back on their wartime experiences (in Washington, that is, not in Europe). World War I animated the spirit of the New Deal and provided the blueprint for national crisis planning. As Leuchtenburg famously put it, the New Deal was "the analogue of war."[112]

The reverse, however, could also be true: war—or more precisely, national security—could be the analogue of the New Deal. Roosevelt's October 1937 quarantine speech in Chicago, warning of a threat from Japan but delivered at the dedication of a PWA-built bridge, thus marked the threshold to a new era of "national security" as the term shifted from being mostly about socioeconomic problems to being entirely about foreign policy threats. The marriage of the speech's substance to its occasion was not a coincidence, and it was concerned as much with domestic politics as geopolitics. The quarantine metaphor allowed Roosevelt to explain to his audience, at an instantly recognizable level, the need to use government power to protect the people from a fast-spreading danger that was too large and too destructive to confront with normal means. "Biopolitics," observes the philosopher Ian Hacking, "has the standard feature of a risk portfolio," something Roosevelt understood intuitively.[113]

From the summer of 1937, Roosevelt became more worried about the world crisis than about the economic crisis. Despite continued systemic problems that came to the fore in a recession that year, the Depression was now a manageable problem, but Germany and Japan were literally on the march. As we shall see in Chapter 5, most Americans did not share their president's alarm, and support for a more activist foreign policy, even one that stopped short of outright military intervention, was small. What better way to build support for a more activist global role than to fall back on the ideological basis that had saved the country from the Depression and handed FDR the greatest popular mandate in American history? In several speeches between 1937 and 1941—shrewdly described by political scientist Harold Lasswell, then an analyst for War Communications Research at the Library of Congress, as an exercise in political "ground laying"—Roosevelt repeatedly invoked the phrase "national security" to explain America's stakes in the world crisis, using it nearly as many times in those four years alone as all other presidents before him combined.[114]

Roosevelt's new vision of national security was clear from this rhetorical barrage. The defense of the United States meant much more than simply defending territory or lives: at "a time of peril unmatched in the history of the nations of all the world," it meant nothing less than "the total defense of the people of the United States of America."[115] In the same way Social Security promised to protect Americans against all manner of socioeconomic threats, even if those threats weren't posing an imminent danger to every individual—consider that at even the worst point of the Depression, most Americans still had a job; or that most people paying into Social Security in the 1930s were healthy and not about to retire—Roosevelt's preemptive call to safeguard national security promised the same government protections for citizens against global threats like Germany and Japan, even if they were, for the moment, remote and distant.

One evening in 1940, between Christmas and New Year's Eve, Roosevelt brought all these strands together in his most important foreign-policy message since the "quarantine" speech in Chicago. "This is not a fireside chat on war," he informed the American people. "It is a talk on national security." Evoking the emergency of the Depression, and the power of government to fight it and thereby ensure social security, Roosevelt made it clearer than he ever had before that this new emergency required a similar response. "Tonight, in the presence of a world crisis, my mind goes back eight years to a night in the midst of a domestic crisis." He reminisced about his first inaugural address and recalled that Americans "met the issue of 1933 with courage and realism." Now, though France and most of Europe were conquered and Britain and China were on the verge of defeat, he was confident Americans would "face this new crisis—this new threat to the security of our nation—with the same courage and realism." Turning to one of the main intellectual pillars of the New Deal, he confessed that while "there is risk in any course we may take ... the course that I advocate involves the least risk now and the greatest hope for world peace in the future." The prevailing uncertainty was being managed through careful preparation: "We are planning our own defense with the utmost urgency" through a "realistic, practical military policy, based on the advice of our military experts." This plan, and others, would also ensure the economic welfare of the American people because the two types of security (social and national) had become indivisible. "I would ask no one to defend a democracy which in turn would not defend everyone in the nation against want and privation." With the solidarity of the nation renewed, with the "splendid cooperation between the Government and industry and labor" united in their own defense in an unparalleled emergency, greater even than the Civil War, Roosevelt invoked what instantly became one of his most famous political calls to arms:

> We must be the great arsenal of democracy. For us this is an emergency as serious as war itself. We must apply ourselves to our task with the same resolution, the same sense of urgency, the same spirit of patriotism and sacrifice as we would show were we at war.

Insuring the nation through a massive armament program, not just for America but also for other countries, was protective in both the near- and long-term. It would, he promised, give "hope for the defense of our civilization and for the building of a better civilization in the future."[116]

———

BY THE EARLY TWENTIETH CENTURY, governments of industrial states in Europe and North America had increasingly committed themselves to providing for the general welfare of their citizens and subjects. This shift in the basis of state responsibility may have been gradual, but it was startling nonetheless. The slow revolution in social governance, propelled by the quest for security, thrilled planners like Merriam and Tugwell and alarmed economists like Knight and Hayek. Even to its adherents, then, the idea that a more capacious "national security" was becoming the basis of American self-defense was novel and disorienting. In the absence of any conceptual coherence, advocates of this new worldview set out to define this new doctrine of national security. If the protection of the territorial sovereignty of the continental United States was no longer the basis of national self-defense, what should replace it?

Edward Mead Earle wanted to find out. "It is of the utmost importance," he wrote in early 1938, "that the United States reexamine its whole policy of national defense."[117] After earning his doctorate at Columbia, Earle made his name at the Institute for Advanced Study in Princeton; by the late 1930s, he was one of the leading international relations scholars of the era. He was staunchly pro-British and anti-Nazi and hoped the United States would enter the world crisis to tilt the balance against fascism, and from 1938 his energies reflected this objective rather than arcane theoretical debates among scholars. Supported by a large grant from the Carnegie Corporation, in 1939 Earle began holding a permanent, invitation-only seminar to determine the nature of this new strategic concept being called "national security." Earle shared Roosevelt's capacious view that security was holistic, and no longer simply the defense of the nation's borders from physical attack, so he invited a wide range of experts—political scientists, military analysts, historians, economists, and practicing diplomats—to his seminar. After much deliberation Alfred Weinberg, appropriately enough a historian of manifest destiny, drafted the seminar's working definition: "National security is the condition in which external attack, direct or indirect, by armed force or other means, upon the nation's territorial domain, rights, or vital interests is not likely to be made or, if made, to succeed."[118]

This was a useful definition, and it perfectly fit the seminar's ultimate goal of building support for a broader American threat perception that could in turn provide a platform to build a forward-looking strategic posture. For seminar member DeWitt Poole, a career foreign-service officer whose expertise was Russia, older notions of "basic security" would no longer do under modern conditions. Weinberg's definition was an improvement because it allowed for "extended security" that usefully "goes beyond the bare fact of continued existence and embraces 'rights' and 'vital interests' of unlimited geographical scope."[119] In his book *Manifest Destiny*, published six years earlier, Weinberg himself had anticipated such thinking: "immediate self-preservation and permanent security are logically distinct goals. Expansion in behalf of security is really a defense against a possible and future rather than an actual and immediate danger."[120] This all dovetailed nicely with Earle's own view that "defense or security was not merely a crisis phenomenon, but an obligation of statecraft at all times" that required "the extension of our diplomatic and of indeed our military frontiers beyond our mere territorial possessions. . . . If defense is conceived as security in a larger sense," he concluded, "the initiative can be ours."[121]

———

EARLE AND HIS COLLEAGUES played an important role in defining national security, but the hard conceptual groundwork had already been done by economic and social planners. All geostrategists and military analysts had to do was apply the basis of socioeconomic security to quickly changing world conditions, and the transformation of national security into a doctrine of defense against external threats was complete. But the process had its origins in domestic social planning.

The social planners' arguments—which were also the basis for Roosevelt's electoral mandate and the legitimacy of the New Deal itself—helped change the dynamics of decision-making at the national level and redraw the fundamental contract between government and citizens. At home, the New Deal rested on a set of basic notions: modern industrial society had become much more interdependent, and therefore more intricate and complex, than any previous society in history; the socioeconomic crisis of the Depression enabled the federal government to exercise unprecedented power; the wielding of this power was vital to protect the security of citizens who were powerless to protect themselves against punitive threats that were systemic, and thus often remote, from the daily experience of citizens themselves; if government didn't maximize its power to address the emergency now, the crisis would deepen and worsen, eventually posing an existential threat to the nation itself; systemic planning was needed to turn fearful uncertainty into managed risk. Absent such thinking, the basic security of the American people was under threat. Everything in the modern world was connected, argued Merriam, from unemployment to industrial strife to fascism to foreign invasion, "and it is plain that these are all social problems."[122]

As social planners and New Dealers often recognized, their program to ensure social security had precisely the logic suitable for a program of national security. The "American standard of living and national defense are not inconsistent but complementary," Merriam argued in 1941. "We can have guns and butter too with our resources and our organization."[123] That was because the motivations for social security and national security were the same. The United States, concluded Epstein, had once been "the most self-sustaining of all industrial nations," but such independence was no longer possible, thus requiring a new system of social security.[124] On the lack of a program for ensuring social security, Rubinow similarly lamented that "in this country . . . we have often delayed our thinking until confronted by an overwhelmingly critical situation and then like children tried to solve the most complicated problem in an hour, just because we have been neglecting it all along."[125] Lasswell, not coincidentally some-one who studied political psychology in both the domestic and foreign political realms, brought all these parts together in his 1935 book *World Politics and Personal Insecurity.* "Let us assume that over the coming years the United States will live in a situation of increasing domestic and exter-nal insecurity," he reasoned; if that turned out to be the case, American social planning and foreign policy would have to make drastic adjust-ments, ideally in tandem. The United States had thus far "been relatively free from the play of the international and of the interclass balance of power," but assuming that it would continue to remain free from these struggles was foolish.[126]

Merriam, Epstein, Rubinow, and Lasswell had each arrived at a key insight: economic laissez-faire was akin to geopolitical free security, and pretending that these complex systems would eventually correct them-selves would prove disastrous, especially when there was now a vision of governance that could meet systemic threats directly. With self-sustaining autonomy no longer possible in the modern world, and with complex, fast-moving crises likely to recur, it was no longer possible for Americans simply to let things happen and respond to the consequences afterward. The rise of fascism abroad, and the threat of its surge at home, brought many on the far left to support the New Deal as a provider of both social security and national security. At home and abroad, the "fight for social and national security" was one and the same, declared Earl Browder, the leader of the Communist Party USA. In a remarkable call for common-front solidarity with liberals, Browder judged that, while the New Deal wasn't proper socialism, it was the best Americans could hope for in a violently insecure world. While "the Spanish and Chinese peoples are fight-ing our battles for us," he concluded, the "New Deal is still a serious effort to defend social and national security, to preserve democracy, to maintain peace, to keep America on the path of progress."[127] In 1938, the Southern Conference for Human Welfare, a biracial, anti–Jim Crow organization founded in Alabama with a significant CPUSA presence, made a similar Popular Front–style call for "an American peace policy, such as proposed by President Roosevelt, to promote the national security of our country, to curb aggression, and assist the democratic peoples of the world to preserve peace, liberty, and freedom."[128]

The systemic social planning that emerged in the late-nineteenth and early-twentieth centuries has become so commonplace today it's difficult to appreciate its novelty at the time. The complex nature of the modern condition required societies—and their governments—to actively plan for preferred outcomes and then manage the process to achieve those outcomes. As specialists themselves put it, "planning is the hallmark of modernity."[129] Over a half-century that crested in the interwar period, planning—social, city, town, agricultural, health, family—emerged as a profession in its own right. The infrastructural needs of growing cities like New York and Chicago required urban planners to mitigate the problems arising from rampant expansion. The growth of cities also required town planners to design suburbs and the "new towns" and "garden cities" that were being built just beyond the cities' suburban fringe. Industrialism required social planners to identify the sources of the crisis in working and living conditions and offer solutions to them, and it required social workers to have a plan to help those in need. And all of the above spurred the emergence of professional community organizing in the 1920s. The rise of planning was a broad, diverse phenomenon: sometimes it emerged from universities, such as the University of Chicago's School of Social Work, but more often social groups—especially those founded by women, for women—devised their own plans and formed their own organizations to carry them out. In other words, planners, often in consultation with local and national politicians, envisioned desired ends and then drew up detailed plans that calibrated various means to achieve them.[130]

Planning evolved as conditions changed and, as the problems of modernity became more difficult and dangerous, planning became more systematic. By the 1930s, the planning of geography, infrastructure, social welfare, and economic security—or, often, all of them together—had become as sophisticated a profession as any. But planning continued to develop in response to the problems it sought to alleviate. Those on the front lines of implementing social policy called for much grander, more integrated levels of government-run social planning than previously thought possible.[131] "Planning," observed Merriam, was a system for "free nations to organize their political machinery so as to facilitate the achievement of their common objectives."[132]

———

THE PLANNING PROCESS—using available means to achieve a desired end—is also the basic calculus of military strategy. The purpose of both planning and strategy is to reduce the complexity of an immediate, systemic problem and offer realistic solutions to addressing it. They are two kinds of problem-solving, with many of the same defining traits and methods. According to one of the foremost social planners of the twentieth century, Columbia University's Alfred J. Kahn, planning is the process of "translating social goals into effective programs" in which "the general goal formulations serve as the points of departure for planning." This required planners to make critical "allocation decisions" through the devising of "a sequence of means-ends relationships."[133] Gunnar Myrdal, the Swedish economist who had done much to interpret American race relations, thought of planning in similarly strategic terms. Planning, he wrote in 1960, consists of "conscious attempts . . . to coordinate public policies more rationally in order to reach more fully and rapidly the desirable ends for future development." Indeed, for Myrdal, "Coordination *is* planning."[134] Unsurprisingly, Merriam's National Resources Planning Board (NRPB), a quintessentially New Deal institution Roosevelt and Ickes established under a different name in 1933, made a seamless transition from planning the domestic economy to planning a society at war.[135]

The new ideas of ensuring social welfare that reached maturation in the interwar period were in fact similar to another new, distinctly modern type of coordinated planning that was also maturing at that very time: grand strategy. There are varying definitions of grand strategy, but in essence it seeks not simply to win a battle, or even a war, but also to manage international conditions over the longer term. It is modern planning on the grandest conceivable scale.[136] Strategy is virtually timeless, as old as the recording of history itself, but until the first half of the twentieth century it was also understood in the fairly narrow terms of finding ways to win battles in order to win wars.[137] Even the strategists shaped by the global wars of empire in the eighteenth century (such as the Seven Years' War) and the sprawling wars of popular ideologies in the nineteenth (the Napoleonic Wars) saw their task as ultimately defined by what happened on the battlefield. But, Earle noted in 1941, the advent of what we now call globalization—including the projection of military power on a global scale—called for a new kind of strategic vision, one that was "not exclusively or even primarily a problem for the professional soldier," because "the long arm of military affairs now reaches into virtually every phase of life including economics, psychology, education, public health."[138]

In the United States this new theory of grand strategy complemented the other new way of thinking about the world: national security. In fact, Earle's Princeton seminar was set up to provide definitional precision not only to national security but also to grand strategy.[139] While national security identified the problem of insecurity, grand strategy devised solutions. Both grand strategy and national security presumed that Americans needed to think about the terms of survival in the modern world in the most capacious terms possible. Because the world was interdependent and complex, it was also infinitely dangerous. Survival was no longer just a matter of repelling direct, physical threats as they happened to emerge; it required anticipating threats, reacting to them before they became direct, and responding to them in ways that would prevent them from emerging again. Just as domestic economic problems required complex new ways of thinking about social welfare, the world crisis required a starkly new way of thinking about foreign and defense policies.

This new way of thinking didn't just remain theoretical. The War and Navy departments increased their formal exercises in war-gaming and threat assessment, and planning intensified from the mid-1930s onward. In essence, war planners and strategic planners were little different than urban planners or social planners: means and ends had to be devised based on a combination of evidence and imagination, and they needed calibration to achieve their objectives. But planning also had to be designed realistically, with the actual tools and methods of implementation in mind, and this hadn't always been the military's strong suit. With the exception of War Plan Orange for hostilities with Japan, planning for which began almost a decade before World War I, US military planning lacked the systematic attention to detail or the grand strategic vision needed for thinking about future warfare. The military established systematic planning divisions after the haphazard, trial-and-error mobilization of the Great War, and the army set up the War Plans Division as a fifth branch of the General Staff in 1921. It wasn't just the increasing complexity of warfare that demanded systematic planning; it was the prospect of total war on a scale that would surely dwarf the Civil War and the World War I. As Dwight Eisenhower, then an Army Major, put it in 1931, "modern war" had become "essentially dual in nature—combatant and industrial."[140]

In seeking to avoid the "drift" and "improvised methods" of 1917–1918, the Army's Draft Mobilization Plan of 1936 warned, "War is no longer simply a battle between armed forces in the field—it is a struggle in which each side strives to bring to bear against the enemy the coordinated power of every individual and every material resource at its command. The conflict extends from the soldier in the most forward line to the humblest citizen in the remotest hamlet in the rear." From the mid-1930s on, the Army and Navy cooperated more integrally on war planning, and war-gaming became more sophisticated as the various color-coded war plans, by which single colors designated a single country, were integrated in the Rainbow war plans that began in 1939.[141] Over the objections of many in the army and navy, Roosevelt insisted on the creation of a new intelligence service, the Office of Strategic Services, that, like the Rainbow plans, codified strategic "prevision" and thereby completed the legitimation of what was once the domain of futurist writers like Homer Lea.[142] When the United States entered World War II, Roosevelt set up a new body, the Joint Chiefs of Staff, to further embed integrated, grand-strategic planning in war operations.[143]

The old way of thinking, presentist rather than futurist, still sometimes proved hard to eradicate. As late as December 1937, William C. Bullitt, ambassador to France and one of FDR's closest foreign-policy advisers, could warn that "there is no basis of policy more unreal or disastrous than the apprehension of remote future dangers."[144] Yet it's difficult to think of a sentiment more out of step with the ethos of the New Deal: the apprehension of remote future dangers was its very purpose. Bullitt, an old Wilsonian and apostle for the League of Nations, should have realized this, but his confusion hints at the revolutionary newness of Roosevelt's vision. When he unveiled his ambition for what became the Social Security Act, in his 1935 State of the Union address, Roosevelt argued, "Its greatest advantage is that it fits logically and usefully into the long-range permanent policy of providing the . . . security which constitute as a whole an American plan for the betterment of the future of the American people."[145] Or as he put it during a fireside chat while the Social Security legislation was being debated in Congress, "We must begin now to make provision for the future." His national insurance plan aimed to do this by managing the risks of life's probable challenges. "Provisions for social security," he promised, "are protections for the future."[146] This was the guiding principle for national security, too, as Earle explained in terms that could easily have been drawn from the national-insurance principle that had guided Social Security planning only a few years before: "In defense or in war it is better to be prepared for things which may never occur than to have things occur for which one is not prepared."[147]

Thus the program of national self-defense that was now being relabeled as "national security" wasn't simply an accompaniment to social security; the two weren't just opposite sides of the same coin. Rather, national security was in large part *the result of* social security. To be sure, when Roosevelt escalated his foreign-policy rhetoric after 1936–1937, he did so in direct response to the deterioration of the world crisis. But his response could have taken many different forms. The form that it actually did take—national security—was a product of his own liberal politics in which the government's main role was to protect the people's security, something he had made explicit time and again. By the same token, the New Deal had created an expectation among the American people that the government would identify threats and provide protection against them. The first step to ensuring Americans' security was to protect them from the economic crisis; the next was to protect them from the world crisis.

———

ROOSEVELT HAD KNOWN nothing but crisis, with the Depression and World War II making his presidency a sustained exercise in managing overlapping states of emergency. But by January 1944, after eleven years in the White House, he could envision a possible return to a normal state of affairs. With the defeat of the Axis powers likely, and with the national economy basically back to full employment and signaling a new era of postwar prosperity, Roosevelt could have been excused for using his annual State of the Union address as a victory lap. Instead, he returned to an old theme that had defined his presidency from the outset: the scourge of insecurity, and the nation's responsibility to address it through the collective power of government.

Perhaps it was the bouts of flu and bronchitis that his doctor said had kept Roosevelt away from Capitol Hill and forced him to deliver his State of the Union as a fireside chat over the radio. Perhaps it was the sheer exhaustion he felt after recently returning from wartime summit meetings in Cairo and Tehran. Perhaps it was frustration with an uncooperative

Congress, a body that even some Republicans were damning as "The House of Reprehensibles."[148] Or perhaps it was, as he indicated in his speech, a concern that Americans were becoming complacent with victory in sight. Whatever the reason, Roosevelt's tone that evening was pleading, lacking its usual warmth and self-confidence and relying more heavily on a stern, almost prophetic admonishment.

While it was true, Roosevelt began, that the United States and its allies were winning the war, "I do not think that any of us Americans can be content with mere survival." A narrow focus on the most basic security of the nation's economy or on the basic integrity of the nation's borders was self-defeating. There was no going back to laissez-faire economics or an "ostrich isolationism" in foreign policy. Americans instead had to determine their own fate rather than leave it to the whims of other forces, be they financial markets or foreign dictators. This required pursuing "one supreme objective for the future," which Roosevelt claimed—not for the first time—"can be summed up in one word: Security." Invoking his own Four Freedoms, he argued that "Freedom from fear is eternally linked with freedom from want." This meant enacting a new domestic regime of redistributive taxation, price controls, and a program of national service to draft workers into factories just as Selective Service was drafting servicemen into the military. The centerpiece of the speech was what Roosevelt termed "economic truths," a series of longstanding progressive goals for affordable housing, access to education, and a decent living wage, that amounted to "a second Bill of Rights under which a new basis of security and prosperity can be established." The ultimate objective couldn't have been clearer: "All of these rights spell security," not only for Americans but for all people, because "unless there is security here at home there cannot be lasting peace in the world." Although this "economic bill of rights" had only eight provisions, instead of ten, Roosevelt unveiled it as an update of the original social contract of 1791 for the modern age.[149]

The idea for an "economic bill of rights" had originated a few years before with the NRPB, whose task was to offer inspiration not merely for the New Deal's grand plans but, just as importantly, on how the government could make those plans a reality. Charles Merriam, the NRPB's vice-chair who saw its mission as devising "a plan for national planning," first came up with the idea of an "economic bill of rights" to guarantee a comfortable standard of living for all American citizens in 1940–1941.[150] The idea appealed to the president but he temporarily shelved it, worried how an increasingly conservative Congress that was hostile to further rounds of socioeconomic planning would react. Even more pressing was the war he had to win.

The NRPB nonetheless kept planning for economic security, and in 1942 published its findings in an impressively detailed, 652-page report entitled *Security, Work, and Relief Policies*. The report outlined a plan for the "assurance of minimum security" because "without social and economic security there can be no true guarantee of freedom." Unlike in previous eras, individuals, or even individual states, were unable to confront the challenges of the modern age; that responsibility resided with the federal government. "If we take these objectives as seriously as we take national defense—and they are indeed a fundamental part of national defense—the ways and means of obtaining the objectives are already at hand." To reach as wide an audience as possible, the NRPB compiled a summary of the exhaustive report's key passages in a pamphlet, the title of which, *After the War—Toward Security*, gestured toward its central message.[151]

By 1944, however, Roosevelt was pushing against the tide of recent political momentum, and if his State of the Union message seemed bold and ambitious, even "radical" to some, it was because he knew his task would be difficult. By then even liberal economists were placing their hopes for postwar prosperity in continued economic expansion instead of more spending on another round of New Deal programs. In such a climate, Roosevelt's call for an "economic bill of rights" fell flat. The speech unsurprisingly brought a recent Wall Street rally to an end, but even trade unions objected to the president's call for higher taxes and national service. In fact, the speech did little more than provide the NRPB with an epitaph, given that Congress had already abolished it a few months before.[152]

These battles were a sign of things to come. Over time, there proved to be a key difference between social security and national security: the scope of government involvement. Even though social security was more directly involved in the daily lives of Americans, there was significant room for private interests to share the role in ensuring people's security. National security was different: if distant countries really did pose a threat to the security of the United States, there was no feasible way private interests could address such challenges. For many Americans, insurance companies and other corporations not only partnered but supplanted the government in providing for their social security.[153] But even in the aggregate, if such a thing were possible, private corporations couldn't keep Germany or Japan or some future enemy at bay. Private interests would of course help the government address national security threats from overseas, but always as a junior partner. Even at their most powerful there was never any prospect of corporations supplanting or replacing the federal government in protecting the national security—certainly not in the 1930s and '40s, but not even at the peak strength of the military-industrial complex during the Cold War. The irony here is acute: Americans' social security at home was becoming less statist than their national security abroad. It didn't start out that way, but this basic, fundamental dynamic has held fast ever since.

[5]

WHY WE FIGHT

FRANK CAPRA JOINED the army five days after the Japanese attack on Pearl Harbor. This was a common story for millions of American men during the war, but Capra was no ordinary GI. One of Hollywood's most celebrated film directors, he had by the time of his army commission won three Oscars for Best Director—then a record and still the second-most in history—and served as head of both the Directors Guild of America and the Academy of Motion Picture Arts and Sciences. Capra had no military experience, and was in his mid-forties, so he wasn't of much use to the army as a soldier. But he did have a talent few others in the army shared: storytelling.

While the government and the American people were still dealing with the shock of Pearl Harbor, Army Chief of Staff General George C. Marshall summoned Capra to Washington. Capra was joining the Signal Corps, where army films were made. His orders were to produce a series of training films for the millions of other American men who were also being inducted into the military for the first time in their lives. The urgency couldn't have been greater: after the mobilization for the Great War, the US military had drastically shrunk; by 1940, it had only the world's seventeenth-largest army, and Americans were no longer acculturated to the presence of a powerful military in American society. While Marshall still had plenty of uniformed personnel to show the new recruits how to fire a rifle, march in formation, and set up a field camp, he was short on people who could inspire enthusiasm for the cause. What he wanted from Capra, then, was a motivational tool, not simply to boost morale but to explain to millions of new soldiers why they were there—because, Marshall suspected, "*the reason why* was hazy in their minds." They might be raw recruits now, he told Capra, but American soldiers would prove to be "superior to totalitarian soldiers, *if*—and this is a large if, indeed—they are given answers as to *why* they are in uniform, and *if* the answers they get are *worth* fighting and dying for."[1]

Marshall's orders were ringing in Capra's ears as he left the Chief of Staff's office. The instructions seemed straightforward—"Tell our young men *why* they are in uniform, *why* they must fight"—but Capra found them almost insurmountably difficult. The reason why just seemed too abstract. But he soon hit upon an elegant solution: he would use the enemies' own words against them. His first task was to watch Leni Riefenstahl's 1935 film *Triumph of the Will,* a work of Nazi propaganda that was all the more disturbing for being one of the most technically brilliant films ever made; at the time only two copies existed in the United States, and Capra had to get a special security clearance just to see it. *Triumph of the Will* convinced him that he should produce an American worldview to counter the Nazis'. Using newsreel footage, plus clips from captured German and Japanese military films, Capra's movie series would be America's response to Riefenstahl and Adolf Hitler. "Use the enemy's own films to expose their enslaving ends," he told his crew. "Let our boys hear the Nazis and Japs shout their own claims of master-race crud—and our fighting men will *know* why they are in uniform."[2] Capra's ideological counternarrative, based on individual rights, democracy, religious freedom, and autonomous local communities instead of nationalist aggression, conquest, and tyranny, would push back against the Axis bid for world domination. The battle between these two worldviews would determine the fate of the world. That's what Marshall's army would be fighting for.

Thus was born *Why We Fight,* a landmark documentary series eventually totaling seven films that was mandatory viewing for all new recruits in the US Army. These films attuned viewers to the ultimate stakes of what Roosevelt had called the global division "between human slavery and human freedom."[3] In the first film, *Prelude to War* (1942), Vice President Henry Wallace framed the conflict as "a fight between a free world and a slave world," while the narrator of the sixth film, *The Battle of China* (1944), portrayed the war as "the struggle of freedom against slavery, civilization against barbarism, good against evil. Upon their victory depends the future of mankind." This was why Americans could no longer avoid the war: remaining neutral was actually taking a position that would lead to the enslavement of the whole world, including the United States. "We simply did not want to understand that our individual and national problems were, and always will be, dependent upon the problems of the whole world," *Prelude to War*'s narrator solemnly intoned. While it seemed "impossible to convince a farm-boy in Iowa . . . that he should go to war because of a mud hut in Manchuria," Capra's orders were to convince the farm boys of America otherwise.[4]

Prelude to War was an instant success with its backers in Washington. Marshall and Secretary of War Henry L. Stimson were delighted that Capra had produced such a powerful message, and after a private screening at the White House, Franklin Roosevelt pushed for it to be available to the public. *Prelude to War* won Capra another Oscar, this time for Best Documentary, and the other six films in the series went on to receive a general release in Allied countries throughout Europe and Asia—including the Soviet Union. Winston Churchill was a particular fan, bringing reels of Capra's movies with him on board to watch while his ship crossed the Atlantic on the way to meet Roosevelt. While *Prelude to War* was a box-office disappointment, and while it's unclear just how much the *Why We Fight* message actually sunk in with its target audience of US Army soldiers, the movies collectively stand as one of the clearest statements of America's wartime aims and ideology.[5]

"Tell our young men *why* they are in uniform, *why* they must fight"— it was a deceptively simple task of obviously enormous importance. But it was also a strange one. The curious question isn't "Why did Americans fight?" but actually "Why did Americans need to be told why they fought?" To the people living in any of America's allied nations—in Britain, France, China, the Soviet Union, and elsewhere in Europe and Asia— who were suffering from constant barrages of artillery, gunfire, bombing, invasion, occupation, and atrocities, the question of why they fought didn't even need posing, let alone answering. Their cities were in flames and rubble. Their people, most of them noncombatants, were dying by the thousands, in some places by the millions. Why Britons or Russians or Chinese fought was self-evident: they fought to save their lives and the lives of their families, and for the very survival of their country. There was nothing remote about their war. Tellingly, wartime propaganda in Britain and the Soviet Union didn't bother asking why the people fought; its aim was instead to maintain morale in the midst of suffering, to steel resolve for an ultimate victory that for a long time seemed unattainable, and to prevent internal division by uniting the nation around a common cause.[6] If the war seemed abstract to the farmers of Iowa, it was very real to the farmers of Manchuria.

For Americans, the situation was somewhat different. Japan had attacked them, and the legitimate cause for war was obvious. But the Japanese had struck a naval base on a colony in the middle of the Pacific Ocean, almost twenty-five hundred miles from the nearest US state. That didn't make the assault on Pearl Harbor any less deadly or tragic (and the accompanying Japanese attack on the US-held Philippines was even more brutal), but the distance did little to clarify the ultimate stakes of the war, especially if the United States itself was in little peril. "To the question: What are we fighting for? there is no single or simple answer," for the simple reason that Americans "have never seen a bomb drop and know nothing about the war except by hearsay," reflected the historian Carl Becker during the war.[7] Before Pearl Harbor, it may have been natural to ask, as the New York Times defense correspondent Hanson Baldwin did, "For what should we fight?"[8] Afterward, however, it made less sense. Yet while Hawai'i had been attacked, Iowa remained safe. Thus the need for Why We Fight.

In describing the free world's fight against slavery, Capra relied on an approach that was becoming a familiar theme in US foreign policy: the government's duty to protect citizens against the variety of threats they faced in the modern, interconnected world. Capra's earlier films, such as Mr. Deeds Goes to Town (1936), You Can't Take It with You (1938), and Mr. Smith Goes to Washington (1939), reflected a populist celebration of what one historian has called "the folkways of ordinary people" and their struggles with the corruptions of modern industrial democracy. Even though Capra mostly kept his political views private, his films were widely interpreted as celebrations of American social democracy and the New Deal in particular. While he had been initially wary of the United States getting involved in foreign conflicts, his conversion to an anti-Nazi, anti-fascist politics was inspired by a "Quarantine Hitler" rally in Los Angeles he attended in 1938. Eager to do his duty, and harassed by rising suspicions of "foreign-born" Hollywood filmmakers, Capra was thus Roosevelt's perfect wartime messenger.[9]

Despite Capra's political diffidence, the Why We Fight movies regularly invoked the New Deal—workers, unions, government assistance—to elevate American liberty over German and Japanese tyranny. All countries had been hit hard by the Depression, intoned the narrator of Prelude to War, but unlike the Axis powers the United States "faced it in a democratic way" through programs like Social Security and the Civilian Conservation Corps (CCC). By similarly chronicling the struggle of ordinary people in Europe and Asia against the forces of tyranny—the ruin of cities and the slaughter of civilians are constantly on screen in the *Why We Fight* films—Capra's documentaries drew their energy from the powerful currents of his Hollywood populism.

It was no coincidence, moreover, that General Marshall was himself a New Dealer. One of the highlights of his career was overseeing army-run CCC camps in South Carolina, Oregon, and Washington state. For him, he told the venerable General John J. Pershing, working with civilians this way was "a major mobilization and a splendid experience for the War Department and the army."[10] Marshall's belief in the New Deal, not just that it was necessary in a time of emergency but a positive good for the moral health of the nation, was deep, and unlike other army commandants he happily called on the Works Progress Administration to help build and repair CCC facilities. In fact, the first time Roosevelt and Marshall ever met was in the fall of 1937, during FDR's western tour—which ended with him delivering the "quarantine" speech in Chicago—when Marshall's troops from Vancouver Barracks in Washington paraded before the president during his visit to the Bonneville Dam. Marshall was invited to board the presidential train car, and while he wasn't impressed with the sycophantic officials who swarmed around Roosevelt, he was inspired by the president himself.[11]

Marshall also believed in the power of cinema. To give CCC workers some light relief, he would often project movies onto the side of a large truck. His commandeering of Capra's talents marked the start of an intimate relationship between Hollywood and the US military, with the armed forces providing film studios with advice, equipment, personnel, and authentic battle footage in exchange for the promotion of ideas and images that would support the war effort.[12]

But there was more to *Why We Fight* than the romance of film or the democratic promise of the New Deal. Celebrations of the superiority of the American way of life were prominent in *Why We Fight*, but they were not in themselves a justification to fight. The New Deal had extended Americans' economic and social security in the face of an immediate danger. War would now extend national security against a different danger. Capra's films showed little nuance in claiming not just that the American way of life was rivaled, or even challenged, by German and Japanese "slavery," but that Americans were threatened by literal enslavement should

Germany and Japan be victorious in Europe and Asia and eventually invade of North America. This palpable sense of danger marked a critical difference from previous justifications for why Americans fought: in 1898, William McKinley portrayed Spanish atrocities as a stain on humanity but not as a threat to America; in 1917, Woodrow Wilson wanted to save democracy for the good of civilization rather than the safety of Americans. In 1941–1942, by contrast, Roosevelt argued that Europe's fate, and Asia's, were also America's. Capra followed Roosevelt's lead, and together they argued that the advance of tyranny, wherever it occurred, was a direct threat to the very survival of the United States and its people. There was no more isolation; there was no more free security. In advancing such an argument, radical at the time but commonplace by the era of the Korean and Vietnam wars (which produced their own *Why We Fight* equivalents of *Why Korea* and *Why Vietnam*), Capra's movies helped change the strategic basis of American warfare.[13] They helped invent national security.

————

THE WORLD IN WHICH Capra made his *Why We Fight* films, and the world those films portrayed, had been shaped by the forces of globalization that the Depression had slowed but not stopped. Ever since the late nineteenth century, technological advances in transportation and communication had made the world appear smaller and more accessible. These new technologies were also sources of enhanced power, a reality felt perhaps most acutely by those who lacked them. Without the dreadnought or the submarine, without "a latest model aeroplane," Marcus Garvey noted with bitter realism, whites would never yield African Americans the respect and security they needed and deserved.[14] In the modern world, power came from the ability to harness technology for political ends.

Spurred in large part by these technological advances, between 1890 and the Great War the transnational circulation of people, goods, ideas, and capital increased dramatically. Globalization fluctuated after 1914—stalling during the war, reviving in the 1920s, stalling again with the Depression—but the technological innovation that made it possible kept progressing. By the escalation of the world crisis in the 1930s, technology had changed everyone's mental map of the world, making possible a lifestyle that collapsed previously unbridgeable distances. In making *Why We Fight,* for instance, Capra himself thought nothing of commuting regularly between Washington and Los Angeles in a way that would have seemed like something from science fiction only a decade or two before. But the war also revealed the dual-use implications of the technologies that made globalization possible, as machines could be used just as easily to kill people as to bring them closer together. While this ease of overpowering the barriers of natural geography was liberating for Capra, it could also be threatening to the security of countries, like the United States, that had traditionally relied on the free security of the protective moats of the Atlantic and Pacific oceans.[15]

Technological advances thus changed the perspective of the map and gave rise to what astonished observers simply referred to as "a new geography." The measurable distances between locations hadn't changed, but people's imagination of distance had completely.[16] For many, such as a continental commuter like Capra, the new travel convenience was liberating. But for others, such as Charles Merriam, it required a whole new perspective, most obviously geopolitical for all countries but also social and political for each individual country. "The growth of communication and transportation alone has overturned the boundary lines of authority, geographically, and has in effect set up a new world," he observed in 1934. "The units of organization have been upset." This new world emerging, and the cataclysmic war it created, would soon lead Merriam to embrace an international society governed by a federated world state. But in 1934, it led him to pose the kind of uncomfortable questions that caused anxiety worldwide:

> We may ask, what would a map of the world show if it were reconstructed by some bold hand, endeavoring to reorganize the social and economic realities of our time within new political boundary lines? Or what would the map of almost any of the individual nations be if its organization were shaped in accord with the social facts of the present time?[17]

After the war, at another moment of intense international tension, Merriam proposed a "World Bill of Rights" to safeguard the security of people everywhere, since the persistence of insecurity meant the inevitable outbreak of more conflict.[18] But other internationalists, even those sympathetic to the notion of a world society, were more realistic. As Archibald MacLeish put it toward the end of the war, the victorious powers would be the ones to determine the world's "geography, its actual shape and meaning in men's minds."[19] This was the shape, and the meaning that filled it, that did much to give form and substance to new American ideas about national security.

These globe-tightening changes partly resulted from new communications technology. Transcontinental telegraph and radio brought people together, but they also raised potential threats to American security by enabling enemy forces to coordinate across the great distances that had been America's traditional shield. Commercial radio also enabled leaders to reach directly to the people, and not just of their own country, which could certainly bind people closer together but could also allow for the spread of internal dissent or fearmongering. In their different ways, Adolf Hitler's and Franklin Roosevelt's uses of radio were at the leading edge of innovation in political communications. And as Riefenstahl and Capra demonstrated, the power of the moving image was no less forceful, with the same film able to foster political and social unity in one country and foment instability in another.[20]

Yet as Marcus Garvey knew, nothing captured both the promise and peril of the new globalizing technologies more than the airplane. It was the "airman's view" of the world that changed the conceptual landscape of geography, in turn giving rise to a new sensibility of "Air-Age Globalism."[21] The new science of "aerography" allowed people to explore the hidden currents of the atmosphere that had remained as inaccessibly unknown as the hidden depths of the oceans.[22] While aviation was a product of the very first years of the twentieth century, and while it was a factor in the Great War, it didn't begin to realize its full potential until the height of the Machine Age. Charles Lindbergh announced this potential in 1927, when he became the first person to fly solo across the Atlantic, departing Long Island as a daredevil and landing just over thirty-three hours later in Paris as an international sensation. By the 1930s, aviation had brought the world closer together than ever before, increasing the range of long-distance travel and the frequency of transnational encounters. And while air travel was still too expensive to become a genuinely mass pursuit (unlike the radio or the automobile), it was becoming accessible enough: passenger numbers increased nearly tenfold in the 1930s.[23] Either way, its apparent promise of endless freedom quickly captured the populist imagination—the first-ever Oscar winner for Best Picture was *Wings* (1927), a silent film about two World War I fighter pilots vying for the affection of the same woman, and two of Capra's first movies of the sound era were *Flight* (1929) and *Dirigible* (1931).

The growth of airlines, especially Pan American, connected the United States to other countries more intimately than ever before—not just to nearby Latin America but also to Europe, Asia, and Africa—leading Pan Am's president to envision, in 1939, "America's frontiers pushed back to infinity."[24] On the assumption that flight would bring people closer together, which in turn was assumed to be a precondition for peaceful relations, aviators such as Elizabeth Lippincott McQueen of the Women's International Aeronautic Association became peace planners.[25] "Planes was dropping and going out from everywheres," the humorist and aviation enthusiast Will Rogers remarked when transiting through Ostend, Belgium, during a trip to Europe in the same year Lindbergh crossed the Atlantic. Ostend reminded Rogers of the railroad junctions of the Midwest, but this time, instead of connecting at Saint Louis for the train to Claremore, Oklahoma (Rogers's hometown), you could catch a flight to Amsterdam, Berlin, Warsaw, or Copenhagen. "Here I am," he marveled, "for no apparent reason, able to fly from London, England, to Moscow, Russia, in two days, part of it over a country that we laugh at and look on as backward and primitive."[26] By allowing countries to hop over centuries of painful industrial development, aviation would be the great leveler of international society. Its possibilities to change the world were endless.

But aviation was also more potentially menacing than anything else, too, and not just because civilian air travel was still incredibly dangerous (Rogers himself died in a plane crash in 1935). Just as a passenger airplane could bring people to distant continents, a military aircraft could unleash destruction to distant countries. By 1936–1937, the German and Italian aerial bombing of cities in Spain and Ethiopia, and the Japanese bombing of cities in China—including the siege of Shanghai that moved Roosevelt to give his quarantine speech—had dramatized the destructive possibilities of airpower. Now, military strategists and planners predicted, trench warfare between fixed positions of infantry would become as irrelevant as the bow and arrow, because bombers simply could fly over them and, as the pioneering air strategist Billy Mitchell foresaw in 1919, destroy "an enemy's great nerve centers . . . so as to paralyze them to the greatest extent possible."[27] As Jeffrey Engel has noted, World War II would be "an airman's war."[28]

This harrowing vision didn't stop at the battlefield: the bomber could also destroy the centers of industrial production that equipped armies and navies, also laying waste to the industrial cities and the people who lived in them. "The next war is going to be all in the air," Rogers predicted. Armies struggling over a few yards of terrain—"that's museum stuff," far removed from "the real war of the future." Instead, in the "next war you don't want to Look Out; you want to Look Up."[29] The president of the National Security League argued that the two greatest perils facing Americans were communists and foreign bombers: "we could at any time be subjected to ready attack by the smallest foreign nation able to build a Zeppelin," he told a crowd in 1923; "we are not isolated or protected by the Atlantic and yet we have no real defense ready."[30]

Even though its numbers were dwindling, the National Security League's heightened threat perception was an extreme vanguard of a wider (if ill-defined) sense of dread. After all, if bombers could fly over armies, they could fly over borders and oceans, too. Although the British, with the Channel suddenly unable to offer a complete protective barrier in the age of airpower, felt more acutely vulnerable to the threat of aerial bombing, Americans felt newly vulnerable, too.[31] "What will the future hold for us?" Mitchell asked matter-of-factly in 1930. "Undoubtedly an attack on the great centers of population," with the "civilian population driven out" of Chicago, Detroit, Pittsburgh, and Washington. Another aviation expert predicted "the termination of New York." The very complexity that made modern societies so dynamic and wealthy also made them uniquely vulnerable: it took only the destruction of one component to bring the whole interdependent system to a halt.[32] "With life unbearable or perhaps not even supportable," one air strategist hypothesized, bombed-out Americans would have little choice but "to yield to the will of an enemy with effective independent air action."[33] The ultimate consequence of airpower—the end of over a century of free security for the continental United States—could not have been more profound.

World War II would soon reaffirm, with harrowing ferocity in cities like London, Dresden, Tokyo, Hiroshima, and Nagasaki, the old relationship between warfare and fire. The new technologies had exponentially increased the destructive capacity of firepower, yet this was already evident before the world war broke out in China in 1937 and Europe in 1939. Henry Stimson had once hoped that international law would one day lead to the end of armed conflict; he was, after all, the secretary of state who oversaw implementation of the Kellogg-Briand Pact that outlawed war altogether. But he had also been a preparedness stalwart in the Great War, and one of the National Security League's more prominent members, before becoming Franklin Roosevelt's secretary of war in 1940.

In 1933, he foresaw how liberal internationalism would have to overcome interstate war. International law remained his fondest hope. "Yet the truth," he acknowledged, was that "in the world at large, political and commercial inter-connection had already so far developed that war anywhere in the world . . . is always a potential danger to the rest of civilization. It is like a prairie fire; and a war once started in any portion of the earth is likely to envelop the whole. Nowhere can war be neglected as entirely innocuous to the rest of the world."[34]

THOSE CONCERNED ABOUT America's new, sudden vulnerabilities in an interconnected world focused obsessively on the disappearance of free security. Geopolitically, the United States still lived in a safe neighborhood; that was in part a function of its mainland being far away from its main peer competitors, but it was also a result of being surrounded by other states that were much weaker. Geographically, however, advanced naval and aviation technology made the protective oceans much narrower. For this reason, free security was a luxury of a bygone era, wrote the distinguished Columbia historian Allan Nevins in 1940 during the Battle of France: "Isolation in the days of the frigate was a different concept from isolation in the days of the 'flying fortress' [the B-17 bomber] with a 3,000-mile radius at 265 miles an hour."[35] Edward Mead Earle, once a subscriber to the theory of free security, saw its disappearance as a sudden break with tradition, and as solely the product of the "political and technological developments of the last twenty-five years."[36]

To internationalists, this meant that reliance on a traditional strategy of hemispheric defense was no longer tenable. The hemispheres couldn't be sealed off from each other anymore, and even if this was something of a historical fallacy—regions of the world had never in fact been sealed off, and people from east and west had always mingled, traded, and often fought—the Monroe Doctrine was still a powerful article of faith in American political culture. Thanks to the shrinkage of geography, internationalists had a compelling case that the world was too small for Americans to assume they were automatically protected from encroachment and even attack. For one thing, Madison, Wisconsin—seen as an isolationist bastion—was geographically closer to China and Russia than it was to Argentina or Chile, and in an age of airpower, which eliminated the distinction between circuitous distance-over-water and direct distance-over-land, this meant that the old assumptions for the requirements of defense would have to be reconsidered.[37] But even the protective barrier of the oceans was uncertain, made clear by the fact that the first naval battle of the war, in December 1939, was between German and British ships off the coast of Argentina. Geographers and political scientists—some of them, like Isaiah Bowman, close to Roosevelt, and others, such as Halford Mackinder and Nicholas Spykman, among the most distinguished figures in the field—expounded on the new, horizonless geopolitical landscape, providing internationalist policymakers with a working theory of the necessity of intervention.[38] As Daniel Immerwahr points out, when Roosevelt called the conflict "a global war," he was the first president ever to use that word in public.[39] This was no coincidence, for it was also Roosevelt, as we've seen, who popularized the term "national security" to refer to a doctrine of national self-defense that actually had no geographical limits.

Internationalists worried that the new military technologies could threaten Americans not by projecting firepower from afar but by conquering territory in the western hemisphere. US military intelligence in the Philippines, Hawai'i, Peru, and elsewhere across the Pacific, along with the FBI at home, worried about pro-Japanese, anti-colonial activists undermining American and European rule in ways that would imperil broader American national security.[40] Even more ominously, if the Nazis knocked out British sea power they could gain a foothold in the Americas, seize control of the hemisphere's strategic natural resources, build airstrips and army bases close enough to the United States to mount bombing operations, and eventually launch a ground invasion.[41] The War Department thus began building its own airstrips even before American entry into the war, using private airlines like Pan Am to maintain a fictive adherence to the official neutrality of most countries in the hemisphere.[42] The construction of US bases in Latin America became public after Pearl Harbor, but under an umbrella of collective security amongst equal sovereign states rather than the narrower goal of protecting US national security. This was a diplomatic necessity, given Roosevelt's own Good Neighbor policy, but it also made strategic sense as US entry into the war, combined with the stalemate on the Eastern Front, made a German incursion into South America, and the resort to collective security, all the more unlikely.[43]

Even so, the underlying premise of resistance to Germany and Japan was American self-defense, both in the more capacious sense of "national security" just then emerging but also in the narrower, more traditional sense of safeguarding territorial sovereignty and protection from physical attack. For this reason, Secretary of State Hull said Americans had everything to fear from the Germans' "steadily expanding conquest" that had global ambitions.[44] If "the French army was the first line of defense of the United States," as Roosevelt purportedly said in 1938, then by 1940–1941 the US security position was in deep crisis.[45] The most plausible invasion scenario was a German defeat of Britain, which would result in the Nazi seizure of much of the Royal Navy, which could in turn enable the Germans to challenge the US Navy for command of the Atlantic, expand their reach into the western hemisphere, and eventually encircle and then conquer the United States itself. The fate of the world—or, at least, of America's place in the world—was therefore at stake. The survival of Britain was paramount, for "if we lose in the Atlantic," Marshall declared, "we lose everywhere."[46] This was why, Roosevelt said, "the best defense of Great Britain is the best defense of the United States."[47] Roosevelt often invoked the defense of common values, such as democracy, to explain America's stakes in the war, but the defense of Britain was more urgent—"not because of any sentimental attachment to the land of Shakespeare, Keats and leafy lanes," presidential speechwriter Robert Sherwood put it, but because of the "duty to promote the interests of our national security."[48]

The era of free security, from the end of the War of 1812 in 1815 to the crisis years of World War II in 1940–1941, coincided with British naval supremacy in the Atlantic and an informal Anglo-American partnership: with the end of British supremacy came the beginning of the end of free security. "The oldest and simplest principle of American security rests on its geographical separation from Europe," the distinguished diplomatic historian Richard Van Alstyne wrote in 1944, in one of the first scholarly assessments of how World War II had changed the basic security parameters of the United States. The fall of France and the risk that Britain would follow suit had confronted Americans with a problem they hadn't faced "since 1776: that American independence and freedom of action cannot tolerate the existence of a predatory conqueror in control of the coastline of western Europe." The prospect of this very worst-case scenario "altered this long-standing system of American security" and "invoked questions for the United States which had never been asked in the nation's history." Americans had taken the British protective shield for granted, and only now, with its very existence threatened, did they realize it. "The traditional idea of American security," Van Alstyne concluded, "was founded on the belief that distance was a permanent protection." That distance could now be overcome and open the only route an invader could take to the United States.[49]

Should Britain surrender, then the worst-case scenario—a direct attack on the continental United States, followed by a full-scale invasion—would become that much more realistic. This strategic nightmare had been a small if powerful current in the American worldview since Homer Lea summoned up the specter of a Japanese occupation of California in 1909, but it had never seemed plausible until 1940–1941. Experts testified before Congress that the widely reprinted 1927 Tanaka Memorial, a supposed Japanese blueprint for world conquest later shown to be a hoax, proved that the United States wasn't immune from attack, and Capra's *Why We Fight* films for the army invoked the Tanaka Memorial alongside *Mein Kampf* as examples of the threat Americans faced.[50] In the summer of 1940 William C. Bullitt, Roosevelt's ambassador to the recently subjugated France, expressed not just the fear, but the humiliation that stemmed from such fear, when he asked Americans whether they wished to share the fate of the French: "Do you want to see Hitler in Independence Hall making fun of the Liberty Bell?"[51]

This heightened sense of vulnerability wasn't just confined to official channels or expert strategists; it was also reflected in the broader contemporary culture. By the summer of 1940, shortly after the fall of France and as Britain was facing a German invasion, 45 percent of Americans told pollsters that the Axis powers would "attack us on our own territory as soon as possible."[52] Each of the seven *Why We Fight* documentaries featured animated maps illustrating in frighteningly realistic detail how the conquest of North America would unfold, with Germany and Japan invading via South America, or over the North Pole, if they won their wars in Europe and Asia. Hollywood produced a run of films in the 1939–1941 period depicting a besieged Britain holding the line of civilization against the onslaught of barbarism. *The Sea Hawk* (1940), starring Errol Flynn, brought the point home by dramatizing the heroic story of Elizabethan England standing fast against the ambitions of Philip II of Spain to expand his empire not just to England, but ultimately its American colonies.[53] After Pearl Harbor, Joe DiMaggio's brother called from San Francisco to tell the baseball star that the beloved family restaurant on Fisherman's Wharf had to close due to the imminent Japanese invasion.[54] That same year, the American Society of Civil Engineers took it upon itself to start planning for a rebuilding program once US cities were flattened by enemy bombers.[55]

The imagination of painter Thomas Hart Benton was even more garish than the nation's engineers. Benton had been a pioneer of Regionalism, a style that celebrated (some say invented) the American pastoral heartland. His contempt for laissez-faire capitalism, his Capraesque celebration of the common man, his support for the New Deal, and his liberal hostility to communism and fascism in equal measure animated his paintings through the 1930s. But even though he was skeptical of direct US military intervention in the world crisis, he shared the growing unease at the growth of German and Japanese power. In 1938, he etched a lithograph, *Approaching Storm*, that portrayed a farmer peacefully plowing his fields (possibly in Iowa) while clouds gathered just over the horizon. After Pearl Harbor, Benton painted a series of gruesome murals collectively known as *The Year in Peril*. Perhaps the most frightening was simply entitled *Invasion*, which depicts fascist soldiers pillaging the United States, its cities bombed, its women raped, its children murdered. Although Benton's purpose was to alert the complacent American people to the danger they were in—he wanted, he later recalled, "to wake up the middle west to the grimness of our national situation"—his paintings were too much even by the standards of government propaganda, and after a brief showing at the Metropolitan Museum in New York they were quietly moved out of sight and into storage.[56]

Opponents of intervention—a varied group of pacifists, nativists, and even some genuine isolationists who really did want to seal off the United States from the rest of the world; their goal was to quarantine America, not Japan or Germany—argued that the likes of Capra, Benton, and Van Alstyne were simply fearmongering, and that the United States remained free from the threat of invasion. But as Stephen Wertheim has shrewdly observed, during the crucible period of 1938–1942, the question of invasion didn't actually matter for internationalists because their whole argument was that continental or even hemispheric safety against a physical attack was no longer the baseline of American national defense.[57] Security now meant something much more than what Robert Osgood dismissed as "its lowest common denominator," repelling a direct physical invasion.[58] Indeed, this was the whole point of the new, more capacious doctrine of "national security." When making the case in 1938 for greater military spending, Roosevelt himself even explicitly separated the two:

"our national defense is . . . inadequate for purposes of national security and requires increase for that reason."[59]

It's unlikely this revolutionary turn in American threat perception came about by some sort of presidentially directed intelligent design; more likely, it evolved between the wars, with the Japanese invasion of China in 1937, the German invasion of Poland in 1939, and especially the German conquest of France in 1940 as the catalytic period in which evolution sped up and produced a new mindset about the measurable risks facing the United States. Not everyone evolved in this way, of course, but for those who did the logic of the more expansive national security vision was irrefutable. In a tightly interconnected world, the United States was more vulnerable, and had to adjust its defensive measures accordingly, even if enemy forces weren't lurking just over the horizon waiting to strike, because that day would surely come. "Nothing seems to me more foolish than a policy designed to assure that if we must fight, the fighting shall be upon our own territory," Dean Acheson told an audience of skeptical students at Yale University in 1939, where the anti-interventionist group America First would soon be founded. "I think it clear that with a nation, as with a boxer, one of the greatest assurances of safety is to add reach to power."[60]

Edward Mead Earle's seminar at Princeton once again led the way in codifying the scale of America's new front line of defense. Seminar members agreed that self-defense was now global—in the Atlantic, yes, and in Britain and France, yes, but not just there. The United States was at risk everywhere. This is what Earle and his colleagues meant when they set about defining the new term of art "national security."[61] Until 1940, Earle himself had still retained faith in the oceans' ability to ensure the nation's free security, but the fall of France and the threat to Britain quickly transformed his view. Even after that point, however, many Americans still believed in free security, but to Earle that seemed foolish. "On the contrary," he wrote in his 1941 polemic *Against this Torrent*, which disseminated the Princeton seminar's findings to a wider audience, "with the possible exception of Secession, we have never before faced a crisis of such moment to our future." Protecting US security required more than simply "meeting an enemy at the water's edge," and there was no defensive barrier "behind which we can take refuge." The answer was a "military policy" that "must be offensive in the sense of enabling us, if necessary, to seize and keep the initiative at whatever points our interests may be threatened." This necessitated a total break with traditional statecraft, because "conventional military standards and time-honored concepts of defense are no longer relevant to our security."[62] This was because the very nature of safety in the modern world had changed irrevocably. "Security is a broad concept," Earle explained; "as distinguished from mere defense, it is concerned less with resistance to attack than with the formulation and enforcement of policies which will make attack less likely and, failing this, to assure that the chances of successful resistance will be as great as possible." Earle confessed he "doubted, in fact, whether talk of physical invasion has any but minor relevance" to security considerations at all, a dismissal of the traditional requirements of self-defense that was audacious in its sweeping totality.[63]

UNFORTUNATELY FOR EARLE and his fellow internationalists, other Americans were not so audacious. Not everyone believed the fundamentals of world order had changed so much, even with the era's technological revolutions, and so they wouldn't accept that American security requirements, let alone the definition of national self-defense, should change as well. Perhaps this is why War Department researchers discovered that for all the acclaim from film critics and military leadership, Capra's *Why We Fight* films actually made limited headway in convincing enlisted men that their country was in direct danger from Germany or Japan. Why they fought, it turned out, had little to do with protecting house and home and more to do with participating in a national adventure and enjoying the camaraderie that comes from being part of a group.[64] For many Americans, just because the world was getting smaller did not mean that threats to the United States had become bigger.

Skeptics abounded. Most diplomatic historians no longer use the term "isolationist" to describe the objections many Americans had to a more robust international role. The word itself was coined in the late 1930s, as a political epithet rather than a neutral descriptor, to discredit people who wanted the United States to stay out of the regional wars in Europe and Asia. Many Americans who opposed intervention in foreign wars were in fact as deeply internationalist as they were deeply antiwar; they wanted their country to be involved in the political affairs of the world, just not at the barrel of a gun. Thus not all anti-interventionists were antisemites, nativists, fascist sympathizers, or even nationalists. Many were pacifists who believed that "Hitler is terrible" but that war was even worse: as one internationalist, a Protestant missionary in China, wrote in the days after the Nazi invasion of Poland, "should we sacrifice our young men, or maim and cripple them," merely to determine whether the British Empire or the German Empire was supreme?[65] To be sure, there were plenty of Americans who were genuine isolationists, who did want to seal the United States off from the rest of the world. But to refer to all of the noninterventionists as "isolationists" gives a misleading impression of the cohesiveness of noninterventionism before 1942.[66]

Noninterventionists simply saw a different world than internationalists. Faraway places with odd-sounding names still didn't matter to American defense for a simple reason: they did not matter to Americans themselves. Referring to the British Isles and Southeast Asia, two of the most vulnerable points in the resistance to Axis aggression, America Firster John T. Flynn called for Roosevelt to launch "a defense program designed to protect this country and not engage in adventures from the Firth of Forth to Dong Dang."[67] Referring to the same remote border crossing between China and Vietnam, which the Japanese had used to invade Indochina in 1940, and which in turn triggered ever-tightening US sanctions against Japan, John B. Trevor asked Americans: "Do you want to pour out American blood in torrents to determine whether France, England, Germany or Japan shall rule Dong Dang or any other God-forsaken tropical hell-hole?" The rhetorical question didn't need repeating, but Trevor did so anyway: "*What does that mean to you?*"[68] To anti-interventionists, the answer was obvious. "I am anticipating the day when the possession of Tibet and Afghanistan will be represented as vitally necessary to the security of Kansas and Nebraska," complained another skeptic. "There is no logical end to this elastic conception of 'security' short of the conquest of the whole world."[69]

Dong Dang, Tibet, and Afghanistan were far away, and the technological revolution that so impressed—and worried—internationalists actually brought comfort to noninterventionists because it would make the United States more secure, not more vulnerable, against remote and distant threats. Aviation, for example, "offers not only the hope of increased security at home," claimed Billy Mitchell, but also, because it would more easily bring people together, "the greatest civilizing element in the future." Warfare would still exist, but "future wars will again be conducted by a special class, the air force, as it was by the armored knights in the Middle Ages." But all that would happen elsewhere, and if the United States built up a sufficient air force, "it is hard to visualize how an enemy could gain a footing on land in a country such as the United States."[70] That was in 1925, and the years between Mitchell's early treatise on airpower and the onset of World War II saw enormous advances in the projection of airpower—witnessed not least by the suffering civilians of Ethiopia, Spain, and China—yet that did little to change noninterventionist minds. Few could challenge the expertise of Charles Lindbergh, who testified to Congress, and told millions of others on speaking tours and over the radio, that US airpower gave the country a firm shield against attack.[71] Roosevelt himself inadvertently reinforced the point when he declared at the outset of rearmament, in 1940, that his goal was to build an air force "capable of overcoming any attack against us."[72] Noninterventionists perceived even the very measures Roosevelt pursued to nudge the United States deeper into the world crisis—the quarantine speech, Lend-Lease—as ways of outsourcing the fighting and thus keeping America out of the war.[73]

Moreover, in economic terms, according to a 1936 War Department study, "the United States is almost self-contained industrially. There exist within its borders in ample quantities the labor, power, facilities and, with certain important exceptions, all the raw materials necessary in war," and those it lacked (such as rubber and hemp) it could import from the Philippines or the British Empire. Easy access to overseas commodities was severed after 1941, but by then US companies were beginning to produce synthetic rubber and other goods that would soon make up for any shortfalls. The United States also had a large domestic market that, even in the midst of the Depression, could function with little reliance on foreign trade, and it had a surplus of workers so that both the military and industry would never be short of personnel. "It is almost impossible to assume a situation," the war planners confidently predicted, "where the population would be in danger of suffering actual hardships in war due to a lack of personnel to produce the necessities of life."[74] Americans had a further advantage in that the dollar was commonly used in international commerce, something the Japanese began to realize when a gold-based dollar exchange they used through a Wall Street bank became vulnerable to sanctions.[75]

Be it militarily or economically, then, the continental United States still enjoyed enough of the blessings of free security to make "national security" a debatable proposition rather than a settled geopolitical fact. "Alone, our nation is unconquerable," Lindbergh boasted in 1940, and though his racist and antisemitic views make it difficult to read his geopolitical views dispassionately—he went on to say that the United States should try to broker a peace in Europe before the white race committed suicide—he had a point about the strength of basic US defense. This was the logic behind the Ludlow Amendment, introduced perennially with broad support through the later 1930s but never ratified, which called for a national referendum on whether to go to war except in cases of a foreign attack or invasion against US soil.[76]

The endurance of free security did not, of course, mean that US foreign interests were risk-free. The world was unquestionably more dangerous in 1939 than it was in 1929 or 1919. But the realities of world politics did mean that the United States could still take for granted that it would not suffer the same fate that befell many other countries, including France, Russia, and China: invasion and occupation. Even Britain had come under direct attack, and a very realistic threat of invasion, in 1940, with many times more civilian deaths than the United States suffered over the course of the whole war. The frequency of ground invasion and aerial bombing meant that anywhere from 70 to 80 percent of the sixty million fatalities in World War II were civilians; of those civilians, a mere twelve thousand—maybe one-quarter of one-tenth of one percent of the worldwide total—were from the United States, some based in Hawaiʻi and the Philippines but the vast majority resulting from service in an active theater of war with the US Merchant Marine or the Civil Air Patrol.[77] Other countries thus looked enviously upon America's extremely fortunate geopolitical position; it was, Stalin noted, "in an impregnable position."[78] If the terms of American foreign policy had changed so that the lowest common denominator of defense—safety from physical attack—was no longer the decisive factor, it nonetheless remained a compelling argument for nonintervention. Indeed, it was still, unsurprisingly, one of the most frequently invoked reasons for staying out of the war. If the Germans couldn't even cross the narrow English Channel to invade Britain, Flynn asked in the spring of 1941, how was it remotely possible they could cross the Atlantic Ocean to invade the United States?[79]

Internationalists sometimes had a difficult time overcoming the logic of free security, even as they were strenuously making the case for intervention on the grounds of national defense. Stimson, who had compared the prospect of war to a prairie brush fire, also subscribed to the classic free-security formulation that "Our geographical situation between two great oceans and between neighboring nations who presence gives us no cause for alarm affords us a unique position of national security."[80] A year before the outbreak of war in Europe, General Marshall had reassured the troops that the United States wasn't like the nations of Europe who had clear enemies and "can plan for national defense along definite lines." America, by contrast, had a fortunate "geographical location" that made it "literally impossible to find definite answers for such questions as: who will be our enemy in the next war; in what theatre of operations will that war be fought; and, what will be our national objective at that time?"[81] In 1939, the preeminent interventionist Walter Lippmann described the United States as "an island lying between two great oceans; the heart of it is invulnerable and the nation can never be conquered or intimidated."[82] As late as November 1941, Treasury Secretary Henry Morgenthau could still argue, in laying out a grand strategy for opposing German expansion, "We are protected by two oceans—let us exploit that protection while distance is still a potent barrier."[83]

Roosevelt could hardly wave such logic away because he had once accepted it himself. Because "our position in the world is unparalleledly secure," he wrote in 1928, it was only "the most excited of the Admirals" who would "seriously consider the possibility of invasion."[84] And should that invasion one day come, however unlikely? Eight years later as president, Roosevelt provided an answer that, knowingly or not, paraphrased Jules Jusserand's geopolitical benediction nearly forty years earlier: "Of all the Nations of the world today we are in many ways most singularly blessed. Our closest neighbors are good neighbors. If there are remoter Nations that wish us not good but ill, they know that we are strong; they know that we can and will defend ourselves and defend our neighborhood."[85]

The opponents of intervention went by different names, and although "isolationism" still is the most common, it isn't the most accurate—that instead falls to "continentalism," or what the scholar Campbell Craig terms "free-security continentalism."[86] Continentalists took the narrowest possible view of American defense, with the American Legion codifying "the term 'continental limits of the United States'" as "the area comprised in the states of the Union and the District of Columbia."[87] This was a simple definition that served the noninterventionists' purposes well, for even by 1941 the equally simple geopolitical logic of the day held that the continental United States remained free from the threat of a direct attack.

The foremost proponent of continentalism was the iconoclastic historian Charles Beard, for whom "national defense means defense of the American heritage—the land, people, and institutions on this continent . . . protected from foreign invasion."[88] But the idea enjoyed broad support among the establishment elite, too. Yale's Samuel Flagg Bemis, the most distinguished diplomatic historian of the era and another believer in continentalism, broadened the "defense of the continental homeland" to include Alaska, but the requirements of self-defense remained narrow. Continentalism, argued Bemis, was the Founders' policy, and had provided America's "proper place in the world" until the misadventures of 1898 and 1917 had skewed the American diplomatic tradition and sent it careening off in misguided directions. "The continental position has always been the strength of the United States in the world," Bemis concluded. "It is a safe ground on which to watch and wait for a better world."[89] This was the logic underpinning the more nationalistic versions of noninterventionism, reflected in Lindbergh's America First organization and Beard's theory of how "Continental Americanism" would provide "a foreign policy for America."[90]

Until the late 1930s, army war planners also doubted the need for US forces to be engaged beyond the western hemisphere. They saw their mission, as Army General Stanley D. Embick put it in Beardian terms, as defined by a mission of "continentalism" that presumed US strategic self-sufficiency and focused on defending US territorial sovereignty.[91] Army continentalism fell out of strategic favor in the year before Pearl Harbor, but even as late as October 1941 war planners were assuming that US entry in the war would mean fighting to defend the western hemisphere from Axis encroachment, not deploying men and resources to Europe and Asia.[92] General Hugh Drum acknowledged that "both the Philippines and Hawaii might be lost to us without materially affecting the safety of the continental United States."[93] The navy, of course, had a more expansive, globalist vision, but until 1938–1939 it could not prevail over the narrower continentalist view of American security requirements.

The leading opponent of intervention was Herbert Hoover. In 1932, when he was pressed to respond to Japan's invasion of Manchuria, Hoover told his cabinet that "he would fight for [the] Continental United States as far as anybody, but he would not fight for Asia," and in the intervening years his view had not changed.[94] Nor had the former president, whom Roosevelt had defeated in 1932, gone quietly into retirement. From 1937, as Roosevelt inched closer to a more interventionist posture, Hoover met him each step of the way with regular broadsides against getting involved in the war. "One test is positive" in deciding whether the nation should go to war, he said in 1938: "There must be no foreign soldier on—or over—our soil." An armed encroachment into the western hemisphere would also warrant an armed US response in kind. But aside from those reasons, the United States had no business in the world crisis.[95]

Hoover, who had traveled the world and consulted with foreign governments throughout his life, was a particular problem for Roosevelt and the internationalists because he was difficult to tar as an "isolationist." In fact, much of his anti-interventionism after 1937, right up to Pearl Harbor, was conditioned by his desire to use official US neutrality to organize food aid and humanitarian relief for Nazi-occupied Europe. The British teamed up with the Roosevelt administration to oppose Hoover's humanitarian mission; the last thing internationalists wanted was to help prop up the Nazi regimes in Europe, however well-intentioned Hoover's plan was. Hoover thought this was morally obscene. In his mind, the Nazis were odious but they posed no security threat to the United States. And from its position of safety, the United States was in a unique position to offer assistance to the starving masses of war-torn Europe. The "potential might of this nation is the strongest thing in the whole world," he declared to a national radio audience. Just as in previous wars, Washington could raise whatever sized army it needed for defense. "The defense of America is not dependent upon any other nation, for America cannot be defeated." Hoover's solution to the world crisis, aside from food relief to Europe, was similar to his defense policies when he was president: a new program of military preparedness so as to protect not just the North American continent but the western hemisphere. With America's strength, that should be easy enough to do.[96] By contrast, in fact, policies like Lend-Lease would only weaken the United States by denying it the armed force needed to defend American soil, a distinction that revealed the gulf between Hoover's traditional notion of self-defense and the Roosevelt revolution in national security.[97]

Hoover's anti-intervention critique contained another argument that gave it such credence and power: the pursuit of security would come at the cost of liberty. Not coincidentally, Hoover wasn't only the nation's foremost critic of intervention, but also its foremost critic of the New Deal. Ever since the 1932 election, when he and Roosevelt argued about the proper role of government in American society, Hoover had been a strident critic of the new liberal welfare-regulatory state. This was in keep-ing with the politics of many anti-interventionists; while there were too many exceptions to draw a straight line between anti-statism and anti-interventionism—too many progressives were happily statist but also principally opposed to war on any grounds, while some internationalists, such as Walter Lippmann, were sharply critical of the New Deal—there was a strong correlation between those who feared big government in both domestic policy and foreign affairs. Even prominent anti-interventionists who had supported the New Deal in its early stages recoiled from what they felt was an abuse of power as the regulatory state grew after 1935.[98] And Hoover, who variously castigated the New Deal as "gigantic social-ism" and "fascistic" and charged that the Roosevelt administration had "a pronounced odor of totalitarian government," was certainly one of them.[99] Taking sides in the war would eventually require going to war, Hoover cautioned, and going to war would in turn require an exponen-tial growth of government that could only threaten American liberty on a scale surpassing the New Deal. If Americans traded their liberty for a false sense of security, then the outcome would be bitterly ironic because in fact "the first security of men has been lost."[100] "We know that with preparedness our freedom is in no danger from invasion," Hoover said during another national radio speech, this time only a few weeks before Pearl Harbor. "On the other hand, by sending our boys overseas" to fight in a protracted global war, "the destruction of freedom in America is so certain."[101] Hoover's fears of a loss of freedom at home seemed all too clear because it's precisely what had happened in 1917–1918, and in 1941 the looming war was already, even before US entry, on a far vaster scale than the Great War.

Others shared Hoover's concern. Even before the New Deal, Beard al-ready saw the federal government as a Hobbesian "leviathan," and though he withheld judgment after Roosevelt's first year in office he still darkly detected a "collectivist" future for America.[102] Beard's biggest fear was that waging a world war would only make the "leviathan" grow and, choosing a metaphor to reflect government power at its fullest, "herd the American people into Roosevelt's quarantine camp."[103] Rearmament, and wartime executive powers, had the potential to dwarf even the New Deal's accumulation of governmental power. "It is quite conceivable," warned a congressional report, "that the democracies might attain a military vic-tory over the aggressors only to find themselves under the domination of economic authority far more concentrated and influential than that which existed prior to the war."[104] Roosevelt's incremental escalation of US intervention in the Battle of the Atlantic without congressional authorization, including drastic measures such as the occupation of Iceland, led Flynn to declare that the nation had reached "the beginning of the end of Constitutional Government in the United States."[105] But one didn't have to be a reactionary like Flynn to worry about the growth of an all-powerful military government. When the director of the National Recovery Administration, Hugh Johnson, quit the Roosevelt administration over concerns about governmental overreach, he became a prominent anti-interventionist.[106] David Mitrany, an international relations theorist and colleague of Earle's at the Institute for Advanced Study in Princeton, warned in 1934 that social and economic planning was becoming harnessed to the securitization of national life, which in turn could lead to its militarization. In "the new conception of national security," as Mitrany put it, the inevitable confluence of social planning with war planning could only lead to the military dominance of society.[107]

———

MAYBE IT DIDN'T matter that Americans disagreed about the world; maybe events would have pushed them into the war regardless of how they felt and how they argued. Either way, what did matter was the direction of US foreign and military policies, for they could have taken one of many different directions for many different reasons. And, ultimately, that direction was largely set by the commander in chief, who himself thought as audaciously and as expansively as the most forward-thinking internationalists. All the innovative thinking about geography and technology would have remained literally academic, lost to a seminar room in Princeton, had the foremost believer in geopolitical change not also happened to be the president of the United States.

Franklin Roosevelt's internationalism was not a sudden development in response to Axis aggression. From his childhood he had a fascination for the sea, and he avidly read the works of Alfred Thayer Mahan. Like Mahan, Roosevelt saw the oceans as connective highways that created a "world-wide arena." He served as Wilson's Assistant Secretary of the Navy during the entire period of the Great War, when aviation and submarines changed the strategic calculus of "national defense." From childhood until he was stricken with polio at the age of thirty-nine, he was a frequent international traveler. He had a deep Episcopal faith—"a strong religious feeling and . . . a very personal one," Eleanor Roosevelt once said—at a time when much of American Protestantism was theologically liberal and devoutly internationalist. He was also, more prosaically, a passionate stamp collector. All this helped create an expansively globalist mindset in the person who was president when the world crisis escalated in the 1930s.[108]

Roosevelt's first task as president was to pull the United States back from the brink of an economic apocalypse that threatened not just prosperity but American democracy itself. In foreign affairs, virtually everything that happened during his first term—the Good Neighbor policy, the abandonment of currency stabilization at the London Economic Conference, the first Neutrality Acts—pulled the United States away from the world as it dealt with the Depression. But from his 1937 quarantine speech in Chicago through the attack on Pearl Harbor, nobody did more to change the dynamic of American geopolitics.

Yet as Roosevelt realized from the response to his quarantine address, Americans were not yet ready to adopt a more interventionist role in world politics. "The country as a whole," he noted with alarm several months after the German invasion of Poland, "does not yet have any deep sense of world crisis." Once understandable, such complacency was now dangerous, but public opinion still moved too slowly toward this realization. "What worries me," he told a confidant on another occasion, "is that public opinion . . . is patting itself on the back every morning and thanking God for the Atlantic Ocean (and the Pacific Ocean)."[109] Revealingly, the *Chicago Daily Tribune* removed its lone reporter from China in 1937, for lack of reader interest, not long before the quarantine speech.[110]

As president, then, Roosevelt needed to convince the American people they (and their government) needed to play a more active role in the world, much as he had convinced them of the need for an emergency economic program in 1933. For this reason, John A. Thompson, the historian who has done the most excavational work on the subject, notes that Roosevelt engaged in "the exaggeration of American vulnerability" by arguing that the United States faced existential risks from foreign threats even if the realization of those threats was unrealistic and largely theoretical.[111] Roosevelt did so partly for strategic reasons—there's no reason to doubt that he sincerely believed the United States was at risk—but, with polls showing a majority opposed to entering the war right up to the fall of 1941, he also did so for domestic political reasons.[112]

As late as 1937, even without US membership in the League of Nations, Roosevelt held out hope that collective security could alleviate another world war. But such slim hopes faded from his grand strategy once it was clear that only something more robust than condemnatory public opinion or an amorphous collective will would be needed to push back the Germans and Japanese. Roosevelt realized this even as many noninterventionists at home, especially the large peace movement, and American allies continued to place their trust in nonviolent collective action.[113] In the summer of 1941, while on a speaking tour of the United States, the British scientist and internationalist Julian Huxley called for the creation of a "Security Club," the member nations of which would "collaborate in some system of pooled security." Huxley had in mind a formal international body to oversee cooperative consultation, but he also envisioned the pooling of the various national arms industries into one single project, so that arms races wouldn't spiral out of control and undermine international stability.[114] In Britain, where support for the League of Nations ran high, planners argued that collective security offered the best way for each nation to preserve its own security from attack and invasion.[115] But in the United States, where the League had always been divisive, support for collective security was weak.[116] Roosevelt wasn't opposed to it in principle, and his quarantine speech was actually premised on the idea of nations acting together, in concert, to isolate Japan. But the failure to check Japanese aggression, and the outbreak of war in Europe, made it clear that an effective system of collective security was not the solution.

What replaced collective security, much less continental defense, was American national security. This did not mean that the United States should necessarily act alone; in a war of truly global scope, alliances would be vital. But it did mean that Americans would ensure their security first and foremost on their own terms; any alliance relationships, however close and collaborative, would in essence be either ad hoc arrangements to meet an immediate crisis, or structured vertically, not horizontally, with US interests and power at the top. "It is axiomatic that the United States should encourage collective security and seek friendly relationships with other nations," war planners concluded in 1943. "But it cannot be too often emphasized . . . that collective security is not a substitute for power," for the simple reason that existing systems of collective security hadn't yet figured out how to harness the collective power of its members. It was instead "wise policy for the United States to be strong and to orient its policy toward arrangements with other states which will give security to our territory and to the ideas which we think worth while."[117] The social/national security dyad thus began to see its first fissure. The system of Social Security was, as Roosevelt himself put it, nothing more than "the collective security of the willingness of his fellows to cooperate through the use of government to help him and each other."[118] But with no world government able to provide a channel for attaining US security in the international system, the federal government was left to fulfill this obligation to its citizens.

In rejecting more horizontal forms of collective security, in which power would be dispersed through sharing it among equal sovereign states, Roosevelt strove to avoid Woodrow Wilson's mistakes in 1917–1919. Whereas Wilson had brought the United States into war in 1917 for the collective good of humanity, Roosevelt instead sounded the national alarm bell, warning Americans again and again that they needed to arm themselves and prepare for war not for the general wellbeing of others but for their own safety. In two solemn speeches upon the outbreak of war in Europe, he imparted "a simple but unalterable fact" of modern international relations: "When peace has been broken anywhere, the peace of all countries is in danger"; and, more directly, "war anywhere necessarily hurts American security."[119] "Frankly and definitely there is danger ahead," he bluntly warned in his "arsenal of democracy" speech—"danger against which we must prepare." Dangers that even, ultimately, included a German invasion of the continental United States and the eradication of the American way of life.[120]

In May 1941, nearly a year after the fall of France but a full six months before Pearl Harbor, Roosevelt took the extraordinary step of declaring a state of "unlimited national emergency." Even if, like the quarantine address, the declaration of emergency was a characteristically symbolic testing of the waters rather than an actual new policy, it nonetheless marked a change of direction. Invoking the most famous line from his 1933 inaugural, "The only thing we have to fear is fear itself," Roosevelt reassured his radio audience that they had faced an emergency before, and that, because they trusted him, he had led them out of that emergency into an era of domestic security. To meet a new systemic crisis, he was asking for their trust once again. Even if German armies weren't massed along the Canadian border or Japanese ships gathering off the coast of

California, the United States faced as serious a threat to its very existence as it ever had:

> Some people seem to think that we are not attacked until bombs actually drop in the streets of New York or San Francisco or New Orleans or Chicago. But they are simply shutting their eyes to the lesson that we must learn from the fate of every Nation that the Nazis have conquered.
>
> . . . the attack on the United States can begin with the domination of any base which menaces our security—north or south.
>
> . . . Our Bunker Hill of tomorrow may be several thousand miles from Boston. Anyone with an atlas, anyone with a reasonable knowledge of the sudden striking force of modern war, knows that it is stupid to wait until a probable enemy has gained a foothold from which to attack. Old-fashioned common sense calls for the use of a strategy that will prevent such an enemy from gaining a foothold in the first place.

To do otherwise was to deny the human imperative of "simple self-preservation." In essence, it would be "suicide." Roosevelt concluded,

> If we believe in the independence and the integrity of the Americas, we must be willing to fight, to fight to defend them just as much as we would to fight for the safety of our own homes. It is time for us to realize that the safety of American homes even in the center of this our own country has a very definite relationship to the continued safety of homes in Nova Scotia or Trinidad or Brazil.[121]

Later, not long after the Japanese attack on Pearl Harbor, he said that the Axis powers had revealed a "single plan" for "their ultimate goal, the conquest of the United States."[122]

Adopting a threat perception based on American national security, however, did not necessarily mean that the United States would go it alone. There was still a place for alliances; indeed, military planners believed the only way they could overcome the combined forces of Germany and Japan was to fight alongside allies. Victory in a global conflict would simply not be possible without acknowledging the necessity of coalition warfare. As Wilson had done a quarter-century before, Roosevelt turned to a familiar flammable metaphor to explain the urgent need for both security and allies. Before the United States was formally at war, that meant aiding the countries holding back the tide of fascism. "Well, let me give you an illustration," he said to reporters at a December 1940 press conference, only ten days before anointing the nation as the arsenal of democracy. "Suppose my neighbor's home catches fire, and I have a length of garden hose four or five hundred feet away. If he can take my garden hose and connect it up with his hydrant, I may help him to put out his fire." There was no point in asking the neighbor to return the hose—it would likely be damaged, most probably beyond repair. And that wasn't the point anyway; it was good sense to prevent a fire from spreading through the community. Helping your neighbor wasn't an act of charity, but an act of self-defense. In March 1941, the Lend-Lease Act formalized this form of strategic fire insurance. To lead the program, Roosevelt appointed not a general or an admiral but the most powerful New Dealer: Harry Hopkins, an old Social Gospel progressive who in the previous eight years headed the Works Progress Administration, the Federal Emergency Relief Administration, and the Civil Works Administration, as well as serving a stint as Secretary of Commerce.[123]

This was all for public consumption, but behind closed doors Roosevelt delivered much the same message, albeit with a slightly different purpose: not to convince a reluctant people to come to his way of thinking, but to mobilize the energies of the government for the monumental task ahead. And that wouldn't be possible unless US foreign-policy planners were all of one mind. "I believe that the fundamental proposition is that we must recognize that the hostilities in Europe, in Africa, and in Asia are all parts of a single world conflict," Roosevelt wrote in in January 1941, in reply to a plea for guidance from his ambassador in Tokyo. It was perhaps his clearest statement yet that was free of all the baggage that normally comes with public rhetoric. "We are engaged in the task of defending our way of life . . . Our strategy of self-defense must be a global strategy which takes account of every front and takes advantage of every opportunity to contribute to our total security."[124]

Roosevelt may have been corresponding with one of his key diplomats, but he applied this same global logic to military defense by similarly prodding his military commanders to think more expansively about American security, and plan accordingly. As we have seen, until the late 1930s planners in the War and Navy Departments had assumed that the baseline of America's defensive requirements should focus on protecting the western hemisphere from foreign attack, but no further. Not long after delivering his quarantine speech in October 1937, Roosevelt started pushing them to think more broadly.[125] The process would be uneven right up to Pearl Harbor, but the first result, the 1938 Naval Act, was driven by the need for "a Navy in sufficient strength to guarantee our national security, but not for aggression; to insure our national integrity; and to support our national policies."[126] A year later, the integrated "Rainbow" war plans replaced the single-color war plans whereby, for instance, Orange represented Japan, Black represented Germany, Red represented Britain, and so on. By contrast, the five different Rainbow plans operated on the assumption that the United States would be engaged in coalition warfare often beyond the western hemisphere. Rainbow Five was the most expansive—and, it turned out, the most prescient—in envisioning a global war between two grand coalitions, but all of the Rainbow plans marked a sharp break with past planning.[127]

Dovetailing with the elaborately complex Rainbow plans was a contrastingly straightforward strategic assessment famously known as Plan Dog. Authored by one individual, Navy Admiral Harold Stark, Plan Dog worked on the assumption that a German victory would be a direct threat not just to the western hemisphere but more specifically to the continental United States. Although later historians exaggerated its powers of foresight (Stark completely misread Japan, for instance), Plan Dog provided a basic template for America's grand strategy in the war soon to come. "Should Britain lose the war," Stark wrote, "the military consequences to the United States would be severe" because Americans "would find ourselves acting alone, and at war with the world." Stark acknowledged that it was the "fundamental requirement of our military position that our homeland remain secure against successful attack," but achieving that basic objective now required the projection of power beyond the western hemisphere, possibly including the dispatch of large numbers of troops to Europe.[128] Plan Dog originated within the Navy, but it also reflected an emerging military consensus on the new needs of basic American security. In the spring of 1941, Army planners similarly concluded that a global two-front war for US security was likely: "The conflict being now a world conflict, there can be no security for the United States or any of the other countries that are resisting the would-be conqueror states so long as any one of the latter is taking and holding new positions."[129]

Making America an "arsenal of democracy" meant rebuilding the warfare state of 1916–1918, but on a much bigger scale befitting a much bigger war. During the Great War, Roosevelt himself had been a strident advocate of preparedness—so strident that it nearly cost him his job in the Navy Department—and even recommended creating a Council of National Defense in 1915.[130] Unlike the acrimonious debates of 1916, preparedness was broadly supported in 1940. With some notable exceptions, such as the Christian pacifist movement, both internationalists and noninterventionists agreed that the world had suddenly become a much more dangerous place and that it was only prudent for the United States to begin a program of rearmament, just in case. Rearmament was nothing more than a prudent measure of "blitzkrieg insurance," Grenville Clark, a Wall Street lawyer who had once led the preparedness drive during the Great War, said in the summer of 1940 as he helped draft the new Selective Service Act providing for the first peacetime draft in American history.[131]

Even anti-interventionists agreed on the need for a robust military. Herbert Hoover believed that the "greatest assurance from aggression against us is preparedness for defense" because America would then be "respected not only for our justice but for our strength," while Beard and Lindbergh concurred that prudence dictated military preparedness.[132] In response to objections from one of the few groups to oppose preparedness, economic libertarians, Roosevelt argued that rearmament was good security insurance in both senses: for national security against potential foreign threats, and for socioeconomic security against unemployment.[133] And of those who still held out against war mobilization, the president accused critics of "playing politics with the national security of America today."[134] Such currents of "old-line Tory Republicanism" aided and abetted—"unconsciously perhaps," Roosevelt conceded—the fascists and communists who were also hoping to see liberal democracy fail in America and around the world.[135]

If this fault line on the proper role of government seems familiar, it's because rearmament drew on the same institutional foundations of economic planning and social security that animated the New Deal in the first place. Practically as well as ideologically, the war effort was itself an extension of the New Deal. The newly created Defense Plant Corporation, for instance, was housed within one of the New Deal's signature agencies, the Reconstruction Finance Corporation, to ensure a smoothly efficient rearmament program alongside the War Production Board.[136] The Office of Price Administration was established in 1941 to ensure inflation didn't become a problem.[137] Having overseen CCC camps during the Depression and then served in the War Plans Division as the world crisis escalated, General George Marshall brought a New Dealer's talent for using government resources in planning and strategizing to his work when Roosevelt made him the key to the mobilization program as Army Chief of Staff in 1940.[138] Marshall's description of Selective Service—"a scientific, a democratic, and an economical method for maintaining a defensive force"—struck all the New Deal's ideological high notes.[139] So, too, with the 1939 relaunch of the General Intelligence Division, did another massive arrogation of power over internal security by the FBI.[140] It's little wonder that economic libertarians objected to rearmament and the inevitable government economic controls that would follow; what's surprising is that so many other conservatives actually backed rearmament and the peacetime draft. Hoover, we have seen, believed preparedness was a good national insurance policy, while business executives such as Alfred Sloan of General Motors felt that rearmament could protect the economy and safeguard the nation so long as government worked with business to ensure that spending didn't overwhelm and distort normal economic behavior.[141]

The program of war production did just that, and more. Beginning in 1940, and continuing for the duration of the war, the United States undertook the largest arms buildup in modern history, supplying enough weapons, vehicles, and supplies not just for its own war but for a substantial part of its allies' campaigns. The result, one defense analyst reflected after the war, was "the triumph of the machine."[142] In the second half of 1940 alone, government spending on rearmament was 50 percent more than all private investment that year.[143] Each of the service branches grew exponentially, with the smallest, the Marine Corps, expanding twentyfold.[144] Initially, with Marshall's support but fueling the anger of noninterventionists like Senator William Borah, much of this military growth actually came directly from New Deal appropriations, via the Ickes-led Public Works Administration and the Hopkins-led Works Progress Administration—which by the eve of war had vastly outspent the War and Navy departments' own budgets. Pointedly, three of the ships in the Battle of Midway (the *Yorktown,* the *Enterprise,* and the *Vincennes*) had been built by PWA workers.[145]

Rearmament, Lend-Lease, and the waging of a global conflict on two transoceanic fronts across three continents pulled the US economy out of the Depression and set the stage for an era of unparalleled prosperity. Sloan and other business leaders were comfortable with this statist turn in economic life because it unfolded mostly on business-friendly terms.

Despite Roosevelt's continuing commitment to New Deal reforms, this was no accident: if an earlier generation of progressives like Walter Weyl had diagnosed capitalist inequality as the source of insecurity, Roosevelt turned that logic on its head by harnessing the power of capital to the security of the nation and turning that power loose on America's enemies through a warfare state that would win the war *and* end the Depression.[146]

But Roosevelt soon lost control of this process. The war superseded the New Deal, a development FDR himself lamented and tried to moderate by introducing his "economic bill of rights" in January 1944, but it was too late. Advancing the increasingly intertwined goals of national security and economic prosperity, the war marked the apogee of the state, but in heavily delimited ways. At the outset, in 1940, Roosevelt vowed to embark upon "a national defense program that reaches into the home of every one of our citizens." He was true to his word, just not in the way he had anticipated or with results he had intended.[147]

––––––

ROOSEVELT'S NATIONAL security revolution made victory in World War II possible. But it also permanently changed the foundations of America's relationship with the rest of the world. The heightened, perhaps exaggerated, threat perception that resulted from bringing the country into the war lowered the threshold for a US response to potential international threats and raised the stakes of inaction to them. As Roosevelt warned when asking Congress to prepare for war by funding a massive national rearmament program, "It is dangerous to prepare for a little defense. It is safe only to prepare for total defense."[148] This search for complete security may have been necessary in 1940–1941, but it would prove difficult to turn off after the war.

The effects of Roosevelt's grand strategy, then, were genuinely revolutionary, marking a complete overturn of the old order and the ushering in of the new. In the fateful summer of 1940, in a commencement address at the University of Virginia, he declared that the United States could not survive as "a lone island in a world dominated by the philosophy of force."[149] It was something he might well have learned from Mahan, one of the first Americans to envision the nation's security as inextricably bound up with the fortunes of an interdependent modern world. Either way it was a concept Roosevelt had invoked before, at the end of World

War I, in urging Americans not to reject the League of Nations and embrace a "Chinese wall policy of isolation."[150] The idea made sense: a lone island of democracy in a world of totalitarian states would likely not survive for long, at least not as a democracy. But it was also startingly new because it turned the entire American diplomatic tradition on its head. Going back to the founding of the republic, previous generations of Americans had relished their status as an exemplary lone island among a world of monarchical empires. Safety had come from separation.

If Roosevelt was right, and separation was no longer possible, then safety would have to come from not just integration within the international system, but domination over it. Woodrow Wilson had made a start toward this conclusion but never actually reached it. For Roosevelt and the internationalists who supported him, the ability to reshape the system itself would be the ultimate protector of the United States in a shrinking, dangerous world.

As is often the case, it took a foreign perspective to appreciate the significance of Roosevelt's strategic innovation. During the rare occasions during the war when Allied leaders were able to meet in person, conference dinners were usually lavish, boozy affairs, with endless toasts of endless praise for how the Allies had shown courage, generosity, and grit in the face of the Nazi onslaught. But for one such toast during the Yalta summit, in the winter of 1945, Stalin put aside the florid rhetoric and offered a perfect summary of FDR's statecraft. Proposing a toast to Roosevelt's health, Stalin began by conceding that he and Churchill "had had relatively simple decisions" in taking their countries to war: "They had been fighting for their very existence against Hitlerite Germany." Roosevelt had been in a different, more difficult, situation because his "country had not been seriously threatened with invasion." Stalin hailed FDR's ability to overcome this conundrum with a new "broader conception of national interest." Even though "his country was not directly imperilled," Stalin concluded, Roosevelt had nonetheless "been the chief forger of the instruments which had led to the mobilization of the world against Hitler." Touched by the Soviet leader's praise, and probably impressed by his insight, Roosevelt replied that in reinventing American national defense, his goal had simply been "to give to every man, woman and child on this earth the possibility of security and wellbeing."[151]

[6]

THE AMERICAN WAY

IN THE TURBULENT TIME between 1914 and 1941, as they grappled with the unprecedented crises of world wars and economic catastrophe that called into question the very future of the United States, Americans invented a number of traditions to soothe the nerves of their anxious nation. Several foundational, supposedly timeless concepts of American nationhood took form in this era of continual existential crisis, among them "the American Dream" and "American exceptionalism." But perhaps the most important of all was "the American Way of Life," a distinct vision that encompassed everything that American society had stood for—democracy, capitalism, prosperity, opportunity, individual liberty—since the founding of the republic. The whole notion that there was a distinct American Way emerged in the 1930s alongside the New Deal's reform of government. At a time of archaeological discoveries and the rise of ethno-racial nationalism, when the notion of "civilization" became not just a popular but a defining vision of the United States, the American Way perfectly expressed what Americans thought was best about their national experiment: it was individualistic but also social, traditional but also progressive, faith-based but also tolerant, with an economy that naturally balanced demand-side consumerism with supply-side industrialism.[1]

Yet beneath the American Way's veneer hid contradictions that also defined the national experience: America could be free and democratic, certainly, but it could also be unforgivingly intolerant. Nothing captured this tension between comforting myth and uncomfortable reality more poignantly than a photograph taken in 1937. In the foreground is a group of African Americans in Louisville, Kentucky, left destitute by one of the worst floods in US history, lining up for government relief. Behind them—and, pointedly, above them—is a billboard sponsored by the National Association of Manufacturers, proclaiming in bold letters the "World's Highest Standard of Living." Below this headline, but above the queue of African Americans seeking assistance, is the billboard's main image, portraying an advertiser's ideal of an American family, with a father, mother, daughter, son, and cute little dog—all white, even the pet—traveling in their shiny new car. The contrast could not have been more painfully stark.

The person who took the picture, Margaret Bourke-White, was one of the most talented photographers of the twentieth century. A pioneering, fearless photojournalist working in Henry Luce's magazine empire, Bourke-White rushed to Louisville to document the flood. When she saw the line of Black relief-seekers in front of the NAM billboard, she immediately realized how "incongruous" and painfully full of "irony" the scene was.[2] This keen sense of paradox, and an uncanny instinct for uncovering powerfully symbolic imagery, had made Bourke-White one of the most respected photojournalists in the world—during the war she took official portraits of Roosevelt, Churchill, Stalin, Gandhi, Wendell Willkie, George S. Patton, and Cordell Hull—but her politics helped, too. She was by temperament and politics a New Dealer, alongside Dorothea Lange probably the most insightful visual chronicler of Depression-ravaged America, and her photos of farmers, miners, and workers, Blacks, whites, and immigrants, regularly adorned the front covers and pages of *Life.* Bourke-White also took dozens of photos of New Deal works projects—her shot of the massive Fort Peck Dam in Montana, for instance, graced the cover of November 23, 1936 issue of *Life,* a little under a year before Roosevelt took his western tour to celebrate the Bonneville and Grand Coulee dams while on his way to give his quarantine speech in Chicago. She then became a war photographer, embedded with US troops as they moved across North Africa and into Europe; to capture the most dramatic images, she even rode along on US bombing missions over Germany (probably not that terrifying for someone who used to take photos while perched on one of the Chrysler Building's gargoyle eagles, some 800 feet above the streets of Manhattan). Margaret Bourke-White was as highly attuned to New Deal liberalism's modernist symbiosis of national security and social security as a Harold Ickes or a Charles Merriam. But, unlike them, she also recognized its contradictions.[3]

African Americans had of course always felt these tensions. At the height of a war to defeat Nazi discrimination, end tyranny, and save democracy, Mary McLeod Bethune emphasized them so that others would know about them, too. As head of the National Association for Colored Women, an advisor to First Lady Eleanor Roosevelt and Secretary of War Henry Stimson, and the lone woman in Franklin Roosevelt's Black Cabinet, Bethune was a New Dealer. But she also knew the limits of liberalism. She observed that while African Americans were still being deliberately held in poverty and segregation, their right to vote denied, they were also asked to help defend "the American way of life—in its ideals of equality of all men before the law, and opportunities for the fullest possible development of the individual." Blacks were willing to do their part in the fight against German Nazism, but American racism was preventing them from breaking "out into the free realm of democratic citizenship." To Bethune, the fundamental issue facing America was obvious: "What, then, does the Negro want? His answer is very simple. He wants only what all other Americans want": nothing less than the full blessings of "American civilization." Denying this goal was tantamount to a betrayal of the American Way and American civilization, and thus a betrayal of the very purpose of America's war effort. "As long as America offers less," she concluded, "she will be that much less a democracy. The whole way is the American way."[4]

One side of Roosevelt's national security revolution was geographical: potential threats to the United States were treated as clear and present dangers no matter where they were in the world, and no matter their plausibility of actually reaching US shores. Another was the new social contract the New Deal signed with the American people, to use the power of government to ensure their economic security. But those weren't the only sides, or even the most important. The key problem for internationalists was that geopolitical logic came down on the side of anti-interventionists like Hoover and Lindbergh: the United States was actually never in danger of being attacked by the Axis powers. This is where a third side of national security came in: in an interdependent world, American values were just as much a part of national defense as US territory.[5] "There comes a time in the affairs of men when they must prepare to defend, not their homes alone, but the tenets of faith and humanity on which their churches, their governments and their very civilization are founded," Roosevelt explained in his 1939 State of the Union address. "The defense of religion, of democracy and of good faith among nations is all the same fight. To save one we must now make up our minds to save all."[6]

The key issue for Americans was not just "why we fight" but "what we defend." The war, and the confusion before Pearl Harbor about America's stakes in it, forced internationalists not only to clarify what Americans stood for, and what defined the culture and values of their nation, but to emphasize the clear and present danger that the Germans and Japanese posed to them. Internationalists argued that this war, more than any other before it, would define the values of the world for generations to come. "We speak most frequently in geographic terms when we speak of war," celebrated poet and Librarian of Congress Archibald MacLeish told Union College's class of 1941, but "geography and war are smaller than the truth. For the true battleground is not an extent of land at all or even an ocean or sea. It is larger still. It is the minds of young men."[7]

That battle for hearts and minds would determine the world war as much as combat between tanks and planes. It was why Americans needed to safeguard their values exactly as they would safeguard their territory, not just with the impressive warfare state but through newly established ideological weapons like the Office of War Information and the Voice of America radio network. They needed to build a global "empire of ideas."[8] There were "certain freedoms which we think are essential everywhere," Roosevelt explained in his 1940 State of the Union address. "We know that we ourselves shall never be wholly safe at home unless other governments recognize such freedoms."[9] Merriam put it more plainly the following year: the United States "finds itself ringed around by hostile forces vowing the extermination of democracy and the reduction to practical slavery of its peoples."[10]

And yet, just like the New Deal itself, national security was born with a major racial blind spot, one that Bourke-White captured on film and Bethune experienced but to which even a progressive like Merriam was oblivious: millions of Americans, after all, had been experiencing slavery, either real or "practical," for centuries, and were continuing to do so. It was a blind spot that would affect US foreign policy for generations to come.

―――――

AMERICA'S CAUSE in the war was to safeguard liberty. But what kind? If anti-interventionists like Herbert Hoover worried that the expansive pursuit of security would endanger liberty, internationalists feared the exact opposite. The world had become so dangerous, they warned, that if Americans did not protect their national security under its more expansive terms, they would be forced to hunker down and create what Harold Lasswell famously called "the garrison state," a country ruled by a government vested with near-total authority, undemocratic, militaristic, and aggressive. Japan was a garrison state; so was Germany. If the United States tried to survive the world crisis in self-imposed isolation, it too would become a garrison state, because external threats would be allowed to grow to such an extent that only total isolation under military rule would ensure security.[11] The implications of Lasswell's theory were clear: the pursuit of national security wasn't a threat to liberty, but rather the only way of protecting liberty from totalitarian threats in an interdependent world.

This wasn't a new idea—both Woodrow Wilson and Theodore Roosevelt had issued similar warnings in 1917—but in the crisis of the late 1930s it seemed more compelling than ever before. Internationalists warned that staying aloof from the war would inevitably lead to America becoming a garrison state of "state capitalism, super-regimentation and totalitarianism."[12] Edward Mead Earle pointed out that while a new course of action meant accepting new risks, "doing nothing may involve the greatest risks of all," especially the near-certainty that the United States would become "a besieged fortress."[13] Reinhold Niebuhr predicted that the pursuit of a narrow hemispheric security would trigger an unlimited arms race and result in "a gigantic navalism," while Dean Acheson warned that "the destructive consequences to our constitutional guarantees of individual liberty cannot be over-estimated."[14] Secretary of State Hull thought it was obvious that in the event of a German victory "our national security would require" Americans to adopt all the traits of a garrison state: "continuous devotion of a very great part of all our work and wealth for defense production, prolonged universal military service, extremely burdensome taxation, unending vigilance against enemies within our borders, and complete involvement in power diplomacy."[15] In his most prominent speeches on the war, Franklin Roosevelt conveyed a similar message, warning in his "arsenal of democracy" speech that if the United States tried to stay completely out of the conflict "we would have to convert ourselves permanently into a militaristic power on the basis of a war economy."[16] Becoming a garrison state would mean sacrificing the New Deal entirely, for a permanent war footing would rob the federal government of time, personnel, initiative, and above all money that could otherwise be devoted to improving the socioeconomic security of Americans.[17]

Internationalists thus made a strong case that national security would be the savior of social security and political liberty. But what exactly was at risk, and what exactly were Americans protecting? Roosevelt's Four Freedoms laid out an overall ideological case, and Capra's *Why We Fight* movies stressed freedom and democracy. But there was more to it than those abstractions. For a half-century, Americans had been grappling with a nation, and a world, changing at a dizzying pace. The Industrial Revolution of the late nineteenth century, the social changes it triggered—urbanization and the new immigration—and the life-changing inventions it spawned—electricity, indoor plumbing, the automobile, aviation, germ theory, oil, petrochemicals—made the United States of 1940 wholly unrecognizable from the United States only fifty years before. The Great War, and especially the Great Depression, also confronted Americans with the most searching types of existential questions a nation can face. The slow closing of the long era of free security, the last of the "tormenting manifestations of our modem predicament" that Richard Hofstadter identified as the sources of a deep national psychological crisis, raised even deeper doubts about the United States in the world.[18] Americans responded by answering these questions in ways that both confirmed the idea of the nation they thought they'd always lived in and recast the nation for a new, industrial, global era.[19]

Americans had survived this existential crisis, Roosevelt believed, because "we have learned to think as a nation. And out of that process we have learned to feel as a nation." The crisis had "given us as a people," he declared on another occasion, "a new understanding of our Government and of ourselves."[20] This was crucial if the United States was to survive the world crisis. In its ruling in the 1940 case of *Minersville School District v. Gobitis,* the Supreme Court intoned that "National unity is the basis of national security," and the new national identity was designed to meet this standard.[21] That fall, on the eve of Germany's launching the Blitz against London, Roosevelt made a similar case. "It is not a change from the American way of life to advocate or legislate a greater and a speedier preparedness," he declared at the dedication of a national park created by the New Deal. "It is a positive protection to the American way of life." Just as Britons were rallying together in the face of German bombing, Americans also had to create a new solidarity. "We, in this hour, must have and will have absolute national unity for total defense."[22]

At the heart of this process of understanding, of national self-awareness, and of forging unity was the invention of several traditions in the interwar period. All of these invented traditions sanctified the supposedly timeless characteristics of American political culture. They were useful myths in a moment of national crisis, not entirely fictitious but not all that historically accurate, either. They were based on a selective reading of a useable past so that Americans could think of themselves as a single, cohesive, undivided nation in a time of global turmoil.

One of these invented traditions was the nation's Judeo-Christian heritage, a new idea that distinguished the democratic United States as a haven of religious liberty from the "godless and soulless" Nazi Germany as the enemy of all religion (not just Judaism), and thus of democracy itself.[23] For Roosevelt in particular, this concept had the virtue of being true: he appointed more Jews and Catholics to his administration than any other president before him and was careful to be as ecumenically inclusive as possible. Part of this was good politics—it would have been impossible for a New York Democrat to succeed otherwise—but it also stemmed from Roosevelt's own deep religious convictions, which were neither formal nor theological but powerful all the same.[24] Through new organizations like the National Conference of Christians and Jews, liberal Protestant clergy and Jewish rabbis also joined forces to promote a biblically sanctified yet acceptably generic idea of "brotherhood" in which Protestants, Catholics, and Jews could all celebrate their common religious heritage as the wellspring of American democracy. Unknown to Americans until the interwar era, the idea that the United States had a Judeo-Christian heritage provided Roosevelt with a wartime glue with which to bind Americans together in a "tri-faith" nation of Protestants, Catholics, and Jews.[25]

The invention of the Judeo-Christian tradition also allowed Roosevelt to frame the war as a fight for cultural survival. In October 1941, in a speech to mark "Total Defense Day," Roosevelt stated that he had in his possession documents proving that "if Hitler wins" he would implement "a plan to abolish all existing religions," including in the pluralistic, tolerant United States. The property of religious institutions would be seized; religious leaders would be imprisoned or worse; the freedom to worship, the protection of which Roosevelt had announced as a major US war aim earlier in the year, would be abolished. "In the place of the churches of our civilization, there is to be set up an International Nazi Church. . . . And in the place of the Bible, the words of *Mein Kampf* will be imposed and enforced as Holy Writ. And in the place of the cross of Christ will be put two symbols—the swastika and the naked sword. The god of Blood and Iron will take the place of the God of Love and Mercy. Let us well ponder that statement which I have made tonight."[26]

For internationalists, "the American Way" was also a perfect vehicle for capturing what needed defending in an anarchic, dangerous world, but it was even more useful because anti-interventionists also thought of the United States, in Herbert Hoover's words, as "the sanctuary for the ideals of civilization."[27] With continentalism looking increasingly untenable, internationalists raised the ideological stakes of the great debate over intervention. As Chester H. Rowell, the internationalist editor of the *San Francisco Chronicle,* put it, "We have here . . . a challenge which goes to the very fundamentals of civilization itself. It goes to the fundamentals of *our* sort of civilization."[28] With the "sequence of evil" triggered by Axis expansionism, American civilization seemed at risk of being extinguished forever.[29] The issue was how to protect it.

In a similar vein, one of the most common themes Roosevelt used to legitimate the New Deal was that it was squarely in keeping with the American Way. The National Recovery Administration, organized labor, care for the unemployed, access to affordable housing, protections for workers against strikebreakers, a liberal public education, regulation of finance, assistance to farmers—all were justified as expressions of the "American way of life."[30] And with New Dealers like Hopkins, Ickes, and Marshall at the helm of America's war effort, it was easy to equate a regulatory economic state at home with a protective national security state abroad as expressions of the American Way. To the men about to be inducted in the nation's first-ever peacetime draft, Roosevelt expressed his gratitude to those who were willing to meet "our country's pressing need for a stronger defense, and its vital meaning to you, your family, and the whole Nation." The operative social contract was in the official title of the draft, Selective Service. The "task before us today," Roosevelt concluded, "is as compelling as any that ever confronted our people, and I would add that each of us must willingly do his bit if we are to hold fast our heritage of freedom and our American way of life—our national existence itself."[31]

But even more was at stake. In World War I, Americans had briefly conflated their own security with the defense of western civilization. Now, in an even greater world war, they saw their national security as bound up with the *rescue* of a modern civilization that was already being destroyed.

To "restore and reconstitute the ordered life that Americans have known," Walter Lippmann wrote in June of 1940, as France was falling to the Germans, they would have to meet their responsibility as the guardians of civilization. Only the United States, "a citadel so strong in its defenses," could wield enough power to ensure that "the world can eventually be redeemed and pacified and made whole again. This is the American destiny." Yet hearing voices of protest from the likes of Herbert Hoover and Charles Lindbergh, Lippmann worried that "our unready and unwilling hands" might fail to seize this destiny. This wasn't just America's fate, but the world's. "Either we shall fulfill that destiny," he warned, "or the world we have lived in will perish beyond hope of an early or an easy resurrection."[32]

DESPITE WHAT ITS ADHERENTS claimed, however, the national unity on which national security depended was not inclusive, and the democracy it celebrated was only partial. Too many Americans were either deliberately left out of the national project, or deliberately marginalized within it, for it to be either truly national or truly democratic in scope. This included national security, which had already begun to show its darker side at the moment of its inception. Security came at a price often paid by the people already forced to the margins of American life.

Accustomed to disappointment from the false dawns of the Civil War, the Spanish-American War, and World War I, Black thinking on the liberating potential of war was both hopeful and cautious. On the cautiously hopeful side was the Double V campaign for victory over fascism and Nazism abroad that would also enable victory over racism at home.[33] Typically, Capra was also hopeful. During the war he produced several other documentaries alongside the *Why We Fight* films, including the surprisingly radical *The Negro Soldier* in 1944.[34] The film begins with a sermon in which a Black preacher compares the war to a rematch of the heavyweight bout between the white German Max Schmelling and the African American Joe Louis, who was then serving in the Army. "This time it's a fight not between man and man but between nation and nation, to fight for the real championship of the world to determine which way of life shall survive: their way or our way. This time we must see to it that there is no return engagement, for the stakes this time are the greatest men have ever fought for. And what are the stakes?" They couldn't be clearer:

people would either be ruled by the laws of the US Constitution or by the dictates of *Mein Kampf.* "The liberty of the whole earth depends on the outcome of this contest."

This resounding message was to be expected from a government-produced film directed by Frank Capra. Others were more skeptical for a simple reason: as the radical economist Scott Nearing put it, American race relations "occupy a frontier of conflict which is beyond the pale of organized society" with "the Negro race . . . held in its subject position by the dominant white race through organized violence."[35] Du Bois editorialized that while "economic security" might be considered "the chief question before the race," no advancement was possible without safety from violence.[36] In 1947, with the promise of a new world still possible but increasingly doubtful, Du Bois asked his readers to imagine a young, white, British woman—a stand-in representing white society in Europe and the United States—who lived in a comfortable home, had a nice family, and didn't have to worry about being safe, fed, and generally content. "It will in all probability not occur to her," Du Bois chided, "that the system which sustains the security, leisure, and comfort she enjoys is based on the suppression, exploitation, and slavery of the majority of mankind." What Du Bois wanted, what Bethune had called for, was for the illusion to shatter, and for access to a life of basic security to be open to everyone.[37]

As Du Bois knew all too well, this was easier demanded than attained. Even while serving in the military to fight for the American Way and against Nazi discrimination, enlisted Black men reported a segregated system of physical harassment, lower pay, daily humiliation, and wretched conditions.[38] In 1936, Howard University political scientist Ralph Bunche, who would later win a Nobel Peace Prize, gave one of the most powerful analyses of the paradoxes of Black insecurity. Race, Bunche explained, might be a "pseudo-scientific" construct, but racism was very real and posed "danger for the future peace and development of the world." Only when "society guarantees economic security to all peoples" would the sources of racial conflict disappear. Without economic security, the poorest in society, usually people of color, would unite in resistance, and then "Race war . . . will be merely a side-show to the gigantic class war which will be waged in the big tent we call the world."[39]

African Americans were right to be wary about future progress, for their security concerns, at home and abroad, were rarely taken seriously by those in power. Ironically, though, some Black ideas about international politics, namely the prospect of a race war, were not just taken seriously but adopted by advocates of white supremacy. Shortly after the outbreak of war in 1939, Lindbergh resurrected the dysgenic predictions of Lothrop Stoddard and Madison Grant during the Great War to portray World War II as a race war. According to Lindbergh, an internally divided white European civilization was unnecessarily weakening itself and paving the way for world domination by "a pressing sea of Yellow, Black, and Brown" led by hordes of "the Mongol and Persian and Moor." The European civil war was "blind, insatiable, suicidal," Lindbergh warned, "a war in which the White race is bound to lose, and the others bound to gain, a war which may easily lead our civilization through more Dark Ages if it survives at all." This nasty pun touched on Lindbergh's deepest fear of a combined decline of both race and civilization. It was "time to turn from our quarrels and to build our White ramparts again." Indulging in a kind of reactionary intersectionality, Lindbergh drew on gendered notions of peace and strength:

> Our civilization depends on peace among Western nations, and therefore on united strength, for Peace is a virgin who dare not show her face without Strength, her father, for protection. We can have peace and security only so long as we band together to preserve that most priceless possession, our inheritance of European blood, only so long as we guard ourselves against attack by foreign armies and dilution by foreign blood.[40]

Lindbergh's remarkable screed, published in *Reader's Digest,* one of the most widely read magazines in the country, was extreme as a matter of public discourse. But it wasn't rare. Lindbergh himself repeated it in comments not long after Pearl Harbor.[41] But even wartime liberal internationalists, putatively in favor of African Americans civil rights, drew strict limits on the extent to which the "brotherhood" of national security liberalism would even attempt to transcend racial discrimination at home and abroad.[42]

Women like Mary McLeod Bethune and Margaret Bourke-White were among the era's most active internationalists, particularly in campaigns for peace, voting rights, and social justice, though they too would be disappointed by the results of the new security prerogative. Many of these causes led women's groups, such as the Women's International League for Peace and Freedom, and prominent peace crusaders like Jane Addams and

Emily Balch, to see themselves as "citizens of the world" and promote collective security of a kind practiced by the League of Nations. For the most part, that meant leaving aside, or often openly disdaining, the more directive policy of "national security" Roosevelt was in the midst of creating. "The cause of world security," declared Florence Guertin Tuttle, founder of the Woman's Pro-League Council, "takes precedence. It is fundamental. It is more than a movement. It is a crusade." And it was more important than national security. To be sure, the New Deal's deliverance of Social Security fit well within the politics of many women's groups, but like other peace campaigners they recoiled from a doctrine of national security that was inherently more militarized than collective security or other forms of conflict resolution like arbitration.[43]

This skepticism about national solutions to international problems might have stemmed from the fact that women were deliberately marginalized within the New Deal's welfare state. Programs like Social Security not only excluded African Americans as much as possible, they also hardened the codification of women's "proper" role within society—namely, as family matrons rather than breadwinners—a traditionalism that was even reflected in such sharply divergent views of conservative economists like Frank Knight and progressive social planners like Abraham Epstein.[44] This was true for both men and women: post–Great War military policies and the New Deal all tightly linked masculinity to labor and femininity to motherhood, which in turn hardened the ostracization of gays and lesbians in American society.[45] Some women themselves even embraced a traditional role as the best way to facilitate national security during the war. Shortly after Pearl Harbor, Cornelia Rogers, head of the Women's Division of the National Security League, admonished women that "Our children need us as greatly" as the war effort because childcare was itself a component of national security. To those women who were moving into factory jobs or agitating for a greater public role in the war effort, Rogers had some advice: "Let us remember that there is much quiet and undramatic work that must be done, and that we as women must continue to do." So, "Stop complaining. Keep on with your job. Be kind, courteous and patient."[46]

Neither the NSL's characteristically reactionary position nor the impositions of New Deal social norms, however, reflected the dominant strain of women's thought on the world crisis. By the end of the 1930s, American women were also becoming concerned about national security in an increasingly anarchic and dangerous world. This reflected an internationalist sensibility, which by 1939 had led even many pacifists to a reluctant acceptance of the potential need to use force, but also the fact that women were now at the forefront of many professions—not only as members and leaders of nongovernmental organizations but also as journalists, missionaries, and academics—that were inherently transnational. This helped foster an acute understanding of the world crisis, which in turn led many women to modify their multilateralist vision of collective security toward an acceptance of American power and support for Roosevelt's grand strategy. To be sure, for the most part, women's internationalist groups continued to promote collective security, though with the United States taking a leadership role and using military means to enforce its mandate. But within that vision, women's groups fully embraced Roosevelt's blending of social and national security as laid out in the Four Freedoms and the Economic Bill of Rights. "Security cannot be found until every country is able to provide adequate opportunities for earning a livable living, and until each country can develop its economic resources through unfettered trade relations with other countries," Esther Caukin Brunauer of the Commission on a Permanent World Society wrote in 1940. "Such economic prosperity for one nation will not mean security unless all countries enjoy similar opportunity." Yet, Brunauer cautioned, this would only be possible if the United States had a more expansive view of its own security needs, and the willingness to deploy all its resources to protect it. She believed women had "a privilege as well as a duty to help with the concrete, specific things that must be done to defend that democracy and also to take part in formulating the policies behind the defense effort."[47]

FROM THE VERY OUTSET, national security forced the international visions of women and people of color to conform to a dominant narrative about the legitimate concerns over peace, security, and empire. In most cases, those two visions did not combine well, although until the 1960s it was rarely to the detriment of the state.

When marginalized groups challenged the dictates of national security, they found themselves at war with their own government. This wasn't just a sequel to the civil-liberties violations of the Great War era, but an institutionalization of them, run by a recently established parallel alphabet soup of New Deal–style government security agencies—OFF, OWI, FNB, OSS, COI, OCD, FAC, and of course the FBI—that monitored "foreign" nationalities and suspected subversives and, as Roosevelt put it, handled "information and data bearing on national security."[48] Meanwhile, the ORR (Office of Radio Research), a Rockefeller Foundation–funded unit based at Princeton, began analyzing foreign-language domestic radio broadcasts to ensure that immigrant communities weren't disseminating subversive propaganda or secret information to the enemy.[49]

Japanese Americans, immediately singled out as a security risk after Pearl Harbor, learned this lesson in an especially hard way. The war against Germany was horrific, but it paled in comparison with the actual race war between Japan and the United States.[50] The direct racial competition between Asians and whites was further complicated by the involvement, either suspected or real, of African Americans. In the fall of 1940, the FBI reported to the War Department that "Pro-Japanese propaganda among negroes in the United States is a phase of Japanese 'Holy War' in . . . her pan-Asiatic anti-white race movement."[51] This was ominous for both Blacks and Japanese given the name on the cover of the report—FBI Director J. Edgar Hoover—but the security services didn't have to fabricate either Japanese support for anti-colonial, anti-American activists or pro-Japanese sympathies among some African Americans; there was plenty of that already. In a different version of a Double V strategy, Mittie Maude Lena Gordon, a Chicago civil rights campaigner, had been calling for Afro-Asian solidarity for a decade before the war in the hopes of ending not only colonialism but also Jim Crow; she was arrested shortly after Pearl Harbor.[52]

Gordon's fate foreshadowed the crackdown on Japanese Americans, more than 120,000 of whom were forcibly moved from their homes on the west coast and detained in internment camps; US citizens accounted for roughly two-thirds of the total. This violation of civil liberties, one of the worst in American history, was explicitly justified under the remit of national security and administered by yet another three-letter official acronym, the WRA (War Relocation Authority).[53] The public, especially on the west coast, generally approved, and popular culture lent its support. The hero of *Little Tokyo, USA,* a viciously racist but popular 1942 film about supposedly traitorous Japanese in the United States, foils a plot to sabotage the American war effort from within. The movie's final lines summed up the nation's prevailing mood: "Be vigilant, America." This vigilance extended beyond US shores, as the United States teamed up with South American nations like Peru to lock down or expel their Japanese populations and ensure hemispheric security.[54]

Fittingly, though, Japanese internment in the United States wasn't motivated by only racism or overblown fears of domestic sabotage: it was, as the WRA's acronymic name implied, also an extension of the New Deal. Just as Roosevelt's "war on crime" was a vital component of the New Deal, Japanese internment was profoundly shaped by liberal notions of planning and development. The context may have been social control under wartime conditions, but the ability of the government to carve out an isolated space of exception offered liberals a planning opportunity that was too good to pass up. Internment wouldn't just keep the nation safe; through a targeted school curriculum, and the assistance of hundreds of social workers, it would also enable the government to turn Japanese Americans into better citizens.[55]

Japanese internment was the most extreme example of national security vigilance, but it wasn't unusual. Roosevelt set the general tone as early as May 1940, a full eighteen months before the United States was at war, when he warned, "Today's threat to our national security is not a matter of military weapons alone. We know of new methods of attack. The Trojan Horse. The Fifth Column that betrays a nation unprepared for treachery." Just as ominous was "an added technique for weakening a nation at its very roots": the "dissemination of discord."[56] A month later, Roosevelt signed the Smith Act into law, which effectively criminalized antiwar politics by giving the authorities the power to decide whether dissent was tantamount to treason. One of the many ironies of Japanese internment is that, while the Japanese were wrongly suspected of plotting against America (only a week after Pearl Harbor, Secretary of the Navy Frank Knox publicly declared that Japanese "Fifth Columnists" in Hawai'i had facilitated the attack), the Germans actually did so. Pro-German groups, such as the Nazi sympathizers that tried to infiltrate Hollywood, and the far-right Christian Front, abounded in a way that groups sympathetic to Italy and Japan did not.[57]

While Japanese sabotage and espionage in the United States were for the most part nonexistent, there were episodes, rare but real, of German-sponsored subversive activities. One episode led to a precedent-setting Supreme Court ruling, reassuring to some but troubling to others, that allowed the government to try unlawful enemy combatants—that is, those who didn't follow the laws of war—in military rather than civilian courts. In the summer of 1942, eight German military agents, two of them US citizens, landed in two groups on the Atlantic shores of Long Island and northern Florida. Some of the agents voluntarily surrendered to the authorities; others had to be caught. All were tried by a military tribunal, and the six who hadn't surrendered themselves and confessed were sentenced to death. In *Ex parte Quirin,* the court ruled that since the men had slipped "secretly and covertly" through "military and naval lines and defenses of the United States" that had been expressly authorized by the commander in chief, they had effectively waived their right to the official status of enemy combatant.[58] The ruling was tortured, doubted even by some of the judges who officially agreed with it, but made possible by the indefatigable, highly irregular and ethically dubious backstage intrigue of Justice Felix Frankfurter to have the court confirm the president's authority in a national security emergency.

Frankfurter wasn't just any justice: he was personally close to both Roosevelt and Stimson, and consulted with them regularly, in private, on cases before the court, including *Quirin.* From the bench, as a stalwart liberal, he was also one of the staunchest defenders of the New Deal. As a Jewish immigrant whose family left Europe when he was a boy, arriving in the United States unable to speak a word of English yet going on to study and teach law at Harvard while also consulting with Roosevelt about New Deal appointments and policies, and then, finally, becoming a Supreme Court justice, Frankfurter was also understandably patriotic. The year before *Quirin,* he wrote the majority opinion in *Gobitis,* which was partly based on the decidedly un-legalistic argument that "National unity is the basis of national security." And in a remarkably unguarded speech in New York, right in the middle of the *Quirin* deliberations, he explained exactly what he meant by national unity and national security. The nation, he told the students at his alma mater, City College, needed "spiritual unity" in order to prevail in "a war to save civilization." Victory for America would settle "the difference between a free society and a concentration camp." He accused "self-destructive isolationism" of undermining the nation's "security and decency." And in a final nod to both the New Deal's enduring metaphorical persona and the era's invented traditions for an era of insecurity, Frankfurter left a parting message for the assembled students: "The ideal that holds us together is our sincere respect for the common man whatever his race or religion."[59]

OTHER THAN IN ROOSEVELT'S many speeches—State of the Union addresses, Inaugural addresses, Fireside Chats—probably the clearest, sharpest call for defending the American Way as a matter of national security came from the media mogul Henry Luce, in February 1941, only a month after Roosevelt had delivered his Four Freedoms speech to Congress. Luce had almost single-handedly reinvented American journalism in the 1930s with his magazines *Time, Life,* and *Fortune* (and, later, *Sports Illustrated*). His stewardship of this media empire could be highly political, but he was also a peerless spotter of talent, including Margaret Bourke-White. After seeing some of her photography, Luce signed her to work for *Fortune* before moving her to *Life,* where she remained for the rest of her career despite their political differences.

Luce, a business-friendly Republican, hated the New Deal, and he disliked Roosevelt personally, too. But he was also an ardent internationalist who, like Walter Lippmann, believed the United States had a destiny to fulfill as a great power that would change the world. Born in China to Presbyterian missionary parents, Luce didn't live in the United States until he was thirteen, when he moved to Connecticut to attend boarding school, and later Yale. He left China two years after the fall of the Qing Dynasty and one year before the onset of the Great War that upended the treaty-port system and stimulated the rise of modern Chinese nationalism. By the early twentieth century, American Protestant missionaries were ecumenical, liberal, and cosmopolitan, and thoroughly embedded within the progressive movement. Luce's missionary parents shared that progressivism and cosmopolitanism, but in Connecticut he imbibed a different sort of faith, one shared by earlier generations of American missionaries: a belief in the global providential mission of God's chosen nation, the United States.[60]

In February 1941, with the country still gripped by the great debate over the war, Luce wrote an article for *Life* that he hoped would bring Americans around to supporting outright intervention. In fact, to him, the whole notion that the country was still at peace was absurd: "All this talk about whether this or that might or might not get us into the war is wasted effort. We are, for a fact, *in* the war." The real questions were why and how the United States should wage it. Luce's answer, immediately apparent in the article's blunt and simple title, was that the United States should use the war to establish "The American Century."

Doing so wasn't just an act of cultural expansionism, to remake the world in an American image purely for the sake of it. Historians have made much of the American Century's hubris, and rightly so, but Luce's rationale was primarily defensive, not offensive.[61] The tightly interconnected modern world made it impossible to avoid not just war, but the causes of war: poverty, nationalism, dictatorship. An American Century was the only thing that could preserve US autonomy in the modern world and protect the American way of life from predatory great powers and mass movements. It was not a new idea—James Monroe had equated the protection of "peace and happiness" with territorial sovereignty when laying down his eponymous doctrine in 1823. But while Monroe's horizon had retrenched, hemispheric limits, Luce's—and Roosevelt's—was limitlessly global.[62]

"Now that we are in this war, how did we get in? We got in on the basis of defense," Luce wrote. "Even that very word, defense, has been full of deceit and self-deceit." He explained:

> To the average American the plain meaning of the word defense is defense of the American territory. Is our national policy today limited to the defense of the American homeland by whatever means may seem wise? It is not. We are *not* in a war to defend American territory. We are in a war to defend and even to promote, encourage and incite so-called democratic principles throughout the world. The average American begins to realize now that that's the kind of war he's in. And he's halfway for it. But he wonders how he ever got there, since a year ago he had not the slightest intention of getting into any such thing. Well, he can see now how he got there. He got there via "defense."

The American debate over whether to fight was not, Luce believed, grounded in objective reality but in competing "picture-patterns" in the national psyche. This was because Herbert Hoover and the anti-interventionists had actually got it right: "If the entire rest of the world came under the organized domination of evil tyrants, it is quite possible to imagine that this country could make itself such a tough nut to crack that not all the tyrants in the world would care to come against us." No American "can honestly say that as a pure matter of defense—defense of our homeland—it is necessary to get into or be in this war." But with the national security revolution, defending territorial sovereignty was no longer the sole criterion of defense. Luce taunted the anti-interventionists by asking "whose Dong Dang and whose Democracy" Americans should fight for. Protecting American values and morals was just as important, not simply as a virtue in itself but because it would allow Americans to create a safer world, for themselves as well as others. "America is responsible, to herself as well as to history, for the world-environment in which she lives. Nothing can so vitally affect America's environment as America's own influence upon it." The final conclusion was inescapable: because Americans needed the world to be more in tune with their ideals, they must be "the powerhouse from which the ideals spread throughout the world." It was not a matter of Christian benevolence, but American interest and safety. "It is in this spirit that all of us are called . . . to create the first great American Century."[63]

(7)

THE BATTLE OF BEDFORD FALLS

POOR GEORGE BAILEY. While personal triumphs and accolades had gone to others, he endured the disappointment of dashed hopes his entire life. After passing up an early investment opportunity, he'd missed out on the boom in plastics. After scrimping and saving, he'd missed out on a lifetime dream of traveling the world. A good student in high school, he'd even been denied the chance to go to college as he minded the family business so that his younger brother Harry could realize his potential, first at football and then in business. Then came World War II, which only compounded George's humiliation. While his boyhood friends and kid brother were becoming heroes overseas—downing Japanese fighters over the Pacific, winning the Silver Star for bravery against German tanks in North Africa, storming the beaches of Normandy—George had to stay home, in Bedford Falls, New York, "4-F on account of his ear" that he damaged when rescuing Harry from the icy waters of a nearby lake when they were children. While the rest of his generation were on one of the greatest adventures in history, fighting tyranny and defending freedom in Europe and Asia, George kept busy organizing scrap drives at home. Instead of "parachuting into France," like Ernie the cab driver, "George fought the Battle of Bedford Falls."

George Bailey wasn't real, of course. As the protagonist of *It's a Wonderful Life*, Frank Capra's 1946 film about the deceptively ordinary courage of everyday sacrifice, George has become one of modern culture's true heroes. By the end of the film, surrounded by friends and family, he's revealed to be the "richest man in town" despite his dire financial straits. The Battle of Bedford Falls is supposed to reinforce this message of everyday heroism, and on one level it does. But it also reinforces then-novel and now-standard ideas about America's place in the world, especially the nature of the external threats the United States faced. The scene in which George wages the Battle of Bedford Falls is comic, as he haplessly marshals women, children, and old men to do their bit for the war by recycling paper, rubber, and scrap metal.[1] He's the only able-bodied man left in town. The fiercest enemy George faces is a crotchety old man who doesn't want to turn off his lights during a nighttime blackout—knowing, just as George most certainly does, that the likelihood of a German or Japanese air raid on a small mill town in upstate New York is pretty small. *It's a Wonderful Life* makes it clear that George's inability to fight overseas was deeply humiliating because that's where modern wars were fought: the American home front was not a war front. To be a war hero, a young man needed to go to war—and in the 1940s, as it was in the Great War before and has been ever since, the war was most certainly not found in places like Bedford Falls, New York.

The condition of war was very different for every other major power fighting in World War II. In China, Japan, Britain, France, Germany, Italy, and the Soviet Union—to say nothing of many other smaller nations—the home front *was* a war front, often the *only* war front. All of these countries except Britain suffered invasion and occupation at some point, often through the enemy's scorched-earth tactics, and while Britain escaped outright invasion it was pummeled from the skies for several years. For those countries that were attacked and invaded, the war turned everything completely upside down, opening social and cultural wounds that wouldn't heal for decades. By contrast, the only fighting in the forty-eight states of the United States consisted of incendiaries attached to a handful of Japanese balloons that floated across the Pacific and landed in Oregon, killing six people. To be sure, the American empire saw heavy combat: Hawai'i and Alaska, which weren't yet states, saw battle in 1941 and 1942–1943, respectively, and the Philippines experienced particularly brutal warfare during the Japanese invasion and occupation. But, uniquely among the major belligerents of the war, the sovereignty of the United States itself and the physical safety of its citizens were never at risk, even indirectly. When Franklin Roosevelt told Americans in 1944 that "our national security does not end at our borders," he was telling a half-truth: US national security certainly did not *end* at the border—it *began* there.[2]

As with *It's a Wonderful Life*, the notion that the front lines of American national security lay far offshore was repeated so often in popular culture that it soon became the very fabric of political culture. War films led the way. In *They Were Expendable,* his 1945 epic of the Japanese conquest of the Philippines, director John Ford drew an equally sharp line between the heroism of wartime service overseas and the distinctly unheroic home front. After holding off and then sinking several enemy vessels in Filipino waters, yet ultimately proving unable to prevent the Philippines from falling to the Japanese, Navy lieutenants John Brickley and Rusty Ryan are ordered home to the States to train the recruits who will mount the counteroffensive to take back the islands and defeat Japan. Though this is clearly vital war work, Brick and Rusty at first refuse to go back to a safe and indulgent country, and they have to be ordered to get on the next evacuation flight by the general in charge. Even then, Rusty, the gruff but gallant Navy lieutenant played by John Wayne, attempts to rush off the plane right before it taxis for takeoff and has to be pulled back inside.

William Wyler drew that line even more starkly in his 1946 Oscar-winning film *The Best Years of Our Lives,* a tragic story of the difficulties faced by veterans returning to postwar civilian life. In the case of sailor Homer Parrish, returning from the Pacific theater to his family's modest house in middle-American Boone City, it means watching his mother weep in sadness to see the hooks that have replaced his two missing hands. Homer can't look his fiancée, Wilma, in the eye even though she says this physical deformity doesn't matter. Others, such as Army sergeant Al Stephenson, find it difficult to work with people who haven't experienced the hardships of war. Air Force bombardier Fred Derry, while outwardly unscathed, bears deep psychological scars expressed only in PTSD-fueled nightmares that prevent his smooth reentry into civilian life.

Their own experiences in World War II made deep impressions on Capra, Ford, and Wyler. Ford and Wyler witnessed fighting up close, with Ford coming under fire while filming in the Pacific, including at Midway. Wyler earned his first Oscar for directing the unabashedly prowar film *Mrs. Miniver* (released in 1942 but filmed in 1941, before the United States was at war), which portrayed embattled England as the last line in the defense of western civilization. During the war, Wyler flew on bombing missions over Europe; on one, his sound technician, flying in the same squadron, was killed when his plane was shot down. *Best Years* screenwriter Robert Sherwood had been wounded while fighting in France during the Great War and spent World War II as Franklin Roosevelt's chief speechwriter. And although Capra felt insecure, perhaps even a bit guilty, about spending the war in the United States, he produced films that shaped how Americans—most of whom, even military personnel like Capra, never left the country—interpreted the war.[3]

The global onslaught of the Axis powers, and then the creeping spread of global communism after the war, fueled a heightened American threat perception that gave rise to a permanent doctrine of national security. Stretching the conceptual bounds of national security even further than Roosevelt had during the war, the onset of the Cold War marked the final stage in the evolution of American defense. According to the national security doctrine that took shape by 1947, the defense of the continental United States, while still important, was no longer even the theoretical "common denominator" it had been during the war. As George Bailey discovered, American national security had become almost completely untethered from the physical security of the United States itself. Intentionally or not, Capra's films charted this subtle but important shift in self-defense. In his wartime *Why We Fight* films, America's enemies are intent on eventually invading the United States. Yet in *It's a Wonderful Life*—a movie partially set during the war but filmed shortly after it—the whole notion that the United States needed defending was played for laughs. America's lines of defense were now far from American shores.

Jimmy Stewart, the Hollywood legend who played George Bailey, eventually got to play a real national security hero in the 1955 movie *Strategic Air Command*. This time, Stewart was Robert "Dutch" Holland, a star third baseman for the St. Louis Cardinals called up for active duty in the air force. His wife, Sally, vents her frustration as Dutch is sent on long missions thousands of miles from home, high above the Arctic Circle and the Pacific Ocean. She doesn't see him anymore, and she doesn't see the point; she understood when he was overseas in World War II, but not now. "But there *is* a *kind* of war," Dutch replies, equally frustrated that Sally doesn't get it. "We've got to stay ready to fight, without fighting. That's even tougher."

The over-the-horizon distance of US defense wasn't just the stuff of Hollywood. Strategists and policymakers alike agreed that the defense of the United States began far from—and indeed might never even reach—the United States. Grayson Kirk, a Columbia University political scientist (and later president) who served in the State Department as a wartime planner, noted the offshore nature of US security just as the war was winding down. "No threat to the United States will originate in this hemisphere; if our security is endangered, the threat will come from across one of our frontier oceans." To meet those threats, Kirk predicted with tragic foresight, the United States would have be proactive and "be able to intervene . . . whenever and wherever necessary for the protection of our own interests." US national self-defense had become virtually separate from the immediate defense of the nation. "We no longer are free to assume," he concluded, "that by preventing a foreign war from coming to our shores we will have fulfilled the highest demands of national security."[4]

The war induced such globalist thinking from more unlikely corners, too. Few made such a dramatic conversion as Yale's Samuel Flagg Bemis, probably the most eminent diplomatic historian of his era and along with Charles Beard one of the prominent "continentalists" who opposed intervention in the late 1930s. Before 1941, Bemis had argued that the Founders had established a continental foreign policy that served the country well until the embrace of imperialism in 1898 set the country on a misguided global path that, by 1937, had brought it to the edge of an unnecessary war the Founders themselves would have avoided. But after 1945, Bemis reversed himself, arguing that the war against Germany and Japan showed that the continentalist strategy wasn't sanctified by tradition but was instead "retrograde," unsuitable for the modern age. Now, with the Soviet challenge arising, Bemis argued that the global balance of power, not an impregnable fortress of continental or even hemispheric defense, was the key to US safety. "American security and defense" against the spread of communism, he wrote, would be decided on "a first line, in Europe," and not in the western Atlantic as he had always argued before.[5]

Kirk and Bemis did not write in a vacuum. It took two years of strategic planning, and convincing Congress and the public to follow along, but by 1947–1948 President Harry Truman and his administration had completed—and made permanent—the national security revolution Franklin Roosevelt started in 1937–1938. In November 1948, the new National Security Council confirmed the new basis of American strategic defense. Communist provocations, NSC planners concluded in a landmark report known as NSC 20–4, "clearly demonstrate that the ultimate objective" of the Soviet Union "is the domination of the world." The authors of NSC 20–4 conceded that Soviet forces were "not capable of sustained and decisive direct military attack against US territory or the Western hemisphere," and that "the USSR could not . . . successfully undertake an invasion of the United States as long as effective US forces remained in being." But they also concluded that none of that mattered, because the extent of US national security was now worldwide. Thus a "concentration of hostile power . . . would pose an unacceptable threat to the security of the United States" whether or not it was poised to attack the United States. "The gravest threat to the security of the United States . . . stems from the hostile designs and formidable power of the USSR, and from the nature of the Soviet system." To ensure survival in the modern world, the American way of life couldn't tolerate any systemic challengers, anywhere.[6] Thoroughly internationalized, American national security had become something of a paradox.

THE COLD WAR'S embedding of national security within the American worldview wasn't inevitable, however. The trajectory of World War II initially followed that of all other US wars: rapid mobilization from a very small military foundation, then equally rapid demobilization once the fighting was over. Some Americans were of course already suspicious of the Soviet Union, and had been for decades; anti-communism was about as natural an impulse in American political culture as anything could be. But dislike and fear are two different emotions, and at the end of the war it wasn't obvious why Americans should fear for their position in the world. At the end of the war, General George Marshall himself proudly declared, "For the first time since assuming this office nearly six years ago, it is possible for me to report that the security of the United States is entirely in our own hands."[7]

This made sense. If, as observers like Grayson Kirk claimed, free security disappeared with the Japanese attack on Pearl Harbor and the German advance in Europe, the outcome of the war brought it roaring back to life.[8] In 1939, the United States had two remote but plausible threats in Japan and Germany. In 1941, both of those powers became America's enemy and posed risks to US security—perhaps not in terms of a direct attack, but a logical threat to vital US interests in an interdependent world. Franklin Roosevelt admitted as much in the midst of the war, gently chiding the people of Washington state during a 1944 visit: "You've dreamt of Japanese marching up the streets of Bremerton or Seattle tomorrow morning," yet "we knew also that Japan did not have the naval and air power to carry the threat into effect"—and, he could have added, it didn't even matter whether the Japanese invaded Seattle or not.[9]

In fact, for political reasons, most of Roosevelt's national security warnings came in the years before 1942. Once the United States was officially at war, especially as the war began to turn in the Allies' favor in 1943–1944, the risk to US security receded. By 1945, the Allied victory had completely smashed Japanese and German power, and even the ostensible victors—Britain, China, France—literally lay in ruins. This was also the case for the devastated Soviet Union, the only state remaining that was powerful enough to pose even a theoretical challenge to the United States. Even if American power in 1945 was, as Paul Kennedy points out, "artificially high" because of a unique confluence of circumstances, the result of the war nonetheless elevated US power to a scale the world hadn't seen since the height of the Roman Empire. While others were not so fortunate, Americans could be forgiven if they once again took their security for granted.[10]

The War Department certainly seemed to do so. Before the end of the war, Army officials started planning for the demobilization that would surely follow victory in the war. As early as the spring of 1943, Marshall directed the commanding general of the Army Service Forces to begin secretly planning for postwar demobilization. The resulting report—written only eighteen months into America's war, before any Allied troops had even landed in Europe, let alone turned the tide of the war—predicted that "the United States will emerge as the strongest military power in the world and will remain for at least several post-war years in a state of preparedness for action in widely dispersed areas." The primary needs for widely dispersed armed forces would be the defense of the western hemisphere, the safeguarding of access to critical natural resources outside the hemisphere, and a US contribution to an "International military force" to occupy defeated nations and maintain a modicum of global security. But even under those terms, War Department planners foresaw a rapid drawdown of the vast majority of military personnel, because none of these goals required a large military. Secretary of War Henry Stimson endorsed the report and told the chiefs of staff to begin contemplating a return to peace, when they would have a force larger than they had before 1941 but nowhere as large as during the war.[11] The plan went public in September 1944, and the following February the War Department announced it would release 250,000 men per month once the war was over in Europe.[12] The Navy was slower to accept demobilization, but it too had firm plans in place before the end of the war.[13] Tellingly, in the absence of an obvious enemy, wartime collaboration between the Army and Navy began to break down as they failed to reach a consensus on the size and scope of the postwar military.[14] Bemis called it "the Great Let-Down of 1945–1947" and lamented that through "demoralization and disillu-sion" Americans had squandered many of the advantages they had won in the war.[15]

Other branches of government also started anticipating the transition to peace. Officials from the Treasury Department and the War Produc-tion Board began planning for peacetime reconversion in May 1943, the Labor Statistics Bureau warned of mass postwar unemployment in Au-gust, and the Federal Advisory Council, which met every quarter to offer advice to the Federal Reserve banks, recommended in November that the government should start winding down military contracts so that private companies, and by extension American workers, weren't caught flat-footed by the end of the war.[16] In 1944, the Office of War Mobilization, which spearheaded wartime production and was run by New Dealer and future secretary of state James F. Byrnes, was renamed the Office of War Mobi-lization and Reconversion.[17] That same year, Congress passed the GI Bill—its original intent reflected in its official legislative name, the Servicemen's Readjustment Act—as "a New Deal for veterans."[18] The GI Bill reflected the prevailing mood among GIs themselves. As one general commanding troops in Italy put it, "the man overseas wants to know only one thing: what provisions are being made for his return to normal living."[19]

Expectations about the return of peace, and peacetime conditions, spilled over into public discourse. The end of the war would presumably not only bring victory, and the return to normalcy at home, but security for the nation. Wasn't that why the United States had entered the war in the first place? In early 1945, with Allied victory all but certain, private banks such as the Provident Loan Society began adjusting their lending strategies on the expectation that peacetime would lead to higher demand for mortgages and small-business loans.[20] This was but one of a multi-tude of ordinary pressures for an end to the emergency. "Let there be no illusion," lamented Nathaniel Peffer, a Columbia political scientist and onetime China correspondent for the *New York Tribune*, as the war drew to a close. "The appeal of this will be tremendous, and perhaps, if not counteracted, irresistible. It is probably what the majority of the Ameri-can people instinctively and spontaneously would prefer." In contrast, like his colleague Grayson Kirk, Peffer thought it was vital for the United States to maintain its military readiness in the name of national security, for the defeat of Germany and Japan had done nothing to erase the new struc-tural realities of world politics that had made American security perma-nently vulnerable.[21]

The return of free security also meant, perhaps counterintuitively, that Americans were returning to ideas of collective security on their grandest scale. For a brief moment at the end of the war, when Kirk noticed "an unprecedented public interest in the principle of an international security organization," many Americans placed their hopes for an enduring peace in highly internationalist solutions to the problem of world order.[22] These visions of world federalism, shared atomic energy, and the pooling of natural and industrial resources flourished when Americans felt the least threatened. It may seem contradictory, but precisely because insecurity reached a low, Americans felt they could afford to be inventive with their security arrangements. The push for collaborative internationalism correspondingly hit a new high. Wendell Willkie's account of his 1942 world tour, *One World,* was a runaway bestseller, and at the time of its founding the United Nations was more popular among Americans than it ever would be again. "The people of the United States muffed the ball over twenty years ago" when it spurned the League of Nations, one leading educator wrote as the war drew to a close; "there seems to be firm desire on the part of the entire nation that we not make the same mistake again."[23]

Sentiments of one-worldism even found their way into that most jingoistic corner of popular culture, the war movie. In *Objective, Burma!* (1945), one of Errol Flynn's last major films, a *Schenectady Gazette* reporter is embedded with a platoon in the China-Burma-India theater. To his surprise, he meets a GI from the same city in upstate New York. "What do you know? It's a small world, isn't it?" the GI exclaims. The reporter, who has followed American soldiers across the Pacific to Asia, agrees. "Yes, and it's getting smaller. And if only more folks back home would realize that Crane Street, Schenectady runs all the way to Burma, this would be the last war."

———

ALONGSIDE DEMOBILIZATION, part of the gradual return to normalcy was the winding down of the draft. Congress renewed the Selective Service Act, originally passed in 1940, twice after the end of the war, but with an eye to an orderly transition from war to peace and never with the intention of making the draft permanent. Marshall hoped instead for congressional authorization of Universal Military Training (UMT), which was not conscription but would instead train every man in the United States in basic skills so that they wouldn't need long to become soldiers or sailors or airmen if another war broke out.[24] Marshall saw UMT in much the same way that New Deal works programs, such as his beloved Civilian Conservation Corps, "strengthen the spiritual and moral fiber of our people."[25] UMT would create a reserve that could quickly augment the kind of small, professional military the United States traditionally had. Marshall thought a permanent draft would be too controversial—and deemed too expensive—in an era of peace and security, but he opposed a large all-volunteer force on the grounds that some things were best left to the public sphere. "When you try to purchase an army on the open market," he told the Senate Foreign Relations Committee in metaphorical language that echoed Wilson on fire insurance and Roosevelt on Social Security, "you cannot possibly afford it." Only government could do the job.[26] With all this in mind, Marshall recommended UMT to Truman as a replacement for Selective Service in May 1945, three days before the German surrender.[27]

Truman needed little convincing, and not just because he respected Marshall: UMT was a quintessentially liberal project that had animated the New Deal right from the very beginning and fit squarely within Truman's own liberalism. Experts argued that it would, for example, facilitate the Democratic Party's recent turn toward civil rights by providing African Americans with skills they were otherwise being denied due to segregation and poverty.[28] After receiving Marshall's recommendation, Truman gave a speech on UMT as the basis of "a long range program of national military security" before a joint session of Congress. He couched it in terms that would have described any of the New Deal's works programs: the training and educating of otherwise idle young men, the imparting of special skills useful in all sorts of jobs, the lowering of illiteracy, and the development of "the ideals of responsible American citizenship."

Yet Truman's main reason for UMT wasn't social security but national security. There was peace in the world for the first time in nearly fifteen years, but it would last "only so long as we remain strong. We must face the fact that peace must be built upon power." Truman was worried first and foremost about American complacency and underpinning that complacency—though he didn't use the term—was free security, no longer a blessing but a curse for officials in Washington. "Never again can we count on the luxury of time with which to arm ourselves," the president warned:

In any future war, the heart of the United States would be the enemy's first target. Our geographical security is now gone—gone with the advent of the robot bomb, the rocket, aircraft carriers and modern airborne armies. The surest guaranty that no nation will dare again to attack us is to remain strong in the only kind of strength an aggressor understands—military power.

The fact that Truman had to remind his audience that the "day of the minute man who sprang to the flintlock hanging on his wall is over," and that should "another national emergency should come, there would be no time for this complicated training," speaks to the power of the systemic obstacle he now faced. If the American people felt insecure, it wasn't because of a foreign power; it was because of fears that the transition to peace would revive mass unemployment. In the face of these widespread assumptions, Truman's plea could not have been any clearer: refusing to maintain military strength, through measures like UMT, would make a great difference between preparedness and vulnerability, and that difference "may be the margin between the survival and the destruction of this great nation."[29] Other commentators agreed. "We cannot gamble with our national existence," one pro-UMT writer argued in *Scientific Monthly;* "the stakes are too big." None was more authoritative than the American Legion: UMT would keep America "forever safe from attack."[30]

Despite Legion backing, Truman's call for UMT went unheeded, and Marshall knew why. "We lack at the moment a proper perspective," the architect of victory in World War II told the annual convention of the Salvation Army, then meeting in Kansas City, Missouri, only a month after Truman's special address to Congress:

We see the peaceful countryside of America unscarred by war, and here in the Mississippi Valley in particular, you are most remote from violent scenes of war. We are busily engaged in welcoming home each month a million and a half of our young men returning to their normal civil occupations. We simply cannot comprehend the disruption of governments, and the complete destruction of cities and homes, that has taken place in the world. We read the discussions in the press and listen to the descriptions and opinions on the radio but these give us only a remote appreciation of the chaotic state of the world beyond the boundaries of the continental United States.[31]

Marshall's worries were well-founded. The end of the war saw the rapid fading of a sense of danger, and without a new adversary, even one as remote as Germany or Japan, there was little prospect that Americans would assume their rightful "leadership of the greatest and most beneficent movement in world history for the good of mankind."[32] As the end of the war approached, American families looked forward to welcoming their sons home, and they called for the military to expedite what was already a surprisingly expeditious demobilization process. This pressure, growing even before the final defeat of Germany and Japan, intensified into 1946. Americans, Secretary of the Navy James Forrestal admonished shortly after the surrender of Japan, "should not delude ourselves into thinking or acting as though we were still the military giant which we were two months ago. We certainly are not." Unfortunately for Forrestal, though, Americans didn't mind their suddenly reduced stature.[33]

—————

ALREADY, HOWEVER, Washington was building a system to prevent another descent into world war, and it was no coincidence that the architecture for this system was based on the principles of regulatory liberalism—what historians have aptly termed "a New Deal for the world."[34]

The idea was simple: for a century, a largely unregulated US economy had experienced repeating cycles of boom and bust. Over time, the booms kept getting bigger, but so did the busts. The United States was getting richer as it generated historic levels of economic growth, but the recessions of 1837, 1857, 1873, and 1893 were each, in their time, the greatest-ever economic crisis in American history. This wild ride continued into the twentieth century, as the cycle of boom and bust kept expanding, even as the Progressives started regulating the economy in small ways and even as the managerial revolution in American business brought more professionalism to commercial activity. The cycle may have continued if not for the cold shock of the Depression, an economic crisis that soon became an existential social, political, and cultural crisis equaled in gravity only by the Civil War (as FDR repeatedly pointed out). Roosevelt's solution, the New Deal programs that established broad regulatory and welfare states for the first time, did not solve the Depression, but it did bring an end to the sense of crisis and provide Americans with a foundation on which to rebuild their economy and democracy.[35]

1941 had the same shock effect on foreign policy as 1929 did on the economy. There was a widespread feeling that just as laissez-faire had created the conditions for the Depression, "isolationism" had enabled laissez-faire world politics that created the conditions for World War II. "An antonym for isolationism is security," Representative Jacob Javits, a liberal Democrat who later became one of the Cold War's leading authorities on national security issues, told his colleagues in Congress in the summer of 1947.[36] Americans had made a mistake in rejecting Wilsonianism and the League, and Truman, Marshall, and others urged Americans not to make the same mistake again. "In our desire to leave the tragedy of war behind us," Truman said in his UMT speech to Congress, "we must not make the same mistake that we made after the first World War when we sank back into helplessness." Marshall told the Salvation Army much the same thing: "America courts disaster for herself and for the world if she again falls into a state of disinterested weakness and fails to fulfill her responsibility." In trying to avoid another World War I, Americans had inadvertently helped cause World War II. They must, Truman and Marshall implored, never do so again.[37]

Providing social security for the world, then, would also ensure national security for the United States. As foreign-affairs analyst Merze Tate had put it during the war, "There is no security for any state unless it be a security in which all neighbors share."[38] This is why someone like John McCloy, one of Stimson's closest aides in the War Department, could say that the "world looks to the U.S. as the one stable country to insure the security of the world" without sounding like a dreamy idealist.[39] Or how a freshman Republican from the hard-edged, anti–New Deal class of the 1946 midterms could argue on the floor of Congress that "the safety and security of the world is indeed our problem and the solution of that problem our real safety; that succor of starving and enslaved peoples is indeed our obligation."[40] Just like the New Deal, there were two sides to this new liberal international order—political and economic—which Roosevelt had explained were "all parts of a consistent whole" to create a world "in which plain people in all countries can work at tasks which they do well, exchange in peace the products of their labor, and work out their several destinies in security and peace."[41] It all amounted, he said on another occasion, to "the great design of security and peace."[42]

Politically, the United States pushed for the establishment of a new international parliament to replace the League of Nations. Like the League, the United Nations, initiated at the Dumbarton Oaks conference in Washington in 1944 and finalized at a major conference in San Francisco in 1945, provided a forum where countries could discuss, and even legislate, problems of international peace and security. Unlike the League, however, there was no pretense that the UN would provide a system of collective security; nor were all members considered equals, as the five permanent members of the Security Council each had a veto over any UN declarations or legislation.[43]

Americans also took the lead in organizing a regulated world economy, not just for the good of others but for Americans, too. Roosevelt's logic was simple: "abundance at home depends upon organization for order and security in the world," and international security was impossible without stable economies in Europe and elsewhere.[44] In 1944, at a ski resort in Bretton Woods, New Hampshire, the Allies met to agree on a new framework that was based on currency stabilization through fixed exchange rates (pegged to the price of gold in US dollars) and two new multilateral institutions, the World Bank to encourage development and the International Monetary Fund to assist economies in distress. Three years later, representatives from 23 countries convened in Geneva to sign the General Agreement on Tariffs and Trade (GATT), setting rules to encourage more open international trade.[45]

The same time GATT came to life, June 1947, the Truman administration added a massive fiscal stimulus to jump-start its new economic order—known, fittingly enough, as the Marshall Plan. The immediate reason for the name was that it was Marshall, now Truman's secretary of state, who announced it in a commencement speech at Harvard, but the deeper symbolic links between Marshall, the New Deal, and the national security revolution were even more important. One Senator dubbed the Marshall Plan "a World-wide WPA scheme"—as criticism, but liberal internationalists would surely have taken it as praise—while a Congressman was more categorical in brandishing it "outright Communism."[46] Still, Marshall, hailed by supporters as "the greatest national security and peace-enforcement weapon of all time," had broad assent because the dollars his Plan sent to fund the relief and recovery of Europe's capitalist economies were as shrewd an investment against international social collapse as the WPA and other New Deal programs had been against the economic crisis of the 1930s.[47] Even if this "New Deal synthesis," as the historian Michael J. Hogan aptly calls it, didn't make Europe more like the United States socially or politically, it fused the two together in an effective strategic alliance to safeguard all types of internal and external security.[48]

Truman's conception of national security was thus the same as Franklin Roosevelt's; the Cold War didn't result from his departing from Roosevelt's principles, but in applying them. Truman explained as much in his State of the Union address in the fateful year of 1947. Much had changed in a short period: internationally, the fitful dialogue between Washington and Moscow was breaking down and a new era of crisis was beginning; domestically, the 1946 midterms saw the fiercely anti–New Deal Republicans take control of Congress for the first time in nearly fifteen years. But the basics of national security remained the same as they were when Roosevelt forged them in the 1930s. "National security does not consist only of an army, a navy, and an air force," Truman said to Congress. "It rests on a much broader basis. It depends on a sound economy of prices and wages, on prosperous agriculture, on satisfied and productive workers, on a competitive private enterprise free from monopolistic repression, on continued industrial harmony and production, on civil liberties and human freedoms—on all the forces which create in our men and women a strong moral fiber and spiritual stamina."[49]

The "shadow of the garrison state" also loomed large, just as it had in 1940–1941. One fear was that the needs of national security would overwhelm American democracy. But the prevailing concern, as Harold Lasswell had expressed it before the war, was that neglecting the needs of national security would eventually, inevitably, endanger the American way of life by necessitating the militarization of US politics and economics, and of society itself. Should Soviet power in Europe grow unchecked, George F. Kennan warned as Congress debated the Marshall Plan in the summer of 1947, Americans would have to make "not only a major and costly readjustment of our political-military strategy but also changes in our domestic life."[50]

Kennan need not have worried. By this time, national security as the overriding organizing principle for US foreign policy had come roaring back to life—not just strategically but culturally, as a Senate resolution to officially designate February 12–22 as "National Security Week" indicated.[51] By 1947, when the nation was debating the Cold War measures the Truman administration was calling for, invoking "national security" to justify any number of objectives had already become commonplace. It may have made some sense to portray the extraction of oil deposits off the coast of California or building the Saint Lawrence Seaway as vital on grounds of national security, less so the helping of farmers by setting a profitable floor for the price of wool, providing federal subsidies for commercial shipping, or ensuring "the health and well-being of the Nation's children" by providing families with "nutritious agricultural commodities."[52] This was a vision of defense so flexible it could include almost anything, yet its very flexibility was precisely why it was so powerful. If national security meant more than territorial self-defense, it could, for ulterior motives but also in good faith, be used in almost any circumstance—even if those circumstances, such as children's nutrition, bore little relation to pre-1937 notions of national self-defense.

———

BY 1947, the embedding of "national security" in political culture was only possible because the risks to US security now appeared to be elevated. The reason—the breakdown of Soviet-American relations and the onset of the Cold War—is familiar, and historians continue to argue over the culpability and underlying dynamics of increasing tension between the two superpowers. But when tracing the solidification of national security in the American worldview, it doesn't actually matter who (if anyone) started the Cold War. Because of the conceptual and political framework built by Franklin Roosevelt and others in the late 1930s and early 1940s, because the war vindicated the strategic legitimacy of this framework, and because continual advances in military technology kept tightening the interconnections of the modern world, American threat perception was already, automatically, on high alert. Thus when a competitor like the Soviet Union—with a large military and an ideology that was completely antithetical in every single way to American liberal democratic capitalism—appeared to project its power for aggressive purposes, Americans were primed to see an existential threat rather than a normal geopolitical competitor. Ideological anti-communism was important to the American calculus, of course, but it wasn't determining.[53] The Soviets could have been fascists or imperialists or religious fundamentalists or dynastic monarchists, and they would just as quickly have been deemed a national security threat if they possessed a combination of military power and hostile ideological intent that made them a plausibly expansionist power unwilling to participate in a US-created liberal capitalist order.

George Fielding Eliot grasped this conundrum facing US foreign policy at the end of the war. Eliot was one of the nation's foremost military analysts, frequently writing commentary on war and defense in leading newspapers and periodicals, and at the end of the war he called for the United States to maintain sizeable armed forces. But he was also a devoted internationalist who believed that the bedrock of world peace was the UN and the rule of international law. Eliot's hardheaded idealism—his blended belief in the might of America and the right of the UN—wasn't all that unusual in 1945–1946; other hardheaded idealists, including some who would become notoriously hawkish in the Cold War, like John Foster Dulles, shared it. For Eliot as for Dulles, international law would provide international equality, stability, and justice, and therefore peace. But Eliot, like Dulles, put so much faith in international law because that very law reflected Anglo-American norms that Americans would happily abide.

And if others wouldn't abide by the right of international law? Then the might of America would have to step in—not as a matter of global altruism, but as a matter of basic safety. Eliot explained:

> There is no longer any such thing as national defense as we have thought of it in the past. There is such a thing as national security, but security is to be obtained either through the establishment of world law, or by a military position of offensive readiness—or rather, counteroffensive readiness—so formidable as to be beyond challenge.

Americans and their like-minded allies (Eliot had also lived in Canada and Australia) had "two objectives" in the postwar world: "the final enthronement of law as governing the affairs of all mankind; and to survive." If one of these objectives had to give way, it would have to be the former, and in that situation the United States would have to seek "the imposition of our authority on the whole world . . . forced upon us as the sole remaining means of self-preservation." This was the tragedy that another hardheaded idealist (actually, Christian realist), Reinhold Niebuhr, identified elsewhere. Eliot put it as straightforwardly as possible:

> There is no security except total security. There is no security except global security. There is no security for any nation that is not security for all. Anything less is a fatal illusion, a compromise with

death. Security, so considered, must therefore be the primary object of American military and foreign policy.[54]

Eliot's dilemma was eventually solved when Americans abandoned their strongest hopes for the UN and sought a partial victory in organizations like NATO.

The very sharp irony here is that Franklin Roosevelt himself believed that a postwar "just and durable peace," to use a phrase that was common among liberal internationalists during the war, was possible only as long as Washington and Moscow could cooperate on key issues of international security. During the war, Roosevelt went to unusual lengths to work with Stalin, and at one point even speculated that Soviet communist planning and American liberal planning were coming to a "convergence" of social democracy.[55] That may have been far-fetched, even when Roosevelt said it, but it revealed the importance he placed on continued cooperation between the United States and the Soviet Union. Any chance of that died with Roosevelt in April 1945, but it's unlikely Washington and Moscow would have continued their wartime condominium of power even had Roosevelt lived. And with a capacious national security sensibility in place, it was extremely unlikely that the hardening of Soviet power in eastern Europe, and the spread of communism to anti-colonial nationalist movements in Asia, would have failed to stimulate an elevated global risk assessment in Washington. Near-universal acceptance of the new theory of "totalitarianism"—that illiberal, anti-democratic political systems concentrating absolute power in a centralized state were fundamentally the same, whether they were fascist or communist—and that international communism was a "monolithic" enemy were made possible by the new doctrine of national security, and together they made it virtually inevitable that Soviet-American relations would deteriorate.[56]

NATIONAL SECURITY HAD its prewar theorists and architects, most notably Edward Mead Earle and Walter Lippmann, but they were relatively sparse; politicians and policymakers actually did most of the codification before 1942. But after the war, the likes of Earle and Lippmann were not so rare.

Earle's title as the chief theorist of national security fell to Arnold Wolfers, a Swiss-born political scientist at Yale who studied and taught in Germany before settling in the United States in 1933. Most of Wolfers's programmatic writing on national security would come in the 1950s, but he began collecting his thoughts on the topic as the war wound down, in a course at Yale called "Foundations of National Power" and then in a series of guest lectures at the National War College in Washington shortly after the war. A nation's first priority, he taught his students, was the integrity of its sovereignty. Traditionally that meant defending borders, but that definition was far too narrow for the world created by World War II. Security now required nations to protect themselves not just from physical attack but also "economic objectives of promoting the welfare of their countries" and "Ideological objectives" such as "promoting democratic institutions elsewhere."[57] Wolfers was also building Yale, especially the Institute of International Studies, into a center for the study of national security.[58] Beyond New Haven, around the same time, Wolfers joined Mead and others in drafting a Brookings Institution report on how the war had permanently changed the terms of US security: sovereign territory was now only one aspect of national self-defense.[59]

Wolfers was both broader and more precise at the National War College two years later, perhaps reflecting the clarifying deterioration of Soviet-American relations. Nations in the postwar world, he began, "are primarily concerned with what we call security, that is the preservation of their rights and possessions, primarily their territorial integrity and independence." The United States had operated differently, due to the long-standing effects of free security. "This country before this war was so little aware of the problem of its security," he explained with some exaggeration, that in the State Department "there was nobody there who was primarily concerned with the problem of security" and that "the bulk of the population is so little security-minded." The war changed everything, however, and security was becoming "a primary consideration." But in a world where no peer competitor could attack the United States—indeed, where the United States didn't really even have a true peer competitor— what did that exactly mean? Americans "feel more secure in a world in which things are ordered according to our principles," and so this logically led to a grand strategy in which "security, welfare and order are the three main objectives." This was, as we have seen, precisely the formulation that social planners like Isaac Rubinow and Charles Merriam had advanced a decade before, and it was precisely the basis for the regulatory "New Deal for the world" policies that the Roosevelt and Truman administrations had already put in place.

Wolfers's lecture was aimed at National War College students—military officers being prepared for leadership positions—but also in the audience that day was George F. Kennan, like Wolfers a resident fellow at the college after his return from duty in the US Embassy in Moscow. In the discussion following the lecture, Kennan asked a question about the scope of America's new defense posture. Wolfers, he said, had drawn a geographical distinction between lines of "inner" and "outer" defense, with the western hemisphere representing the inner line and the rest of the world representing the outer. Kennan could accept that distinction so long as "we should not concentrate too much attention on an inner line of defense as opposed to an outer one, which is perhaps itself vital." Wolfers quickly replied, "Or to believe that the inner line is really our main line of defense. It is a kind of glorified isolationism if we say we won't be isolationists but will limit ourselves to hemisphere defense and aid the Latin American republics. That still keeps us on the inner, the last-ditch defense line." Which is where, Wolfers and Kennan agreed, the United States must not be.[60]

Kennan has rightly gone down in history as the architect of containment, the grand strategy designed to keep Soviet communism at bay. This was a forward-looking strategic doctrine, one that sought to stay on the front foot to meet potential challenges to US security wherever they emerged, anywhere in the world. Kennan was a foreign-policy realist, famously ill-disposed to what he derided as the "legalistic-moralistic" impulse in the American diplomatic tradition.[61] Americans, he felt, were too prone to launching ideological crusades against foreign threats; they instead had to learn to discipline themselves to identify only the actual threats to US security, whatever their ideological character. By 1946–1947, Kennan had identified the Soviet Union as one of these threats, and warned about it in two famous documents: the "Long Telegram" of February 1946, and an article in *Foreign Affairs,* published under the pseudonym "X," in July 1947. In both, Kennan called for an American strategy that would resist communist expansion wherever it appeared. Yet the containment strategy he recommended was just as ideological as the tradition he dismissed, premised as much on the protection of a liberal, democratic, capitalist *American* way of life as on the protection of more "realist" security interests. In fact, Kennan went so far as to suggest that containment wouldn't just protect the American way but invigorate it. "Surely," Mr. X said of the communist challenge, "there was never a fairer test of national quality than this." In the face of the communist challenge, Americans should be vigilant, not fearful, and express "a certain gratitude to a Providence which, by providing the American people with this implacable challenge, has made their entire security as a nation dependent on their pulling themselves together and accepting the responsibilities of moral and political leadership that history plainly intended them to bear." Henry Luce, who came from the same Presbyterian tradition and shared a similar religious outlook, couldn't have put it better himself.[62]

Kennan's containment strategy, however, was not necessarily a new departure in American national security policy. For one thing, his strategic vision was in line with the leading theorists of national security. Just as he had productive exchanges with Wolfers, he also learned from Edward Mead Earle. When he was devising his own course at the National War College, Kennan relied heavily on *Makers of Modern Strategy,* one of the many venues where Earle articulated his vision, not just because the book was already canonical in the field but for lack of anything else: the field of grand-strategic studies was still very small. Earle's plan for security was innately preemptive, just like containment, based as it was on a "military policy" that "must be offensive in the sense of enabling us, if necessary, to seize and keep the initiative at whatever points our interests may be threatened."[63]

In fact, the conceptual foundations of Kennan's strategy of containment predated Earle, as containment bore the exact same hallmarks as Roosevelt's strategic outlook. Containment was an almost exact replica, conceptually at least, of Roosevelt's 1937 "quarantine" proposal: the only two differences were that containment relied on the projection of US power, alone if necessary, whereas the quarantine would have been a system of collective security; and, of course, that containment was actually implemented. But the core similarities are striking. Containment functioned much like an international quarantine, keeping the contagion of communism at bay by isolating it in places where it already existed and couldn't spread to infect "healthy" societies. Not coincidentally, Americans pathologized communism as a contagious disease; the solution, said the US Chamber of Commerce in a common analogy, was "inoculation" against "the insidious disease of Communism."[64] And just as Roosevelt recognized that the catastrophic scale of the Depression meant that the New Deal needed to prioritize security first and foremost because democracy couldn't survive without a baseline of security, Kennan's Long Telegram warned that the "tired and frightened" people of Europe "are less interested in abstract freedom than in security."[65] Absent security, communism would thrive. In the case of the American economy of the 1930s, only the federal government could provide security; in the case of European politics of the 1940s, only the United States could provide security. Without vigorous state intervention in both cases, everything would be lost.

Kennan didn't invent these ideas; he inherited and expanded them. As intelligent as they were, Kennan, Wolfers, and others who thought systematically about national security in the early Cold War didn't add anything theoretically or conceptually new. Their ideas about threats to the United States were exercises in confirming an existing theory by rounding it out in light of new circumstances. The Cold Warriors found that the theory of American security that anti-Nazi and anti-fascist internationalists had laid down a decade still worked. The national security strategists of the early Cold War corroborated the earlier theory here, made minor corrections and adjustments there, but in essence the Roosevelt theory of international risk and threat had been tested and validated.

―――――

KENNAN'S *FOREIGN AFFAIRS* article marked the end of a flurry of activity in the first half of 1947 that put the United States in a permanent state of military readiness. Beginning with the Truman Doctrine in March, and punctuated by the Marshall Plan announcement in June, US threat perception converged, nearly unanimously, on a strategic perspective that saw the Soviet Union as both willing and able to do great harm to the United States. "There were few divisions between American policymakers over US security objectives," observes Melvyn Leffler. "Disputes were emerging, but they focused on tactics and priorities, not objectives" or the nature of the threat.[66] Once it had decided that cooperation, even compromise, with the Soviets was no longer tenable, the Truman administration implemented what Kennan called "measures short of war"—rearmament, intelligence gathering, espionage, alliance-building, propaganda, economic assistance—as the advance guard of containment. But Kennan also knew full well the extent to which national security would have to be insured by military might. As he told his students at the National War College only a few weeks before he sat in on Wolfers's lecture, "You have no idea how much it contributes to the general politeness and pleasantness of diplomacy when you have a little quiet armed force in the background."[67]

After the stutter-step of postwar demobilization, Kennan and his colleagues in Washington soon had more than just "a little" armed force at their disposal. Beginning in 1947, the Truman administration embarked on a program of military mobilization that put the nation on a permanent war footing. The impact was profoundly enduring, not just on politics and foreign policy but also on American law and government.[68] Scholars have variously termed the basis of this war footing an "ideology of national preparedness," "institutionalized preparedness," or simply "peacetime military preparedness" that normalized the temporary, emergency mobilization efforts of 1916–1918 and 1940–1942.[69] To do so, it needed a new permanent system that was always fit for purpose, not just hastily assembled in an ad hoc moment of crisis, and that would prevent, as Assistant Secretary of War John McCloy put it, "the retrogression to fixed positions which follows a successful war."[70] The solution came in July 1947, the same month Mr. X unveiled containment, in one of the single most important pieces of congressional legislation in American history, one that changed not only the character of US foreign and military policies but of American society itself: the National Security Act.[71]

Before 1947, the War Department (for the army) and the Navy Department were separate institutions. While the president was the commander in chief, and theoretically had the final say over the direction of strategy and operations, in practice the War and Navy departments were locked in a state of constant competition and thus were difficult to manage; they also both cultivated supporters in Congress, who controlled the military budget. It was a system almost designed to be inefficiently difficult. But the unprecedentedly complex nature of World War II, which required combined operations around the world, revealed that it was possible for the services not only to cooperate, but to function effectively together within a larger system. In the postwar geopolitical moment, argued Robert Patterson, Stimson's successor as secretary of war, it made no sense to revert back to the old ways and base the "nation's security establishment . . . on one organization in peace and another in war."[72]

For Truman, this was a longstanding interest. In 1944, when still a senator, he vowed that the unification of the service branches would provide "complete integration that will consider the national security as a whole." The United States could no longer afford to maintain its tradition of peacetime unpreparedness and haphazard mobilization in the face of crisis; instead, it needed a new "Department of National Security."[73] As president, Truman wanted to formalize this wartime cooperation in a new "comprehensive and continuous program of national security." Reform was essential, and Americans "would be taking a grave risk with the national security" without it.[74] He was supported by Marshall, whose affinity for New Deal planning informed his thinking. Army planners used landmark studies on public administration by Leonard D. White—a colleague of Charles Merriam's at the University of Chicago who also worked as a public planner in the Roosevelt administration—to shape their approach to service unification.[75]

Originally called the National Military Establishment, Truman and Marshall's plan was significantly watered down by the time it passed as the National Security Act in July 1947. Partly this was due to intense rearguard action by the Navy Department, which feared losing its stature, autonomy, and generous appropriations (historically much greater than the army's); not coincidentally, Navy officials shared little of the Army's interest in public administration but had extensive experience in the corporate world.[76] Partly it was due to fears that the new NME, which one critic excoriated as "a bureaucratic monstrosity" with "a militaristic national high command," would corrode democracy.[77] Senator George Aiken spoke for many when he warned that the Act's centralization of executive war powers, not just in the hands of the president but in an unelected national security bureaucracy, was "only a short step from a radical departure in our concept of government itself."[78]

Aiken's concerns, alongside Navy opposition, led to the ultimate passage of a compromise bill, but the National Security Act was a major departure fully deserving its label as "the Magna Charta of the national security state."[79] In one single piece of legislation, the National Security Act formally created the National Security Council (NSC), the Central Intelligence Agency (CIA), the Joint Chiefs of Staff (JCS), the Office of the Secretary of Defense (OSD), and the National Security Resources Board (NSRB); it also created the United States Air Force (USAF) as a separate service branch and unified it with the Army and Navy—"our three arms of national security," George Fielding Eliot called them—in a single defense establishment.[80] UMT was a nonstarter in 1946, but two years later Congress went much further and approved a permanent peacetime draft with the Selective Service Act. The National Military Establishment became the Department of Defense (DOD) in 1949—the same year that the North Atlantic Treaty Organization (NATO) was founded in Washington. Congress rounded out the new system with the creation of the National Security Agency (NSA) in 1952.

Collectively, these executive departments and agencies represented the culmination of Franklin Roosevelt's national security revolution. Through a significant enhancement of its powers, the federal government had promised to ensure the security of the American people even if there was no clear and present danger to threaten them. At heart, this new system was an attempt to turn uncertainty into risk, and in turn to institutionalize the management of risk for the United States in the world and formalize forward planning as the best form of risk management. It was a New Deal for the world, certainly—not just in the overall objective, but in method. Thus the NSC, CIA, JCS, OSD, NSRB, USAF, DOD, NATO, and NSA, alongside partner institutions like the IMF, GATT, UN, and Atomic Energy Commission (AEC, established in 1946), were the last of the New Deal's alphabet agencies.

Ironically, the passage of the New Deal for the world marked the peak of the New Deal at home. At this point, domestic social welfare lost much of its momentum, and the original bond between social security and national security began to crack. Truman's attempt to extend the New Deal, a set of social welfare programs he called the Fair Deal that included the provisions for universal health care lacking in Roosevelt's Social Security Act, got nowhere, even as the institutionalization of the national security state was mostly complete by 1947. Yet it was precisely the escalation of national security that stunted the growth of social security. Social security, and all it represented, was not dead, but it now switched places with national security as the nation's top priority and took a back seat when it came time to disburse federal funds. Much of this had to do with the postwar red scare. As with the first red scare after the Great War and Japanese internment during World War II, the perceived requirements of national defense led to a domestic purge of those who were suspected of aiding and abetting a hostile foreign power. In that moment of the early Cold War, the pressures of McCarthyism were so intense that they forever warped the government's mandate to protect the American people, bending it in unforeseen ways toward military defense and away from domestic welfare. Once inseparably entwined, social security and national security had begun to go their separate ways.

As consequential as the National Security Act was, it did not mark a new departure or start a new era in US foreign policy or grand strategy. It was instead the culmination of a longer process that had begun a decade before. Thus the scholars who have historicized "national security" and dated its origins to the early Cold War, even to the National Security Act itself, have begun the story at its end. The expansive doctrine of threat perception known as "national security" crystallized in the National Security Act, as well as in the other momentous policies of the first six months of 1947, but it solidified in a form initially molded, imperfectly, by Woodrow Wilson, and then perfected by Franklin Roosevelt. The Cold War was thus a catalyst, not a cause, for the national security state. While it's true that a permanent peacetime national security state was a result of the Cold War, the ideas and perceptions that made it possible coalesced and took shape in the 1930s.[81] That shape has remained more or less intact since 1947.

EPILOGUE

SECURITY NATION

WHEN FRANKLIN ROOSEVELT declared, in 1939, that Americans "must prepare to defend, not their homes alone, but the tenets of faith and humanity on which their churches, their governments and their very civilization are founded," it was a revolutionary new concept of defense. But a little over a decade later, when Dwight Eisenhower stated, as a simple matter of fact, that "the purpose of America is to defend a way of life rather than merely to defend property, homes, or lives," he was paraphrasing a now-conventional wisdom.[1] When Roosevelt told Americans, in 1944, that "our national security does not end at our borders," he was clarifying a bracingly new idea that was only just beginning to take hold in political culture. Only eighteen months later, in early 1946, military officials could reflexively assume "that the defense of a nation . . . must begin beyond its frontiers."[2] Today, when we take these assertions of basic security requirements as natural, we forget the suddenness with which they emerged and the speed with which they were accepted.

When Harry Truman completed Franklin Roosevelt's national security revolution, US national security became like the ever-expanding universe. Expansion created momentum for further expansion as new spheres of national security created yet more spheres, in a process that kept replicating itself through the Cold War and beyond. After 1945, US officials deemed western Europe and Japan to be essential to safeguarding American national security. Korea lay outside these essential spheres of security. But when Korean communist forces crossed the 38th parallel into the southern half of the peninsula, Truman instantly recognized the inescapable logic that boxed him in: if Japan was essential to the United States, and Korea was essential to Japan, then Korea was essential to the United States.[3] As a result, as in 1943 or 1944, US troops were once again fighting in faraway places they had never heard of, let alone been able to place on a map, for the intuitive reason that the enemy was bent on the destruction of the American way of life, and that if Americans didn't fight them in Korea, they'd end up fighting them in Pleasant Valley, Idaho, or Bedford Falls, New York.

This logic led, also inescapably, to security theories that derived directly from the relatively new sciences of geopolitics and international relations and which, in turn, gave further momentum to the expansion of US security requirements. One was credibility, another deterrence.[4] The most notorious version was probably the domino theory, first articulated by Dwight Eisenhower in 1954. When a reporter asked the president, "would you mind commenting on the strategic importance of Indochina to the free world? I think there has been, across the country, some lack of understanding on just what it means to us," Eisenhower replied that if Vietnam fell to communism, it would set off a chain reaction leading to the fall of other countries and regions, denying the United States and its key allies, such as Japan, the strategic natural resources and territory vital to remain secure. A process triggered in Indochina would thus likely end in Australia or Japan—and, by implication, eventually America itself. "So," he concluded, "the possible consequences of the loss are just incalculable to the free world."[5]

It's surprising that Eisenhower was the first to use the specific metaphor of falling dominoes, for it was probably the most natural way of analogizing national security. It was precisely this domino logic that led Roosevelt to mount US opposition to German and Japanese expansionism—including in regions like Indochina. In 1940–1941, when internationalists like Henry Luce and incredulous anti-interventionists argued over whether the defense of the frontier outpost of Dong Dang was a matter of US security, they were arguing over the domino theory, and in turn over the logic of national security itself. Luce won the argument, and the result has reverberated ever since.[6] "What would they have us abandon to the enemy?" a Navy admiral asks a reluctant pilot who's sent on a difficult mission in James A. Michener's Korean War novel *The Bridges at Toko-Ri*. "Korea? Then Japan and the Philippines? Sooner or later Hawaii?" Unlike Eisenhower's warning, but much like Homer Lea's, this domino theory did not stop in the Pacific: "Maybe California, Colorado. Perhaps we'd stabilize at the Mississippi."[7]

Like something from astrophysics, the domino theory had no theoretical end. Because US interests had a global scope, American security requirements were also global. If communism was everywhere, then the United States had to be everywhere. This defined both the means and ends of US grand strategy in the Cold War and beyond. This in turn required global military preparedness, which Eisenhower's secretary of state, John Foster Dulles, described to a congressional committee as "insurance against aggression." By 1953, when Dulles spoke to Congress, the American presence was found all over the world, often in regions that had never before been in the US sphere of influence. "That is not yet the case everywhere," Dulles cautioned. "But where it is the case, there is more security." This global strategy was necessary because the threat Americans faced was thought to be limitless. "When any nation falls a victim to Soviet aggression," Dulles explained, "the Soviet Union becomes stronger, and United States safety is lessened. It is as simple as A, B, C. . . . If Soviet communism is permitted to gobble up other parts of the world one by one, the day will come when the Soviet world will be so powerful that no corner of the world will be safe, including our corner."[8]

Dulles's strategy, described by the historian Richard Immerman as an "Empire of Security," was no different than Roosevelt's arguments about German and Japanese aggression.[9] As Exhibit A, Dulles may as well have displayed the maps of how the enemy would invade America from Frank Capra's *Why We Fight*.

Dulles's statecraft was in keeping with the nightmare visions of Roosevelt and Capra that the enemy could invade American shores. Cold War leaders constantly warned Americans that the fighting might be happening elsewhere for now, but the United States was next. That was all the more believable in the atomic age, particularly when the Soviet Union became a nuclear power in 1949, which is when free security's slow death finally reached its end.[10] Truman was especially blunt: humanity would "go back to the Dark Ages if we have another world war," he said during the conflict in Korea. "And if a third world war should come, we will not be in the position that we have been in the other two. We will be a battlefront. We can look forward to destruction here, just as the other countries in the Second World War."[11] When Soviet leader Nikita Khrushchev publicly blustered that he could rain missiles down on the United States, he privately boasted that "main street Americans have begun to shake from fear for the first time in their lives."[12] He wasn't wrong: in the late 1950s and early 1960s, Americans went on a civil-defense building spree, hoping to survive a nuclear apocalypse by digging out bomb shelters in their backyards and basements.[13]

———

BUT AMERICAN PURPOSE in the Cold War wasn't entirely reactive. If the pursuit of security meant, as the State Department's Walt Rostow put it in 1962, that the United States needed "to create the kind of world environment it desires," then Americans couldn't wait for threats to emerge.[14] US officials had to act preemptively to manage risk—as Dulles had put it, just like an insurance policy. This strategic concept was also part of the New Deal inheritance. "No old defense is so strong that it requires no further strengthening and no attack is so unlikely or impossible that it may be ignored," Roosevelt had warned the American people in the spring of 1940, when calling on Congress to fund the massive rearmament program. "The clear fact is that the American people must recast their thinking about national protection."[15] But this, too, created the problem of open-ended commitments. In 1969, as Americans were reeling from the catastrophe in Vietnam, Eugene Rostow, Walt's older brother who had also served in the State Department, was interviewed by the *New Yorker*'s William Whitworth. Unchastened, the elder Rostow defended the war as necessary to maintain a global balance of power with communism. Whitworth found this unconvincing, even troubling: "We have the balance in order to deal with the problem, and we have to deal with the problem in order to preserve the balance. The theory is eating its own tail."[16]

In winning their argument with the skeptics of internationalism, then, Roosevelt, Luce, Truman, and Dulles created a whole new set of problems. One might be called the security paradox: the pursuit of greater security merely leads to greater insecurity. Territorial expansion, either through outright conquest or the installation of client regimes, has long been a way for states to ensure their own security. But the American security paradox was different, as different as the extraterritorial American imperium itself. The logic chain of the domino theory, indeed of national security itself, had nothing to limit it. Thus the expansion of security didn't extend the periphery, but expanded the center by proliferating it into many peripheries. In 1961, when an American war in Vietnam was still only a terrible prospect, a reporter asked Secretary of State Dean Rusk the same question Eisenhower had been posed in 1954: why should the United States risk "becoming bogged down in peripheral war such as in the jungles of southeast Asia"? "Because," Rusk patiently explained, "if you don't pay attention to the periphery, the periphery changes. And the first thing you know the periphery is the center. I mean, peace and security are world-wide."[17] John F. Kennedy put it in more specific geographical terms. Britain's defensive frontier traditionally lay along the Rhine, Kennedy noted, but "American frontiers are on the Rhine and the Mekong and Tigres and the Euphrates and the Amazon. There is no place in the world that is not of concern to all of us."[18] This logic may have helped expand American security, but it also expanded American vulnerabilities, in turn generating new fears for American national security and the need for further expansion. US national security, in other words, became its own zero-sum game.[19]

As Johnson, Rostow, and Rusk discovered, this logic led them straight from the Rhine to the Mekong (the Tigris and Euphrates would come a half-century later). The United States went to war in Vietnam for many reasons, but most important was the need to uphold America's credibility that it would enforce containment as a matter of national security. The fight this time happened to be in Vietnam, but it could be any-where; and if Americans ignored it, thinking they were secure, it would eventually come to the United States. This globally stretched logic made intuitive sense to Kennedy and Johnson, who as young men had both seen combat in the remotest reaches of the south Pacific.[20] "The battle against Communism must be joined in Southeast Asia with strength and determination . . . or the United States, inevitably, must surrender the Pacific and take up our defenses on our own shores," then Vice President Johnson told John F. Kennedy, invoking the specter of the garrison state, in 1961. "The basic decision in Southeast Asia is here. We must decide whether to help these countries to the best of our ability or throw in the towel in the area and pull back our defenses to San Francisco and [a] 'For-tress America' concept."[21] Or as Johnson, now president, warned National Security Adviser McGeorge Bundy during the critical period of escalation in 1964–1965, "if you start running from the Communists, they may just chase you right into your own kitchen."[22] Even after he had made the "ba-sic decision" to go to war, Johnson's logic held: "It is better to do it there," he told a crowd of US troops girding for deployment to South Vietnam, "than it is in Honolulu."[23] And his faith in Roosevelt's national security revolution didn't fade in retirement, even though he'd been forced from office by the very war that revolution had produced. The "minute we look soft, the would-be aggressors will go wild," he told his former aide and biographer Doris Kearns. "We'll lose all of Asia and then Europe and we'll be an island all by ourselves." It was only when Americans had recognized "that Hitler could take over America" that they realized they could only protect US security by being a guarantor of international security.[24]

Johnson's error was to lead the nation's quest for security down a dead end in Vietnam. Undersecretary of State George Ball, a dovish critic inside the Johnson administration, observed that in pursuing containment in Southeast Asia to uphold US credibility for strength, Johnson was undermining America's credibility for good judgment.[25] It may never have mattered, though, had the war not gone so badly. When a gung-ho solider asked Michael Herr, a skeptical journalist who covered the war for *Esquire* magazine, "Would you rather fight them here or in Pasadena?" Herr thought to himself, "*Maybe we could beat them in Pasadena.*"[26] America's national security logic made just as little sense from the Vietnamese perspective. "We did not attack your country," communist leaders replied when an American asked them, long after the war was over, why they had fought. "You came to our country."[27]

Not surprisingly, Franklin Roosevelt was Lyndon Johnson's political role model. LBJ got his start in politics as a New Dealer, working for Harry Hopkins's Works Progress Administration as head of the WPA's National Youth Administration, before winning election to Congress as a New Deal Democrat in 1937. When he became president himself, he promised to enact a wide range of ambitiously progressive programs—on health, education, housing, immigration, and, most famously, civil rights—he collectively labeled the Great Society. "It is a Society where no child will go unfed, and no youngster will go unschooled. Where no man who wants work will fail to find it," he declared when first unveiling the idea to an audience in Ohio. "Where peace and security is common among neighbors and possible among nations. This is the world that waits for you. Reach out for it now."[28] Johnson explicitly couched the Great Society as an extension of the New Deal. "If you will give us the mandate," he vowed at a rally during the 1964 campaign, "we will go back to that Capital City on the Potomac and we will take the programs that were started by Franklin Delano Roosevelt and carried on by Harry S. Truman . . . and we will build a greater America."[29] By electing him, Johnson promised at a campaign stop in Chicago, Americans would "pledge ourselves to democracy's greatest tradition, the New Freedom of Wilson, the New Deal of Roosevelt, the Fair Deal of Harry S. Truman."[30]

It was entirely fitting for Johnson to include himself in this gallery of liberal heroes, although part of the reason why was not yet apparent in 1964. Wilson, Roosevelt, Truman, and Johnson were not just all liberal Democrats, and not just architects of the most ambitious reform programs in American history: they were also the major war presidents of the twentieth century. That's no coincidence. All of them saw their role first and foremost as the executor of a social contract that provided a baseline of security for the American people. Wilson, as this book has shown, was both part of this tradition yet also outside it, for he began a revolution in security that fizzled out soon after he launched it. But once Roosevelt took up the Wilsonian mantle and expanded upon it, he permanently changed the trajectory of security at home and, especially, abroad.

While fellow liberal Democrats like Truman and Johnson followed in Roosevelt's wake, conservative Republicans like Herbert Hoover and Dwight Eisenhower, instinctively cautious about big government, large public expenditures, and foreign wars of abstract beginnings and uncertain endings, took a different course. As president, both Hoover (in Manchuria) and Eisenhower (in Indochina and the Middle East) had been pushed to fight but chose not to. Eisenhower even argued the very same year he invoked the domino theory, "I just don't believe you can buy 100 percent security in every little corner of the world where someone else wants to start trouble."[31] Such skepticism became especially pronounced further to the right. "It does not follow," said Senator Robert A. Taft, the unofficial spokesman of hard-edged conservatism, "that because we desire the freedom of every country in the world we must send an American land army to that country to defend it. If we commit ourselves to more than we can carry out, we weaken the whole nation."[32] Like Hoover, Taft also bitterly opposed the New Deal and Fair Deal, and gave his name to the legislation that weakened one of the New Deal's signature achievements, the Wagner Act that fully legalized trade unions.

If the disaster in Vietnam saw the end of Lyndon Johnson's political career, it did not mark the end of the national security revolution. But Vietnam did fundamentally change things, scrambling ideological convictions and partisan loyalties much as the civil rights revolution reversed political identities on race. On matters of security, in both foreign policy and domestic politics, Democrats and Republicans switched places—not completely, but enough to completely unsettle the existing order. There was, Mary Dudziak has shown, a brief open window when national security created space for real change in American race relations, but that window closed as Vietnam and civil rights seemed to fail alongside each other in the mid-1960s, culminating in the burning twin cities of Detroit in 1967 and Saigon in 1968.[33] Johnson tried to rescue himself by promising, as Roosevelt had done three decades before, internal security as well as national security. "No right is more elemental to our society than the right to personal security and no right needs more urgent protection," he proclaimed, although his topic wasn't social welfare or minority civil rights, but crime. That he delivered these remarks on bolstering law enforcement on Monday, March 8, 1965—the day in between the first two aborted marches from Selma to Montgomery, the first of which was known as Bloody Sunday for a brutal police attack on peaceful, unarmed activists—indicated the nation's direction of travel.[34] As Elizabeth Hinton has documented, to achieve socioeconomic reform, liberalism compromised itself from within, just as it had during the New Deal, by promising to ensure personal security against domestic enemies of criminals as well as national security against foreign enemies. Asian communists were not the only ones posing a security problem, Johnson told a delegation of law enforcement officials in 1966: "We are today fighting a war within our own boundaries."[35]

This was nearly the undoing of liberalism, as the Democratic Party fractured and Republicans picked up the pieces. The war in Vietnam took a toll on domestic reform as well, and Martin Luther King was exactly right when he blamed the war for destroying the Great Society.[36] Liberals and progressives increasingly began to see social security and national security not as mutually constitutive but contradictory. Conservatives moved along the same path but in the opposite direction, embracing the national security state with unprecedented fervor while simultaneously trying to topple the social security state the New Deal and Great Society had built.

———

AFTER THE NATION had recovered from its humiliation in Vietnam, Americans reinforced their commitment to ensuring freedom elsewhere so as to protect it at home. In fact, post-Vietnam presidents deepened the reciprocal relationships between security and values and the foreign and the domestic. "As we meet tonight," Jimmy Carter declared at the height of the Iran hostage crisis and the Soviet invasion of Afghanistan, "it has never been more clear that the state of our Union depends on the state of the world. And tonight, as throughout our own generation, freedom and peace in the world depend on the state of our Union."[37] In 2005, in the midst of another crisis in the Middle East that tested Americans' resolve as well as US power, George W. Bush used his second inaugural address to proclaim, "The survival of liberty in our land increasingly depends on the success of liberty in other lands. . . . America's vital interests and our deepest beliefs are now one."[38]

This totalistic vision of security was reflected in domestic society, as well. Not long after its inception, leaders figured out that they could build support for just about any initiative as long as they described it as vital for national security. Despite his doubts, Eisenhower did not follow the example of his fellow Republicans Hoover and Taft and attack the New Deal. He instead built support for infrastructure projects he valued, such as the Saint Lawrence Seaway and the Interstate Highway System, by tethering them to the requirements of national security.[39] On the same principle, the Pentagon became one of the world's leading centers of technological innovation, not only by conducting its own research and development but by partnering with universities and corporations or simply underwriting research in the private sector.[40]

Eisenhower may have lamented this "military-industrial complex" as he left office, but little could be done to slow, let alone halt, its growth.[41] The expansion of the national security state in fact continued, unabated by disasters like Vietnam—even though some Pentagon officials soon recanted their faith in national security and bloated defense spending and called for the demilitarization of US foreign policy.[42] And with it grew the concentration of executive war powers, with the presidency eclipsing Congress to the point of irrelevance on most matters of national security, military defense, and foreign policy. The urgent demands of protecting the nation from any and all manner of threats gave the president tremendous latitude in foreign affairs. Through this broadening latitude Arthur Schlesinger traced the emergence of an "imperial presidency" that continued gaining power at the expense of other branches despite changing times. "National security," Schlesinger argued, "is the contemporary version of Lockean prerogative" justifying the suspension of normal laws restraining executive power.[43] The once-distinct lines between peacetime and wartime blurred.[44] The national security revolution thus created a permanent state of emergency, to the point that the emergency's exceptional nature became the norm. Scholars of executive war powers agree that, whatever his intentions, it all began with Franklin Roosevelt.[45]

The security preoccupation crept into many other facets of American society, and not all of them as salubrious as easier shipping through the beautiful Thousand Islands. The embedding of national security in the national political culture led to a creeping militarization of society—perhaps not as dire as Harold Lasswell's "garrison state" or LBJ's "Fortress America," but something altogether different in American history.[46] Even Lasswell could get carried away, calling in 1950 for Congress to establish an annual national holiday, "National Security Day," so that Americans could celebrate what they were defending and remind themselves of why they were in a state of permanent readiness, brandishing George Kennan's "all measures short of war."[47]

Other domestic products of the national security revolution were much more pernicious. The carceral state targeted African Americans at wildly disproportionate rates, while at the same time enormous annual defense budgets and frequent wars triggered a flow of surplus weapons and other military hardware to police departments and prisons in the United States, thereby militarizing domestic law enforcement as counterinsurgency and, later, counterterrorism.[48] Highly racialized fears of crime coupled with often-racialized fears of foreign enemies turned the rapidly suburbanizing nation into a different kind of fortress America—one that did battle with itself in moral panics like the federal government's "war on drugs."[49] Domestic surveillance and persecution of alleged subversives, which quickly came to include people who were demonstrably not national security risks (such as civil rights activists, labor organizers, immigrant groups, and antiwar protestors), were direct products of Roosevelt's security revolution.[50] The classification of state secrets correspondingly metastasized—to the extent that, by 2022, the federal government literally did not know how many top-secret documents were out there—and, as a result, the twin phenomena of leaking and whistleblowing grew, too.[51]

National security made people do strange things, like break in to someone's psychiatrist's office in search of embarrassing information—as happened to Daniel Ellsberg, the former Pentagon official turned whistleblower who, having turned against the Vietnam War, leaked the Pentagon Papers in 1971. The burglar, Egil Krogh, received instructions from the White House that Ellsberg was a national security threat and had to be stopped. Krogh had some misgivings about his assignment, but the "key is the effect that the term 'national security' had on my judgment. The very words served to block critical analysis."[52] Reflecting on Vietnam in retirement, Lyndon Johnson might have thought the same thing.

But like the potential death of the ever-expanding universe, there was always a chance that the constant creation of new security interests would lead the whole system to collapse upon itself. This is what happened when the United States went to war in Vietnam, and again in Iraq in 2003. Instead of evaluating the severity of a threat, assessing the risks, and then acting or perhaps waiting to see what happened, national security officials sometimes felt they needed to act preemptively.[53] They had an incentive to react to a potential threat, no matter how remote, as if it were imminent: they had information the public lacked, they were the ones who could identify dangerous threats from obscure but hostile sources, and they were the ones who would suffer the consequences if they let a threat slip through. Edward Mead Earle once noted that, in national security strategy, "A wise nation does not abandon the known and the certain for the unknown and the uncertain."[54] Strategists who came after Earle put his principle to the test. In late 1989, in the heady days after the fall of the Berlin Wall, Undersecretary of Defense Paul Wolfowitz cautioned against large cuts to the Pentagon's budget, terming US military power "a prudent hedge against uncertainties."[55] Later, terrified but also emboldened by 9/11, George W. Bush's vice president referred to this same principle in more extreme terms as "the one percent doctrine": for Dick Cheney, a threat with only a one percent chance of harming the United States was best treated as a total certainty.[56] Around the same time, Under Secretary of Defense Douglas Feith called it "anticipatory self-defense."[57] In a crisis atmosphere, such caution is very human.[58] But as Bush, Cheney, Wolfowitz, and Feith found out, their quest for total security could create new problems of its own.

———

DESPITE ALL THE WARNINGS issued by Truman, Kennedy, Johnson, and others that fighting could one day reach American shores, the United States did not suffer a major attack from a foreign enemy until September 11, 2001. The 9/11 attacks caused one of the most profound, disorienting shocks to the nation in its entire history, not least in how Americans articulated it. Leaders struggled to arrive at a terminology to categorize the attacks, even though, strictly speaking, they already had the language to do so:

more than anything else, the 9/11 attacks violated the security of the nation. Yet they weren't labeled as such because, until that point, "the security of the nation" referred to physical attacks against the sovereign United States in the abstract. It summoned up remote theoretical possibilities that would happen only if Americans let their guard down elsewhere in the world. Seeking to marginalize so-called isolationists, Walter Lippmann once referred to the "continental homeland" as if it were separate from the nation that security policy was designed to protect; Henry Luce did something similar in his "American Century" article by dismissing the "defense of our homeland" as the pertinent issue. The real action, Lippmann and Luce implied, happened elsewhere.[59] At the dawn of the Cold War, when containment was being implemented and Americans started worrying about domestic communist subversion, officials had to resort to awkward formulations like "internal national security"—or, in J. Edgar Hoover's words, "the internal security of this nation"—to draw a distinction between the two types of threat.[60]

After 9/11, George W. Bush started using a new phrase that no other president before him had uttered, and "homeland security" quickly became the preferred technical description for the nation's plight in the age of terror.[61] In commissioning a post-9/11 "National Strategy for Homeland Security," Bush wanted answers to questions he himself had inadvertently raised: "What is 'homeland security' and what missions does it entail? What do we seek to accomplish, and what are the most important goals of homeland security?" While he waited, he reassured Americans that "We will prevail" against anyone who threatened not just US territory but "our way of life."[62]

Some answers came from the new Office of Homeland Security, set up in the weeks after 9/11 and initially located within the White House, just as the National Security Council staff had been in 1947. "Our Nation learned a terrible lesson," read one line from the OHS report, and it was that "American soil is not immune to evil or cold-blooded enemies capable of mass murder," Americans were on the cusp of a "long struggle to protect our Nation," not unlike the Cold War except in one crucial respect: this time the battleground was the United States. The report then defined homeland security with a precision that had eluded any official attempt to codify national security: "Homeland security is a concerted national effort to prevent terrorist attacks within the United States, reduce America's vulnerability to terrorism, and minimize the damage and recover from attacks that do occur." Seeing terrorism in this light reinforced the idea, which framed much of the initial reaction to 9/11 and certainly the official response, that al Qaeda struck at the United States for what it was and the values it stood for, not what it did in the world.[63]

As Amy Kaplan has observed, "homeland security" seemed a perfect fit for the "war of terror" because it connotes a sense of embattled belonging, of being under siege in one's own home, and of sharply demarcating between insiders who belong and outsiders who do not. And unlike "national security," which in the World War II era was new in content as well as form, homeland security echoed older, darker currents of American history. It became the preferred term of art for government officials, and it provided the name of a sprawling new government institution, the Department of Homeland Security (DHS). Yet after 9/11, "homeland security" never caught in the broader political culture or popular imagination like "national security."[64]

The paradox of having two separate government agencies pursuing both national security *and* homeland security deepened when the *New York Times* reported in 2017 that DHS "is increasingly going global."[65] But this oxymoron was actually not a new phenomenon either—it, too, started during the New Deal. When he was Roosevelt's secretary of the interior, Harold Ickes undertook a similar transformation of a previously insular government institution. (This was, of course, the same Ickes who also headed the PWA and was on stage with the president when he delivered the "quarantine" speech in Chicago in 1937.) Operating under the guise of national security, Ickes pushed the Department of the Interior outward, in search of strategic resources to help the United States and its Allies mobilize for war. At first this meant securing raw materials from America's colonial territories, from Alaska to the Philippines, but from there it was an easy step to branch out to other parts of the world. In expanding the range of his department, Ickes created a titular paradox, aptly called by the historian Megan Black the "global interior."[66] As the 9/11 Commission's report put it, in a way Ickes would have surely appreciated, "the American homeland is the planet."[67]

———

JUST AS ROOSEVELT and Ickes responded to a changing world by identifying, and responding to, new threats to the nation's security, observers over the last several decades have pointed to new sources of danger and called for these dangers to be treated as national security threats. "We know that food security is national security," as one of the supporters of congressional legislation known as the Food Security is National Security Act put it.[68] Some called on Congress to regulate social media as a national security issue.[69] And one of the leading voices for action on climate change (although also one of the world's biggest sources of emissions) was the US national security establishment.[70]

In perceiving the outlines of these complex newer problems in the dim twilight of the Cold War, nobody was as visionary as Jessica Tuchman Mathews. Perhaps drawing inspiration from the lessons about strategic shortsightedness and miscalculation chronicled by her mother, the celebrated historian Barbara Tuchman, in the spring of 1989 Mathews published an article, "Redefining Security," in *Foreign Affairs* that was every bit as seminal as Kennan's "X" article on containment four decades before. Mathews warned that human-caused environmental decline was "altering the basic physiology of the planet" that, if "left unchecked," would have "irreversible" consequences. Population growth, the degradation of ostensibly renewable resources like fisheries and forests, soil erosion, and unequal land ownership were combining to generate an unprecedented crisis. That would be bad enough, but the worst problem of all was global warming from spiraling carbon emissions. Climate change, Mathews explained to an audience that had likely never come upon the problem before, meant that "the planet is warmed *un*naturally." It would inevitably lead to unpredictable and extreme weather and thus crop failure, rising sea levels, social dislocation, mass migration, and war. But environmental decline was a problem even without the outbreak of armed conflict, for without a properly functioning environment life on earth would on its own eventually become unsustainable. The crisis demanded "a sizable shift in priorities" not unlike the epochal strategic shift Roosevelt and Truman brought about during and after World War II. Once again, "the need for a new diplomacy," even if it might "encroach upon what we now think of as the prerogatives of national governments," was acute. Mathews instead called for genuinely collective security, not the partial kind that NATO practiced, but a new system that transcended the nation-state and was multilateral, equitable, and global. "The 1990s," she declared, "will demand a redefinition of what constitutes national security."[71]

Mathews foresaw, with remarkable prescience, the crisis now confronting Americans and the world. It's a totally new crisis, from a confluence of new challenges, that will require a similarly novel way of perceiving and responding to them. These challenges, nonmilitary in nature—having to do with gender, climate change, environmental degradation, pandemics, famine, migration, inequality, and human rights—fell under a new category of "human security" that emerged in the late 1990s from what Mathews identified as "a growing sense that individuals' security may not in fact reliably derive from their nation's security."[72]

This was new thinking, indeed. But following it through will require an ontological change even more profound and consequential than the shift Roosevelt started in 1937. And considering how long it's been since Americans have had to reconceptualize their threat perception, it won't be easy. To do so, there won't be very much cultural or political capital to use, at least not from living memory, as no one is left who remembers what national defense was like before national security. It's difficult to re-think something that is now part of the body politic's basic instinct.

The end of the Cold War led experts to claim that "the United States is required to *think* again" about its national security.[73] Similarly, after 9/11, Americans widely began to feel that they lived in "a newly security-conscious world" demanding multiple "redefinitions" of national security.[74] Those diagnoses may have made sense at the time but they've left few traces, because such efforts at rethinking and redefining merely led back to the same places they started. People in every era since World War II have perceived themselves to be living in a time of unparalleled fear and danger, whether that danger comes from Japanese saboteurs within, communists with nuclear missiles, or terrorists with suicide bombs. The duck-and-cover drills and civil-defense programs of the Cold War were propelled by the same mindset as the domestic counterterrorism operations of more recent decades. Every era seems to require a strategic rethink or geopolitical reset, yet the foundations of American threat perception have remained consistent since the late 1930s: threats can be distant and remote but they can also one day be clear and present, so it's always better to assume the latter; if threats aren't addressed preemptively, they will one day wreak damage on the United States; threats are not just physical but ideological and cultural, in both method and substance; protecting the American way of life is just as vital as protecting territory. This basic matrix of threat perception has become broader and more sophisticated since the New Deal era, and it's become deeply, perhaps irrevocably, embedded within American government and society. But it's still the same basic matrix.

Perhaps the answer lies in completely casting off "national security" altogether, though that seems unlikely; it's just too tightly woven into the fabric of American society. More likely to succeed are efforts to thoroughly rebrand "national security" in the way Mathews called for in 1989. No less a figure than Melvyn Leffler, the US diplomatic historian and key innovator of the concept of "national security," certainly thinks so. In 2021, Leffler called for a "wholesale rethinking" by which US national security strategy would "rearrange its priorities and spend more money on the most dire and most likely threats" emanating from the environment, disease, and technology.[75] This is a courageous, compelling call to a new kind of arms. But it will take another politician with Roosevelt's gifts to make it work.

Whoever it is will also have to contend with renewed momentum in the opposite direction. Responding to the resurgence of traditional great-power rivalries and return of geopolitical tensions, other countries have even adopted the national security terminology and mindset: Britain set up its own National Security Council, headed by a National Security Adviser, in 2010, joining Argentina, Canada, India, Israel, Japan, New Zealand, Norway, and other countries.[76] Under Xi Jinping, China has been especially preoccupied with national security, establishing the Central National Security Commission in 2013 and imposing a "national security law" on Hong Kong in 2020. The purpose is to officially codify, and broadly popularize, what Xi calls the "comprehensive national security concept" for the party, the state, communist ideology, and the nation so that Beijing can help "the seeds of national security to take root and sprout."[77] It's unclear whether Xi or other Chinese leaders appreciate the irony of their adopting what was once, by invention and tradition, a uniquely American term.

While some American commentators feel that old conventions make no sense in the recent, turbulent era of public-health emergencies and clashing populisms on the far-left and far-right, national security identities seem as entrenched as ever.[78] Indeed, they seem to be coming full circle. In 2023, national security hawks in Congress declared China "an existential threat to our nation" in much the same way their congressional forebears demonized the Soviet Union.[79] Old divisions over national security are also reopening. Conservative Republicans are once again questioning the need for an internationalist foreign policy in faraway places. When justifying his 2019 decision to withdraw US troops from Syria, Donald Trump puzzled why Americans should care when "we are 7,000 miles away."[80] Later, he wondered why Taiwan actually mattered to US national security when it was "9,500 miles away."[81] During the fractious congressional debate over whether to continue sending aid to Ukraine, Republicans argued that while there was "concern about the safety, security and sovereignty of Ukraine . . . the American people have those same concerns about our own domestic sovereignty and our safety and our security."[82] Ron DeSantis, who sought his party's presidential nomination in 2024, expressed the same kind of reaction to Bush's second inaugural address in 2005. Echoing anti-interventionist feelings in 1941 about the unimportance of an obscure outpost like Dong Dang, DeSantis wrote "I remember being stunned" in a campaign autobiography. "Does the survival of American liberty depend on whether liberty succeeds in Djibouti?"[83]

J. D. Vance, Trump's running mate in the 2024 election, made a similar point during the campaign. Before going to law school, Vance had joined the Marines and was deployed to Iraq. But he became a fierce critic of George W. Bush's forever wars in the Middle East and the underlying theories of limitless national security that propelled them, and later, as a US senator, he opposed sending aid to Ukraine. In accepting the Republican nomination for vice president, Vance said that patriotic Americans "love this country not only because it's a good idea, but because in their bones they know that this is their home, and it will be their children's home, and they would die fighting to protect it." Ohio and Kentucky were home; the Middle East and Ukraine were not. Vance promised that he and Trump would "send our kids to war only when we must," and the only thing that qualified was the defense of the homeland. To Vance, the principles that made America great, such as democracy and religious freedom, were worth protecting, but only if they were under threat at home. "People will not fight for abstractions," he declared in a speech that condemned the wars in Iraq and Afghanistan as misguided crusades, "but they will fight for their home."[84]

As if moving in sync in the opposite direction, Joe Biden, a self-styled latter-day New Dealer invoking FDR as his political hero, reclaimed the national security tradition for liberal Democrats, linking pro-labor, social-welfare policies at home with a robust liberal internationalism abroad. After the chaos of the Trump presidency, the Biden administration moved swiftly to reinstate the old verities. National Security Advisor Jake Sullivan renewed the Rooseveltian social/national security dyad with particular vigor in a major speech at the Brookings Institution.[85] In a symbolic gesture, Biden in one of his first acts as president made a point of officially "renewing" the NSC system and promising the "revitalization of our national security and foreign policy institutions."[86] And he explained his resolute opposition to Russia's 2022 invasion of Ukraine in terms— "an unusual and extraordinary threat to the national security"—that echoed Roosevelt on China and Poland and Truman on Korea and Germany.[87] Yet Biden also heeded warnings by analysts such as Jessica Mathews about new existential threats. "The world is changing, and it's changing rapidly," he said in explaining why his administration's National Security Strategy paid so much attention to climate, health, and food issues. "And we have to gain control of our own destiny within that change."[88] Yet more conventional crises, warfare in eastern Europe and the Middle East, have bedeviled Biden's national security strategy.

————

ROBERT MCNAMARA KNEW these dilemmas, and the disasters they can lead to, better than most. As secretary of defense under both Kennedy and Johnson from 1961 to 1968, McNamara was one of the main architects of the war in Vietnam, so much so that many called it "McNamara's war." Yet after harboring private doubts as early as 1963—not just about the war's tactics, but its very purpose—he started to raise troubling questions, in 1966, to an audience he knew would get the word out. "We still tend to conceive of national security almost solely as a state of armed readiness, a vast, awesome arsenal of weaponry," he said in a speech to an annual convention of newspaper editors. "We still tend to assume that it is primarily this purely military ingredient that creates security. We are haunted by this concept of military hardware."[89]

After the strain of managing a war he no longer believed in led him nearly to a nervous breakdown, McNamara left the Pentagon in early 1968, at the height of the Tet Offensive. Both he and Johnson knew he was no longer the right person for the job. He then went to head the World Bank, where he turned a fairly moribund institution into a dynamo of international development. In the 1980s, McNamara poured his energies into campaigning for nuclear arms control, and hopefully elimination one day, before publishing a 1995 memoir about the war in Vietnam in which he admitted, for the first time publicly and so unambiguously, "we were wrong, terribly wrong. We owe it to future generations to explain why."[90]

A national conversion of this kind seems remote, which is alarming given that the world doesn't seem to be getting any safer. Security threats, however they're defined, exist, and sometimes they require a military response. But McNamara discovered the hard way what happens when a pursuit of national security becomes an obsession and armed force becomes a first resort rather than the last. This is a particular problem when the obsession prevents action against new threats requiring imaginative new responses. Franklin Roosevelt faced this problem in his day, and he was able to solve it, sometimes for better, sometimes for worse. Yet his very success trapped later generations of policymakers, confining them to national security goals and methods that didn't necessarily apply, let alone work, in later circumstances. Given the challenges we now face, not just from interstate warfare but from climate change and (potentially) artificial intelligence, breaking through these Rooseveltian constraints has itself become a national security crisis of the utmost urgency. The basic terms of national self-defense are long overdue for another reinvention.

NOTES

INTRODUCTION

1. See Alan Dawley, *Struggles for Justice: Social Responsibility and the Liberal State* (Cambridge, MA: Harvard University Press, 1991); David M. Kennedy, *Freedom from Fear: The American People in Depression and War, 1929–1945* (New York: Oxford University Press, 1999); Jennifer Klein, *For All These Rights: Business, Labor, and the Shaping of America's Public-Private Welfare State* (Princeton: Princeton University Press, 2003); Mariano-Florentino Cuéllar, *Governing Security: The Hidden Origins of American Security Agencies* (Stanford: Stanford University Press, 2013); and Aziz Rana, *The Two Faces of American Freedom* (Cambridge, MA: Harvard University Press, 2014).

2. Helena Rosenblatt, *The Lost History of Liberalism: From Ancient Rome to the Twenty-First Century* (Princeton: Princeton University Press, 2018), 260–264. For a genealogy of liberalism, see Duncan Bell, *Reordering the World: Essays on Liberalism and Empire* (Princeton: Princeton University Press, 2016), 62–90.

3. I first made this argument in Andrew Preston, "Monsters Everywhere: A Genealogy of National Security," *Diplomatic History* 38 (June 2014): 477–500, esp. 487–491. For a related argument, see Mark Neocleous, "From Social to National Security: On the Fabrication of Economic Order," *Security Dialogue* 37 (September 2006): 363–384. Peter Roady, *The Contest over National Security: FDR, Conservatives, and the Struggle to Claim the Most Powerful Phrase in American Politics* (Cambridge, MA: Harvard University Press, 2024), also intertwines socioeconomic security and national security, but, in contrast to my approach, sees the two as always mutually constitutive and coexisting from the very beginning of Roosevelt's presidency. This book, most notably in Chapter 4, argues instead that a domestic doctrine of social security was the wellspring of an international doctrine of national security

4. Franklin D. Roosevelt, Message to Congress on Appropriations for National Defense, July 10, 1940, *APP*, https://www.presidency.ucsb.edu/node/209802.

5. John Deutch, "The United States: The Making of National Security Policy," in *The Making of National Security Policy: Security Challenges of the 21st Century*, ed. Meir Elran, Owen Alterman, and Johannah Cornblatt (Tel Aviv: Institute for National Security Studies, 2011), 50.

6. Quoted in Robert Dallek, *Flawed Giant: Lyndon Johnson and His Times, 1961–1973* (New York: Oxford University Press, 1998), 154.

7. Edward Mead Earle, "Notes on the Term Strategy," *Naval War College Information Service for Officers* 2 (December 1949), 4; Earle, rough draft of "The Foundations of American Foreign Policy, 1939–1950," n.d., box 34, Edward Mead Earle Papers, Seeley G. Mudd Library, Princeton University.

8. Harold D. Lasswell, *National Security and Individual Freedom* (New York: McGraw-Hill, 1950), 51. Emphasis in original.

9. Arnold Wolfers, "The Pole of Power and the Pole of Indifference," *World Politics* 4 (October 1951): 39–63, 51.

10. Arnold Wolfers, "'National Security' as an Ambiguous Symbol," *Political Science Quarterly* 67 (December 1952): 481–502, 483, 490, 489.

11. Robert Endicott Osgood, *Ideals and Self-Interest in America's Foreign Relations: The Great Transformation of the Twentieth Century* (Chicago: University of Chicago Press, 1953), 5.

12. Morton Berkowitz and P. G. Bock, *American National Security: A Reader in Theory and Policy* (New York: Free Press, 1965), x. Emphasis in original.

13. Melvyn P. Leffler, *A Preponderance of Power: National Security, the Truman Administration, and the Cold War* (Stanford: Stanford University Press, 1992), 13.

14. Melvyn P. Leffler, "National Security," in *Safeguarding Democratic Capitalism: U.S. Foreign Policy and National Security, 1920–2015* (Princeton: Princeton University Press, 2017), 319–320, 324. This is the latest version of an essay that has been revised since first published in 1991.

15. Graham Allison and Gregory F. Treverton, "Introduction and Overview," in *Rethinking America's Security: Beyond Cold War to New World Order,* ed. Graham Allison and Gregory F. Treverton (New York: W. W. Norton, 1992), 16.

16. Quoted in Robert R. Bowie and Richard H. Immerman, *Waging Peace: How Eisenhower Shaped an Enduring Cold War Strategy* (New York: Oxford University Press, 1998), 44–45.

17. Melvyn P. Leffler, "National Security," in *Explaining the History of American Foreign Relations,* ed. Michael J. Hogan and Thomas G. Paterson, 2nd ed. (New York: Cambridge University Press, 2004), 133.

18. Quentin Skinner, "Language and Political Change," in *Political Innovation and Conceptual Change,* ed. Terence Ball, James Farr, and Russell L. Hanson (Cambridge: Cambridge University Press, 1989), 13.

19. On keywords, see Daniel T. Rodgers, *Contested Truths: Keywords in American Politics since Independence* (New York: Basic Books, 1987). For specific examples, see Geoffrey M. Hodgson, "Social Darwinism in Anglophone Academic Journals: A Contribution to the History of the Term," *Journal of Historical Sociology* 17 (December 2004): 428–463; Samuel Moyn, *The Last Utopia: Human Rights in History* (Cambridge, MA: Harvard University Press, 2010); Mary L. Dudziak, *War Time: An Idea, Its History, Its Consequences* (New York: Oxford University Press, 2012); David Armitage, "Is There a Pre-History of Globalisation?" in *Foundations of Modern International Thought* (Cambridge: Cambridge University Press, 2013), 33–45; and Matthew Specter, *The Atlantic Realists: Empire and International Political Thought Between Germany and the United States* (Stanford: Stanford University Press, 2022). My approach is probably closest to Timothy Mitchell's investigation of the concept of "the economy" and how this basic notion didn't become theory or practice until the interwar period. Before then, just as with "national security," the economy meant something very different than to what it does today. See Timothy Mitchell, "Fixing the Economy," *Cultural Studies* 12 (1998): 82–101; Mitchell, "Rethinking Economy," *Geoforum* 39 (May 2008): 1116–1121; and Mitchell, "Economists and the Economy in the Twentieth Century," in *The Politics of Method in the Human Sciences: Positivism and its Epistemological Others,* ed. George Steinmetz (Durham, NC: Duke University Press, 2005), 126–141.

20. Ronnie D. Lipschutz, "On Security," in *On Security*, ed. Ronnie D. Lipschutz (New York: Columbia University Press, 1995), 8; emphasis in original. For leading examples, see Barry Buzan, *People, States and Fear: An Agenda for International Security Studies in the Post-Cold War Era*, 2nd ed. (Boulder, CO: Lynne Rienner, 1991); Ole Waever, "Securitization and Desecuritization," in Lipschutz, *On Security*, 46–86; Barry Buzan, Ole Waever, and Jaap de Wilde, *Security: A New Framework for Analysis* (Boulder, CO: Lynne Rienner, 1998); and Thierry Balzacq, ed., *Securitization Theory: How Security Problems Emerge and Dissolve* (New York: Routledge, 2011). For other international relations approaches, see David Campbell, *Writing Security: United States Foreign Policy and the Politics of Identity* (Minneapolis: University of Minnesota Press, 1992); Peter J. Katzenstein, ed., *The Culture of National Security: Norms and Identity in World Politics* (New York: Columbia University Press, 1996); Paul A. Chilton, *Security Metaphors: Cold War Discourse from Containment to Common House* (New York: P. Lang, 1996), 22–24, 57–65; David A. Baldwin, "The Concept of Security," *Review of International Studies* 23 (January 1997): 5–26; and Ronald R. Krebs, *Narrative and the Making of US National Security* (New York: Cambridge University Press, 2015). For a thoughtful assessment of various types of "security," see David A. Welch, *Security: A Philosophical Investigation* (Cambridge: Cambridge University Press, 2022).

21. For "intermestic," see Campbell Craig and Fredrik Logevall, *America's Cold War: The Politics of Insecurity* (Cambridge, MA: Harvard University Press, 2009). See also Julian E. Zelizer, *Arsenal of Democracy: The Politics of National Security—From World War II to the War on Terrorism* (New York: Basic Books, 2010).

22. For example, Leffler's most penetrating insights into the conceptual nature of national security are made in reference to US foreign and military policies between 1945–1952; see Melvyn P. Leffler, "The American Conception of National Security and the Beginnings of the Cold War, 1945–1948," *American Historical Review* 89 (April 1984): 346–381, 347–349, 378–380; Leffler, *Preponderance*, 10–15, 159–164, 209–210, 309–311, 355–360, 488, 496–498; and Leffler, *The Specter of Communism: The United States and the Origins of the Cold War, 1917–1953* (New York: Hill and Wang, 1994), 128–130.

23. On this general dynamic, see R. B. J. Walker, *Inside / Outside: International Relations as Political Theory* (Cambridge: Cambridge University Press, 1992); and, specifically for national security, Emily S. Rosenberg, "Commentary: The Cold War and the Discourse of National Security," *Diplomatic History* 17 (April 1993): 277–284, 283; Robert Latham, *The Liberal Moment: Modernity, Security, and the Making of Postwar International Order* (New York: Columbia University Press, 1997), 92–95; and Neocleous, "From Social to National Security," 364.

24. Wolfers, "National Security," 483.

25. Daniel Larsen, "Before 'National Security': The Espionage Act of 1917 and the Concept of 'National Defense,'" *Harvard National Security Journal* 12 (2021), https://harvardnsj.org/2021/06/28/before-national-security-the-espionage-act-of-1917-and-the-concept-of-national-defense/. For an important study that locates the origins of "national security" in World War I, see Mark R. Shulman, "The Progressive Era Origins of the National Security Act," *Dickinson Law Review* 104 (2000): 289–330. My conclusions differ from Shulman's, however, in that I argue that World War I marked a false start in the evolution of national security, as will be apparent from Chapters 2 and 3.

26. For examples of timelessness, see Amos A. Jordan and William J. Taylor Jr., *American National Security: Policy and Process* (Baltimore: Johns Hopkins University Press, 1981); James Chace and Caleb Carr, *America Invulnerable: The Quest for Absolute Security from 1812 to Star Wars* (New York: Summit, 1988); Ernest R. May, "National Security in American History," in Allison and Treverton, *Rethinking America's Security*, 94–114; John Lewis Gaddis, *Surprise, Security, and the American Experience* (Cambridge, MA: Harvard

University Press, 2004); William O. Walker III, *National Security and Core Values in American History* (New York: Cambridge University Press, 2009); and Laura K. Donohue, "The Limits of National Security," *American Criminal Law Review* 48 (Fall 2011): 1573–1756.

27. See, for example, P. G. Bock and Morton Berkowitz, "The Emerging Field of National Security," *World Politics* 19 (October 1966): 122–136, esp. 122–124; Norman A. Graebner, ed., *The National Security: Its Theory and Practice, 1945–1960* (New York: Oxford University Press, 1986); Harold Hongju Koh, *The National Security Constitution: Sharing Power After the Iran-Contra Affair* (New Haven: Yale University Press, 1990); Rosenberg, "Commentary"; Michael J. Hogan, *A Cross of Iron: Harry S. Truman and the Origins of the National Security State* (New York: Cambridge University Press, 2000); Elisabeth Åsbrink, *1947: Where Now Begins* (New York: Other Press, 2017); Joseph Darda, *Empire of Defense: Race and the Cultural Politics of Permanent War* (Chicago: University of Chicago Press, 2019); and Daniel W. Drezner, "How Everything Became National Security: And National Security Became Everything," *Foreign Affairs* (September/October 2024): 122–135. Leffler is something of an exception: although most of his analysis of national security is rooted in the origins of the Cold War, he does link it to the World War II era in causally important ways. See Leffler, *Preponderance*, 20–24; and Leffler, *Specter*, 23–32. From IR theory, see Michael Mandelbaum, *The Fate of Nations: The Search for National Security in the Nineteenth and Twentieth Centuries* (New York: Cambridge University Press, 1988); and Barry Buzan and Lene Hansen, *The Evolution of International Security Studies* (Cambridge: Cambridge University Press, 2009). It is, however, more appropriate to date the advent of the national security *state* to the postwar era, as the permanent institutionalization of relationships between research, industry, technology, capital, and government didn't happen until the Cold War: Linda Weiss, *America Inc.? Innovation and Enterprise in the National Security State* (Ithaca, NY: Cornell University Press, 2014).

28. Daniel Yergin, *Shattered Peace: The Origins of the Cold War and the National Security State* (Boston: Houghton Mifflin, 1977), 193–220. For Thompson's foundational work on the concept of national security, see John A. Thompson, *A Sense of Power: The Roots of America's Global Role* (Ithaca, NY: Cornell University Press, 2015). This book is a synthesis of several of his influential articles: Thompson, "The Exaggeration of American Vulnerability: The Anatomy of a Tradition," *Diplomatic History* 16 (January 1992): 23–43; Thompson, "Another Look at the Downfall of 'Fortress America,'" *Journal of American Studies* 26 (December 1992): 393–408; Thompson, "Conceptions of National Security and American Entry into World War II," *Diplomacy & Statecraft* 16 (2005): 671–697; and Thompson, "The Geopolitical Vision: The Myth of an Outmatched USA," in *Uncertain Empire: American History and the Idea of the Cold War,* ed. Joel Isaac and Duncan Bell (New York: Oxford University Press, 2012), 91–114. But see also Michael S. Sherry, *In the Shadow of War: The United States since the 1930s* (New Haven: Yale University Press, 1995), xi, 29–44; David Reynolds, *From Munich to Pearl Harbor: Roosevelt's America and the Origins of the Second World War* (Chicago: Ivan R. Dee, 2001), 128–129, 179–186; and Douglas T. Stuart, *Creating the National Security State: A History of the Law That Transformed America* (Princeton: Princeton University Press, 2008).

29. See, however, the suggestive exceptions of Rosenberg, "Commentary," 278; and Sherry, *In the Shadow of War,* 31–32. To be sure, others have drawn compelling causal links between the New Deal Roosevelt's epochal foreign policy, most notably Elizabeth Borgwardt, *A New Deal for the World: America's Vision for Human Rights* (Cambridge, MA: Harvard University Press, 2005); and David Ekbladh, *The Great American Mission: Modernization and the Construction of an American World Order* (Princeton: Princeton University Press, 2009). I examine some of these links as they relate to national security in Chapter 7. However, these important books concentrate on, respectively, human rights and international

development, and are not concerned with ideas of national security per se or the policy origins of the national security state. The same is true for transnational histories of the New Deal: for the leading examples, see Daniel T. Rodgers, *Atlantic Crossings: Social Politics in a Progressive Age* (Cambridge, MA: Harvard University Press, 1998); and Kiran Klaus Patel, *The New Deal: A Global History* (Princeton: Princeton University Press, 2017).

30. On warfare to welfare and domestic state-building, see Elizabeth Kier and Ronald R. Krebs, eds., *In War's Wake: International Conflict and the Fate of Liberal Democracy* (Cambridge: Cambridge University Press, 2010); James T. Sparrow, *Warfare State: World War II Americans and the Age of Big Government* (New York: Oxford University Press, 2011); Jennifer Mittelstadt, *The Rise of the Military Welfare State* (Cambridge, MA: Harvard University Press, 2015); and Olivier Burtin, *A Nation of Veterans: War, Citizenship, and the Welfare State in Modern America* (Philadelphia: University of Pennsylvania Press, 2022).

31. Rosenberg, "Commentary," 277–278.

32. Charles A. Beard, *The Idea of National Interest: An Analytical Study in American Foreign Policy* (New York: Macmillan, 1934), 407.

33. Hans J. Morgenthau, *In Defense of the National Interest: A Critical Examination of American Foreign Policy* (New York: Alfred A. Knopf, 1951); Hans J. Morgenthau, "What Is the National Interest of the United States? *Annals of the American Academy of Political and Social Science* 282 (July 1952): 1–7; and Hans J. Morgenthau, "Another 'Great Debate': The National Interest of the United States," *American Political Science Review* 46 (December 1952): 961–988.

34. See, respectively, Stephen D. Krasner, *Defending the National Interest: Raw Materials Investments and U.S. Foreign Policy* (Princeton: Princeton University Press, 1978); and Peter Trubowitz, *Defining the National Interest: Conflict and Change in American Foreign Policy* (Chicago: University of Chicago Press, 1998).

35. H. W. Brands, "The Idea of the National Interest," *Diplomatic History* 23 (April 1999): 239–261, 239. Wolfers came up with a similar, if more vaguely worded, definition of the national interest: Wolfers, "'National Security' as an Ambiguous Symbol," 481.

36. This is actually close to how Morgenthau posited the difference between national security and the national interest: Hans J. Morgenthau, *Politics among Nations: The Struggle for Power and Peace* (New York: Alfred A. Knopf, 1948), 440. On how the doctrine of necessity creates justificatory space for war, see Judith N. Shklar, *The Faces of Injustice* (New Haven: Yale University Press, 1990), 71–73.

37. Bock and Berkowitz, "Emerging Field of National Security," 135.

38. Fen Hampson, "Decanting the National Interest," *Harvard International Review* 1 (April/May 1979): 35–36, 35.

39. Corey Robin, *Fear: The History of a Political Idea* (New York: Oxford University Press, 2004); Joanna Bourke, *Fear: A Cultural History* (London: Virago, 2005).

40. Franklin D. Roosevelt, Letter of Greeting to the United Methodist Council, January 17, 1938, American Presidency Project (hereafter *APP*), https://www.presidency.ucsb.edu/node/209048.

41. Andrew Preston, "The Fearful Giant: National Insecurity and U.S. Foreign Policy," in *Ideology in U.S. Foreign Relations: New Histories*, ed. Christopher McKnight Nichols and David Milne (New York: Columbia University Press, 2022), 169–184.

42. For a contrary view, see Gaddis, *Surprise*, 13.

43. Calvin Coolidge, Fourth Annual Message, December 7, 1926, *APP*, https://www.presidency.ucsb.edu/node/206730.

44. See Ira Katznelson, *Fear Itself: The New Deal and the Origins of Our Time* (New York: Liveright, 2013), a book which has deeply informed my overall approach to national security.

45. Ioannis D. Evrigenis, *Fear of Enemies and Collective Action* (Cambridge: Cambridge University Press, 2009).

46. Judith N. Shklar, *Political Thought and Political Thinkers*, ed. Stanley Hoffmann (Chicago: University of Chicago Press, 1998), 3–19, esp. 12 for the clearest expression along these lines.

47. Brett Gary, *The Nervous Liberals: Propaganda Anxieties from World War I to the Cold War* (New York, 1999), 5–8. See also John M. Owen IV, *Liberal Peace, Liberal War: American Politics and International Security* (Ithaca, NY: Cornell University Press, 1997); Latham, *Liberal Moment*; David Ciepley, *Liberalism in the Shadow of Totalitarianism* (Cambridge, MA: Harvard University Press, 2007); and G. John Ikenberry, *A World Safe for Democracy: Liberal Internationalism and the Crises of Global Order* (New Haven: Yale University Press, 2020). For a clear expression of Cold War "national security liberalism," see Lasswell, *National Security and Individual Freedom*. On liberalism's multiplicity, see Gary Gerstle, "The Protean Character of American Liberalism," *American Historical Review* 99 (October 1994): 1043–1073; and Alan Brinkley, *The End of Reform: New Deal Liberalism in Recession and War* (New York: Vintage, 1996), 8–10.

48. Mary Douglas, *Risk and Blame: Essays in Cultural Theory* (London: Routledge, 1992), 39.

49. Thompson, "Exaggeration."

50. On liberal ambivalence about the growth of the state, depending on how it grew and for what purposes, see Anne M. Kornhauser, *Debating the American State: Liberal Anxieties and the New Leviathan, 1930–1970* (Philadelphia: University of Pennsylvania Press, 2015).

51. Shklar herself made this very point about Roosevelt: Judith N. Shklar, *Ordinary Vices* (Cambridge, MA: Harvard University Press, 1984), 69–70.

52. For the most incisive contrary view, see Samuel Moyn, *Liberalism against Itself: Cold War Intellectuals and the Making of Our Times* (New Haven: Yale University Press, 2023). See also Steven M. Gillon, *Politics and Vision: The ADA and American Liberalism, 1947–1985* (New York: Oxford University Press, 1987); and Jennifer A. Delton, *Rethinking the 1950s: How Anticommunism and the Cold War Made America Liberal* (New York: Cambridge University Press, 2013).

53. Charles Tilly, "War Making and State Making as Organized Crime," in *Bringing the State Back In*, ed. Peter B. Evans, Dietrich Rueschemeyer, and Theda Skocpol (Cambridge: Cambridge University Press, 1985), 169–191; James C. Scott, *Against the Grain: A Deep History of the Earliest States* (New Haven: Yale University Press, 2017), 240–243, 268n23.

54. Lauren Benton and Lisa Ford, *Rage for Order: The British Empire and the Origins of International Law, 1800–1850* (Cambridge, MA: Harvard University Press, 2016), 85–116; Lauren Benton, Adam Clulow, Bain Attwood, eds., *Protection and Empire: A Global History* (Cambridge: Cambridge University Press, 2017).

55. See, for example, Peter Silver, *Our Savage Neighbors: How Indian War Transformed Early America* (New York: W. W. Norton, 2008).

56. Quoted in Christopher Clark, *Time and Power: Visions of History in German Politics, from the Thirty Years' War to the Third Reich* (Princeton: Princeton University Press, 2019), 65.

57. "Roosevelt Against Inconclusive Peace," *New York Times*, January 13, 1918.

1. THE BLESSINGS OF FREE SECURITY

1. Alexis de Tocqueville, *Democracy in America*, ed. Harvey C. Mansfield and Delba Winthrop (Chicago: University of Chicago Press, 2000), 265–274 (quoted on 265). For Toc-

queville scholarship that doesn't examine free security, see Sheldon S. Wolin, *Tocqueville Between Two Worlds: The Making of a Political and Theoretical Life* (Princeton: Princeton University Press, 2001), aside from a brief mention on 256; Hugh Brogan, *Alexis de Tocqueville: A Life* (New Haven: Yale University Press, 2007); Alan Ryan, *On Tocqueville: Democracy and America* (New York, 2014); and Olivier Zunz, *The Man Who Understood Democracy: The Life of Alexis de Tocqueville* (Princeton: Princeton University Press, 2022). On Tocqueville's world travels and America's "geographical isolation," see Jeremy Jennings, *Travels with Tocqueville Beyond America* (Cambridge, MA: Harvard University Press, 2023), 65.

2. Not every historian accepts the premise of free security: see William H. Goetzmann, *When the Eagle Screamed: The Romantic Horizon in American Diplomacy, 1800–1860* (New York: Wiley, 1966); Frederick Merk, *The Monroe Doctrine and American Expansionism, 1843–1849* (New York: Alfred A. Knopf, 1966); John Lewis Gaddis, *Surprise, Security, and the American Experience* (Cambridge, MA: Harvard University Press, 2004), 7–33; and Charles N. Edel, *Nation Builder: John Quincy Adams and the Grand Strategy of the Republic* (Cambridge, MA: Harvard University Press, 2014), 55–184.

3. George F. Kennan, *American Diplomacy, 1900–1950* (Chicago: University of Chicago Press, 1951), 3.

4. For example, see Andrew Preston, *Sword of the Spirit, Shield of Faith: Religion in American War and Diplomacy* (New York: Alfred A. Knopf, 2012), 10–11.

5. Samuel Huntington, *The Soldier and the State: The Theory and Politics of Civil-Military Relations* (Cambridge, MA: Harvard University Press, 1957), 222–226. By arguing that industrialism created an absence of war, however, Huntington reversed the proper cause and effect: it was instead the absence of the necessity of war that helped spur industrialization. For more, see Paul Kennedy, *The Rise and Fall of the Great Powers: Economic Change and Military Conflict from 1500 to 2000* (New York: Random House, 1987), 242–243; Michael Mann, *The Sources of Social Power,* vol. 2: *The Rise of Classes and Nation-States, 1760–1914* (Cambridge: Cambridge University Press, 1993), 377, 490–491; Charles S. Maier, *Among Empires: American Ascendancy and Its Predecessors* (Cambridge, MA: Harvard University Press, 2006), 195.

6. Quoted in Christopher McKnight Nichols, *Promise and Peril: America at the Dawn of a Global Age* (Cambridge, MA: Harvard University Press, 2011), 79.

7. David C. Hendrickson, *Peace Pact: The Lost World of the American Founding* (Lawrence: University Press of Kansas, 2003); François Furstenberg, "The Significance of the Trans-Appalachian Frontier in Atlantic History," *American Historical Review* 113 (June 2008): 647–677; Thomas Richards Jr., *Breakaway Americas: The Unmanifest Future of the Jacksonian United States* (Baltimore: Johns Hopkins University Press, 2020). Partisan politics, much of it caused by foreign policy, also threatened to dissolve the union: James Roger Sharp, *American Politics in the Early Republic: The New Nation in Crisis* (New Haven: Yale University Press, 1993).

8. *Federalist* 29, January 9, 1788, in Alexander Hamilton, James Madison, and John Jay, *The Federalist: With Letters of Brutus,* ed. Terence Ball (Cambridge: Cambridge University Press, 2003), 132. All references to the *Federalist Papers* are from this edition.

9. *Federalist* 3, November 3, 1787; *Federalist* 4, November 3, 1787, 9, 12–13. On the theorizing, see Max M. Edling, *A Revolution in Favor of Government: Origins of the U.S. Constitution and the Making of the American State* (New York: Oxford University Press, 2003), 73–146; Hendrickson, *Peace Pact;* and Charles Edel, "Extending the Sphere: A Federalist Grand Strategy," in *Rethinking American Grand Strategy,* ed. Elizabeth Borgwardt, Christopher McKnight Nichols, and Andrew Preston (New York: Oxford University Press, 2021), 83–105.

10. *Federalist* 24, December 19, 1787, 113.

11. *Federalist* 25, December 21,1787, 115.

12. *Federalist* 41, January 19,1788, 195. The two uses are in *Federalist* 29, January 9,1788, 132; and *Federalist* 70, March 15,1788, 344.

13. Timothy J. Shannon, *Indians and Colonists at the Crossroads of Empire: The Albany Congress of 1754* (Ithaca, NY: Cornell University Press, 2000), 83–89.

14. *Federalist* 8, November 20,1787, 30–35.

15. *Federalist* 41, 197.

16. *Federalist* 41, 196–197.

17. Hamilton to Washington, April 14,1794, *Founders Online,* https://founders.archives .gov/documents/Hamilton/01-16-02-0208-0002. See also *Federalist* 23, December 18,1787, 106–110.

18. *Federalist* 70, 344.

19. Sylvia R. Frey, *Water from the Rock: Black Resistance in a Revolutionary Age* (Chapel Hill: University of North Carolina Press, 1991). For the British, see Maya Jasanoff, *Liberty's Exiles: American Loyalists in the Revolutionary World* (New York: Alfred A. Knopf, 2011); and Alan Taylor, *The Internal Enemy: Slavery and War in Virginia, 1772–1832* (New York: W. W. Norton, 2013). On Spanish Florida, see Nathaniel Millett, *The Maroons of Prospect Bluff and Their Quest for Freedom in the Atlantic World* (Gainesville: University Press of Florida, 2013); and Matthew J. Clavin, *The Battle of Negro Fort: The Rise and Fall of a Fugitive Slave Community* (New York: New York University Press, 2019).

20. Quoted in Andy Doolen, *Territories of Empire: U.S. Writing from the Louisiana Purchase to Mexican Independence* (New York: Oxford University Press, 2014), 27–28.

21. Quoted in Adam Rothman, *Slave Country: American Expansion and the Origins of the Deep South* (Cambridge, MA: Harvard University Press, 2005), 85. More generally, see Ashli White, *Encountering Revolution: Haiti and the Making of the Early Republic* (Baltimore: Johns Hopkins University Press, 2010), 124–165; and Daniel Immerwahr, "Burning Down the House: Slavery and Arson in America," *Journal of American History* 110 (December 2023): 449–473, 460–464.

22. Quoted in Laurent Dubois, *Avengers of the New World: The Story of the Haitian Revolution* (Cambridge, MA: Harvard University Press, 2004), 225. Although even then, some white Southerners, among them John C. Calhoun, scoffed at the idea that Haiti was a threat: Robert G. Parkinson, *The Common Cause: Creating Race and Nation in the American Revolution* (Chapel Hill: University of North Carolina Press, 2016), 650–651.

23. Roger Brown, *The Republic in Peril: 1812* (New York: Columbia University Press, 1964); Alan Taylor, *The Civil War of 1812: American Citizens, British Subjects, Irish Rebels, and Indian Allies* (New York: Alfred A. Knopf, 2010). Moreover, as Taylor notes, Southerners feared the British would use the conflict to threaten the survival of slavery.

24. Quoted in Edel, *Nation Builder,* 119.

25. Eliga H. Gould, *Among the Powers of the Earth: The American Revolution and the Making of a New World Empire* (Cambridge, MA: Harvard University Press, 2012).

26. Jasper M. Trautsch, *The Genesis of America: US Foreign Policy and the Formation of National Identity, 1793–1815* (New York: Cambridge University Press, 2018).

27. See, respectively, *Federalist* 28, December 26,1787, 131; and *Federalist* 41, 197, 199.

28. *Philadelphia Evening Post,* February 22,1804. For a strategic analysis explaining why, see Robert W. Tucker and David C. Hendrickson, *Empire of Liberty: The Statecraft of Thomas Jefferson* (New York: Oxford University Press, 1990), 95–100; and Francis D. Cogliano, *Emperor of Liberty: Thomas Jefferson's Foreign Policy* (New Haven: Yale University Press, 2016).

29. Patrick Griffin, *American Leviathan: Empire, Nation, and Revolutionary Frontier* (New York: Hill and Wang, 2007); Amy S. Greenberg, *Manifest Manhood and the Antebel-*

lum American Empire (New York: Cambridge University Press, 2005); Emily Conroy-Krutz, *Christian Imperialism: Converting the World in the Early American Republic* (Ithaca, NY: Cornell University Press, 2015). For a related argument, see also Peter Silver, *Our Savage Neighbors: How Indian War Transformed Early America* (New York: W. W. Norton, 2008). On the shakiness of US sovereignty in Louisiana, see Robert Lee, "Accounting for Conquest: The Price of the Louisiana Purchase of Indian Country," *Journal of American History* 104 (March 2017): 921–942.

30. Thomas Jefferson, Inaugural Address, March 4, 1801, American Presidency Project, https://www.presidency.ucsb.edu/node/201948.

31. C. Vann Woodward, "The Age of Reinterpretation," *American Historical Review* 66 (October 1960): 1–19, quoted on 2.

32. There is no historiography of free security per se, though historians have often alluded to it without examining it in detail or using the term itself. For a suggestive example, see Thomas R. Hietala, *Manifest Design: Anxious Aggrandizement in Late Jacksonian America* (Ithaca, NY: Cornell University Press, 1985), 176. There are, however, a few notable exceptions: Alex Roland, "Technology, Ground Warfare, and Strategy: The Paradox of American Experience," *Journal of Military History* 55 (October 1991): 447–468, 458–461; David Reynolds, *From World War to Cold War: Churchill, Roosevelt, and the International History of the 1940s* (Oxford: Oxford University Press, 2006), 297–298; Campbell Craig and Fredrik Logevall, *America's Cold War: The Politics of Insecurity* (Cambridge, MA: Harvard University Press, 2009); and Robert Kagan, *The Ghost at the Feast: America and the Collapse of World Order, 1900–1941* (New York: Alfred A. Knopf, 2023).

33. Fareed Zakaria, "The Myth of America's 'Free Security,'" *World Policy Journal* 14 (Summer 1997): 35–43. Despite this basic problem, isolationism can be a useful lens if used carefully. For leading examples, see Christopher McKnight Nichols, *Promise and Peril: America at the Dawn of a Global Age* (Cambridge, MA: Harvard University Press, 2011); and Charles A. Kupchan, *Isolationism: A History of America's Efforts to Shield Itself from the World* (New York: Oxford University Press, 2020).

34. Arthur M. Schlesinger Jr., *The Imperial Presidency* (1973; Boston: Houghton Mifflin, 2004), x. Walter Lippmann held a similar view: see Lippman, *U.S. Foreign Policy: Shield of the Republic* (Boston: Little, Brown, 1943), 49; and Lippman, *U.S. War Aims* (Boston: Little, Brown, 1944), 197. For a much more nuanced view, see Kupchan, *Isolationism,* 35–38.

35. Abraham Lincoln, "Address Before the Young Men's Lyceum of Springfield, Illinois," January 27, 1838, in *The Collected Works of Abraham Lincoln,* vol. 1, ed. Roy P. Basler (New Brunswick, NJ: Rutgers University Press, 1953), 109.

36. Kevin Phillips, *The Cousins' Wars: Religion, Politics, and the Triumph of Anglo-America* (New York: Basic Books, 1999); see also Taylor, *Civil War of 1812.*

37. Stéphane Roussel, *The North American Democratic Peace: Absence of War and Security Institution-Building in Canada-US Relations, 1867–1958* (Kingston, ON: Queens-McGill University Press, 2004).

38. See, most recently, Jay Sexton, *The Monroe Doctrine: Empire and Nation in Nineteenth-Century America* (New York: Hill and Wang, 2011).

39. Quoted in Edel, *Nation Builder,* 173.

40. Woodward, "Age of Reinterpretation," 2.

41. Max M. Edling, *A Hercules in the Cradle: War, Money, and the American State, 1783–1867* (Chicago: University of Chicago Press, 2014), 237.

42. Edling, *Hercules,* 223.

43. Gautham Rao, *National Duties: Custom Houses and the Making of the American State* (Chicago: University of Chicago Press, 2016).

44. I have relied heavily here on Edling, *Hercules,* with figures from Table C.2, 240.

45. On nineteenth-century American government, see William J. Novak, "The Myth of the 'Weak' American State," *American Historical Review* 115 (June 2008): 752–772; Brian Balogh, *A Government Out of Sight: The Mystery of National Authority in Nineteenth-Century America* (New York: Cambridge University Press, 2009); Desmond King and Robert C. Lieberman, "Ironies of State Building: A Comparative Perspective on the American State," *World Politics* 61 (July 2009): 547–588; Gary Gerstle, *Liberty and Coercion: The Paradox of American Government from the Founding to the Present* (Princeton: Princeton University Press, 2015), 17–123; and Nicolas Barreyre and Claire Lemercier, "The Unexceptional State: Rethinking the State in the Nineteenth Century (France, United States)," *American Historical Review* 126 (June 2021): 481–503. Though for a complicating analysis that emphasizes region to demonstrate the weakness of the state in the interior, see Andrew Shankman, "Toward a Social History of Federalism," *Journal of the Early Republic* 37 (Winter 2017): 615–653. For accounts that focus on the fiscal-military state, see Steven Watts, *The Republic Reborn: War and the Making of Liberal America, 1790–1820* (Baltimore: Johns Hopkins University Press, 1987); Ira Katznelson, "Flexible Capacity: The Military and Early American Statebuilding," in *Shaped by War and Trade: International Influences on American Political Development,* ed. Ira Katznelson and Martin Shefter (Princeton: Princeton University Press, 2002), 82–110; Sheldon D. Pollack, *War, Revenue, and State Building: Financing the Development of the American State* (Ithaca, NY: Cornell University Press, 2009); and Edling, *Hercules.* For an overview, see R. M. Bates, "Government by Improvisation? Towards a New History of the Nineteenth-Century American State," *Journal of Policy History* 33 (July 2021): 287–316.

46. "The Addition to the Capitol," July 4, 1851, *The Papers of Daniel Webster,* series 4: *Speeches and Formal Writings,* vol. 2, ed. Charles M. Wiltse (Hanover, NH: University Press of New England, 1988), 619–620.

47. Michael H. Hunt, *The American Ascendancy: How the United States Gained and Wielded Global Dominance* (Chapel Hill: University of North Carolina Press, 2007), 70; Richard Hume Werking, *The Master Architects: Building the United States Foreign Service, 1890–1913* (Lexington: University Press of Kentucky, 1977), 3, 7, 18, 257n17.

48. Megan Black, *The Global Interior: Mineral Frontiers and American Power* (Cambridge, MA: Harvard University Press, 2018), 23–24; Pekka Hämäläinen, *Indigenous Continent: The Epic Contest for North America* (New York: Liveright, 2022), 432–433.

49. Werking, *Master Architects,* 9–11; Warren Frederick Ilchman, *Professional Diplomacy in the United States, 1779–1939: A Study in Administrative History* (Chicago: University of Chicago Press, 1961), 81.

50. Ilchman, *Professional Diplomacy,* 34.

51. Quoted in Werking, *Master Architects,* 15.

52. Quoted in Frank Ninkovich, *Global Dawn: The Cultural Foundation of American Internationalism, 1865–1890* (Cambridge, MA: Harvard University Press, 2009), 75.

53. Robert L. Beisner, *From the Old Diplomacy to the New, 1865–1900,* 2nd ed. (Arlington Heights, IL: Harlan Davidson, 1986), 28. Morton Keller similarly describes the State, War, and Navy departments as "weak, thinly staffed, relatively inconsequential agencies of government until the last years of the nineteenth century" and that "the contrast with their British counterparts . . . was dramatic." Morton Keller, *Affairs of State: Public Life in Late Nineteenth-Century America* (Cambridge, MA: Harvard University Press, 1977), 317.

54. Ninkovich, *Global Dawn,* 74.

55. Werking, *Master Architects,* 20–66.

56. The Civil War, when passports were required for internal security reasons, was a brief exception: Craig Robertson, *The Passport in America: The History of a Document* (New York: Oxford University Press, 2010); John Torpey, *The Invention of the Passport:*

Surveillance, Citizenship and the State (Cambridge: Cambridge University Press, 2000), 93–103, 117–120.

57. Kelly Lytle Hernández, *Migra! A History of the U.S. Border Patrol* (Berkeley: University of California Press, 2010), 26–28, 32–36.

58. The following discussion doesn't include the volunteer or state militias, and instead focuses on the size of permanent personnel within the regular branches of the armed services. Admittedly, neglecting the militias in some ways leads to an underestimation of the size of the nineteenth-century American military, particularly in the antebellum period, and thus a possibly skewed comparison with Europe, where militias were uncommon. But I have deliberately not included militias for two reasons: one, by their very nature they were in large part private and autonomous and not appendages of the government; two, also by their very nature, they were amateurish and incompetent, and regular military personnel wanted little to do with them. As George Washington observed during the Revolution, "*No Militia* will ever acquire the habits necessary to resist a regular force." During the Mexican War, Mexicans called the poorly behaved US militia forces "Vandals vomited from Hell"; even their American comrades considered them little more than a "lawless drunken rabble." It is thus doubtful that excluding the militia distorts my analysis. Washington to Samuel Huntington, September 15,1780, *Founders Online*, https://founders.archives.gov/documents/Washington/03-28-02 -0147 (emphasis in original); Allan R. Millett and Peter Maslowski, *For the Common Defense: A Military History of the United States of America*, rev. and expanded (New York: Free Press, 1994), 136–137, 149–150; Jerry Cooper, *The Rise of the National Guard: The Evolution of the American Militia, 1865–1920* (Lincoln: University of Nebraska Press, 1997), 1–22.

59. These figures don't include the Confederate armed forces, which, in the absence of detailed records, had an estimated total wartime force of anywhere between 600,000 and 1.5 million. See James M. McPherson, *Battle Cry of Freedom: The Civil War Era* (New York: Oxford University Press, 1988), 306–307n41; and John M. Sacher, *Confederate Conscription and the Struggle for Southern Soldiers* (Baton Rouge: Louisiana State University Press, 2021), 4, 185–197.

60. "Military Personnel on Active Duty," Susan B. Carter et al., eds., *Historical Statistics of the United States*, vol. 5: *Governance and International Relations* (Cambridge: Cambridge University Press, 2006), Table Ed26-47, 354; "Number in the Armed Forces—United Kingdom, 1855–1980," B. R. Mitchell, *British Historical Statistics* (Cambridge: Cambridge University Press, 1988), Labour Force Table 6, 121.

61. C. A. Bayly, "The British Military-Fiscal State and Indigenous Resistance: India, 1750–1820," in *The East India Company*, vol. 5: *Warfare, Expansion and Resistance*, ed. Patrick Tuck (London: Routledge, 1998), 222.

62. Fareed Zakaria, *From Wealth to Power: The Unusual Origins of America's World Role* (Princeton: Princeton University Press, 1998), 128–130.

63. See John H. Schroeder, *Shaping a Maritime Empire: The Commercial and Diplomatic Role of the American Navy, 1829–1861* (Westport, CT: Greenwood Press, 1985).

64. Brian McAllister Linn, *The Echo of Battle: The Army's Way of War* (Cambridge, MA: Harvard University Press, 2007), 15–38.

65. "State Employment for Austria-Hungary, France, Great Britain, Prussia-Germany, and the United States, 1760–1910," Mann, *Rise of Classes and Nation-States*, Table 11.7, 393. While it is true that violent conflict between North and South didn't end in 1865, and that the US Army still occupied the old Confederacy past 1870, it is nonetheless remarkable that so few troops remained in service. On the continuation of the Civil War past 1865, see Gregory P. Downs, *After Appomattox: Military Occupation and the Ends of War* (Cambridge, MA: Harvard University Press, 2019).

66. Barreyre and Lemercier, "Unexceptional State"; see also Peter Baldwin, "Beyond Weak and Strong: Rethinking the State in Comparative Policy History," *Journal of Policy History* 17 (January 2005): 12–33. These important articles do not examine war or the military.

67. Webster, "Addition," 619.

68. Quoted in Stephen W. Sawyer, "Beyond Tocqueville's Myth: Rethinking the Model of the American State," in *Boundaries of the State in US History*, ed. James T. Sparrow, William J. Novak, and Stephen W. Sawyer (Chicago: University of Chicago Press, 2015), 71.

69. Lawrence A. Scaff, *Max Weber in America* (Princeton: Princeton University Press, 2011), 64.

70. Katznelson, "Flexible Capacity," 97–98; Balogh, *Government Out of Sight*, 138, 158, 189; William B. Skelton, *An American Profession of Arms: The Army Officer Corps, 1784–1861* (Lawrence: University Press of Kansas, 1992), 228–230. For the best overall account, see William D. Adler, *Engineering Expansion: The U.S. Army and Economic Development, 1787–1860* (Philadelphia: University of Pennsylvania Press, 2021).

71. Todd Shallat, *Structures in the Stream: Water, Science, and the Rise of the U.S. Army Corps of Engineers* (Austin: University of Texas Press, 1994).

72. Edward M. Coffman, *The Old Army: A Portrait of the American Army in Peacetime, 1784–1898* (New York: Oxford University Press, 1986), 43.

73. Balogh, *Government Out of Sight*, 194–200, 205–213.

74. Zakaria, *From Wealth to Power*, 53n33.

75. Katznelson, "Flexible Capacity."

76. Russell F. Weigley, *History of the United States Army* (New York: Macmillan, 1967), 139–143; Roger J. Spiller, "Calhoun's Expansible Army: The History of a Military Idea," *South Atlantic Quarterly* 79 (Spring 1980): 189–203. On Calhoun's successful efforts to create a professional officer corps as the foundation of the expansible army, see Skelton, *American Profession of Arms*. More generally, see Paul A. C. Koistinen, *Beating Plowshares into Swords: The Political Economy of American Warfare, 1606–1865* (Lawrence: University Press of Kansas, 1996), 73–101.

77. "Military Personnel on Active Duty," Table Ed26-47.

78. "Military Personnel on Active Duty," Table Ed26-47.

79. Jay Sexton, *Debtor Diplomacy: Finance and American Foreign Relations in the Civil War Era, 1837–1873* (Oxford: Clarendon, 2005), 9, 19.

80. Edling, *Hercules*, 213–215, 230–232. The Spanish-American War was different, funded largely through raising internal taxation, especially on the consumption of "vice" goods such as alcohol and tobacco: Hugh Rockoff, *America's Economic Way of War: War and the US Economy from the Spanish-American War to the Persian Gulf War* (Cambridge: Cambridge University Press, 2012), 57–62.

81. Millett and Maslowski, *For the Common Defense*, 123–157; Skelton, *American Profession of Arms*, 109–259.

82. In addition to the above discussion of *The Federalist*, see Edling, *Revolution in Favor of Government*.

83. Kenneth R. Stevens, *Border Diplomacy: The Caroline and McLeod Affairs in Anglo-American-Canadian Relations, 1837–1842* (Tuscaloosa: University of Alabama Press, 1989).

84. Webster to Henry Stephen Fox, 4/24/1841, *Papers of Daniel Webster, Series 3: Diplomatic Papers, 1841–1852*, vol. 1 (Hanover, NH: University Press of New England, 1987), 67–68.

85. John Fabian Witt, *Lincoln's Code: The Laws of War in American History* (New York: Free Press, 2012), 111–117. On Webster's norm in subsequent theoretical and legal considerations of force, see also Chris Brown, "After 'Caroline': NSS 2002, Practical Judgment,

and the Politics and Ethics of Preemption," in *The Ethics of Preventive War*, ed. Deen K. Chatterjee (Cambridge: Cambridge University Press, 2013), 31–36.

86. Sexton, *Monroe Doctrine*, 49–50, 56–58; quoted in Edel, *Nation Builder,* 175.

87. Edel, *Nation Builder,* 174–176.

88. Sexton, *Monroe Doctrine,* 50–62.

89. "Address of July 4, 1821," in *John Quincy Adams and American Continental Empire: Letters, Papers and Speeches,* ed. Walter LaFeber (Chicago: University of Chicago Press, 1965), 45.

90. Dean B. Mahin, *One War at a Time: The International Dimensions of the American Civil War* (Washington, DC: Brassey's, 1999), 218–238, 269–285 (quotations on 220). On the Grand Design, see Stève Sainlaude, *France and the American Civil War: A Diplomatic History* (Chapel Hill: University of North Carolina Press, 2019), 110–125. On Lincoln's international strategy, see also Kevin Peraino, *Lincoln in the World: The Making of a Statesman and the Dawn of American Power* (New York: Crown, 2013).

91. Jay Sexton, "Anglophobia in Nineteenth-Century Elections, Politics, and Diplomacy," in *America at the Ballot Box: Elections and American Political History,* ed. Gareth Davies and Julian E. Zelizer (Philadelphia: University of Pennsylvania Press, 2015), 98–117.

92. Brian DeLay, *War of a Thousand Deserts: Indian Raids and the U.S.-Mexican War* (New Haven: Yale University Press, 2008), 288; Amy S. Greenberg, *A Wicked War: Polk, Clay, Lincoln, and the 1846 U.S. Invasion of Mexico* (New York: Alfred A. Knopf, 2012), 84–85, 97–98.

93. Howard Jones, *Union in Peril: The Crisis Over British Intervention in the Civil War* (Chapel Hill: University of North Carolina Press, 1992); Mahin, *One War at a Time,* 58–82, 142–160, 286–300; Sexton, *Debtor Diplomacy,* 95–104, 202–241.

94. John Townshend to Calhoun, December 22,1845, *Papers of John C. Calhoun,* 28 vols. (Columbia: University of South Carolina Press for South Caroliniana Society, 1959–2003), 22:354–355.

95. Calhoun, "Speech on His Slavery Resolutions in Reply to James F. Simmons," December 20,1847, *Papers of John C. Calhoun,* 24:188–189. In general, see Hietala, *Manifest Design,* 13–14.

96. Matthew Karp, *This Vast Southern Empire: Slaveholders at the Helm of American Foreign Policy* (Cambridge, MA: Harvard University Press, 2016); Matthew Karp, "Grand Strategy of the Master Class: Slavery and Foreign Policy from the Antebellum Era to the Civil War," in Borgwardt, Nichols, and Preston, *Rethinking American Grand Strategy,* 106–122. During the Civil War, the Confederacy abandoned all fears of central authority and consolidated a total warfare state and society that was even more comprehensive than the Union's. See Richard Franklin Bensel, *Yankee Leviathan: The Origins of Central State Authority in America, 1859-1877* (New York: Cambridge University Press, 1990), 94–237.

97. J. L. Granatstein, *Canada's Army: Waging War and Keeping the Peace* (Toronto: University of Toronto Press, 2002), 14–23.

98. Lincoln, Lyceum Address, 109.

99. On tensions in the nineteenth-century Pacific, see Thomas M. Jamison, *The Pacific's New Navies: An Ocean, Its Wars, and the Making of US Sea Power* (New York: Cambridge University Press, 2024).

100. Daniel Immerwahr, *How to Hide an Empire: A History of the Greater United States* (New York: Farrar, Straus, and Giroux, 2019), 50–52.

101. See Robert Burr, *By Force or Reason: Chile and the Balancing of Power in South America, 1830-1905* (Berkeley: University of California Press, 1965); Thomas L. Whigham, *The Road to Armageddon: Paraguay Versus the Triple Alliance, 1866-70* (Calgary: University of Calgary Press, 2017); Thomas L. Whigham, *The Paraguayan War: Causes and Early*

Conduct, 2nd ed. (Calgary: University of Calgary Press, 2018); and Thomas M. Jamison, "The War of the Pacific, Technology and U.S. Naval Development: An International History of Regional War," *Journal of Military History* 82 (October 2018): 1093–1122. On war and South American political development, see Fernando Lopez-Alves, *State Formation and Democracy in Latin America, 1810–1900* (Durham, NC: Duke University Press, 2000); and James E. Sanders, *The Vanguard of the Atlantic World: Creating Modernity, Nation, and Democracy in Nineteenth-Century Latin America* (Durham, NC: Duke University Press, 2014).

102. Quoted in Robert Kagan, *Dangerous Nation: America's Foreign Policy from Its Earliest Days to the Dawn of the Twentieth Century* (New York: Alfred A. Knopf, 2006), 3.

103. Heather Cox Richardson, *West from Appomattox: The Reconstruction of America after the Civil War* (New Haven: Yale University Press, 2007); James Belich, *Replenishing the Earth: The Settler Revolution and the Rise of the Angloworld, 1783–1939* (Oxford: Oxford University Press, 2009), 79–105, 223–260, 331–355, 396–406.

104. Edel, *Nation Builder,* 122–123.

105. Quoted in Ada Ferrer, *Cuba: An American History* (New York: Scribner, 2021), 64. On the western incursion, see Ned Blackhawk, *Violence over the Land: Indians and Empires in the Early American West* (Cambridge, MA: Harvard University Press, 2006), 114–118.

106. On manifest destiny in deeper historical context, see Anders Stephanson, *Manifest Destiny: American Expansion and the Empire of Right* (New York: Hill and Wang, 1995); and Preston, *Sword of the Spirit,* 135–153. On the internal nature of the ideology of manifest destiny, see Hietala, *Manifest Design.* But for a contrary view see Sam W. Haynes, "Anglophobia and the Annexation of Texas: The Quest for National Security," in *Manifest Destiny and Empire: American Antebellum Expansion,* ed. Sam W. Haynes and Christopher Morris (College Station: Texas A&M University Press, 1997), 115–145.

107. Quoted in Richard Drinnon, *Facing West: The Metaphysics of Indian-Hating and Empire-Building* (Minneapolis: University of Minnesota Press, 1980), 402. On Morse, see Joseph W. Phillips, *Jedidiah Morse and New England Congregationalism* (New Brunswick, NJ: Rutgers University Press, 1983); and Richard J. Moss, *The Life of Jedidiah Morse: A Station of Peculiar Exposure* (Knoxville: University of Tennessee press, 1995).

108. Abraham Lincoln, Annual Message to Congress, December 1, 1862, *Collected Works of Abraham Lincoln,* vol. 5 (New Brunswick, NJ: Rutgers University Press, 1990), 537.

109. Quoted in Richardson, *West from Appomattox,* 37.

110. For such views at the time, see Hietala, *Manifest Design,* 173–214; and Alan Taylor, *American Republics: A Continental History of the United States, 1783–1850* (New York: W. W. Norton, 2021).

111. Abraham Lincoln, Second Debate with Stephen A. Douglas at Freeport, Illinois, August 27, 1858, *Collected Works of Abraham Lincoln,* vol. 3, 55. It's highly unlikely he had this in mind, but Douglas's comments bore a strong analogical resemblance to the central moral of Bernard Mandeville's *The Fable of the Bees* (1714), a satirical work of political thought which likened people to bees and argued that it was futile, even unnatural, to stop bees from behaving like the acquisitive, constantly moving animals they are. While Mandeville's influence on Douglas's expansionism is uncertain, his *Fable* did figure in the work of later economists, including Adam Smith, John Maynard Keynes, and Friedrich Hayek. See E. J. Hundert, *The Enlightenment's Fable: Bernard Mandeville and the Discovery of Society* (Cambridge: Cambridge University Press, 1994).

112. Abraham Lincoln, Third Debate with Stephen A. Douglas at Jonesboro, Illinois, September 15, 1858, *Collected Works of Abraham Lincoln,* vol. 3, 115.

113. See, for example, Daniel K. Richter, *Facing East from Indian Country: A Native History of Early America* (Cambridge, MA: Harvard University Press, 2001); Michael Witgen, *An Infinity of Nations: How the Native New World Shaped Early North America* (Phila-

delphia: University of Pennsylvania Press, 2012); Hämäläinen, *Indigenous Continent;* and Ned Blackhawk, *The Rediscovery of America: Native Peoples and the Unmaking of U.S. History* (New Haven: Yale University Press, 2023).

114. DeLay, *War of a Thousand Deserts,* esp. 288–296; Pekka Hämäläinen, *The Comanche Empire* (New Haven: Yale University Press, 2008), 232–238, 292–293, 321–341. Hämäläinen also points out, however, that the Comanches had internal problems of their own that made American military success much easier than it would have been in the 1830s. On the Lakota, see Pekka Hämäläinen, *Lakota America: A New History of Indigenous Power* (New Haven: Yale University Press, 2019).

115. On the power and agency of Indigenous nations, see Blackhawk, *Violence over the Land,* esp. 176–225; John W. Hall, *Uncommon Defense: Indian Allies in the Black Hawk War* (Cambridge, MA: Harvard University Press, 2009); Roger L. Nichols, *Warrior Nations: The United States and Indian Peoples* (Norman: University of Oklahoma Press, 2013); and, more generally, Blackhawk, *Rediscovery of America;* and Kathleen DuVal, *Native Nations: A Millennium in North America* (New York: Random House, 2024).

116. Blackhawk, *Violence over the Land,* 226–266; Karl Jacoby, *Shadows at Dawn: A Borderlands Massacre and the Violence of History* (New York: Penguin, 2008); Ari Kelman, *A Misplaced Massacre: Struggling over the Memory of Sand Creek* (Cambridge, MA: Harvard University Press, 2013); Benjamin Madley, *An American Genocide: The United States and the California Indian Catastrophe, 1846–1873* (New Haven: Yale University Press, 2016).

117. Greenberg, *Wicked War;* Mexican observers quoted in Timothy J. Henderson, *A Glorious Defeat: Mexico and Its War with the United States* (New York: Hill and Wang, 2007), 148, 167, 188. On the mismatch, see Peter Guardino, *The Dead March: A History of the Mexican-American War* (Cambridge, MA: Harvard University Press, 2017).

118. David E. Shi, "Seward's Attempt to Annex British Columbia, 1865–1869," *Pacific Historical Review* 47 (May 1978): 217–238. On Alaska and BC, see Richardson, *West from Appomattox.*

119. Ged Martin, *Britain and the Origins of Canadian Confederation, 1837–1867* (Vancouver: University of British Columbia Press, 1995); David Sim, *A Union Forever: The Irish Question and U.S. Foreign Relations in the Victorian Age* (Ithaca, NY: Cornell University Press, 2013), 70–72, 84–96; William Jenkins, "'Such Bastard Despotism': Fenian Views of Canadian Confederation," in *Globalizing Confederation: Canada and the World in 1867,* ed. Jacqueline Krikorian, Marcel Martel, and Adrian Shubert (Toronto: University of Toronto Press, 2017), 61–78.

120. "Speech on Motion for an Address to Her Majesty in Favour of Confederation," February 9, 1865, Thomas D'Arcy McGee, *Speeches and Addresses Chiefly on the Subject of British-American Union* (London: Chapman and Hall, 1865), 271, 278.

121. Roussel, *North American Democratic Peace.* See also James Laxer, *Staking Claims to a Continent: John A. Macdonald, Abraham Lincoln, Jefferson Davis, and the Making of North America* (Toronto: House of Anansi Press, 2016).

122. Kennedy, *Rise and Fall of the Great Powers,* 243. Emphasis in original.

123. Henry James, *Richard Olney and His Public Service* (Boston: Houghton-Mifflin, 1923), 105.

124. Richard White, *Railroaded: The Transcontinentals and the Making of Modern America* (New York: W. W. Norton, 2011), 358, 414–418, 429–450; Olney quoted in Gerald G. Eggert, *Richard Olney: Evolution of a Statesman* (University Park: Pennsylvania State University Press, 1974), 142.

125. Olney to Thomas Francis Bayard, July 20, 1895, *Foreign Relations of the United States, 1895,* Part I (Washington, DC: GPO, 1896), 558.

126. Lars Schoultz, *Beneath the United States: A History of U.S. Policy toward Latin America* (Cambridge, MA: Harvard University Press, 1998), 122–124.

127. Quoted in Herring, *From Colony to Superpower,* 6. On Jusserand, see Bradford Perkins, *The Great Rapprochement: England and the United States, 1895–1914* (New York: Atheneum, 1968), 111.

2. THE BATTLE OF PLEASANT VALLEY

1. Ernest Hugh Fitzpatrick, *The Coming Conflict of Nations; or, The Japanese-American War* (Springfield, IL: H. W. Rokker, 1909).

2. On Anglo-American confederation see three books by Duncan Bell: *The Idea of Greater Britain: Empire and the Future of World Order, 1860–1900* (Princeton: Princeton University Press, 2007); *Reordering the World: Essays on Liberalism and Empire* (Princeton: Princeton University Press, 2016); and *Dreamworlds of Race: Empire and the Utopian Destiny of Anglo-America* (Princeton: Princeton University Press, 2020).

3. See, for example, Thomas F. Millard, *America and the Far Eastern Question* (New York: Moffat, Yard, 1909).

4. Susan R. Grayzel, *At Home and Under Fire: Air Raids and Culture in Britain From the Great War to the Blitz* (Cambridge: Cambridge University Press, 2011), 20–92; Richard Scully, *British Images of Germany: Admiration, Antagonism and Ambivalence, 1860–1914* (Basingstoke, UK: Palgrave Macmillan, 2012), 83–130, 261–315; David G. Morgan-Owen, *The Fear of Invasion: Strategy, Politics, and British War Planning, 1880–1914* (Oxford: Oxford University Press, 2017).

5. Lawrence M. Kaplan, *Homer Lea: American Soldier of Fortune* (Lexington: University Press of Kentucky, 2010).

6. Homer Lea, *The Valor of Ignorance* (New York: Harper and Brothers, 1909), 222–307 (quoted at 28, 205).

7. Lea, *Valor of Ignorance,* 156–160, 248–251, 307 (quoted at 192, 158–159). On Lea and the alleged internal threat, see Erika Lee, *The Making of Asian America: A History* (New York: Simon and Schuster, 2015), 130–133.

8. Jordan quoted in Sidney L. Gulick, *Anti-Japanese War-Scare Stories* (New York: F. H. Revel, 1917), 26.

9. Lea, *Valor of Ignorance,* xii.

10. Lea, *Valor of Ignorance,* xix, xxii.

11. Theodore Burton (R-OH) comments, April 15, 1908, *Congressional Record-House,* vol. 42, Part 5, 4777. Burton's argument wasn't unusual: Robert Endicott Osgood, *Ideals and Self-Interest in America's Foreign Relations: The Great Transformation of the Twentieth Century* (Chicago: University of Chicago Press, 1953), 32.

12. "Worked All Sunday for 4 Battleships," *New York Times,* April 27, 1908. In the end, Congress only appropriated funds for two new battleships: Public Law No. 115, House Resolution 20471, May 13, 1908, *Statutes at Large of the United States of America,* vol. 35, Part 1 (Washington, DC: GPO, 1909), 158–159.

13. Sherman quoted in Brian McAllister Linn, *The Echo of Battle: The Army's Way of War* (Cambridge, MA: Harvard University Press, 2007), 55–56; Mahan quoted in John A. Thompson, *A Sense of Power: The Roots of America's Global Role* (Ithaca, NY: Cornell University Press, 2015), 50.

14. Alfred Thayer Mahan, *The Influence of Sea Power Upon History, 1660–1783* (Boston: Little, Brown, 1890), 34.

15. Emory Upton, *The Military Policy of the United States* (Washington, DC: GPO, 1914 [1904]), vii, xii.

16. Linn, *Echo of Battle,* 93–115.

17. Quoted in Allan R. Millett and Peter Maslowski, *For the Common Defense: A Military History of the United States of America,* rev. ed. (New York: Free Press, 1994), 263; on the army's domestic duties, see Millett and Maslowski, *For the Common Defense,* 262–264, and 280 for the German General Staff; and Jerry M. Cooper, "The Army as Strikebreaker: The Railroad Strikes of 1877 and 1894," *Labor History* 18 (1977):, 179–196. On domestic security, see also Linn, *Echo of Battle,* 79–81.

18. Compare spending on the army for fiscal years 1870–1898 (an annual average of $44,941,000) with fiscal years 1899–1904 (an annual average of $150,889,000) in John Joseph Wallis, "Federal Government Expenditure, by Major Function: 1789–1970," Table Ea636–643, *Historical Statistics of the United States,* Part E: *Governance and International Relations,* ed. Susan B. Carter et al. (Cambridge: Cambridge University Press, 2006), 5–92.

19. Between 1880 and 1914, total US military personnel was averaged only about one-third to one-half the size of Italy's, which was consistently only the sixth-largest of European military establishments: Paul Kennedy, *The Rise and Fall of the Great Powers: Economic Change and Military Conflict from 1500 to 2000* (New York: Random House, 1987), Table 19, 203.

20. Theodore Roosevelt, Fourth Annual Message, December 6, 1904, American Presidency Project (hereafter *APP*), https://www.presidency.ucsb.edu/node/206208.

21. Theodore Roosevelt, Second Annual Message, December 2, 1902, *APP,* https://www.presidency.ucsb.edu/node/206194.

22. Henry Adams, *The Education of Henry Adams: An Autobiography* (Boston: Houghton Mifflin, 1918), 363–364.

23. Address before the New York State Bar Association, "The Monroe Doctrine and Some Incidental Obligations in the Zone of the Caribbean," January 19, 1912, *Foreign Relations of the United States, 1912* (Washington, DC: GPO, 1919), 1088.

24. On America's global carceral state, see Alfred W. McCoy, *Policing America's Empire: The United States, the Philippines, and the Rise of the Surveillance State* (Madison: University of Wisconsin Press, 2009); Jeremy Kuzmarov, *Modernizing Repression: Police Training and Nation-Building in the American Century* (Amherst: University of Massachusetts Press, 2012); Stuart Schrader, *Badges without Borders: How Global Counterinsurgency Transformed American Policing* (Oakland: University of California Press, 2019); Moon-Ho Jung, *Menace to Empire: Anticolonial Solidarities and the Transpacific Origins of the US Security State* (Oakland: University of California Press, 2022); and Julian Go, *Policing Empires: Militarization, Race, and the Imperial Boomerang in Britain and the US* (New York: Oxford University Press, 2023).

25. Katherine Unterman, *Uncle Sam's Policemen: The Pursuit of Fugitives across Borders* (Cambridge, MA: Harvard University Press, 2015).

26. Quoted in Linn, *Echo of Battle,* 34, 38, and 11–40 (54–56 for coastal defense).

27. Theodore Roosevelt, Remarks Before the Merchants Club in Chicago, May 10, 1905, *APP,* https://www.presidency.ucsb.edu/node/343607. Roosevelt later returned to the theme in requesting additional funds: Theodore Roosevelt, Special Message, April 14 1908, *APP,* https://www.presidency.ucsb.edu/node/206667.

28. T. Roosevelt, "Remarks Before the Merchants Club."

29. Quoted in Michael H. Hunt, *Ideology and U.S. Foreign Policy* (New Haven: Yale University Press, 1987), 128.

30. A. T. Mahan, *The Interest of America in Sea Power, Present and Future* (Boston: Little, Brown, 1897), 156–157. For a rounded consideration of Mahan's outlook that includes a detailed focus on economic security, see Nicholas A. Lambert, *The Neptune Factor: Alfred Thayer Mahan and the Concept of Sea Power* (Annapolis, MD: Naval Institute Press, 2024).

31. "Admiral Dewey's Reply to Protests Against Naval Increase," *Washington Post,* March 15, 1908.

32. Table of spending figures, 1899–1917, Millett and Maslowski, *For the Common Defense,* 319. For a case study of (limited) modernization, see James C. Rentfrow, *Home Squadron: The U.S. Navy on the North Atlantic Station* (Annapolis, MD: Naval Institute Press, 2014). In general, see Mark Shulman, *Navalism and the Emergence of American Sea Power* (Annapolis, MD: Naval Institute Press, 1995); Dirk Bönker, *Militarism in a Global Age: Naval Ambitions in Germany and the United States before World War I* (Ithaca, NY: Cornell University Press, 2012).

33. Warship tonnage figures, 1880–1914, Table 20, Kennedy, *Rise and Fall of the Great Powers,* 203.

34. Katherine C. Epstein, "The Sinews of Globalization," in *The Cambridge History of America and the World,* vol. 3, *1900–1945,* ed. Brooke L. Blower and Andrew Preston (New York: Cambridge University Press, 2021), 37. Epstein lays out her case in more detail in the pathbreaking article "The Conundrum of American Power in the Age of World War I," *Modern American History* 2 (November 2019): 345–365; see also Katherine C. Epstein, "A Useful Category of Analysis? Grand Strategy and US Foreign Relations from the Civil War through World War I," in *Rethinking American Grand Strategy,* ed. Elizabeth Borgwardt, Christopher McKnight Nichols, and Andrew Preston (New York: Oxford University Press, 2021), 123–242. The examples I've used above are drawn from these three articles.

35. Beverly Gage, *The Day Wall Street Exploded: A Story of America in Its First Age of Terror* (New York: Oxford University Press, 2009), 96–122.

36. Michael J. Green, *By More Than Providence: Grand Strategy and American Power in the Asia Pacific Since 1783* (New York: Columbia University Press, 2017), 78–122; Andrew Preston, "From Dong Dang to Da Nang: The Past, Present, and Future of America's Thirty Years War for Asia," *Diplomatic History* 46 (January 2022): 1–34, esp. 30–33.

37. "Of Course There Will Not Be Any War But Just the Same . . . ," *Chicago Daily Tribune,* August 28, 1910.

38. Jung, *Menace to Empire,* 64–104, 148–186.

39. Brian McAllister Linn, *Guardians of Empire: The U.S. Army and the Pacific, 1902–1940* (Chapel Hill: University of North Carolina Press, 1997), 79–113. On the Philippines specifically, see Christopher Capozzola, *Bound by War: How the United States and the Philippines Built America's First Pacific Century* (New York: Basic Books, 2020), 47–111.

40. John Temple Graves, "Japan Knows Our Weakness," *New York American,* June 5, 1913.

41. See, for example, *Defenselessness of the Pacific Coast: Speech of Hon. James McLachlan of California in the House of Representatives* (Washington, DC: GPO, 1910).

42. John M. Thompson, *Great Power Rising: Theodore Roosevelt and the Politics of U.S. Foreign Policy* (New York: Oxford University Press, 2019), 120–149.

43. Linn, *Guardians of Empire,* 88.

44. Notice of House Resolution 29371, *Congressional Record-House* 46:1, 12/14/1910, 323; see also "War Needs of U.S.," *Washington Post,* December 15, 1910.

45. Edward S. Miller, *War Plan Orange: The U.S. Strategy to Defeat Japan, 1897–1945* (Annapolis, MD: Naval Institute Press, 1991), 23, 41

46. Quoted in Miller, *War Plan Orange,* 41; for Hawai'i, see 29–30, 44–46.

47. Rachel St. John, *Line in the Sand: A History of the Western U.S.-Mexico Border* (Princeton: Princeton University Press, 2011), 134–135. On the impact of Mexican radicalism and nationalism in the region, see Samuel Truett, *Fugitive Landscapes: The Forgotten History of the U.S.-Mexico Borderlands* (New Haven: Yale University Press, 2006); and Kelly Lytle Hernández, *Bad Mexicans: Race, Empire, and Revolution in the Borderlands* (New York: W. W. Norton, 2022).

48. A view prompted as early as 1911, when stray Mexican bullets flew across the border and killed two Americans in Douglas, Arizona: Huntington Wilson to Henry Lane Wilson, April 14, 1911, *Foreign Relations of the United States, 1911* (Washington, DC: GPO, 1918), 456. Even the most sensitive analyst of Pancho Villa's raid on Columbus describes it as politically rational, and even understandable, but militarily "quixotic": Friedrich Katz, "Pancho Villa and the Attack on Columbus, New Mexico," *American Historical Review* 83 (1978), 102.

49. Nancy Mitchell, *The Danger of Dreams: German and American Imperialism in Latin America* (Chapel Hill: University of North Carolina Press, 1999), 160–215.

50. St. John, *Line in the Sand,* 124–138. For "spectacle," see David Dorado Romo, *Ringside Seat to a Revolution: An Underground Cultural History of El Paso and Juárez, 1893–1923* (El Paso, TX: Cinco Puntos Press, 2005), 77–192.

51. S. Deborah Kang, *The INS on the Line: Making Immigration Law on the US-Mexico Border, 1917–1954* (New York: Oxford University Press, 2017), 14–35; St. John, *Line in the Sand,* 131–132.

52. Quoted in Thomas J. Knock, *To End All Wars: Woodrow Wilson and the Quest for a New World Order* (Princeton: Princeton University Press, 1992), 83.

53. George C. Herring, *From Colony to Superpower: U.S. Foreign Relations since 1776* (New York: Oxford University Press, 2008), 395.

54. Quoted in St. John, *Line in the Sand,* 135.

55. Quoted in Megan Threlkeld, *Pan American Women: U.S. Internationalists and Revolutionary Mexico* (Philadelphia: University of Pennsylvania Press, 2014), 87.

56. Jules Witcover, *Sabotage at Black Tom: Imperial Germany's Secret War in America, 1914–1917* (Chapel Hill: University of North Carolina Press, 1989); Dwight R. Messimer, *The Baltimore Sabotage Cell: German Agents, American Traitors, and the U-boat Deutschland During World War I* (Annapolis, MD: Naval Institute Press, 2015). On perceptions of Germany, see Bönker, *Militarism in a Global Age.* British intelligence had actually penetrated US government communications much more thoroughly than the Germans: Daniel Larsen, *Plotting for Peace: American Peacemakers, British Codebreakers, and Britain at War, 1914–1917* (Cambridge: Cambridge University Press, 2021).

57. On Venezuela, Mitchell, *Danger of Dreams,* 64–107. On the DR, Lars Schoultz, *Beneath the United States: A History of U.S. Policy toward Latin America* (Cambridge, MA: Harvard University Press, 1998), 182–189.

58. Brenda Gayle Plummer, *Haiti and the Great Powers, 1902–1915* (Baton Rouge: Louisiana State University Press, 1988). On the reasons for intervention, see Mary A. Renda, *Taking Haiti: Military Occupation and the Culture of U.S. Imperialism, 1915–1940* (Chapel Hill: University of North Carolina Press, 2001), 96–99.

59. Mark T. Gilderhus, *Pan American Visions: Woodrow Wilson in the Western Hemisphere, 1913–1921* (Tucson: University of Arizona Press, 1986), 64–66.

60. St. John, *Line in the Sand,* 139.

61. Ross A. Kennedy, *The Will to Believe: Woodrow Wilson, World War I, and America's Strategy for Peace and Security* (Kent, OH: Kent State University Press, 2009), 27–38.

62. Bönker, *Militarism in a Global Age,* 79–84, 90–97.

63. Stuart H. Perry, "After the War," *North American Review* 200 (November 1914): 732–741, 733, 738–739.

64. John C. G. Röhl, *Wilhelm II Into the Abyss of War and Exile, 1900–1941* (Cambridge: Cambridge University Press, 2014), 212–218, 228–235. Ironically, Germany's imperial plans were modelled closely on US expansionism: Jens-Uwe Guettel, *German Expansionism, Imperial Liberalism and the United States, 1776–1945* (Cambridge: Cambridge University Press, 2012).

65. "116 Nearby Ports Open to Invaders," *New York Times,* January 30, 1916; Howard D. Wheeler, "The Attack on New York," *Harper's Weekly,* December 12, 1914, 556–559.

See also Howard D. Wheeler, *Are We Ready?* (Boston: Houghton Mifflin, 1915), which includes a foreword by General Leonard Wood.

66. A. E. Anderson, "Why We Must Fight Abroad," *Four Minute Men News,* Edition A (n.d. [October 1917]), 5.

67. Osgood, *Ideals and Self-Interest,* 130–133 (quoted on 126).

68. "Noted Men Demand We Arm for War," *New York Times,* December 1, 1914, 1.

69. Homer Lea, *The Day of the Saxon* (New York: Harper and Brothers, 1912).

70. "The Facts Supporting President Wilson's War Message," *Current History* 6 (July 1917): 64–75, 64.

71. Osgood, *Ideals and Self-Interest,* 125.

72. Senate Resolution 371, and discussion, *Congressional Record-Senate* 48:10, August 2, 1912, 10045–10047. For the strategic implications of communications, see David Paull Nickles, *Under the Wire: How the Telegraph Changed Diplomacy* (Cambridge, MA: Harvard University Press, 2003), 103–189; Jonathan Reed Winkler, *Nexus: Strategic Communications and American Security in World War I* (Cambridge, MA: Harvard University Press, 2008); and John A. Britton, *Cables, Crises, and the Press: The Geopolitics of the New International Information System in the Americas, 1866–1903* (Albuquerque: University of New Mexico Press, 2013). For Germany, see Heidi J. S. Tworek, *News from Germany: The Competition to Control World Communications, 1900–1945* (Cambridge, MA: Harvard University Press, 2019). For naval technology, see Katherine C. Epstein, *Torpedo: Inventing the Military-Industrial Complex in the United States and Great Britain* (Cambridge, MA: Harvard University Press, 2014).

73. Munroe Smith, "The German Theory of Warfare," *North American Review* 206 (September 1917): 394–405, 404.

74. "Why We Are Fighting," *Four Minute Men Bulletin* 11 (July 23, 1917), 1–2.

75. David F. Houston, *Eight Years with Wilson's Cabinet, 1913 to 1920,* vol. I (Garden City, NY: Doubleday, Page, 1926), 230. On the broader context of civilizational discourse in US foreign policy, see Benjamin A. Coates, "American Presidents and the Ideology of Civilization," in *Ideology in U.S. Foreign Relations: New Histories,* ed. Christopher McKnight Nichols and David Milne (New York: Columbia University Press, 2022), 53–73.

76. Benjamin Allen Coates, *Legalist Empire: International Law and American Foreign Relations in the Early Twentieth Century* (New York: Oxford University Press, 2016), 142–148.

77. Walter Hines Page to Lansing, January 22, 1916, *Foreign Relations of the United States: Lansing Papers,* 307.

78. Quoted in Neiberg, *Path to War,* 42.

79. For Progressives, see Thompson, *Reformers and War* (Holt quoted on 202). For Christian pacifists, see Richard M. Gamble, *The War for Righteousness: Progressive Christianity, the Great War, and the Rise of the Messianic Nation* (Wilmington, DE: ISI Books, 2003).

80. Quoted in Neiberg, *Path to War,* 101.

81. House to Wilson, August 22, 1914, Arthur S. Link, ed., *The Papers of Woodrow Wilson,* vol. 30 (Princeton: Princeton University Press, 1979), 432–433.

82. Diary entry, August 30, 1914, *The Intimate Papers of Colonel House,* vol. 1: *Behind the Political Curtain, 1912–1915,* ed. Charles Seymour (Boston: Houghton Mifflin, 1926), 299.

83. David C. Atkinson, *The Burden of White Supremacy: Containing Asian Migration in the British Empire and the United States* (Chapel Hill: University of North Carolina Press, 2017). For further comparative context, see also Marilyn Lake and Henry Reynolds, *Drawing the Global Colour Line: White Men's Countries and the International Challenge of*

Racial Equality (Cambridge: Cambridge University Press, 2008); and Jesse Tumblin, *The Quest for Security: Sovereignty, Race, and the Defense of the British Empire, 1898–1931* (New York: Cambridge University Press, 2019).

84. James Slayden speech, May 26, 1908, *Congressional Record-House* 42: 6, 6985.

85. On white, race-based *anti*-imperialism, see Eric T. L. Love, *Race over Empire: Racism and U.S. Imperialism, 1865–1900* (Chapel Hill: University of North Carolina Press, 2004).

86. Quoted in Jung, *Menace to Empire*, 123.

87. Quoted in Romo, *Ringside Seat to a Revolution*, 231.

88. *Chae Chan Ping v. United States*, May 13, 1889, 130 US 581 (1889), https://www.law.cornell.edu/supremecourt/text/130/581. See also Beth Lew-Williams, *The Chinese Must Go: Violence, Exclusion, and the Making of the Alien in America* (Cambridge, MA: Harvard University Press, 2018), 192–193. The original Chinese Exclusion Act did not use security as its rationale, however, instead claiming that Chinese immigration "endangers the good order of certain localities": "An Act to Execute Certain Treaty Stipulations Relating to Chinese," May 6, 1882, *Statutes at Large of the United States of America*, vol. 22 (Washington, DC: GPO, 1883), 58.

89. *Nishimura Ekiu v. United States*, January 18, 1892, 142 US 651 (1892), https://www.law.cornell.edu/supremecourt/text/142/651.

90. W. E. B. Du Bois, "Of the Culture of White Folk," *Journal of Race Development* 7 (April 1917): 434–447, 446.

91. Lothrop Stoddard, *The Rising Tide of Color Against White World-Supremacy* (New York: Scribner, 1920), vi, 301–303.

92. Warren S. Thompson, "Race Suicide in the United States," *Scientific Monthly*, July 1917, 22–35. On Ross, a Progressive and founder of American sociology who taught at Stanford, Indiana, and Wisconsin, see Laura L. Lovett, *Conceiving the Future: Pronatalism, Reproduction, and the Family in the United States, 1890–1938* (Chapel Hill: University of North Carolina Press, 2007), 77–108.

93. Madison Grant, *The Passing of the Great Race: or, The Racial Basis of European History* (New York: C. Scribner, 1916), 67, 200.

94. Henry Fairfield Osborn, "Preface to the New Edition," in Madison Grant, *The Passing of the Great Race; or, The Racial Basis of European History*, rev. ed. (New York: Charles Scribner's Sons, 1918), xiii.

95. John Patrick Finnegan, *Against the Specter of a Dragon: The Campaign for American Military Preparedness, 1914–1917* (Westport, CT: Greenwood Press, 1974), 96.

96. Houston, *Eight Years with Wilson's Cabinet*, 229.

97. Houston, *Eight Years with Wilson's Cabinet*, 229.

98. For Wilson's racial views, see Trygve Throntveit, *Power without Victory: Woodrow Wilson and the American Internationalist Experiment* (Chicago: University of Chicago Press, 2017), 85–121. On Wilson's support for Jim Crow, see Eric S. Yellin, *Racism in the Nation's Service: Government Workers and the Color Line in Woodrow Wilson's America* (Chapel Hill: University of North Carolina Press, 2013). On the racism that was inextricable from rather than inconsistent with Wilson's progressivism, see Stephen Skowronek, "The Reassociation of Ideas and Purposes: Racism, Liberalism, and the American Political Tradition," *American Political Science Review* 100 (August 2006): 385–401. More generally, see William A. Link, *The Paradox of Southern Progressivism, 1880–1930* (Chapel Hill: University of North Carolina Press, 1992); Glenda Elizabeth Gilmore, *Gender and Jim Crow: Women and the Politics of White Supremacy in North Carolina, 1896–1920* (Chapel Hill: University of North Carolina Press, 1996), 147–175; and Michael McGerr, *A Fierce Discontent: The Rise and Fall of the Progressive Movement in America, 1870–1920* (New York: Free Press, 2003), 182–218.

On the respectability of racist and eugenic thinkers, see also Aristide R. Zolberg, *A Nation by Design: Immigration Policy in the Fashioning of America* (Cambridge, MA: Harvard University Press, 2006), 248–250.

99. For a transnational history, see Lake and Reynolds, *Drawing the Global Colour Line.*

100. David Woodward, *The American Army and the First World War* (Cambridge: Cambridge University Press, 2014), 11. On wartime racial restrictions more generally, see Chad L. Williams, *Torchbearers of Democracy: African American Soldiers in the World War I Era* (Chapel Hill: University of North Carolina Press, 2010).

101. Erez Manela, *The Wilsonian Moment: Self-Determination and the International Origins of Anticolonial Nationalism* (New York: Oxford University Press, 2007). On the interwar imperial system, see Susan Pedersen, *The Guardians: The League of Nations and the Crisis of Empire* (New York: Oxford University Press, 2015).

102. Quoted in Osgood, *Ideals and Self-Interest,* 204. For more on Carnegie's views, see Bell, *Dreamworlds of Race,* 42–99.

103. Lothrop Stoddard and Glenn Frank, *Stakes of the War: Summary of the Various Problems, Claims, and Interests of the Nations at the Peace Table* (New York: Century, 1918), esp. 349–368.

104. The single best account is Adriane Lentz-Smith, *Freedom Struggles: African Americans and World War I* (Cambridge, MA: Harvard University Press, 2009).

105. NAACP advertisement, *The Crisis,* August 1917, 158. On the limitations of military service for African Americans, see Jennifer D. Keene, *Doughboys, the Great War, and the Remaking of America* (Baltimore: Johns Hopkins University Press, 2001), 82–104; and Williams, *Torchbearers of Democracy,* 52–61.

106. "Resolutions of the Washington Conference," *The Crisis,* June 1917, 59–60; see also Du Bois, "Of the Culture of White Folk." On Du Bois, see Chad L. Williams, *The Wounded World: W.E.B. Du Bois and the First World War* (New York: Farrar, Straus, and Giroux, 2023).

107. "The Rights of Africans and of Peoples of African Origin," *Advocate of Peace,* April 1919, 102.

108. W. E. B. Du Bois, *Darkwater: Voices from Within the Veil* (New York: Harcourt, Brace, and Howe, 1920), 4. See also his later reflections about the promise and limits of revolutionary change during the Great War in W. E. B. Du Bois, *Dusk of Dawn: An Essay Toward an Autobiography of a Race Concept* (New York: Harcourt, Brace, 1940), 281–289, 303–305. For different explanations of his fleeting moment of optimism, see Mark Ellis, "'Closing Ranks' and 'Seeking Honors': W.E.B. Du Bois in World War I," *Journal of American History* 79 (June 1992): 96–124; and William Jordan, "'The Damnable Dilemma': African-American Accommodation and Protest during World War I," *Journal of American History* 81 (March 1995): 1562–1583.

109. See, for example, Philip Ainsworth Means, "Race Appreciation and Democracy," *Journal of Race Development* 9 (October 1918): 180–188, 187–188. On the racial equality clause, see Naoko Shimazu, *Japan, Race and Equality: The Racial Equality Proposal of 1919* (London: Routledge, 1998); and Margaret MacMillan, *Paris 1919: Six Months That Changed the World* (New York: Random House, 2001), 306–321. On the acceptance of empire, see Manela, *Wilsonian Moment;* and Pedersen, *Guardians.*

110. "Making the World Safe for the White Race," *The Crisis,* September 1925, 232.

111. Quoted in Kennedy, *Will to Believe,* 171.

112. For Wilson, see Thompson, *Woodrow Wilson,* 142–143; for Roosevelt, see Speech to the Illinois Bar Association, "National Duty and International Ideals," April 29, 1916, in *Newer Roosevelt Messages,* vol. 3: *Speeches, Letters and Magazine Articles Dealing with the War, Before and After, and Other Vital Topics,* ed. William Griffith (New York: Current Literature, 1919), 778.

113. Daniel Larsen, "Before 'National Security': The Espionage Act of 1917 and the Concept of 'National Defense,'" *Harvard National Security Journal* 12 (2021), https://harvardnsj .org/2021/06/28/before-national-security-the-espionage-act-of-1917-and-the-concept-of -national-defense/.

114. Amos S. Hershey, "Some Problems of Defense," *Annals of the American Academy of Political and Social Science* 61 (September 1915): 263–269, 263.

115. Hector C. Bywater, *Sea-Power in the Pacific: A Study of the American-Japanese Naval Problem* (Boston: Constable, 1921), 244.

116. Frederic J. Haskin, *The Panama Canal* (Garden City, NY: Doubleday, Page, 1914), 348.

117. Mahan, *Influence of Sea Power,* 33–35; Theodore Roosevelt, Special Message to Congress, January 4, 1904, *APP,* https://www.presidency.ucsb.edu/node/206374.

118. Walter E. Weyl, *The End of the War* (New York: Macmillan, 1918), 68–69.

119. As noted by Wilson scholars themselves. See, for example, Knock, *To End All Wars,* 118; and John Milton Cooper Jr., *Woodrow Wilson: A Biography* (New York: Alfred A. Knopf, 2009), 382–383.

120. Woodrow Wilson, Address to a Joint Session of Congress Requesting a Declaration of War Against Germany, April 2, 1917, *APP,* https://www.presidency.ucsb.edu/node/207620.

121. Quoted in Thompson, *Woodrow Wilson,* 106.

122. Woodrow Wilson, Address at Sea Girt, New Jersey Accepting the Democratic Nomination for President, September 2, 1916, *APP,* https://www.presidency.ucsb.edu/node /206580.

123. Thompson, *Woodrow Wilson,* 148–149.

124. Woodrow Wilson, Address to a Joint Session of Congress, February 26, 1917, *APP,* https://www.presidency.ucsb.edu/node/206610; Woodrow Wilson, Inaugural Address, March 5, 1917, *APP,* https://www.presidency.ucsb.edu/node/207579.

125. Wilson, "Declaration of War Against Germany."

126. Cooper, *Woodrow Wilson,* 388. Preparedness campaigners like Henry Cabot Lodge were exceptions: William C. Widenor, *Henry Cabot Lodge and the Search for an American Foreign Policy* (Berkeley: University of California Press, 1980), 274.

127. Woodrow Wilson, Address to the Seventh Annual Dinner of the Railway Business Association in New York City, January 27, 1916, *APP,* https://www.presidency.ucsb.edu/node /317442.

128. Knock, *To End All Wars,* 119.

129. Weyl, *End of the War,* 143–144.

130. On the early problems, see Nicholas A. Lambert, *Planning Armageddon: British Economic Warfare and the First World War* (Cambridge, MA: Harvard University Press, 2012), 251–254, 268–272, 342–343, 363–364, 423, 502–503. For 1916 and after, see Adam Tooze, *The Deluge: The Great War and the Remaking of Global Order 1916–1931* (London: Allen Lane, 2014), 34–40, 48–49, 206–209.

131. Quoted in Thompson, *Sense of Power,* 104.

132. On the absence of a security guarantee, see Lloyd E. Ambrosius, "Wilson, the Republicans, and French Security after World War I," *Journal of American History* 59 (September 1972): 341–352. On the dilemma of being involved in post-1918 France, see Melvyn P. Leffler, *The Elusive Quest: America's Pursuit of European Stability and French Security, 1919–1933* (Chapel Hill: University of North Carolina Press, 1979). On US participation in the supposedly isolationist 1920s, see Frank Costigliola, *Awkward Dominion: American Political, Economic, and Cultural Relations with Europe, 1919–1933* (Ithaca, NY: Cornell University Press, 1984); Patrick O. Cohrs, *The Unfinished Peace after World War I: America, Britain and the Stabilisation of Europe, 1919–1932* (Cambridge: Cambridge

University Press, 2006); Patricia Clavin, *Securing the World Economy: The Reinvention of the League of Nations, 1920–1946* (Oxford: Oxford University Press, 2013); and Patrick O. Cohrs, *The New Atlantic Order: The Transformation of International Politics, 1860–1933* (Cambridge: Cambridge University Press, 2022).

133. Daniel Immerwahr, *How to Hide an Empire: A History of the Greater United States* (New York: Farrar, Straus, and Giroux, 2019), 219.

134. Albert Bushnell Hart, "The Next War," *New York Times*, February 8, 1920. See also Albert Bushnell Hart, "The Need for a Concord of Nations," *Annals of the American Academy of Political and Social Science* 96 (July 1921): 161–165.

135. Quoted in Sarah Churchwell, *Behold, America: A History of America First and the American Dream* (London: Bloomsbury, 2018), 85.

136. Quoted in Cohrs, *Unfinished Peace*, 303.

3. MORAL INSURANCE

1. Woodrow Wilson, Second Annual Message, December 8, 1914, American Presidency Project (hereafter *APP*), https://www.presidency.ucsb.edu/node/207586. Emphasis added.

2. Woodrow Wilson, Address at Soldiers' Memorial Hall, Pittsburgh, January 29, 1916, *APP*, https://www.presidency.ucsb.edu/node/317413.

3. Woodrow Wilson, Address at the Milwaukee Auditorium, January 31, 1916, *APP*, https://www.presidency.ucsb.edu/node/317546.

4. On the centrality of fire, see Richard White, *The Republic for Which It Stands: The United States during Reconstruction and the Gilded Age, 1865–1896* (New York: Oxford University Press, 2017), 482–492; and Daniel Immerwahr, "All That Is Solid Bursts into Flame: Capitalism and Fire in the Nineteenth-Century United States," *Past & Present* 20 (2024). For Chicago, see Karen Sawislak, *Smoldering City: Chicagoans and the Great Fire, 1871–1874* (Chicago: University of Chicago Press, 1995); and for San Francisco, see Joanna L. Dyl, *Seismic City: An Environmental History of San Francisco's 1906 Earthquake* (Seattle: University of Washington Press, 2017). In general, see Christine Meisner Rosen, *The Limits of Power: Great Fires and the Process of City Growth in America* (Cambridge: Cambridge University Press, 1986); and Marc Schneiberg and Tim Bartley, "Regulating American Industries: Markets, Politics, and the Institutional Determinants of Fire Insurance Regulation," *American Journal of Sociology* 107 (July 2001): 101–146.

5. Dalit Baranoff, "Shaped by Risk: The American Fire Insurance Industry, 1790–1920," *Enterprise & Society* 6 (December 2005): 561–570, 562. Although Benjamin Franklin founded the nation's first fire-insurance company, the Philadelphia Contributorship, in 1752, fire insurance remained uncommon until well into the nineteenth century. On Franklin's company, see Edmund S. Morgan, *Benjamin Franklin* (New Haven: Yale University Press, 2002), 57–58; and Arwen P. Mohun, *Risk: Negotiating Safety in American Society* (Baltimore: Johns Hopkins University Press, 2013), 25–28.

6. A. W. Whitney, "The Conflagration Hazard," in *Yale Readings in Insurance*, ed. Lester W. Zartman (New Haven: Yale University Press, 1909), 242, 245, 248–249.

7. Maynard M. Metcalf, "Fire Insurance and Protection from Fire," *Scientific Monthly* 3 (July 1916), 7.

8. Walter C. Betts, "Fire Insurance Rates and Methods," *Annals of the American Academy of Political and Social Science* 22 (November 1903): 1–14, 13–14; Knight, *Risk, Uncertainty and Profit*, 238–245, 251–258. From slightly different perspectives that reach a similar conclusion, see also Henry W. Farnham, "Government Insurance," in Zartman, *Yale Readings in Insurance*, esp. 394; and Robert Riegel, "Problems of Fire Insurance Ratemaking," *Annals of the American Academy of Political and Social Science* 70 (March 1917): 199–219, 217–218.

9. H. Roger Grant, *Insurance Reform: Consumer Action in the Progressive Era* (Ames: Iowa State University Press, 1979), 71–133.

10. "A Good Servant, but a Bad Master," *Four Minute Men Bulletin* 41 (October 15, 1918), 6.

11. On the growth of overall state capacity during this era, see Stephen Skowronek, *Building a New American State: The Expansion of National Administrative Capacities, 1877–1920* (Cambridge: Cambridge University Press, 1982). On foreign and military affairs specifically, see Fareed Zakaria, *From Wealth to Power: The Unusual Origins of America's World Role* (Princeton: Princeton University Press, 1998); and Daniel Beaver, *Modernizing the American War Department: Change and Continuity in a Turbulent Era, 1885–1920* (Kent, OH: Kent State University Press, 2014).

12. Diary entry, August 30, 1914, *Intimate Papers of Colonel House*, vol. 1, ed. Charles Seymour (Boston: Houghton Mifflin, 1926), 299.

13. G. A. Lynch, "National Defense," *Infantry Journal* 10 (March–April 1914), 628–629.

14. Neiberg, *Path to War*, 125.

15. Robert D. Ward, "The Origin and Activities of the National Security League, 1914–1919," *Mississippi Valley Historical Review* 47 (June 1960): 51–65, quoted at 53; Mark R. Shulman, "The Progressive Era Origins of the National Security Act," *Dickinson Law Review* 104 (2000): 289–330. For the NSL's strategy for public education, see its self-published book: Albert Bushnell Hart and Arthur O. Lovejoy, *Handbook of the War for Public Speakers* (New York: National Security League, 1918).

16. Frederic Louis Huidekoper, *The Military Unpreparedness of the United States* (New York: Macmillan, 1915). For Huidekoper's earlier writings on preparedness, see Huidekoper, "Is the United States Prepared for War?" *North American Review* 182 (February 1906): 161–178; Huidekoper, "Is the United States Prepared for War?—II," *North American Review* 182 (March 1906): 391–407; Huidekoper, *The Truth Concerning the United States Army* (Washington, DC: US Infantry Association, 1911); and Huidekoper, "The United States Army and Organized Militia Today," reprinted from the Infantry Journal, July 1911, Washington, DC, 1911; see also "The Army Unprepared For War, Says F. L. Huidekoper," *New York Times*, February 19, 1911. For his connection to the NSL, see John Whiteclay Chambers, *To Raise an Army: The Draft Comes to Modern America* (New York: Free Press, 1987), 86.

17. Augustus Peabody Gardner, "The Nation's Security. How About Our Army And Navy?," Speech in the House of Representatives, October 16, 1914, House Resolution 372, *Congressional Record-House* 51:16, 16745.

18. Senate Resolution 202, *Congressional Record-Senate* 52:1, December 7, 1914, 7; Lodge speech, *Congressional Record-Senate* 52:2, December 15, 1915, 1603, 1609–1610.

19. John Patrick Finnegan, *Against the Specter of a Dragon: The Campaign for American Military Preparedness, 1914–1917* (Westport, CT: Greenwood Press, 1974), 95–101.

20. The articles were authored by, respectively, George von L. Meyer, Cushing Stetson, and Rupert Hughes, *American Defense* 1 (January 1916), 5–7, 12, 21, 26.

21. "Righteous Peace and National Unity," May 19, 1916, *Newer Roosevelt Messages*, vol. 3, ed. William Griffith (New York: Current Literature, 1919), 789.

22. Robert Endicott Osgood, *Ideals and Self-Interest in America's Foreign Relations: The Great Transformation of the Twentieth Century* (Chicago: University of Chicago Press, 1953), 201.

23. Wilson, Second Annual Message, December 8, 1914.

24. Wilson, Second Annual Message, December 8, 1914.

25. Quoted in David Traxel, *Crusader Nation: The United States in Peace and the Great War, 1898–1920* (New York: Alfred A. Knopf, 2006), 243.

26. Woodrow Wilson, Address delivered at the First Annual Assemblage of the League to Enforce Peace, May 27, 1916, *APP,* https://www.presidency.ucsb.edu/node/206570; see also Woodrow Wilson, Address at Sea Girt, New Jersey Accepting the Democratic Nomination for President, September 2, 1916, *APP,* https://www.presidency.ucsb.edu/node/206580. On the stump speeches, see John A. Thompson, *Woodrow Wilson* (London: Routledge, 2002), 116–117.

27. Christopher Capozzola, *Uncle Sam Wants You: World War I and the Making of the Modern American Citizen* (New York: Oxford University Press, 2008), 173–205; Neiberg, *Path to War,* 122–150. See also, with some focus on NSL activities, Zachary Smith, *Age of Fear: Othering and American Identity During World War I* (Baltimore: Johns Hopkins University Press, 2019).

28. Woodrow Wilson, Inaugural Address, March 5, 1917, *APP,* https://www.presidency.ucsb.edu/node/207579.

29. For the complexity of Roosevelt's views, see Gary Gerstle, *American Crucible: Race and Nation in the Twentieth Century* (Princeton: Princeton University Press, 2001), 44–80. For "America First," see Sarah Churchwell, *Behold, America: The Entangled History of "America First" and "the American Dream"* (London: Bloomsbury, 2018), 41–75.

30. *National Security League: Hearings before a Special Committee of the House of Representatives,* Part 2, December 20, 1918 (Washington, DC: GPO, 1918), 100.

31. Kennedy, *Over Here,* 36. For a different view, see Shulman, "Progressive Era Origins."

32. *National Security League: Hearings . . . ,* Part 3, January 6, 1919 (Washington, DC: GPO, 1919), 249.

33. George B. Duncan, "Military Preparedness: What Does It Mean?" *North American Review* 202 (October 1915): 509–516, 515. On the links between progressivism and preparedness, see Penn Borden, *Civilian Indoctrination of the Military: World War I and Future Implications for the Military-Industrial Complex* (Westport, CT: Greenwood Press, 1989).

34. Neiberg, *Path to War,* 143.

35. Quoted in Peter A. Shulman, *Coal and Empire: The Birth of Energy Security in Industrial America* (Baltimore: Johns Hopkins University Press, 2015), 207.

36. Daniel T. Rodgers, *Atlantic Crossings: Social Politics in a Progressive Age* (Cambridge, MA: Harvard University Press, 1998), 241–266; Jonathan Levy, *Freaks of Fortune: The Emerging World of Capitalism and Risk in America* (Cambridge, MA: Harvard University Press, 2012), 304–307; Hannah Farber, *Underwriters of the United States: How Insurance Shaped the American Founding* (Chapel Hill, 2021). For "group insurance," see Jennifer Klein, *For All These Rights: Business, Labor, and the Shaping of America's Public-Private Welfare State* (Princeton: Princeton University Press, 2003), 18–30. For workplace accident insurance, which did have a significant influence on the growth of the federal social-welfare state, see John Fabian Witt, *The Accidental Republic: Crippled Workingmen, Destitute Widows, and the Remaking of American Law* (Cambridge, MA: Harvard University Press, 2004). On the rapid spread of insurance in the nineteenth century, see (despite their interpretive differences) Viviana A. Rotman Zelizer, *Morals and Markets: The Development of Life Insurance in the United States* (New York: Columbia University Press, 1979); and Sharon Ann Murphy, *Investing in Life: Insurance in Antebellum America* (Baltimore: Johns Hopkins University Press, 2010), with growth statistic on 5. Likewise, despite their differences, on the subtreasury plan see Lawrence Goodwyn, *Democratic Promise: The Populist Moment in America* (New York: Oxford University Press, 1976), 134–139, 149–176, 213–243, 311–316, 565–581; Elizabeth Sanders, *Roots of Reform: Farmers, Workers, and the American State, 1877–1917* (Chicago: University of Chicago Press, 1999); and Charles Postel, *The Populist Vision* (New York: Oxford University Press, 2007), 153–156.

37. I. M. Rubinow, *Social Insurance, with Special Reference to American Conditions* (New York: H. Holt, 1913).

38. Josiah Royce, *War and Insurance* (New York: Macmillan, 1914), x–xi, xx, 64. Emphasis in original. Despite Royce's claim that "the whole subject is new," the pioneering English aviator Edward Purkis Frost had already come up with a similar plan: Edward P. Frost, *Safeguards for Peace: A Scheme of State Insurance Against War* (Cambridge: Cambridge University Press, 1905).

39. Royce, *War and Insurance*, xxix.

40. Ralph Barton Perry, *The Free Man and the Soldier* (New York: C. Scribner's Sons, 1916).

41. "Roosevelt Against Inconclusive Peace," *New York Times*, January 13, 1918.

42. Gerstle, *American Crucible*, 84–85.

43. See Henry Crosby Emery, "Legislation against Futures," *Political Science Quarterly* 10 (March 1895): 62–86; and Emery, *Speculation on the Stock and Produce Exchanges of the United States* (New York: Columbia University Press, 1896). For his life, see Robert Stanley Herren, "Emery, Henry Crosby," *American National Biography* (New York: Oxford University Press, 1999), https://doi.org/10.1093/anb/9780198606697.article.1000511. On his role in the development of risk management in the late nineteenth century, see Levy, *Freaks of Fortune*, 234, 261.

44. Henry C. Emery, *Some Economic Aspects of War* (Washington, DC: GPO, 1914), 9, 20–22. On Emery's business-oriented progressivism, see Cedric B. Cowing, *Populists, Plungers, and Progressives: A Social History of Stock and Commodity Speculation, 1890–1936* (Princeton: Princeton University Press, 1965), 47–49, 108; and Paul Wolman, *Most Favored Nation: The Republican Revisionists and U.S. Tariff Policy, 1897–1912* (Chapel Hill: University of North Carolina Press, 1992), 158, 165–166, 180, 190–191, 208.

45. Woodrow Wilson, Address to the Seventh Annual Dinner of the Railway Business Association in New York City, January 27, 1916, *APP*, https://www.presidency.ucsb.edu/node /317442.

46. Chambers, *To Raise an Army*, 75.

47. "National Defense Outlays and Veterans' Benefits: 1915–1995," *Historical Statistics of the United States*, Part E: *Governance and International Relations*, eds. Susan B. Carter et al. (Cambridge: Cambridge University Press, 2006), Table Ed146–154.

48. "War Expenditure and Total Mobilized Forces, 1914–1919," Table 25, Paul Kennedy, *The Rise and Fall of the Great Powers: Economic Change and Military Conflict from 1500 to 2000* (New York, 1987), 274.

49. See the definitive account in Chambers, *To Raise an Army*.

50. "America's Unfolding Power," *Washington Post*, August 4, 1918.

51. Jennifer D. Keene, *Doughboys, the Great War, and the Remaking of America* (Baltimore: Johns Hopkins University Press, 2001), 8–34; Mark Ethan Grotelueschen, *The AEF Way of War: The American Army and Combat in World War I* (Cambridge: Cambridge University Press, 2007); David Woodward, *The American Army and the First World War* (Cambridge: Cambridge University Press, 2014). On the impact of US forces, see David Stevenson, *With Our Backs to the Wall: Victory and Defeat in 1918* (London: Allen Lane, 2011).

52. Allan R. Millett and Peter Maslowski, *For the Common Defense: A Military History of the United States of America*, rev. and expanded (New York: Free Press, 1994), 338–342; Jerry Cooper, *The Rise of the National Guard: The Evolution of the American Militia, 1865–1920* (Lincoln: University of Nebraska Press, 1997), 153–172.

53. Mark Clodfelter, *Beneficial Bombing: The Progressive Foundations of American Air Power, 1917–1945* (Lincoln: University of Nebraska Press, 2010), 30–32.

54. Kathryn Steen, *The American Synthetic Organic Chemicals Industry: War and Politics, 1910–1930* (Chapel Hill: University of North Carolina Press, 2014).

55. Stephen Meyer III, *The Five Dollar Day: Labor Management and Social Control in the Ford Motor Company 1908–1921* (Albany: State University of New York Press, 1981), 170–171; David Hounshell, *From the American System to Mass Production, 1800–1932: The Development of Manufacturing Technology in the United States* (Baltimore: Johns Hopkins University Press, 1984), 267–268; Vincent Curcio, *Henry Ford* (New York: Oxford University Press, 2013), 86–102.

56. Quoted in Paul A. C. Koistinen, "The 'Industrial-Military Complex' in Historical Perspective: World War I," *Business History Review* 41 (Winter 1967): 378–403, 393.

57. McGerr, *Fierce Discontent*, 298; McAdoo quoted in Bureau of War Risk, Treasury Department, "Uncle Sam's Insurance for Soldiers and Sailors: Answers to Questions You Will Ask," War Risk Insurance Bulletin No. 4, T49.3, November 15, 1917, 3.

58. Albert C. James, "War Risk Insurance," prepared for students at the University of Minnesota, March 1918, 3–4. See also Beth Linker, *War's Waste: Rehabilitation in World War I America* (Chicago: University of Chicago Press, 2011), 28–35.

59. Quoted in K. Walter Hickel, "War, Region, and Social Welfare: Federal Aid to Servicemen's Dependents in the South, 1917–1921," *Journal of American History* 87 (March 2001): 1362–1391, 1365. For Lathrop's vision, see J. C. Lathrop, "The Children's Bureau in War Time," *North American Review* 206 (November 1917): 734–746; and Julia C. Lathrop, "Provision for the Care of the Families and Dependents of Soldiers and Sailors, *Proceedings of the Academy of Political Science in the City of New York* 7 (February 1918): 140–151. For broader context, see Eric Rauchway, *The Refuge of Affections: Family and American Reform Politics, 1900–1920* (New York: Columbia University Press, 2001): 123–153 (127–128 for Lathrop); and, beyond the war, Theda Skocpol, *Protecting Soldiers and Mothers: The Political Origins of Social Policy in the United States* (Cambridge, MA: Harvard University Press, 1992), 480–524.

60. On healthcare, see Jessica L. Adler, *Burdens of War: Creating the United States Veterans Health System* (Baltimore: Johns Hopkins University Press, 2017); on the irony, see Linker, *War's Waste*, 10–34. For earlier precursors, see Skocpol, *Protecting Soldiers and Mothers*, 102–151; and Patrick J. Kelly, *Creating a National Home: Building the Veterans' Welfare State, 1860–1900* (Cambridge, MA: Harvard University Press, 1997).

61. Nancy K. Bristow, *Making Men Moral: Social Engineering During the Great War* (New York: New York University Press, 1996); Mark T. Hauser, "'A Violent Desire for the Amusements': Boxing, Libraries, and the Distribution and Management of Welfare During the First World War," *Journal of Military History* 86 (October 2022): 883–913.

62. W. Elliot Brownlee, "Woodrow Wilson and Financing the Modern State: The Revenue Act of 1916," *Proceedings of the American Philosophical Society* 129 (June 1985): 173–210.

63. Valerie Jean Conner, *The National War Labor Board: Stability, Social Justice, and the Voluntary State in World War I* (Chapel Hill: University of North Carolina Press, 1983); Joseph A. McCartin, *Labor's Great War: The Struggle for Industrial Democracy and the Origins of Modern American Labor Relations, 1912–1921* (Chapel Hill: University of North Carolina Press, 1997). On the wider corporatist context, see Kennedy, *Over Here*, 258–270. On WIB, see Robert D. Cuff, *The War Industries Board: Business-Government Relations during World War I* (Baltimore: Johns Hopkins University Press, 1973).

64. Thomas B. Love, "The Social Significance of War Risk Insurance," *Annals of the American Academy of Political and Social Science* 79 (September 1918): 46–51, 46, 51.

65. Paul H. Douglas, "The War Risk Insurance Act," *Journal of Political Economy* 26 (May 1918): 461–483, 483.

66. Quoted in John Milton Cooper Jr., *Woodrow Wilson: A Biography* (New York: Alfred A. Knopf, 2009), 382.

67. Quoted in Cooper, *Woodrow Wilson*, 375.

68. Quoted in Maureen A. Flanagan, *America Reformed: Progressives and Progressivisms, 1890s–1920s* (New York: Oxford University Press, 2007), 230. Flanagan makes a similar point about the CPI's need to exaggerate the stakes of the war, not because of free security but because of a general uncertainty over American identity. On the CPI, see especially Stephen Vaughn, *Holding Fast the Inner Lines: Democracy, Nationalism, and the Committee on Public Information* (Chapel Hill: University of North Carolina Press, 1980). On the ideological impact the war's geographical remoteness had on the US home front, see Kennedy, *Over Here*, 45–92.

69. Woodrow Wilson, Address to a Joint Session of Congress Requesting a Declaration of War Against Germany, April 2, 1917, *APP*, https://www.presidency.ucsb.edu/node/207620.

70. Sam Lebovic, *State of Silence: The Espionage Act and the Rise of America's Secrecy Regime* (New York: Basic Books, 2023), 43–72; Kaeten Mistry and Hannah Gurman, "The Paradox of National Security Whistleblowing: Locating and Framing a History of the Phenomenon," in *Whistleblowing Nation: The History of National Security Disclosures and the Cult of State Secrecy*, ed. Kaeten Mistry and Hannah Gurman (New York: Columbia University Press, 2020), 16–17; Gerstle, *American Crucible*, 92–93; Moon-Ho Jung, *Menace to Empire: Anticolonial Solidarities and the Transpacific Origins of the US Security State* (Oakland: University of California Press, 2022), 187–231.

71. Capozzola, *Uncle Sam Wants You*, 41–53.

72. Kennedy, *Over Here*, 116–117; Capozzola, *Uncle Sam Wants You*, 193. As Vaughn, *Holding Fast*, points out, most of the worst repression happened at the state and local levels (216). On the federalist nature of CND, see William J. Breen, *Uncle Sam at Home: Civilian Mobilization, Wartime Federalism, and the Council of National Defense, 1917–1919* (Westport, CT: Greenwood Press, 1984).

73. Carl H. Chrislock, *Watchdog of Loyalty: The Minnesota Commission of Public Safety During World War I* (St. Paul: Minnesota Historical Society Press, 1991), x.

74. Quoted in Robert B. Westbrook, *John Dewey and American Democracy* (Ithaca, NY: Cornell University Press, 1991), 197. For Dewey's vision of progressive government emerging from the war, see John Dewey, "Internal Social Reorganization after the War," *Journal of Race Development* 8 (April 1918): 385–400.

75. On progressive intellectuals and the war, see Thompson, *Reformers and War;* and Throntveit, *Power Without Victory.* On progressive antiwar views, see Christopher McKnight Nichols, *Promise and Peril: America at the Dawn of a Global Age* (Cambridge, MA: Harvard University Press, 2011). For the progressives' transnational networks, see James T. Kloppenberg, *Uncertain Victory: Social Democracy and Progressivism in European and American Thought, 1870–1920* (New York: Oxford University Press, 1986); and Daniel T. Rodgers, *Atlantic Crossings: Social Politics in a Progressive Age* (Cambridge, MA: Harvard University Press, 1998). For the progressivism of Creel and the CPI, see Vaughn, *Holding Fast;* and of the army, see Woodward, *American Army and the First World War*, 12–13.

76. Herbert Croly, *The Promise of American Life* (New York: Macmillan, 1909), 311; for Croly's views on US free security, see 7–16.

77. "The End of Isolation," *New Republic*, November 7, 1914, 9–10.

78. Walter Lippmann, "What Program Shall the United States Stand for in International Relations?" *Annals of the American Academy of Political and Social Science* 66 (July 1916): 69–70.

79. Rodgers, *Atlantic Crossings*, 275–290; McGerr, *Fierce Discontent*, 280–298.

80. Croly, *Promise of American Life*, 311.

81. "End of Isolation," 10.

82. Walter Lippmann, "The World Conflict in Its Relation to American Democracy," *Annals of the American Academy of Political and Social Science* 72 (July 1917): 1–10, 8–9.

83. Walter E. Weyl, *The New Democracy: An Essay on Certain Political and Economic Tendencies in the United States* (New York: Macmillan, 1912), 348, 320, 298, 143.

84. Walter E. Weyl, *American World Policies* (New York: Macmillan, 1917), 1, 57.

85. Weyl, *American World Policies,* 227–228.

86. Walter E. Weyl, *The End of the War* (New York: Macmillan, 1918), 72, 210.

87. Randolph Bourne, "The State," in *War and the Intellectuals: Essays by Randolph S. Bourne, 1915–1919,* ed. Carl Resek (New York: Harper and Row, 1964), 71, 72, 73, 77. See also Thompson, *Reformers and War,* 84–86, 147, 158–168, 273–276; and Nichols, *Promise and Peril,* 113–178. For Bourne's feud with Dewey, see Westbrook, *John Dewey and American Democracy,* 195–227.

88. Quoted in Ward, "Origin and Activities," 59. See also Kennedy, *Over Here,* 291; and M. J. Heale, *American Anti-Communism: Combating the Enemy Within, 1830–1970* (Baltimore: Johns Hopkins University Press, 1990), 52–53, 66–67. For the wider context, see Alex Goodall, *Loyalty and Liberty: American Countersubversion from World War I to the McCarthy Era* (Urbana: University of Illinois Press, 2013).

89. "Says We Face Revolution," *New York Times,* October 17, 1919.

90. Beverly Gage, *The Day Wall Street Exploded: A Story of America in Its First Age of Terror* (New York: Oxford University Press, 2009), 127–129.

91. Brian McAllister Linn, *The Echo of Battle: The Army's Way of War* (Cambridge, MA: Harvard University Press, 2007), 139.

92. Madison Grant, "America for the Americans," American Defense Society, 1924.

93. Gage, *Day Wall Street Exploded,* 310.

4. THE BRIDGE IN CHICAGO

1. Franklin D. Roosevelt, Address at Chicago, October 5, 1937, American Presidency Project (hereafter *APP*), https://www.presidency.ucsb.edu/node/208843.

2. "New Bridge Opened," *Chicago Defender,* October 9, 1937.

3. Harry Hansen, *The Chicago* (New York: Farrar & Rinehart, 1942), 263.

4. H. Evert Kincaid, "The Chicago Comprehensive City Plan," *Journal of the American Institute of Planners* 11 (October–December 1945): 23–27, 24.

5. "Outer Drive Bridge," *Chicago Daily Tribune,* October 5, 1937.

6. Nathan Holth, *Chicago's Bridges* (Botley, UK: Shire, 2013), 11–20, 44–45; Patrick T. McBriarty, *Chicago River Bridges* (Urbana: University of Illinois Press, 2013), 48–51.

7. "Reroute Traffic for Dedication of Link Bridges," *Chicago Daily Tribune,* October 3, 1937.

8. Chicago Plan Commission, *The Outer Drive Along the Lake Front, Chicago* (Chicago: University of Chicago Press, 1929), 6, 11, 63.

9. House Resolution 7187, *Congressional Record-House,* January 8, 1926, 1732; House Resolution 7187, *Congressional Record-House,* March 6, 1926, 5191; House Resolution 15333, *Congressional Record-House,* January 14, 1929, 1672.

10. Dennis H. Cremin, *Grant Park: The Evolution of Chicago's Front Yard* (Carbondale: Southern Illinois University, 2013), 133–134.

11. Hansen, *Chicago,* 262.

12. In general, see Roger Biles, *The Fate of Cities: Urban America and the Federal Government, 1945–2000* (Lawrence: University Press of Kansas, 2011), 6–7. On Chicago specifically, see Robert G. Spinney, *City of Big Shoulders: A History of Chicago* (DeKalb: Northern

Illinois Press, 2000), 180–181; and Robert Bruegmann, "Built Environment of the Chicago Region," in *Chicago Neighborhoods and Suburbs: A Historical Guide*, ed. Ann Durkin Keating (Chicago: University of Chicago Press, 2008), 80. The New Deal's longer-term urban impact wasn't always beneficial to cities themselves, however, especially when it came to issues of race: Arnold R. Hirsch, *Making the Second Ghetto: Race and Housing in Chicago, 1940–1960* (New York: Cambridge University Press, 1983).

13. Franklin D. Roosevelt, Remarks at Grand Coulee Dam, October 2, 1937, *APP*, https://www.presidency.ucsb.edu/node/208836. For 1934, see David M. Kennedy, *Freedom from Fear: The American People in Depression and War, 1929–1945* (New York: Oxford University Press, 1999), 246.

14. Roosevelt, Address at Chicago, October 5, 1937.

15. Kathryn S. Olmsted, *The Newspaper Axis: Six Press Barons Who Enabled Hitler* (New Haven: Yale University Press, 2022), 125; Kenneth S. Davis, *FDR, Into the Storm, 1937–1940: A History* (New York: Random House, 1993), 130; James MacGregor Burns, *Roosevelt: The Lion and the Fox* (New York: Harcourt Brace, 1956), 318. See also Richard Norton Smith, *The Colonel: The Life and Legend of Robert R. McCormick, 1880–1955* (Boston: Houghton Mifflin, 1997), 360–364. These are in fact rare instances in which the bridge dedication is even mentioned, and diplomatic historians have completely ignored it.

16. On the importance of the New Deal to Chicago, see Lizabeth Cohen, *Making a New Deal: Industrial Workers in Chicago, 1919–1939* (New York: Cambridge University Press, 1990), esp. 267–289. See also Lyle W. Dorsett, *Franklin D. Roosevelt and the City Bosses* (Port Washington, NY: Kennikat Press, 1977), 85–90; Roger Biles, *Big City Boss in Depression and War: Mayor Edward J. Kelly of Chicago* (DeKalb: Northern Illinois University, 1984), 74–88; Nathan Godfried, *WCFL, Chicago's Voice of Labor, 1926–1978* (Urbana: University of Illinois Press, 1997), 137–149, 187–193; Gregory C. Randall, *America's Original GI Town: Park Forest, Illinois* (Baltimore: Johns Hopkins University Press, 2000); and Larry Bennett, *The Third City: Chicago and American Urbanism* (Chicago: University of Chicago Press, 2010), 150–152.

17. For McCormick, see Olmsted, *Newspaper Axis*, 62–70. For the economists, Angus Burgin, *The Great Persuasion: Reinventing Free Markets since the Depression* (Cambridge, MA: Harvard University Press, 2012), 12–16, 32–54.

18. Cordell Hull, *The Memoirs of Cordell Hull*, vol. 1 (New York: Macmillan, 1948), 544.

19. *The Secret Diary of Harold L. Ickes*, vol. 2: *The Inside Struggle, 1936–1939* (New York: Simon and Schuster, 1953), 213, 268. For FDR's War on Crime, see Anthony Gregory, *New Deal Law and Order: How the War on Crime Built the Modern Liberal State* (Cambridge, MA: Harvard University Press, 2024).

20. Roosevelt to House, October 19, 1937, in *The Roosevelt Letters: Being the Personal Correspondence of Franklin Delano Roosevelt*, vol. 3: *1928–1945*, ed. Elliott Roosevelt (London: Harrap, 1952), 221.

21. *Secret Diary of Harold L. Ickes*, vol. 2, 222; Hull, *Memoirs*, 545; quotations from Stanley Hornbeck to Dorothy Borg, October 24, 1957, Stanley Hornbeck papers, box 34, Hoover Institution Archives, Stanford University. Moreover, as Megan Black argues, it's important to remember that the Department of the Interior was a major actor internationally as well as—indeed, by this point, perhaps even more than—in the United States: Megan Black, *The Global Interior: Mineral Frontiers and American Power* (Cambridge, MA: Harvard University Press, 2018). To epitomize the state's infrastructural and regulatory powers at their most invasive, thereby introducing his theory of "panopticism," Foucault used the story of a medieval village imposing a strict quarantine to deal with an outbreak of the plague: Michael Foucault, *Discipline and Punish: The Birth of the Prison*, trans. Alan Sheridan (London: Allen Lane, 1977), 195–200.

22. 1891 Immigration Act quoted in Mae M. Ngai, *Impossible Subjects: Illegal Aliens and the Making of Modern America* (Princeton: Princeton University Press, 2004), 59.

23. Alison Bashford, *Imperial Hygiene: A Critical History of Colonialism, Nationalism and Public Health* (Basingstoke, UK: Palgrave Macmillan, 2004), 115–136; Alison Bashford, ed., *Quarantine: Local and Global Histories* (Basingstoke, UK: Palgrave Macmillan, 2016). For the American reliance on quarantines as a public-health measure, see Howard Markel, *Quarantine! East European Jewish Immigrants and the New York City Epidemics of 1892* (Baltimore: Johns Hopkins University Press, 1997); Nayan Shah, *Contagious Divides: Epidemics and Race in San Francisco's Chinatown* (Berkeley: University of California Press, 2001); and, in comparative context, Charles Allan McCoy, *Diseased States: Epidemic Control in Britain and the United States* (Amherst: University of Massachusetts Press, 2020), 88–110, 128–145. On polio, see Naomi Rogers, *Dirt and Disease: Polio Before FDR* (New Brunswick, NJ: Rutgers University Press, 1992), esp. 33–44; and Daniel J. Wilson, "A Crippling Fear: Experiencing Polio in the Era of FDR," *Bulletin of the History of Medicine* 72 (Fall 1998): 464–495.

24. Alan L. Olmstead and Paul W. Rhode, *Arresting Contagion: Science, Policy, and Conflicts over Animal Disease Control* (Cambridge, MA: Harvard University Press, 2015).

25. On the anti-Japanese focus of the "yellow peril," see Erika Lee, "The 'Yellow Peril' and Asian Exclusion in the Americas," *Pacific Historical Review* 76 (November 2007): 537–562. For quarantine policies for Asia and Europe, see Amy L. Fairchild, *Science at the Borders: Immigrant Medical Inspection and the Shaping of the Modern Industrial Labor* (Baltimore: Johns Hopkins University Press, 2003). For Angel Island, see Shah, *Contagious Divides*, 183–186; Erika Lee, *At America's Gates: Chinese Immigration during the Exclusion Era, 1882–1943* (Chapel Hill: University of North Carolina Press, 2003), 81–84; and Erika Lee and Judy Yung, *Angel Island: Immigrant Gateway to America* (New York: Oxford University Press, 2010), 10, 35–39, 77–78, 152–153, 218–220. On Asian immigrants as dangerous, see Beth Lew-Williams, *The Chinese Must Go: Violence, Exclusion, and the Making of the Alien in America* (Cambridge, MA: Harvard University Press, 2018). For biopolitics, see Khary Oronde Polk, *Contagions of Empire: Scientific Racism, Sexuality, and Black Military Workers Abroad, 1898–1948* (Chapel Hill: University of North Carolina Press, 2020); and Shanon Fitzpatrick, "The Body Politics of US Imperial Power," in *The Cambridge History of America and the World*, vol. 3, *1900–1945*, ed. Brooke L. Blower and Andrew Preston (New York: Cambridge University Press, 2021), 562–590.

26. Robert Kagan, *The Ghost at the Feast: America and the Collapse of World Order, 1900–1941* (New York: Alfred A. Knopf, 2023), 369–376.

27. Hansen, *Chicago*, 263.

28. "N Lake Shore Dr. Bridge History," http://chicagoloopbridges.com/bridges12/MS12/LSD12-4.html.

29. Ira Katznelson, *Fear Itself: The New Deal and the Origins of Our Time* (New York: Liveright, 2013), 29–57, esp. 47–48 for the relationship between uncertainty and fear.

30. Frank H. Knight, *Risk, Uncertainty and Profit* (Boston: Houghton Mifflin, 1921), 20 (emphasis in original). It was the new availability of statistics and other numerical data in the nineteenth century that made the measurement of risk possible in the twentieth. Although he doesn't mention Knight, see Ian Hacking, *The Taming of Chance* (Cambridge: Cambridge University Press, 1990).

31. Katznelson, *Fear Itself*, 33–34.

32. Quoted in Angus Burgin, "The Radical Conservatism of Frank H. Knight," *Modern Intellectual History* 6 (November 2009): 513–538, 518, 522. For Knight's psychological depression, see Burgin, *Great Persuasion*, 13.

33. Knight, *Risk, Uncertainty and Profit*, 348.

34. Jonathan Levy, *Freaks of Fortune: The Emerging World of Capitalism and Risk in America* (Cambridge, MA: Harvard University Press, 2012), 281–282.

35. Frank H. Knight, "Review of *Economic Stabilization in an Unbalanced World* by Alvin Harvey Hansen," *Journal of Political Economy* 41 (April 1933), 245.

36. Frank H. Knight, "Intellectual Confusion on Morals and Economics," *International Journal of Ethics* 45 (January 1935): 200–220, 216; Frank H. Knight, "The Rôle of Principles in Economics and Politics," *American Economic Review* 41 (March 1951): 1–29, 11.

37. F. H. Knight, "Unemployment: And Mr. Keynes's Revolution in Economic Theory," *Canadian Journal of Economics and Political Science* 3 (February 1937): 100–123, 100–101, 122. On Knight as a beloved but demanding teacher, see Burgin, *Great Persuasion*, 34–35, 44–45.

38. Quoted in Burgin, *Great Persuasion*, 28.

39. Jens Beckert, "What Is Sociological about Economic Sociology? Uncertainty and the Embeddedness of Economic Action," *Theory and Society* 25 (December 1996): 803–840.

40. Quoted in Burgin, *Great Persuasion*, 4. On Knight's heterodoxy, see Burgin, "Radical Conservatism," esp. 515–516, 520–521, 524–529, 535–536; more generally, see also Kim Phillips-Fein, *Invisible Hands: The Businessmen's Crusade Against the New Deal* (New York: W. W. Norton, 2009), 23–24. On Knight's differences with the postwar Chicago School led by Milton Friedman, see also Thomas A. Stapleford, "Positive Economics for Democratic Policy: Milton Friedman, Institutionalism, and the Science of History," in *Building Chicago Economics: New Perspectives on the History of America's Most Powerful Economics Program*, ed. Robert Van Horn, Philip Mirowski, and Thomas A. Stapleford (Cambridge: Cambridge University Press, 2011), 5–6, 23–26; and Daniel Stedman Jones, *Masters of the Universe: Hayek, Friedman, and the Birth of Neoliberal Politics* (Princeton: Princeton University Press, 2012), 89–91.

41. John Maynard Keynes, *A Treatise on Probability* (1921), in *The Collected Writings of John Maynard Keynes*, vol. 8 (Cambridge: Cambridge University Press, 2013), esp. 3–9, 21–38. For Knight and Keynes's fundamental perceptions of risk and uncertainty, see Levy, *Freaks of Fortune*, 327n18. Ideas about probability were from a much older lineage than conceptions of quantifiable risk: see Ian Hacking, *The Emergence of Probability: A Philosophical Study of Early Ideas about Probability, Induction and Statistical Inference* (Cambridge: Cambridge University Press, 1975).

42. Robert Skidelsky, *John Maynard Keynes, 1883–1946: Economist, Philosopher, Statesman* (London: Macmillan, 2003), 286.

43. Keynes, *The Times* (London), January 2, 1934, *Collected Writings of John Maynard Keynes*, vol. 21, *Activities 1931–1939* (Cambridge: Cambridge University Press, 2013), 297. On their interactions, see Skidelsky, *John Maynard Keynes*, 505–511; and Eric Rauchway, *The Money Makers: How Roosevelt and Keynes Ended the Depression, Defeated Fascism, and Secured a Prosperous Peace* (New York: Basic Books, 2015).

44. Skidelsky, *John Maynard Keynes*, 96–98, 286, 366 (quoted on 457).

45. Keynes, *The General Theory of Employment, Interest and Money* (1936), *Collected Writings of John Maynard Keynes*, vol. 7 (Cambridge: Cambridge University Press, 2013), 221.

46. Keynes, "Can America Spend Its Way into Recovery?" *Redbook*, December 1934, *Collected Writings*, vol. 21, 335, 336.

47. Franklin D. Roosevelt, Inaugural Address, March 4, 1933, *APP*, https://www.presidency.ucsb.edu/node/208712.

48. Kennedy, *Freedom from Fear*, 244–248, 363–380; Jennifer Klein, *For All These Rights: Business, Labor, and the Shaping of America's Public-Private Welfare State* (Princeton: Princeton University Press, 2003), 53–161 (quoted on 78). Much of my thinking about

security has been shaped by these two important books, although neither of them examines "national security" as an aspect of broader thinking about security.

49. Jonathan Levy, *Ages of American Capitalism: A History of the United States* (New York: Random House, 2021), 389–392, 399, 416–417; see also Levy, *Freaks of Fortune,* 313–315.

50. Charles E. Merriam, "The Assumptions of Democracy," *Political Science Quarterly* 53 (September 1938): 328–349, 344.

51. Leverett S. Lyon et al., *The National Recovery Administration: An Analysis and Appraisal* (Washington, DC: Brookings Institution, 1935), 558.

52. Franklin D. Roosevelt, Radio Address on the Third Anniversary of the Social Security Act, August 15, 1938, *APP,* https://www.presidency.ucsb.edu/node/209105.

53. Franklin D. Roosevelt, Message to Congress on the Objectives and Accomplishments of the Administration, June 8, 1934, *APP,* https://www.presidency.ucsb.edu/node/208398.

54. Franklin D. Roosevelt, Annual Message to Congress, January 4, 1935, *APP,* https://www.presidency.ucsb.edu/node/208864.

55. Rexford G. Tugwell, *In Search of Roosevelt* (Cambridge, MA: Harvard University Press, 1972), 290.

56. Herbert Hoover, *The Challenge to Liberty* (New York: C. Scribner's Sons, 1934), esp. 38, 171, 176–178, 183–188. For the broader debate, see Eric Rauchway, *Winter War: Hoover, Roosevelt, and the First Clash Over the New Deal* (New York: Basic Books, 2018).

57. Wilbur Cohen oral history, in *The Making of the New Deal: The Insiders Speak,* ed. Katie Louchheim (Cambridge, MA: Harvard University Press, 1983), 155.

58. Ira Jewell Williams, "The Future of Democracy in the United States," *Annals of the American Academy of Political and Social Science* 180 (July 1935): 83–93, 83, 91. See also Ira Jewell Williams, "Does the Commerce Clause Give Power to Dominate All Industry?" *University of Pennsylvania Law Review and American Law Register* 83 (November 1934): 23–36.

59. Lionel Robbins, *Economic Planning and International Order* (London: Macmillan, 1937), 90.

60. F. A. Hayek, *The Road to Serfdom* (London: G. Routledge and Sons, 1944), 90, 89, 99.

61. Tugwell, *In Search of Roosevelt,* 290, 186; see also Rexford G. Tugwell, *The Battle for Democracy* (New York: Columbia University Press, 1935). Many of the New Deal's architects, however, admired the systemic order in Fascist Italy: Katznelson, *Fear Itself,* 59–71, 93–95.

62. Charles E. Merriam, *On the Agenda of Democracy* (Cambridge, MA: Harvard University Press, 1941), 64.

63. George Soule, *The Coming American Revolution* (New York: Macmillan, 1934), 282.

64. Merriam, review of *The Challenge to Liberty* by Herbert Hoover, *American Political Science Review* 29 (February 1935), 133. On the New Deal as a response to Hoover's response to the Depression, see Daniel T. Rodgers, *Atlantic Crossings: Social Politics in a Progressive Age* (Cambridge, MA: Harvard University Press, 1998), 413. On social welfare as conceptually a form of disaster relief, see Michele Landis Dauber, *The Sympathetic State: Disaster Relief and the Origins of the American Welfare State* (Chicago: University of Chicago Press, 2012).

65. J. M. Keynes, "The General Theory of Employment," *Quarterly Journal of Economics* 51 (February 1937): 209–223, 213–224, 222. On Burke's influence, see Tiziano Raffaelli, "Keynes and Philosophers," in *The Cambridge Companion to Keynes,* ed. Roger E. Backhouse and Bradley W. Bateman (Cambridge: Cambridge University Press, 2006), 176.

66. Rexford G. Tugwell, *FDR: Architect of an Era* (New York: Macmillan, 1967), 127.

67. Skidelsky, *John Maynard Keynes*, 236, 418, 564 (quoted on 709).

68. Knight, *Risk, Uncertainty and Profit*, 43–48, 245–247. For a concise explanation of the Keynesian paradox of thrift, see Lance Taylor, *Maynard's Revenge: The Collapse of Free Market Macroeconomics* (Cambridge, MA: Harvard University Press, 2010), 4–5, 167–169.

69. Roy Lubove, *The Struggle for Social Security, 1900–1935* (Cambridge, MA: Harvard University Press, 1968), 34–44 (quoted on 34); Rodgers, *Atlantic Crossings*, 242–243.

70. I. M. Rubinow, *Social Insurance, with Special Reference to American Conditions* (New York: H. Holt, 1913), 3, 7.

71. I. M. Rubinow, *The Quest for Security* (New York: H. Holt, 1934), 20, 22, 31.

72. Lubove, *Struggle for Social Security*, 138–139; Rodgers, *Atlantic Crossings*, 431–432. On Epstein as the coiner of the phrase "social security," see Klein, *For All These Rights*, 80.

73. Abraham Epstein, *Insecurity, a Challenge to America: A Study of Social Insurance in the United States and Abroad* (New York: H. Smith and R. Haas, 1933), 3, 22, 17–18.

74. Epstein, *Insecurity*, 3–6. Later scholars agreed that security and risk were products of the modern industrial condition: see Anthony Giddens, *Modernity and Self-Identity: Self and Society in the Late Modern Age* (Cambridge: Cambridge University Press, 1991); Ulrich Beck, *Risk Society: Towards a New Modernity* (London: Sage, 1992); and Elaine Freedgood, *Victorian Writing about Risk: Imagining a Safe England in a Dangerous World* (Cambridge: Cambridge University Press, 2000).

75. T. S. Eliot, "Notes on Mannheim's Paper," January 10, 1941, J. H. Oldham papers, box 14, folder 6, New College Library Special Collections, University of Edinburgh.

76. Franklin D. Roosevelt, Executive Order 6757, June 29, 1934, *APP*, https://www.presidency.ucsb.edu/node/208449. On CES, see Ann Shola Orloff, "The Political Origins of America's Belated Welfare State," in *The Politics of Social Policy in the United States*, ed. Margaret Weir, Ann Shola Orloff, and Theda Skocpol (Princeton: Princeton University Press, 1988), 70–79; and Kennedy, *Freedom from Fear*, 262–271. On the groundswell, see Alan Brinkley, *Voices of Protest: Huey Long, Father Coughlin, and the Great Depression* (New York: Vintage, 1982), 222–226.

77. Meg Jacobs, *Pocketbook Politics: Economic Citizenship in Twentieth-Century America* (Princeton: Princeton University Press, 2005), 45–49. While he later invoked the Triangle fire as the inspiration for his own reformist politics, Roosevelt, at the time a state senator, refused to support Perkins's proposals, and he even made sure to be out of Albany the day the legislation was voted on: Jean Edward Smith, *FDR* (New York: Random House, 2007), 80–82.

78. Committee on Economic Security, "What the Economic Security Program Means to You," 1935, 1, https://www.ssa.gov/history/reports/ces/cesvol9whatitmeans.html.

79. Quoted in Kennedy, *Freedom from Fear*, 258.

80. *Report to the President of the Committee on Economic Security* (Washington, DC: GPO, 1935), 43.

81. See, for example, Franklin D. Roosevelt, Fireside Chat, September 30, 1934, *APP*, https://www.presidency.ucsb.edu/node/208160; and Franklin D. Roosevelt, Address at Worcester, Mass., October 21, 1936, *APP*, https://www.presidency.ucsb.edu/node/208308.

82. Of his writings in this vein, see esp. I. M. Rubinow, "Government's Obligation for Economic Security," *Annals of the American Academy of Political and Social Science* 178 (March 1935): 59–68; and Rubinow, *Quest for Security*, 338–354, 507–527, 539–548. See also I. M. Rubinow, "Can Private Philanthropy Do It?" *Social Service Review* 3 (September 1929): 361–394; and I. M. Rubinow, "Conflict of Public and Private Interests in the Field of Social Insurance," *Annals of the American Academy of Political and Social Science* 154 (March 1931): 108–116.

83. Epstein, *Insecurity*, 664. On Epstein at the Pennsylvania Commission on Old Age Pensions, see Lubove, *Struggle for Social Security*, 128–129, 138–140. On the national trend, see Klein, *For All These Rights*, 54–67.

84. Adam Smith, *The Wealth of Nations*, vol. 1 (1776), ed. Edwin R. A. Seligman (London: Dent, 1937), 289.

85. See, for example, Arthur B. Adams, *National Economic Security* (Norman: University of Oklahoma Press, 1936), esp. 214–229; compare with his more conventionally conservative faith in the money supply a decade before: Arthur B. Adams, *Profits, Progress and Prosperity* (New York: McGraw-Hill, 1927).

86. Wallace Brett Donham, *Business Adrift* (New York: McGraw-Hill, 1931), 140, 163.

87. Quoted in Katznelson, *Fear Itself*, 229.

88. Klein, *For All These Rights*, esp. 91–94, 107–113, is superb on how and why this process played out (quoted on 11). See also Steven A. Sass, *The Promise of Private Pensions: The First Hundred Years* (Cambridge, MA: Harvard University Press, 1997), 88–144; Jennifer Klein, "The Politics of Economic Security: Employee Benefits and the Privatization of New Deal Liberalism," *Journal of Policy History* 16 (January 2004): 34–65; and, more broadly, Gail Radford, *The Rise of the Public Authority: Statebuilding and Economic Development in Twentieth-Century America* (Chicago: University of Chicago Press, 2013). On the removal of health insurance, see Badger, *New Deal*, 232, 235–238, 243. On the initially limited funding basis of social security, see Martha Derthick, *Policymaking for Social Security* (Washington, DC: Brookings Institution, 1979), 160–161.

89. Quoted in Klein, *For All These Rights*, 115.

90. See the revised edition of Epstein, *Insecurity*, 3rd (rev) ed. (New York: H. Smith and R. Haas, 1936), v–viii, 669–784; and Abraham Epstein, "The Social Security Act," *The Crisis*, November 1935, 333–334. For "timidity," see William Withers, *Financing Economic Security in the United States* (New York: Columbia University Press, 1939), 188.

91. Franklin D. Roosevelt, Acceptance Speech for the Renomination for the Presidency, Philadelphia, June 27, 1936, *APP*, https://www.presidency.ucsb.edu/node/208917.

92. Quoted in Klein, *For All These Rights*, 138.

93. Klein, *For All These Rights*, 78.

94. In addition to the discussion of this in Chapter 2, see "Naval and Coast Defense," *Scientific American*, December 24, 1881, 401; and "Fortifications Bill," *New York Times*, June 26, 1892.

95. For example, see Cordell Hull's usage in 1937, in *The Memoirs of Cordell Hull*, vol. 1 (New York: Macmillan, 1948), 536.

96. Charles Sumner, "The National Security and the National Faith: Guaranties for the National Freedman and the National Creditor," Speech at the Republican State Convention, Worcester, September 14, 1865, (Boston: Press of Geo. C. Rand and Avery, 1865), 5, https://www.loc.gov/item/ca28000957/.

97. Orin Judson Field, "The United States Courts," *North American Review* 190 (July 1909): 74–81, 81.

98. Quoted in William E. Leuchtenburg, *The FDR Years: On Roosevelt and His Legacy* (New York: Columbia University Press, 1995), 51.

99. For the banks, see *National Security Bank v. Price*, 22 F. 697 (1885), https://cite.case.law/f/22/697/; *National Security Bank v. Butler*, 129 US 223, 32 L. Ed. 682, 9 S. Ct. 281 (1889), https://cite.case.law/us/129/223/; "The Treasury Statement," *Wall Street Journal*, July 2, 1891. For the others, see *American Exchange and Review* 27 (June 1875), 193; and "Mrs. La Manna After Her Money," *New York Times*, February 2, 1893.

100. John F. Hume, "Responsibility for State Roguery," *North American Review* 139 (December 1884): 563–579, 571.

101. William Yandell Elliott, *The Need for Constitutional Reform: A Program for National Security* (New York: McGraw-Hill, 1935), 18 (emphasis in original). On Elliott, see Walter Isaacson, *Kissinger: A Biography* (New York: Simon and Schuster, 1992), 61–64, 69–72; and Jeremi Suri, *Henry Kissinger and the American Century* (Cambridge, MA: Harvard University Press, 2007), 110–112 (quoted on 111). On the BAC, see Kim McQuaid, "Corporate Liberalism in the American Business Community, 1920–1940," *Business History Review* 52 (Autumn 1978): 356–364.

102. Herbert Hoover, Radio Address on the Hoarding of Currency, *APP,* March 6, 1932, https://www.presidency.ucsb.edu/node/208450.

103. Herbert Hoover, Telegram to the Chairman of the Republican National Committee on Election Results in Maine, September 13, 1932, *APP,* https://www.presidency.ucsb.edu/node/207511.

104. Herbert Hoover, Annual Message to the Congress on the State of the Union, December 6, 1932, *APP,* https://www.presidency.ucsb.edu/node/207748.

105. Franklin D. Roosevelt, Second Fireside Chat, May 7, 1933, *APP,* https://www.presidency.ucsb.edu/node/208122.

106. Beverly Gage, *G-Man: J. Edgar Hoover and the Making of the American Century* (New York: Viking, 2022), 147–178, quoted on xv. For FDR's War on Crime, see Anthony Gregory, *New Deal Law and Order: How the War on Crime Built the Modern Liberal State* (Cambridge, MA: Harvard University Press, 2024); and for surveillance, see Rhodri Jeffreys-Jones, *We Know All About You: The Story of Surveillance in Britain and America* (Oxford: Oxford University Press, 2017), 75–92. Unsurprisingly, domestic policing was part of the "liberalism of fear": Judith N. Shklar, *Political Thought and Political Thinkers,* ed. Stanley Hoffmann (Chicago: University of Chicago Press, 1998), 11–12.

107. Franklin D. Roosevelt, Address at the National Parole Conference, April 17, 1939, *APP,* https://www.presidency.ucsb.edu/node/209533.

108. Matthew Dallek, *Defenseless Under the Night: The Roosevelt Years, Civil Defense, and the Origins of Homeland Security* (New York: Oxford University Press, 2016).

109. Katznelson, *Fear Itself,* 123–124 (NIRA quoted on 229).

110. Franklin D. Roosevelt, Remarks at Casper, Wyoming, *APP,* September 24, 1937, https://www.presidency.ucsb.edu/node/208778.

111. Roosevelt, Inaugural Address, March 4, 1933. For an example from the campaign, see Radio Address from Albany, "The Forgotten Man," April 7, 1932, *APP,* https://www.presidency.ucsb.edu/node/288092.

112. William E. Leuchtenburg, "The New Deal and the Analogue of War," in Leuchtenburg, *FDR Years,* 35–75, esp. 49–65. See also Michael S. Sherry, *In the Shadow of War: The United States since the 1930s* (New Haven: Yale University Press, 1995), 16–32.

113. Hacking, *Taming of Chance,* 22.

114. "Classification of policy statements of the President," n.d. [1941], Harold Lasswell Papers, Series III, box 180, folder 175, Manuscripts and Archives, Sterling Memorial Library, Yale University. On Roosevelt's public-relations strategy, see Steven Casey, *Cautious Crusade: Franklin D. Roosevelt, American Public Opinion, and the War against Nazi Germany* (New York: Oxford University Press, 2001); and Andrew Johnstone, *Against Immediate Evil: American Internationalists and the Four Freedoms on the Eve of World War II* (Ithaca, NY: Cornell University Press, 2014), 14–16. Presidential usage of "national security" is derived from a basic search in the *American Presidency Project,* a database that includes all presidential public statements from George Washington through to the present: https://www.presidency.ucsb.edu/. Presidents before FDR uttered the phrase a total of 19 times. Roosevelt uttered the phrase 27 times over the course of his presidency, with the majority (16) coming between 1937 and 1941. Even then, the newness of term was reflected in its relative infrequency:

consider that Truman used the phrase a total of 212 times, Eisenhower 244, with all of those in reference to foreign and military affairs and none to socioeconomic conditions.

115. Franklin D. Roosevelt, Address at Chickamauga Dam Celebration, Near Chattanooga, Tennessee, September 2, 1940, *APP*, https://www.presidency.ucsb.edu/node/209931.

116. Franklin D. Roosevelt, Fireside Chat, December 29, 1940, *APP*, https://www.presidency.ucsb.edu/node/209416.

117. Edward Mead Earle, "American Military Policy and National Security," *Political Science Quarterly* 53 (March 1938): 1–13, 4.

118. A. K. Weinberg, "The Meaning of National Security," September 1941, Security Folder, box 33, Edward Mead Earle Papers, Seeley G. Mudd Library, Princeton University (hereafter Earl Papers). On Earle and his Princeton seminar, see Andrew Preston, "National Security as Grand Strategy: Edward Mead Earle and the Burdens of World Power," in *Rethinking American Grand Strategy*, ed. Elizabeth Borgwardt, Christopher McKnight Nichols, and Andrew Preston (New York: Oxford University Press, 2021), 238–253. See also David Ekbladh, "Present at the Creation: Edward Mead Earle and the Depression-Era Origins of Security Studies," *International Security* 36 (Winter 2011/12): 107–141; and Dexter Fergie, "Geopolitics Turned Inwards: The Princeton Military Studies Group and the National Security Imagination," *Diplomatic History* 43 (September 2019): 644–670.

119. D. C. Poole to Earle, October 22, 1941, Security Folder, box 33, Earl Papers.

120. Albert K. Weinberg, *Manifest Destiny: A Study of Nationalist Expansionism in American History* (Baltimore: Johns Hopkins University Press, 1935), 384.

121. Edward Mead Earle, "Political and Military Strategy for the United States," *Proceedings of the Academy of Political Science* 19 (January 1941): 2–9, 8–9.

122. Charles Edward Merriam, *Political Power: Its Composition and Incidence* (New York: McGraw Hill, 1934), 224.

123. Merriam, *Agenda*, 108–109. On this conceptual linking of war and welfare, see also Charles E. Merriam, *The New Democracy and the New Despotism* (New York: McGraw-Hill, 1939), 37, 186.

124. Epstein, *Insecurity* (1933), 657.

125. Rubinow, *Quest for Security*, 571–572.

126. Harold Lasswell, *World Politics and Personal Insecurity* (New York: Free Press, 1935), 214.

127. Earl Browder, Speech in Cincinnati, "Defend the Social and National Security of the American People," January 24, 1939, Earl Browder papers, box 63, Special Collections Research Center, Syracuse University.

128. Quoted in Committee on Un-American Activities, "Report on the Southern Conference for Human Welfare," *Congressional Record-House*, 93:6, June 16, 1947, 7069. On the SCHW, see Glenda Elizabeth Gilmore, *Defying Dixie: The Radical Roots of Civil Rights, 1919–1950* (New York: W. W. Norton, 2008), 268–273.

129. Hilda Blanco, *How to Think About Social Problems: American Pragmatism and the Idea of Planning* (Westport, CT: Greenwood Press, 1994), 20–21.

130. The literature on American planning from 1880 to 1940 is endless, but I have relied on the following in particular. On urban planning, Anthony Sutcliffe, *Towards the Planned City* (Oxford: B. Blackwell, 1981), 88–125; Peter Hall, *Cities of Tomorrow: An Intellectual History of Urban Planning and Design Since 1880*, 4th ed. (Malden, MA: Wiley-Blackwell, 2014); and Eric Mumford, *Designing the Modern City: Urbanism Since 1850* (New Haven: Yale University Press, 2018). On town planning, Edward Relph, *The Modern Urban Landscape: 1880 to the Present* (Baltimore: Johns Hopkins University Press, 1987), 49–75. On social work, Roy Lubove, *The Professional Altruist: The Emergence of Social Work as a Career 1880–1930* (Cambridge, MA: Harvard University Press, 1968); Michael B. Katz, *In the*

Shadow of the Poorhouse: A Social History of Welfare in America, 2nd ed. (New York: Basic Books, 1996), 168–172; and Walter I. Trattner, *From Poor Law to Welfare State: A History of Social Welfare in America,* 6th ed. (New York: Free Press, 1998). Social planners' designs of ends, however, sometimes clashed with social workers' applications of means: see John Ehrenreich, *The Altruistic Imagination: A History of Social Work and Social Policy in the United States* (Ithaca, NY: Cornell University Press, 1985). On community organizing, Neil Betten and Michael J. Austin, *The Roots of Community Organizing, 1917–1939* (Philadelphia: Temple University Press, 1990). On women's planning organizations, Anne Firor Scott, *Natural Allies: Women's Associations in American History* (Urbana: University of Illinois Press, 1991). Many new planning ideas, as well as many of the planners themselves (such as Rubinow and Epstein), came from overseas: see Rodgers, *Atlantic Crossings.*

131. See, for example, Pierce Williams, "Hard-core Unemployment: The Challenge of Permanently Depressed Areas," *Survey Graphic* 27 (June 1938): 346–352.

132. Merriam, *Agenda,* 57.

133. Alfred J. Kahn, *Theory and Practice of Social Planning* (New York: Russell Sage Foundation, 1969), 1, 3, 9, 15.

134. Gunnar Myrdal, *Beyond the Welfare State: Economic Planning and Its International Implications* (New Haven: Yale University Press, 1960), 23, 63. Emphasis in original.

135. See Barry D. Karl, *Charles E. Merriam and the Study of Politics* (Chicago: University of Chicago Press, 1974), 226–283; Marion Clawson, *New Deal Planning: The National Resources Planning Board* (Baltimore: Johns Hopkins University Press, 1981), 176–181; John W. Jeffries, "A 'Third New Deal'? Liberal Policy and the American State, 1937–1945," *Journal of Policy History* 8 (October 1996): 387–409, 394–399; and Patrick D. Reagan, *Designing a New America: The Origins of New Deal Planning, 1890–1943* (Amherst: University of Massachusetts Press, 2000), 168–223. For Merriam's own account of the NRPB, see Charles E. Merriam, "The National Resources Planning Board: A Chapter in American Planning Experience," *American Political Science Review* 38 (December 1944): 1075–1088. For the NRPB's place within a wider political context, see Alan Brinkley, *Liberalism and Its Discontents* (Cambridge, MA: Harvard University Press, 1998), esp. 54–59.

136. Christopher McKnight Nichols and Andrew Preston, "Introduction," in Borgwardt, Nichols, and Preston, *Rethinking American Grand Strategy,* 1–3, 6–14. From a large and constantly growing literature, see esp. Paul Kennedy, ed., *Grand Strategies in War and Peace* (New Haven: Yale University Press, 1991); John Lewis Gaddis, *On Grand Strategy* (New York: Penguin, 2018); and Hal Brands, ed., *The New Makers of Modern Strategy: From the Ancient World to the Digital Age* (Princeton: Princeton University Press, 2023).

137. Hew Strachan, *The Direction of War: Contemporary Strategy in Historical Perspective* (Cambridge: Cambridge University Press, 2013), esp. 26–45.

138. Earle, "Introductory Statement to Seminar," September 26, 1941, Research Files—WWI–WWII, National Defense, box 32, Earle Papers.

139. Preston, "National Security as Grand Strategy."

140. Brian McAllister Linn, *The Echo of Battle: The Army's Way of War* (Cambridge, MA: Harvard University Press, 2007), 139–146 (quoted on 143, 140); Ray S. Cline, *Washington Command Post: The Operations Division* (Washington, DC: Center for Military History, US Army, 1951), 29–32.

141. Quoted in Linn, *Echo of Battle,* 140. On the growth of war planning, see Edward S. Miller, *War Plan Orange: The U.S. Strategy to Defeat Japan, 1897–1945* (Annapolis, MD: Naval Institute Press, 1991); Calvin L. Christman, "Franklin D. Roosevelt and the Craft of Strategic Assessment," in *Calculations: Net Assessment and the Coming of World War II,* ed. Williamson Murray and Allan R. Millett (New York: Free Press, 1992), 216–257; Henry G. Gole, *The Road to Rainbow: Army Planning for Global War, 1934–1940* (Annapolis, MD: Naval

Institute Press, 2003); and Andrew F. Krepinevich Jr., "Transforming to Victory: The US Navy, Carrier Aviation, and Preparing for War in the Pacific," in *The Fog of Peace and War Planning: Military and Strategic Planning under Uncertainty*, ed. Talbot C. Imlay and Monica Duffy Toft (London: Routledge, 2006), 179–204.

142. Matthew Connelly et al., "'General, I Have Fought Just as Many Nuclear Wars as You Have': Forecasts, Future Scenarios, and the Politics of Armageddon," *American Historical Review* 117 (December 2012): 1431–1460, 1434–1436.

143. See Mark A. Stoler, *Allies and Adversaries: The Joint Chiefs of Staff, the Grand Alliance, and U.S. Strategy in World War II* (Chapel Hill: University of North Carolina Press, 2000).

144. Quoted in Frank Ninkovich, *The Wilsonian Century: U.S. Foreign Policy since 1900* (Chicago: University of Chicago Press, 1999), 125–126.

145. Roosevelt, Annual Message to Congress, January 4,1935; Will Brownell and Richard N. Billings, *So Close to Greatness: A Biography of William C. Bullitt* (New York: Macmillan, 1987); David Mayers, *FDR's Ambassadors and the Diplomacy of Crisis: From the Rise of Hitler to the End of World War II* (New York: Cambridge University Press, 2013), 136–143.

146. Franklin D. Roosevelt, Fireside Chat, April 28,1935, *APP*, https://www.presidency .ucsb.edu/node/208619.

147. Edward Mead Earle, *Against This Torrent* (Princeton: Princeton University Press, 1941), 22.

148. Quoted in William L. O'Neill, *A Democracy at War: America's Fight at Home and Abroad in World War II* (Cambridge, MA: Harvard University Press, 1993), 392. For ailments, see Iwan Morgan, *FDR: Transforming the Presidency and Renewing America* (London: Bloomsbury Academic, 2022), 257. For travel, see Katznelson, *Fear Itself*, 195–196, 555n1.

149. Franklin D. Roosevelt, State of the Union Message to Congress, January 11,1944, *APP*, https://www.presidency.ucsb.edu/node/210825. The speech is analyzed well in Cass R. Sunstein, *The Second Bill of Rights: FDR's Unfinished Revolution and Why We Need It More than Ever* (New York: Basic Books, 2004).

150. Quoted in Alan Brinkley, *The End of Reform: New Deal Liberalism in Recession and War* (New York: Alfred A. Knopf, 1995), 246; and Elizabeth Borgwardt, *A New Deal for the World: America's Vision for Human Rights* (Cambridge, MA: Harvard University Press, 2005), 51–52.

151. *Security, Work, and Relief Policies: Report of the Committee on Long–Range Work and Relief Policies to the National Resources Planning Board* (Washington, DC: GPO, 1942), 514, 1, 4; National Resources Planning Board, "After the War—Toward Security," NRPB 107, September 1942.

152. Katznelson, *Fear Itself*, 370–380. For economic growth over planning, see Alan Brinkley, "The New Deal and the Idea of the State," in *The Rise and Fall of the New Deal Order, 1930–1980*, ed. Steve Fraser and Gary Gerstle (Princeton: Princeton University Press, 1989), 105–111; and Brinkley, *End of Reform*, 245–264. For "radical," see Kennedy, *Freedom from Fear*, 784. For Wall Street and unions, see "Advance of Stocks Best of New Year," *New York Times*, January 12,1944; and "Labor Fights Compulsion," *New York Times*, January 12,1944.

153. A revealing exception was one of the most comprehensive social-welfare systems in the country: benefits for service personnel and veterans. See Jennifer Mittelstadt, *The Rise of the Military Welfare State* (Cambridge, MA: Harvard University Press, 2015); and Olivier Burtin, *A Nation of Veterans: War, Citizenship, and the Welfare State in Modern America* (Philadelphia: University of Pennsylvania Press, 2022).

5. WHY WE FIGHT

1. Frank Capra, *The Name Above the Title: An Autobiography* (New York: Macmillan, 1971), 326–327 (emphases in original). Size of the army is from Henry G. Gole, *The Road to Rainbow: Army Planning for Global War, 1934–1940* (Annapolis, MD: Naval Institute Press, 2003), xv.

2. Capra, *The Name Above the Title,* 327, 332. Emphases in original.

3. Franklin D. Roosevelt, Radio Address Announcing an Unlimited National Emergency, May 27, 1941, American Presidency Project (hereafter *APP*), https://www.presidency.ucsb.edu/node/209607.

4. The film scripts aren't easy to find, even online, so all quotation from the films is from my own transcriptions. The National Archives has made all seven films freely available on YouTube: https://youtube.com/playlist?list=PLugwVCjzrJsXwAiWBipTE9mTlFQC7H2rU&si=lK5BvpBkHKhOG2fL. One historian credits Capra with coining the now-common term "free world": William O. Walker, *The Rise and Decline of the American Century* (Ithaca, NY: Cornell University Press, 2018), 220n19. On the "free world versus slave world" narrative in US wartime propaganda more generally, see Susan A. Brewer, *Why America Fights: Patriotism and War Propaganda from the Philippines to Iraq* (New York: Oxford University Press, 2009), 104–116.

5. Clayton R. Koppes and Gregory D. Black, *Hollywood Goes to War: How Politics, Profits and Propaganda Shaped World War II Movies* (New York: Free Press, 1987), 122–125; Mark Harris, *Five Came Back: A Story of Hollywood and the Second World War* (New York: Penguin, 2014), 217–219, 381–382. For Churchill, see Giles Milton, *The Stalin Affair: The Impossible Alliance that Won the War* (London: John Murray, 2024), 185.

6. On Britain, see Sonya O. Rose, *Which People's War? National Identity and Citizenship in Britain 1939–1945* (Oxford: Oxford University Press, 2003); for film in particular, Clive Coultass, "British Feature Films and the Second World War," *Journal of Contemporary History* 19 (1984): 7–22, 9; Anthony Aldgate and Jeffrey Richards, *Britain Can Take It: The British Cinema in the Second World War* (Oxford: Blackwell, 1986); James Chapman, *The British at War: Cinema, State and Propaganda, 1939–1945* (London: I. B. Tauris, 1998); and Kent Puckett, *War Pictures: Cinema, Violence, and Style in Britain, 1939–1945* (New York: Fordham University Press, 2017). On Russia, see Karel C. Berkhoff, *Motherland in Danger: Soviet Propaganda during World War II* (Cambridge, MA: Harvard University Press, 2012). Even Japanese wartime films largely ignored grand ideological objectives and concentrated on fighting the war: Peter B. High, *The Imperial Screen: Japanese Film Culture in the Fifteen Years' War, 1931–1945* (Madison: University of Wisconsin Press, 2003), 385–395. China's unusual circumstances—a civil war within a world war—meant that propaganda on all sides was even more narrowly focused on achieving victory: see Carolyn Fitzgerald, *Fragmenting Modernisms: Chinese Wartime Literature, Art, and Film, 1937–1949* (Leiden: Brill, 2013); and, more generally, Hans Van de Ven, *China at War: Triumph and Tragedy in the Emergence of the New China 1937–1952* (Cambridge, MA: Harvard University Press, 2018).

7. Carl L. Becker, *How New Will the Better World Be?* (New York: Alfred A. Knopf, 1945), 112.

8. Hanson W. Baldwin, *United We Stand! Defense of the Western Hemisphere* (New York: McGraw-Hill, 1941), 37.

9. Morris Dickstein, *Dancing in the Dark: A Cultural History of the Great Depression* (New York: W. W. Norton, 2009), 399–400, 458–459, 477–495 ("folkways" on 526); Harris, *Five Came Back,* 7–9, 23–28, 41–46, 65–68, 76–79 ("Quarantine Hitler" on 28–29); see also James Chandler, *An Archaeology of Sympathy: The Sentimental Mode in Literature and Cinema* (Chicago: University of Chicago Press, 2013). For Capra's politics, including his

encounter with the Dies Committee, see Joseph McBride, *Frank Capra: The Catastrophe of Success* (New York: Simon and Schuster, 1992), 255–263, 334, 340–342, 390–393. Lary May, *The Big Tomorrow: Hollywood and the Politics of the American Way* (Chicago: University of Chicago Press, 2000), 85–87, situates Capra within a socially conscious "conversion narrative" common to Hollywood films during the Depression.

10. Marshall to Pershing, July 11, 1933, *Papers of George Catlett Marshall*, vol. 1, ed. Larry I. Bland (Baltimore: Johns Hopkins University Press, 1981), 398.

11. On Marshall and the New Deal, see Forrest C. Pogue, *George C. Marshall: Education of a General, 1880–1939* (New York: Viking, 1963), 292–300; and Eric Larrabee, *Commander in Chief: Franklin Delano Roosevelt, His Lieutenants, and their War* (New York: Harper and Row, 1987), 107–109. On meeting with FDR, see Thomas Parrish, *Roosevelt and Marshall: Their Partnership in Politics and War* (New York: W. Morrow, 1989), 75–77.

12. Robert L. McLaughlin and Sally E. Parry, *We'll Always Have the Movies: American Cinema During World War II* (Lexington: University Press of Kentucky, 2006), 19–24.

13. Tom Engelhardt, *The End of Victory Culture: Cold War America and the Disillusioning of a Generation* (New York: Basic Books, 1995), 11–12; Brewer, *Why America Fights*, 163–166, 194–195.

14. Speech by Marcus Garvey, New York, September 7, 1921, *Marcus Garvey and Universal Negro Improvement Association Papers*, vol. 9 (Berkeley: University of California Press, 1995), 192.

15. The literature on early globalization is immense, but see especially Emily S. Rosenberg, ed., *A World Connecting: 1870–1945* (Cambridge, MA: Harvard University Press, 2012). On the ebb-and-flow of globalization, see Ronald Findlay and Kevin H. O'Rourke, *Power and Plenty: Trade, War, and the World Economy in the Second Millennium* (Princeton: Princeton University Press, 2007). Because Findlay and O'Rourke concentrate on economics, however, they overstate the decline of interconnectedness after 1929. On the continuation of other forms of globalization, such as those relating to transportation, communications, and ideology that are the focus in this chapter, see Brooke L. Blower and Andrew Preston, eds., *The Cambridge History of America and the World*, vol. 3: *1900–1945* (New York: Cambridge University Press, 2021). On Capra's assumption that he would make his army documentaries by regularly crisscrossing the United States, see Capra, *Name Above the Title*, 337–339.

16. Alan K. Henrikson, "The Map as an 'Idea': The Role of Cartographic Imagery During the Second World War," *American Cartographer* 2 (1975): 19–53; Susan Schulten, *The Geographical Imagination in America, 1880–1950* (Chicago: University of Chicago Press, 2001); Denis Cosgrove, *Apollo's Eye: A Cartographic Genealogy of the Earth in the Western Imagination* (Baltimore: Johns Hopkins University Press, 2001), 236–248; Jeffrey A. Engel, *Cold War at 30,000 Feet: The Anglo-American Fight for Aviation Supremacy* (Cambridge, MA: Harvard University Press, 2007), 39–41; Jenifer Van Vleck, *Empire of the Air: Aviation and the American Ascendancy* (Cambridge, MA: Harvard University Press, 2013), 89–130 (1943 *Fortune* magazine article quoted on 3); and, on methodology and theory, James Corner, "The Agency of Mapping: Speculation, Critique and Invention," in *Mappings,* ed. Denis Cosgrove (London: Reaktion, 1999), 213–252.

17. Charles Edward Merriam, *Political Power: Its Composition and Incidence* (New York: McGraw-Hill, 1934), 280.

18. Or Rosenboim, *The Emergence of Globalism: Visions of World Order in Britain and the United States, 1939–1950* (Princeton: Princeton University Press, 2017), 222–223.

19. Quoted in Cosgrove, *Apollo's Eye*, 246.

20. David Paull Nickles, *Under the Wire: How the Telegraph Changed Diplomacy* (Cambridge, MA: Harvard University Press, 2003); and Jonathan Reed Winkler, *Nexus: Strategic Communications and American Security in World War I* (Cambridge, MA: Harvard University Press, 2008).

21. Alan K. Henrikson, "FDR and the 'World-Wide Arena," in *FDR's World: War, Peace, and Legacies*, ed. David B. Woolner, Warren F. Kimball, and David Reynolds (New York: Palgrave Macmillan, 2008), 36, 38.

22. Alexander McAdie, "Aerography, The Science of the Structure of the Atmosphere," *Geographical Review* 1 (April 1916): 266–273.

23. Passenger numbers increased from 475,000 in 1932 to over four million in 1941: Van Vleck, *Empire of the Air*, 92.

24. Van Vleck, *Empire of the Air*, 53–103 (quoted on 119).

25. Tamson Pietsch, "Elizabeth Lippincott McQueen: Thinking International Peace in an Air-Minded Age," in *Women's International Thought: A New History*, ed. Patricia Owens and Katharina Rietzler (Cambridge: Cambridge University Press, 2021), 115–135.

26. Will Rogers, *There's Not a Bathing Suit in Russia, & Other Bare Facts* (New York: Albert and Charles Boni, 1927), 41–42, 53.

27. Quoted in Mark Clodfelter, *Beneficial Bombing: The Progressive Foundations of American Air Power, 1917–1945* (Lincoln: University of Nebraska Press, 2010), 33.

28. Engel, *Cold War at 30,000 Feet*, 17.

29. Rogers, *There's Not a Bathing Suit in Russia*, 54, 136.

30. "Menken Warns of Red Peril Here," *New York Times*, November 5, 1923.

31. Engel, *Cold War at 30,000 Feet*, 24–25.

32. Quoted in Michael S. Sherry, *The Rise of American Air Power: The Creation of Armageddon* (New Haven: Yale University Press, 1987), 30, 44.

33. Quoted in Clodfelter, *Beneficial Bombing*, 61.

34. Henry L. Stimson, "Bases of American Foreign Policy during the Past Four Years," *Foreign Affairs* 11 (April 1933): 383–396.

35. Allan Nevins, "Two Views of America's Part," *New York Times*, May 26, 1940. Nevins borrowed this breakdown of different speeds in different eras from an FDR speech ten days before: Franklin D. Roosevelt, Message to Congress on Appropriations for National Defense, May 16, 1940, APP, https://www.presidency.ucsb.edu/node/209636.

36. Earle to MacLeish, November 21, 1941, box 37, Writings, "American Security," Edward Mead Earle Papers, Seeley G. Mudd Library, Princeton University.

37. Eugene Staley, "The Myth of the Continents," *Foreign Affairs* 19 (April 1941): 481–494, 483–486. On the inherent paradox of the Monroe Doctrine, see Jay Sexton, *The Monroe Doctrine: Empire and Nation in Nineteenth-Century America* (New York: Hill and Wang, 2011).

38. All had written on the subject over long careers, but for their views in the fulcrum of the late 1930s and early 1940s, see Halford J. Mackinder, "The Round World and the Winning of the Peace," *Foreign Affairs* 21 (July 1943): 595–605; Nicholas John Spykman, *America's Strategy in World Politics: The United States and the Balance of Power* (New York: Harcourt, Brace, 1942). On Bowman, see Neil Smith, *American Empire: Roosevelt's Geographer and the Prelude to Globalization* (Berkeley: University of California Press, 2004). Edward Mead Earle provided a new Introduction to the 1942 reissue of Mackinder's most influential book: H. J. Mackinder, *Democratic Ideals and Reality: A Study in the Politics of Reconstruction* (New York: Henry Holt, 1942 [1919]).

39. Daniel Immerwahr, *How to Hide an Empire: A History of the Greater United States* (New York: Farrar, Straus, and Giroux, 2019), 223.

40. Erika Lee, *America for Americans: A History of Xenophobia in the United States* (New York: Basic Books, 2019), 184–185, 196–199, 205–210; Moon-Ho Jung, *Menace to Empire: Anticolonial Solidarities and the Transpacific Origins of the US Security State* (Oakland: University of California Press, 2022).

41. David G. Haglund, *Latin America and the Transformation of U.S. Strategic Thought, 1936–1940* (Albuquerque: University of New Mexico Press, 1984). For natural resources, see

Megan Black, *The Global Interior: Mineral Frontiers and American Power* (Cambridge, MA: Harvard University Press, 2018), 84–88, 91–96, 111–114.

42. Van Vleck, *Empire of the Air,* 82–87.

43. Rebecca Herman, *Cooperating with the Colossus: A Social and Political History of US Military Bases in World War II Latin America* (New York: Oxford University Press, 2022).

44. "Secretary Hull's Address of October 26, 1941," in *Peace and War: United States Foreign Policy, 1931–1941* (Washington, DC: GPO, 1943), 56.

45. William Bullitt comments to Juliusz Lukasiewicz, January 1939, *For the President, Personal and Secret: Correspondence between Franklin D. Roosevelt and William C. Bullitt,* ed. Orville H. Bullitt (Boston: Houghton Mifflin, 1972), 304.

46. Quoted in Larrabee, *Commander in Chief,* 50.

47. Franklin D. Roosevelt, Press Conference, December 17, 1940, *APP,* https://www.presidency.ucsb.edu/node/209409.

48. Robert E. Sherwood, *Roosevelt and Hopkins: An Intimate History* (New York: Harper and Brothers, 1948), 228.

49. Richard Van Alstyne, *American Diplomacy in Action: A Series of Case Studies* (Stanford: Stanford University Press, 1944), 9, 52, 394, 399.

50. See, for example, the statement by C. H. French, May 4, 1939, *Neutrality, Peace Legislation, and Our Foreign Policy: Hearings Before the Committee on Foreign Relations, United States Senate* (Washington, DC: GPO, 1939), 635–136; and Admiral Joseph Taussig's testimony, April 22, 1940, *Construction of Certain Naval Vessels: Hearings Before the Committee on Naval Affairs, United States Senate* (Washington, DC: GPO, 1940), 188–190. For the most prominent US reprinting of what was probably a Chinese forgery, see Carl Crow, ed., *Japan's Dream of World Empire: The Tanaka Memorial* (New York: Harper and Brothers, 1942). For historians' skepticism, see John J. Stephan, "The Tanaka Memorial (1927): Authentic or Spurious?" *Modern Asian Studies* 7 (1973): 733–745; and Barak Kushner, *Men to Devils, Devils to Men: Japanese War Crimes and Chinese Justice* (Cambridge, MA: Harvard University Press, 2015), 172–174. On Capra's use of the Tanaka Memorial and other narrative contrivances to portray the Japanese, see John W. Dower, *War Without Mercy: Race and Power in the Pacific War* (New York: Pantheon, 1986), 15–24. The Tanaka Memorial could only earn such widespread credibility, however, because it seemed to confirm the reality of Japanese aggression in East and Southeast Asia, which was indeed reflected in Japan's grand strategy and propaganda. See, respectively, Jeremy A. Yellen, *The Greater East Asia Co-Prosperity Sphere: When Total Empire Met Total War* (Ithaca, NY: Cornell University Press, 2019); and Barak Kushner, *The Thought War: Japanese Imperial Propaganda* (Honolulu: University of Hawai'i Press, 2005).

51. Quoted in John A. Thompson, "Another Look at the Downfall of 'Fortress America,'" *Journal of American Studies* 26 (December 1992): 393–408, 396.

52. John A. Thompson, "Conceptions of National Security and American Entry into World War II," *Diplomacy & Statecraft* 16 (2005): 671–697, 678.

53. For the other movies, see H. Mark Glancy, *When Hollywood Loved Britain: The Hollywood "British" Film 1939–1945* (Manchester: Manchester University Press, 1999); and David Welky, *The Moguls and the Dictators: Hollywood and the Coming of World War II* (Baltimore: Johns Hopkins University Press, 2008). More generally, see Nicholas John Cull, *Selling War: The British Propaganda Campaign Against American "Neutrality" in World War II* (New York: Oxford University Press, 1995); and Susan A. Brewer, *To Win the Peace: British Propaganda in the United States During World War II* (Ithaca, NY: Cornell University Press, 1997).

54. Richard Ben Cramer, *Joe DiMaggio: The Hero's Life* (New York: Simon and Schuster, 2000), 198–199.

55. "Defense of Nation in War Discussed," *New York Times,* January 16,1941.

56. Quoted in Erika Doss, "*The Year of Peril:* Thomas Hart Benton and World War II," in *Thomas Hart Benton: Artist, Writer, and Intellectual,* ed. Douglas Hurt and Mary K. Dains (Columbia: State Historical Society of Missouri, 1987), 35. On Benton's politics, see also Elizabeth Broun, "Thomas Hart Benton: A Politician in Art," *Smithsonian Studies in American Art* 1 (Spring 1987): 58–77. On the invention of a tradition-bound pastoral heartland, see Daniel Immerwahr, "The Pitchfork of History," *New Yorker,* October 23,2023; and Steven Conn, *The Lies of the Land: Seeing Rural America for What It Is—and Isn't* (Chicago: University of Chicago Press, 2023).

57. Stephen Wertheim, *Tomorrow, the World: The Birth of U.S. Global Supremacy* (Cambridge, MA: Harvard University Press, 2020), 90.

58. Robert Endicott Osgood, *Ideals and Self-interest in America's Foreign Relations: The Great Transformation of the Twentieth Century* (Chicago: University of Chicago Press, 1953), 403.

59. Franklin D. Roosevelt, Message to Congress Recommending Increased Defense Appropriations, January 28,1938, *APP,* https://www.presidency.ucsb.edu/node/209359.

60. Dean Acheson, Speech to students at Yale, November 28,1939, Dean Acheson, *Morning and Noon* (Boston: Houghton Mifflin, 1965), 270. On the emergence of an internationalist campaign to sway public opinion between 1937 and 1941, see Andrew Johnstone, *Against Immediate Evil: American Internationalists and the Four Freedoms on the Eve of World War II* (Ithaca, NY: Cornell University Press, 2014).

61. See Daniel Yergin, *Shattered Peace: The Origins of the Cold War and the National Security State* (Boston: Houghton Mifflin, 1977), 194; David Ekbladh, "Present at the Creation: Edward Mead Earle and the Depression-Era Origins of Security Studies," *International Security* 36 (Winter 2011/12): 107–141; Dexter Fergie, "Geopolitics Turned Inwards: The Princeton Military Studies Group and the National Security Imagination," *Diplomatic History* 43 (September 2019): 644–670; and Andrew Preston, "National Security as Grand Strategy: Edward Mead Earle and the Burdens of World Power," in *Rethinking American Grand Strategy,* ed. Elizabeth Borgwardt, Christopher McKnight Nichols, and Andrew Preston (New York: Oxford University Press, 2021), 238–253.

62. Edward Mead Earle, *Against this Torrent* (Princeton: Princeton University Press, 1941), 14–17, 63. On Earle's own conversion from invulnerable free security to vulnerable national security, see Wertheim, *Tomorrow, the World,* 39–40. For examples showing the shift, compare Earle's "National Security and Foreign Policy," *Yale Review* 29 (March 1940): 444–460, esp. 446, 457–460; with his "The Threat to American Security," *Yale Review* 30 (March 1941): 454–480. Even after the shift, Earle's belief in free security made it into his analysis of Alexander Hamilton's diplomacy, in the first edition of his landmark book. E. M. Earle, *Makers of Modern Strategy: Military Thought from Machiavelli to Hitler* (Princeton: Princeton University Press, 1943), 143.

63. Earle, *Against this Torrent,* 29–30, 18.

64. On the limited effect of the films, see James T. Sparrow, *Warfare State: World War II Americans and the Age of Big Government* (New York: Oxford University Press, 2011), 211.

65. William Parsons to "Family," September 6,1939, Myra and William Parsons papers, box 1, Manuscripts and Archives, Sterling Memorial Library, Yale University.

66. See Andrew Johnstone, "Isolationism and Internationalism in American Foreign Relations," *Journal of Transatlantic Studies* 9 (March 2011): 7–20; and Brooke L. Blower, "From Isolationism to Neutrality: A New Framework for Understanding American Political Culture, 1919-1941," *Diplomatic History* 38 (April 2014): 345–376. Wertheim, *Tomorrow, the World,* offers the strongest attack on the use of "isolationism." For a nuanced exploration

of the diversity of isolationism in the early twentieth century, see Christopher McKnight Nichols, *Promise and Peril: America at the Dawn of a Global Age* (Cambridge, MA: Harvard University Press, 2011).

67. John T. Flynn, "Plain Economics," October 26, 1940, *Investigation of Concentration of Economic Power: Final Report and Recommendations of the Temporary National Economic Committee* (Washington, DC: GPO, 1941), 211.

68. Quoted in Stanley K. Bigman, "The 'New Internationalism' Under Attack," *Public Opinion Quarterly* 14 (1950): 235–261, 254n15. Emphasis in original.

69. William Henry Chamberlin, "War: Shortcut to Fascism," *American Mercury,* December 1941, 399.

70. William Mitchell, *Winged Defense: The Development and Possibilities of Modern Air Power—Economic and Military* (New York: G. P. Putnam's Sons, 1925), 19, 112; see also 120–136.

71. Charles Lindbergh, Speech over CBS Radio, "Air Defense for America," May 9, 1940, Lindbergh papers, Series V, box 201, folder 352, Manuscripts and Archives, Sterling Memorial Library, Yale University.

72. Franklin D. Roosevelt, Address at New Washington National Airport, September 28, 1940, *APP,* https://www.presidency.ucsb.edu/node/210478.

73. On the quarantine speech, see "Borah Hails Statement," *New York Times,* October 6, 1937. On Lend-Lease, see "Hoover Condemns War Aid to Soviet," *New York Times,* June 30, 1941; and Hugh S. Johnson, *Hell-Bent for War* (Indianapolis: Bobbs-Merrill, 1941), 7.

74. "Industrial Mobilization Plan," September 1936, RG107, Entry 190, box 10, National Archives and Records Administration, College Park, MD (hereafter NARA). For more historical context, see John A. Thompson, *A Sense of Power: The Roots of America's Global Role* (Ithaca, NY: Cornell University Press, 2015), 176–182, 196–197; Immerwahr, *How to Hide an Empire,* 158.

75. Sherman Miles to Marshall (Memo 31), October 28, 1940, RG165, Entry 184, box 961, NARA.

76. Charles A. Lindbergh, "What Substitute for War?" *Atlantic,* March 1940, 304–308 (quoted on 308). On Ludlow and his amendment, see Manfred Jonas, *Isolationism in America, 1935–1941* (Ithaca, NY: Cornell University Press, 1966), 159–166.

77. Victor Davis Hanson, *The Second World Wars: How the First Global Conflict Was Fought and Won* (New York: Basic Books, 2017), 469–471, 38–39, 494–496.

78. Quoted in Laurence Steinhardt to Hull, August 16, 1939, *Foreign Relations of the United States* (hereafter *FRUS*), *The Soviet Union, 1933–1939* (Washington, DC: GPO, 1952), 776.

79. John T. Flynn, "Can Hitler Invade America?" *Reader's Digest,* April 1941, 1–6.

80. Stimson speech, "Mr. Hoover's Foreign Policy and the Commercial Welfare of the United States," Republican National Committee press release, September 27, 1932, Hornbeck papers, box 402, Hoover Institution, Stanford University.

81. George Marshall, Speech at Maxwell Field, Alabama, September 19, 1938, *Papers of George Catlett Marshall,* vol. 1, 633.

82. Walter Lippmann, "The American Destiny," *Life,* June 5, 1939, 47, 72.

83. "An Approach to the Problem of Eliminating Tension with Japan and Insuring Defeat of Germany," November 17, 1941, *FRUS, 1941,* vol. IV: *The Far East* (Washington, DC: GPO, 1956), 607.

84. Franklin D. Roosevelt, "Our Foreign Policy: A Democratic View," *Foreign Affairs* 6 (July 1928): 573–586, 579.

85. Franklin D. Roosevelt, Address at Chautauqua, August 14, 1936, *APP,* https://www.presidency.ucsb.edu/node/208921.

86. Campbell Craig, "The Not-So-Strange Career of Charles Beard," *Diplomatic History* 25 (Spring 2001): 251–274, 255.

87. Resolution No. 6, "Term 'Continental Limits of The United States' as used in the Authorization for Payment of Traveling and Other Expenses," February 7, 1921, National Executive Committee Resolutions, American Legion Digital Archive, https://archive.legion.org /node/2500.

88. Quoted in Craig, "Not-So-Strange Career," 256. See also David Milne, *Worldmaking: The Art and Science of American Diplomacy* (New York: Farrar, Straus, and Giroux, 2015), 129–130, 151.

89. Samuel Flagg Bemis, *A Diplomatic History of the United States* (New York: H. Holt, 1936), 806, 803, 809.

90. Charles A. Beard, *A Foreign Policy for America* (New York: Alfred A. Knopf, 1940).

91. Mark A. Stoler, "From Continentalism to Globalism: General Stanley D. Embick, the Joint Strategic Survey Committee, and the Military View of American National Policy during the Second World War," *Diplomatic History* 6 (Summer 1982): 303–321; Mark A. Stoler, *Allies and Adversaries: The Joint Chiefs of Staff, the Grand Alliance, and U.S. Strategy in World War II* (Chapel Hill: University of North Carolina Press, 2000), 10–15.

92. "A National Doctrine of War for the United States," n.d. [1941], RG165, Entry 422, box 19, NARA; "War Department Strategic Estimate," October 1941, RG165, Entry 422, box 20, NARA.

93. Quoted in Immerwahr, *How to Hide an Empire*, 165.

94. Quoted in James Chace and Caleb Carr, *America Invulnerable: The Quest for Absolute Security from 1812 to Star Wars* (New York: Summit, 1988), 202.

95. Herbert Hoover, Radio speech to Republican Women's Clubs, January 15, 1938, Herbert Hoover, *Addresses Upon the American Road, 1933–1938* (New York: C. Scribner's Sons, 1938), 302.

96. "Text of Hoover Speech," *New York Times*, May 12, 1941. For his defense policy as president, see Herbert Hoover, Annual Message to Congress, December 3, 1929, *APP*, https://www.presidency.ucsb.edu/node/209213. For humanitarian relief, see Herbert Hoover, *An American Epic*, vol. 4, *1939–1963* (Chicago: University of Chicago Press, 1964), 1–73.

97. "Define Powers in Lease Bill," *Washington Post*, January 17, 1941.

98. Wayne S. Cole, *Roosevelt and the Isolationists, 1932–1945* (Lincoln: University of Nebraska Press, 1983), 37–52, 128–162, 291–296, 383–405.

99. Quoted in William Leuchtenburg, *Herbert Hoover* (New York: Times Books, 2009), 150–151. See also Hoover's own critique in *The Challenge to Liberty* (New York: Charles Scribner's Sons, 1934); and *The Memoirs of Herbert Hoover*, vol. 3: *The Great Depression, 1929–1941* (New York: Macmillan, 1953), 354–356. On the differences between Hoover and Roosevelt, see Eric Rauchway, *Winter War: Hoover, Roosevelt, and the First Clash Over the New Deal* (New York: Basic Books, 2018). On Hoover's suspicion of the liberal state, see William J. Barber, *From New Era to New Deal: Herbert Hoover, the Economists, and American Economic Policy, 1921–1933* (New York: Cambridge University Press, 1985), esp. 189–196.

100. "Thomas Jefferson and The Bill of Rights," April 1943, Herbert Hoover, *Addresses Upon the American Road: World War II, 1941–1945* (New York: D. Van Nostrand, 1946), 383.

101. "New A.E.F. Looms," *New York Times*, November 20, 1941. On fears that Roosevelt's foreign policy was creating an overreach of executive authority, see Justus D. Doenecke, *Storm on the Horizon: The Challenge to American Intervention, 1939–1941* (Lanham, MD: Rowman and Littlefield, 2000), 270–284.

102. Charles A. Beard and William Beard, *The American Leviathan: The Republic in the Machine Age* (New York: Macmillan, 1930); Charles A. Beard and George H. E. Smith, *The Future Comes: A Study of the New Deal* (New York: Macmillan, 1933), 164.

103. Quoted in Milne, *Worldmaking,* 160.

104. *Investigation of Concentration of Economic Power,* 3.

105. Quoted in Cole, *Roosevelt and the Isolationists,* 432.

106. On his concerns about the New Deal, see John Kennedy Ohl, *Hugh S. Johnson and the New Deal* (Dekalb: Northern Illinois University Press, 1985); and about intervention, see Doenecke, *Storm on the Horizon.*

107. David Mitrany, "The Political Consequences of Economic Planning," *Sociological Review* 26 (October 1934): 321–345, 326–327.

108. Robert Dallek, *Franklin D. Roosevelt and American Foreign Policy, 1932–1945* (New York: Oxford University Press, 1979), 3–20; Henrikson, "FDR and the 'World-Wide Arena,'" 35–61; David F. Schmitz, *The Sailor: Franklin D. Roosevelt and the Transformation of American Foreign Policy* (Lexington: University Press of Kentucky, 2021), 9–34; Eleanor Roosevelt, *This I Remember* (New York: Harper, 1949), 346. "National defense" is from Franklin D. Roosevelt, "The Future of the Submarine," *North American Review* 202 (October 1915): 505–508, 508.

109. Quoted in Steven Casey, *Cautious Crusade: Franklin D. Roosevelt, American Public Opinion, and the War Against Nazi Germany* (New York: Oxford University Press, 2001), 24.

110. Kathryn S. Olmsted, *The Newspaper Axis: Six Press Barons Who Enabled Hitler* (New Haven: Yale University Press, 2022), 63.

111. John A. Thompson, "The Exaggeration of American Vulnerability: The Anatomy of a Tradition," *Diplomatic History* 16 (Winter 1992): 23–43.

112. Thompson, *Sense of Power,* 155, 173–176, 181.

113. On the interwar peace movement, see Michael G. Thompson, *For God and Globe: Christian Internationalism in the United States between the Great War and the Cold War* (Ithaca, NY: Cornell University Press, 2015).

114. Julian Huxley, "Armaments and Security," *New Republic,* June 2, 1941, 750.

115. J. M. Spaight, *Pseudo-Security* (London: Longmans, Green, 1928); H. E. Hyde, *The Price of National Security* (London: P. S. King, 1930).

116. Not nonexistent, though: see, for example, Charles E. Merriam, *On the Agenda of Democracy* (Cambridge, MA: Harvard University Press, 1941), 53–54.

117. Analysis Section, M.I.D., "The United States and the Power Cycle," April 1, 1943, RG107, Entry 103, box 280, NARA.

118. Franklin D. Roosevelt, Address at Marietta, Ohio, July 8, 1938, *APP,* https://www.presidency.ucsb.edu/node/209056.

119. Franklin D. Roosevelt, Fireside Chat, September 3, 1939, *APP,* https://www.presidency.ucsb.edu/node/209990; Franklin D. Roosevelt, Message to Congress Urging Repeal of the Embargo Provisions of the Neutrality Law, September 21, 1939, *APP,* https://www.presidency.ucsb.edu/node/210082.

120. Franklin D. Roosevelt, Fireside Chat, December 29, 1940, *APP,* https://www.presidency.ucsb.edu/node/209416.

121. "Unlimited National Emergency." On the emergency's symbolic nature, see David Kennedy, *Freedom from Fear: The American People in Depression and War, 1929–1945* (New York: Oxford University Press, 1999), 493–494.

122. Franklin D. Roosevelt, State of the Union Address, January 6, 1942, *APP,* https://www.presidency.ucsb.edu/node/210559.

NOTES TO PAGES 167–171

123. Roosevelt, Press Conference, December 17, 1940. On Hopkins and Lend-Lease, see George McJimsey, *Harry Hopkins: Ally of the Poor and Defender of Democracy* (Cambridge, MA: Harvard University Press, 1987), 151–161.

124. Roosevelt to Joseph Grew, January 21, 1941, *FRUS, 1941*, vol. IV, 7. For the original plea, see Grew to Roosevelt, December 14, 1940, *FRUS, 1940*, vol. IV: *The Far East* (Washington, DC: GPO, 1955), 469–471.

125. Franklin D. Roosevelt, Greeting on Navy Day, October 8, 1937, *APP,* https://www.presidency.ucsb.edu/node/208849.

126. Carl Vinson comments, February 11, 1938, *Hearings on House Resolution 9218,* 2208.

127. See the definitive treatment in Gole, *Road to Rainbow;* but see also Stoler, *Allies and Adversaries,* 18–35.

128. Harold Stark to Frank Knox, November 12, 1940, Franklin D. Roosevelt Library, http://docs.fdrlibrary.marist.edu/psf/box4/a48b01.html.

129. Stimson to Stanley Hornbeck, June 4, 1941, with enclosure, May 26, 1941 (quoted on 8), RG107, Entry 99, box 4, folder "Far East (Before Dec. 7, 1941)," NARA.

130. Dallek, *Franklin D. Roosevelt,* 10.

131. Draft editorial, June 23, 1940, Grenville Clark papers, box 113, folder 67, Rauner Library Archives and Manuscripts, Dartmouth College.

132. For Hoover, see "American Policies for Peace," radio speech to Republican Women's Clubs, January 15, 1938, Herbert Hoover, *Addresses Upon the American Road, 1933–1938* (New York: C. Scribner's Sons, 1938), 303. For Beard, see Milne, *Worldmaking,* 161–162.

133. Roosevelt, Press Conference, December 17, 1940; Franklin D. Roosevelt, State of the Union Address, January 6, 1942, *APP,* https://www.presidency.ucsb.edu/node/210559.

134. Franklin D. Roosevelt, Campaign Address at Madison Square Garden, October 28, 1940, *APP,* https://www.presidency.ucsb.edu/node/209307.

135. Franklin D. Roosevelt, Radio Address on the Election of Liberals, November 4, 1938, *APP,* https://www.presidency.ucsb.edu/node/209329.

136. Alan Brinkley, *The End of Reform: New Deal Liberalism in Recession and War* (New York: Vintage, 1996), 175–200, 240–245.

137. Meg Jacobs, *Pocketbook Politics: Economic Citizenship in Twentieth-Century America* (Princeton: Princeton University Press, 2005), 179–220.

138. Forrest C. Pogue, *George C. Marshall: Ordeal and Hope, 1939–1942* (New York: Viking, 1966), 120–192; Parrish, *Roosevelt and Marshall,* 84–88.

139. "Statement by General Marshall," *Life,* July 22, 1940, 16.

140. Beverly Gage, *G-Man: J. Edgar Hoover and the Making of the American Century* (New York: Viking, 2022), 227–236.

141. Alfred P. Sloan, "The Economic Aspects of American Defense," *Proceedings of the Academy of Political Science* 19 (January 1941): 127–139.

142. Hanson W. Baldwin, "America at War: The Triumph of the Machine," *Foreign Affairs* 24 (January 1946): 241–252.

143. Jonathan Levy, *Ages of American Capitalism: A History of the United States* (New York: Random House, 2021), 436–461, spending figures on 442. For a detailed study, see Maury Klein, *A Call to Arms: Mobilizing America for World War II* (New York: Bloomsbury, 2013).

144. Aaron B. O'Connell, *Underdogs: The Making of the Modern Marine Corps* (Cambridge, MA: Harvard University Press, 2012), 29–34.

145. Sherwood, *Roosevelt and Hopkins,* 75–76; Kennedy, *Freedom from Fear,* 251–252.

146. Walter E. Weyl, *American World Policies* (New York: Macmillan, 1917), 137–138.

147. Franklin D. Roosevelt, Greeting on Navy Day, October 2, 1940, *APP*, https://www .presidency.ucsb.edu/node/210489. In general, see Sparrow, *Warfare State;* and Mark R. Wilson, *Destructive Creation: American Business and the Winning of World War II* (Philadelphia: University of Pennsylvania Press, 2016). On wartime production, see Paul A. C. Koistinen, *Arsenal of World War II: The Political Economy of American Warfare, 1940–1945* (Lawrence: University Press of Kansas, 2004). On the war superseding, indeed subsuming, the New Deal, see Brinkley, *End of Reform;* John W. Jeffries, "A 'Third New Deal'? Liberal Policy and the American State, 1937–1945," *Journal of Policy History* 8 (October 1996): 387–409; Bartholomew H. Sparrow, *From the Outside In: World War II and the American State* (Princeton: Princeton University Press, 1996); and Jennifer Klein, *For All These Rights: Business, Labor, and the Shaping of America's Public-Private Welfare State* (Princeton: Princeton University Press, 2003), 116–161, 204–257. On the war as the end of the Depression, see J. R. Vernon, "World War II Fiscal Policies and the End of the Great Depression," *Journal of Economic History* 54 (December 1994): 850–868. But for a contrary view, see Alexander J. Field, *The Economic Consequences of U.S. Mobilization for the Second World War* (New Haven: Yale University Press, 2022). On the war as both the apogee of the state and anti-statism, see Alan Brinkley, *Liberalism and Its Discontents* (Cambridge, MA: Harvard University Press, 1998), 85–88.

148. Franklin D. Roosevelt, Annual Budget Message, January 3, 1941, *APP*, https://www .presidency.ucsb.edu/node/210616.

149. Franklin D. Roosevelt, Address at University of Virginia, June 10, 1940, *APP*, https:// www.presidency.ucsb.edu/node/209705; A. T. Mahan, *The Interest of America in Sea Power, Present and Future* (Boston: Little, Brown, 1897), 118–119, 254. Earle said much the same: Edward Mead Earle, "Power Politics and American World Policy," *Political Science Quarterly* 58 (March 1943): 94–106, 100.

150. Quoted in Dallek, *Franklin D. Roosevelt,* 12.

151. "Tripartite Dinner Meeting, Yusupov Palace, Bohlen minutes," February 8, 1945, *FRUS: The Conferences of Malta and Yalta* (Washington, DC: GPO, 1955), 798.

6. THE AMERICAN WAY

1. Wendy L. Wall, *Inventing the "American Way": The Politics of Consensus from the New Deal to the Civil Rights Movement* (New York: Oxford University Press, 2008); Andrew Preston, "Monsters Everywhere: A Genealogy of National Security," *Diplomatic History* 38 (June 2014): 477–500, 496–497; Thomas Borstelmann, *Just Like Us: The American Struggle to Understand Foreigners* (New York: Columbia University Press, 2020), 37–42. For "American Dream," see Sarah Churchwell, *Behold, America: A History of America First and the American Dream* (London: Bloomsbury, 2018). For "exceptionalism," see Ian Tyrrell, *American Exceptionalism: A New History of an Old Idea* (Chicago: University of Chicago Press, 2021), 3, 141–181.

2. Margaret Bourke-White, *Portrait of Myself* (New York: Simon and Schuster, 1963), 150.

3. See her descriptions in Bourke-White, *Portrait of Myself,* 107–113, 122–142; and her photos collected in Sean Callahan, ed., *The Photographs of Margaret Bourke-White* (New York: Bonanza Books, 1972). On her life, see Vicki Goldberg, *Margaret Bourke-White: A Biography* (New York: Harper and Row, 1986).

4. Mary McLeod Bethune, "Certain Unalienable Rights," in *What the Negro Wants,* ed. Rayford W. Logan (Chapel Hill: University of North Carolina Press, 1944), 252–256.

5. Earle, for instance, embedded the protection of values in "national security": Edward Mead Earle, "American Security: Its Changing Conditions," *Annals of the American Academy of Political and Social Science* 218 (November 1941): 189–193.

6. Franklin D. Roosevelt, Annual Message to Congress, January 4, 1939, American Presidency Project (hereafter *APP*), https://www.presidency.ucsb.edu/node/209128.

7. Archibald MacLeish, "To the Class of '41," *New Republic*, June 21, 1941, 718.

8. Justin Hart, *Empire of Ideas: The Origins of Public Diplomacy and the Transformation of U. S. Foreign Policy* (New York: Oxford University Press, 2013), 41–106; Holly Cowan Shulman, *The Voice of America: Propaganda and Democracy, 1941–1945* (Madison: University of Wisconsin Press, 1990).

9. Franklin D. Roosevelt, Annual Message to Congress, January 3, 1940, *APP*, https://www.presidency.ucsb.edu/node/210437.

10. Charles E. Merriam, *On the Agenda of Democracy* (Cambridge, MA: Harvard University Press, 1941), 42.

11. Harold D. Lasswell, "Sino-Japanese Crisis: The Garrison State versus the Civilian State," *China Quarterly* 2 (Special Fall Number, 1937): 643–649; Harold D. Lasswell, "The Garrison State," *American Journal of Sociology* 46 (January 1941): 455–468.

12. Walter Millis, "Is It Internationalism or 'Continentalism,'" *New York Herald Tribune*, May 19, 1940. On Wilson and TR, see Ross A. Kennedy, *The Will to Believe: Woodrow Wilson, World War I, and America's Strategy for Peace and Security* (Kent, OH: Kent State University Press, 2009), 172–175.

13. Edward Mead Earle, *Against This Torrent* (Princeton: Princeton University Press, 1941), 27, 60.

14. Reinhold Niebuhr, "American Foreign Policy," *The Nation*, May 25, 1940, 657; Dean Acheson, speech to students at Yale, November 28, 1939, Dean Acheson, *Morning and Noon* (Boston: Houghton Mifflin, 1965), 272.

15. "Statements by the Secretary of State Before the House Foreign Affairs Committee," January 15, 1941, *Department of State Bulletin*, January 18, 1941, 88.

16. Roosevelt, Fireside Chat, December 29, 1940.

17. Franklin D. Roosevelt, Radio Address Announcing an Unlimited National Emergency, May 27, 1941, *APP*, https://www.presidency.ucsb.edu/node/209607.

18. Richard Hofstadter, *Anti-Intellectualism in American Life* (New York: Alfred A. Knopf, 1963), 42.

19. On the inventions and economic dynamics that profoundly changed the nation, see Robert J. Gordon, *The Rise and Fall of American Growth: The U.S. Standard of Living since the Civil War* (Princeton: Princeton University Press, 2016).

20. Franklin D. Roosevelt, Fireside Chat, October 12, 1937, *APP*, https://www.presidency.ucsb.edu/node/208891; FDR, Acceptance Speech for the Renomination for the Presidency, June 27, 1936, *APP*, https://www.presidency.ucsb.edu/node/208917.

21. *Minersville School Dist. et al. v. Gobitis et al.* 310 US 586 § 8 (1940), https://www.law.cornell.edu/supremecourt/text/310/586.

22. Franklin D. Roosevelt, Address at Dedication of Great Smoky Mountains National Park, September 2, 1940, *APP*, https://www.presidency.ucsb.edu/node/209936.

23. "Secretary Hull's Address of June 20, 1940," in *Peace and War: United States Foreign Policy, 1931–1941* (Washington, DC: GPO, 1943), 53.

24. Andrew Preston, *Sword of the Spirit, Shield of Faith: Religion in American War and Diplomacy* (New York: Alfred A. Knopf, 2012), 315–326.

25. Kevin M. Schultz, *Tri-Faith America: How Catholics and Jews Held Postwar America to Its Protestant Promise* (New York: Oxford University Press, 2011), 15–67. For various approaches to the invention of the Judeo-Christian tradition, see also Mark Silk, *Spiritual Politics: Religion and America Since World War II* (New York: Simon and Schuster, 1988), 40–53; Wall, *Inventing the "American Way"*; Preston, *Sword of the Spirit, Shield of Faith*, 327–341; K. Healan Gaston, *Imagining Judeo-Christian America: Religion, Secularism, and*

the Redefinition of Democracy (Chicago: University of Chicago Press, 2019); and Borstelmann, *Just Like Us,* 39–40.

26. Franklin D. Roosevelt, Address for Navy and Total Defense Day, October 27, 1941, *APP,* https://www.presidency.ucsb.edu/node/210207.

27. Herbert Hoover, "On American Liberty: Broadcast from the Metropolitan Opera," December 7, 1940, Herbert Hoover, *Addresses Upon the American Road, 1940–1941* (New York: C. Scribner's Sons, 1941), 53. See also Charles A. Beard and Mary R. Beard, *The Rise of American Civilization* (New York: Macmillan, 1927).

28. Chester H. Rowell, "The War and the Pacific," in *Defense for America,* ed. William Allen White (New York: Macmillan, 1940), 135. Emphasis in original.

29. Brooks Atkinson, "The Forgotten Moral Issue," *Reader's Digest,* May 1941, 2.

30. See, respectively: Franklin D. Roosevelt, Address to the Representatives of Industry on N.R.A. Codes, March 5, 1934, *APP,* https://www.presidency.ucsb.edu/node/208473; FDR, Fireside Chat, September 6, 1936, *APP,* https://www.presidency.ucsb.edu/node/209049; FDR, Letter on Peace in the Ranks of Labor, September 30, 1939, *APP,* https://www.presidency.ucsb.edu/node/210098, and FDR, Greeting to the American Federation of Labor, November 13, 1940, *APP,* https://www.presidency.ucsb.edu/node/209360; FDR, Radio Address on Cooperation with the Unemployment Census, November 14, 1937, *APP,* https://www.presidency.ucsb.edu/node/208998 and FDR, Annual Message to Congress, January 3, 1940, *APP,* https://www.presidency.ucsb.edu/node/210437; FDR, Message to Congress on Legislation for Private Construction of Housing, November 27, 1937, *APP,* https://www.presidency.ucsb.edu/node/209024; FDR, Statement on the Sit-Down Strikes in Michigan, October 25, 1938, *APP,* https://www.presidency.ucsb.edu/node/209283; FDR, Statement on Education, October 2, 1939, *APP,* https://www.presidency.ucsb.edu/node/210119; FDR, Statement on Signing Two Statutes to Protect Investors, August 23, 1940, *APP,* https://www.presidency.ucsb.edu/node/209898; FDR, Radio Address on the Eighth Year of the New Deal Agricultural Policy, March 8, 1941, *APP,* https://www.presidency.ucsb.edu/node/210634.

31. FDR, Message to Selective Service Registrants, October 16, 1940, *APP,* https://www.presidency.ucsb.edu/node/209224.

32. Walter Lippmann, "America and the World," *Life,* June 3, 1940, 103.

33. Kevin M. Kruse and Stephen Tuck, eds., *Fog of War: The Second World War and the Civil Rights Movement* (New York: Oxford University Press, 2012); Rawn James Jr., *The Double V: How Wars, Protest, and Harry Truman Desegregated America's Military* (New York: Bloomsbury, 2013), 137–196.

34. Stephen Tuck, "'You can sing and punch . . . but you can't be a soldier or a man': African American Struggles for a New Place in Popular Culture," in Kruse and Tuck, *Fog of War,* 110–113; Kathleen M. German, *Promises of Citizenship: Film Recruitment of African Americans in World War II* (Jackson: University Press of Mississippi, 2019), 67–77.

35. Scott Nearing, *Black America* (New York: Vanguard Press, 1929), 212.

36. W. E. B. Du Bois, "The Democrats Speak," *The Crisis,* August 1936, 241.

37. W. E. B. Du Bois, *The World and Africa: An Inquiry into the Part Which Africa Has Played in World History* (New York: Viking, 1947), in W. E. B. Du Bois, *Works, Selections,* vol. 10 / 11, *The World and Africa; and, Color and Democracy,* ed. Henry Louis Gates Jr. (New York: Oxford University Press, 2007), 26.

38. "The Negro in the United States Navy," *The Crisis,* July 1940, 200–201, 210. On conditions for Blacks in the military and their campaigns to improve them, see Kimberley Phillips Boehm, *War! What Is It Good For? Black Freedom Struggles and the U. S. Military from World War II to Iraq* (Chapel Hill: University of North Carolina Press, 2012), 37–84; Christine Knauer, *Let Us Fight as Free Men: Black Soldiers and Civil Rights* (Philadelphia: University of Pennsylvania Press, 2014), 13–32; and Thomas A. Guglielmo, *Divisions: A New*

History of Racism and Resistance in America's World War II Military (New York: Oxford University Press, 2021).

39. Ralph J. Bunche, *A World View of Race* (Washington, DC: Associates in Negro Folk Education, 1936), 25, 32, 96.

40. Charles A. Lindbergh, "Aviation, Geography, and Race," *Reader's Digest,* November 1939, 64, 66, 65, 66–67.

41. "Lindbergh's Remarks at AFC Dinner," *PM,* January 11, 1942, 3.

42. Andrew Preston, "The Limits of Brotherhood: Race, Religion, and World Order in American Ecumenical Protestantism," *American Historical Review* 127 (September 2022): 1222–1251. Generally, see also Leah N. Gordon, *From Power to Prejudice: The Rise of Racial Individualism in Midcentury America* (Chicago: University of Chicago Press, 2015); N. D. B. Connolly, "The Strange Career of American Liberalism," in *Shaped by the State: Toward a New Political History of the Twentieth Century,* ed. Brent Cebul, Lily Geismer, and Mason B. Williams (Chicago: University of Chicago Press, 2019), 62–95; and Joseph Darda, *The Strange Career of Racial Liberalism* (Stanford: Stanford University Press, 2022).

43. Quoted in Megan Threlkeld, *Citizens of the World: U.S. Women and Global Government* (Philadelphia: University of Pennsylvania Press, 2022), 73. For an overview of women's interwar internationalism, see Megan Threlkeld, "Women's Politics in International Context," in *The Cambridge History of America and the World,* vol. 3: *1900–1945,* ed. Brooke L. Blower and Andrew Preston (New York: Cambridge University Press, 2021), 360–380. See also Ian Tyrrell, *Woman's World / Woman's Empire: The Woman's Christian Temperance Union in International Perspective, 1880–1930* (Chapel Hill: University of North Carolina Press, 1991); Leila J. Rupp, *Worlds of Women: The Making of an International Women's Movement* (Princeton: Princeton University Press, 1997); Allison L. Sneider, *Suffragists in an Imperial Age: U.S. Expansion and the Woman Question, 1870–1929* (New York: Oxford University Press, 2008); and Nichols, *Promise and Peril,* 273–290, 296–300, 304–307.

44. Abraham Epstein, *Insecurity: A Challenge to America* (New York: H. Smith and R. Haas, 1933), 23, 50; J. Patrick Raines, "Frank H. Knight's Contributions to Social Economics," *Review of Social Economy* 47 (Fall 1989): 280–292.

45. George Chauncey, *Gay New York: Gender, Urban Culture, and the Making of the Gay Male World, 1890–1940* (New York: Basic Books, 1994), 331–354; Alice Kessler-Harris, "In the Nation's Image: The Gendered Limits of Social Citizenship in the Depression Era," *Journal of American History* 86 (December 1999): 1251–1279; Jennifer Klein, *For All These Rights: Business, Labor, and the Shaping of America's Public-Private Welfare State* (Princeton: Princeton University Press, 2003), 13, 104–107; Margot Canaday, *The Straight State: Sexuality and Citizenship in Twentieth-Century America* (Princeton: Princeton University Press, 2009), 55–173; James T. Sparrow, *Warfare State: World War II Americans and the Age of Big Government* (New York: Oxford University Press, 2011), 203–208; and, more generally, Jonathan Ned Katz, *The Invention of Heterosexuality* (Chicago: University of Chicago Press, 2007). On the effects of the Great War, see Beth Linker, *War's Waste: Rehabilitation in World War I America* (Chicago: University of Chicago Press, 2011).

46. Cornelia Rogers, "Women Advised on War Work," *New York Times,* December 18, 1941.

47. Threlkeld, *Citizens of the World,* 103–123 (quoted on 117, 123). More generally, see Cynthia Enloe, *Bananas, Beaches and Bases: Making Feminist Sense of International Politics* (Berkeley: University of California Press, 2014).

48. Lorraine M. Lees, "National Security and Ethnicity: Contrasting Views during World War II," *Diplomatic History* 11 (Spring 1987): 113–125; Franklin D. Roosevelt, Statement on the Appointment of William J. Donovan as Coordinator of Information, July 11, 1941, *APP,* https://www.presidency.ucsb.edu/node/209759. The acronyms stand for: Office of Facts

and Figures, which became the Office of War Information; Foreign Nationalities Branch, which was housed within the Office of Strategic Services, which was founded in 1941 under the original name of the Office of the Coordinator of Information; Office of Civilian Defense; Foreign Activity Correlation, a unit within the State Department; and the Federal Bureau of Investigation, which got its new name and structure in 1935.

49. Susan J. Douglas, *Listening In: Radio and the American Imagination* (Minneapolis: University of Minnesota Press, 2004), 149.

50. Dower, *War Without Mercy.*

51. "Japanese Propaganda Agencies," Quarterly Summary of National Defense Investigations, November 15, 1940, RG107, Entry 103, box 279, National Archives and Records Administration, College Park, MD.

52. Marc Gallicchio, *The African American Encounter with Japan and China: Black Internationalism in Asia, 1895–1945* (Chapel Hill: University of North Carolina Press, 2000); Moon-Ho Jung, *Menace to Empire: Anticolonial Solidarities and the Transpacific Origins of the US Security State* (Oakland: University of California Press, 2022); Keisha N. Blain, "'The Dark Skin[ned] People of the Eastern World': Mittie Maude Lena Gordon's Vision of Afro-Asian Solidarity," in Owens and Rietzler, *Women's International Thought,* 179–197.

53. Tetsuden Kashima, *Judgment Without Trial: Japanese American Imprisonment During World War II* (Seattle: University of Washington Press, 2003); Erika Lee, *America for Americans: A History of Xenophobia in the United States* (New York: Basic Books, 2019), 183–219. Oddly, however, the FBI didn't support Japanese internment: Beverly Gage, *G-Man: J. Edgar Hoover and the Making of the American Century* (New York: Viking, 2022), 258–261.

54. Thomas Connell, *America's Japanese Hostages: The World War II Plan for a Japanese Free Latin America* (Westport, CT: Praeger, 2002); Erika Lee, *The Making of Asian America: A History* (New York: Simon and Schuster, 2015), 223–227, 243–250.

55. Brian Masaru Hayashi, *Democratizing the Enemy: The Japanese American Internment* (Princeton: Princeton University Press, 2004). For education, see Thomas James, *Exile Within: The Schooling of Japanese Americans, 1942–1945* (Cambridge, MA: Harvard University Press, 1987); and for social work, Yoosun Park, *Facilitating Injustice: The Complicity of Social Workers in the Forced Removal and Incarceration of Japanese Americans, 1941–1946* (New York: Oxford University Press, 2020). For the war on crime, see Anthony Gregory, *New Deal Law and Order: How the War on Crime Built the Modern Liberal State* (Cambridge, MA: Harvard University Press, 2024).

56. Franklin D. Roosevelt, Fireside Chat, May 26, 1940, *APP,* https://www.presidency.ucsb.edu/node/209685.

57. Brian Masaru Hayashi, "Frank Knox's Fifth Column in Hawai'i: The U.S. Navy, the Japanese, and the Pearl Harbor Attack," *Journal of American-East Asian Relations* 27 (2020): 142–168 (quoted on 143). On Hollywood, see Steven J. Ross, *Hitler in Los Angeles: How Jews Foiled Nazi Plots Against Hollywood and America* (New York: Bloomsbury, 2017); and Laura B. Rosenzweig, *Hollywood's Spies: The Undercover Surveillance of Nazis in Los Angeles* (New York: New York University Press, 2017). On the Christian Front, see Charles R. Gallagher, *Nazis of Copley Square: The Forgotten Story of the Christian Front* (Cambridge, MA: Harvard University Press, 2021); and, for a similar instance, Warren Grover, *Nazis in Newark* (New Brunswick, NJ: Transaction, 2003). More generally, see Bradley W. Hart, *Hitler's American Friends: The Third Reich's Supporters in the United States* (New York: St. Martin's Press, 2018); and Rhodri Jeffreys-Jones, *The Nazi Spy Ring in America: Hitler's Agents, the FBI, and the Case That Stirred the Nation* (Washington, DC: Georgetown University press, 2020).

58. *Ex parte QUIRIN,* 317 US 1 § 47 (1942), https://www.law.cornell.edu/supremecourt/text/317/1.

59. Brad Snyder, *Democratic Justice: Felix Frankfurter, the Supreme Court, and the Making of the Liberal Establishment* (New York: W. W. Norton, 2022), 395–405, quoted on 400.

60. Alan Brinkley, *The Publisher: Henry Luce and His American Century* (New York: Alfred A. Knopf, 2010), 6–15; David A. Hollinger, *Protestants Abroad: How Missionaries Tried to Change the World but Changed America* (Princeton: Princeton University Press, 2018), 24–58. On the progressivism of Protestant missions more generally, see Preston, *Sword of the Spirit, Shield of Faith,* 175–197.

61. For treatments that emphasize offense, see Michael J. Hogan, ed., *The Ambiguous Legacy: U.S. Foreign Relations in the "American Century"* (New York: Cambridge University Press, 1999); Andrew J. Bacevich, ed., *The Short American Century: A Postmortem* (Cambridge, MA: Harvard University Press, 2012); and Hart, *Empire of Ideas.*

62. James Monroe, Seventh Annual Message, December 2, 1823, *APP,* https://www.presidency.ucsb.edu/node/205755.

63. Henry R. Luce, "The American Century," *Life,* February 17, 1941, 61–63, 65. Emphasis in original.

7. THE BATTLE OF BEDFORD FALLS

1. Domestic recycling was actually critical to the war effort, even if it weren't always recognized as heroic: see James J. Kimble, *Prairie Forge: The Extraordinary Story of the Nebraska Scrap Metal Drive of World War II* (Lincoln: University of Nebraska Press, 2014).

2. Franklin D. Roosevelt, Radio Address at a Dinner of the Foreign Policy Association, October 21, 1944, American Presidency Project (hereafter *APP*), https://www.presidency.ucsb.edu/node/210407. On World War II in the American empire, see Daniel Immerwahr, *How to Hide an Empire: A History of the Greater United States* (New York: Farrar, Straus, and Giroux, 2019), 171–212. On the totality of social upheaval in most countries, see Aviel Roshwald, *Occupied: European and Asian Responses to Axis Conquest, 1937–1945* (Cambridge: Cambridge University Press, 2023). On the comparative difference of the American experience, see Gerhard L. Weinberg, *A World at Arms: A Global History of World War II* (Cambridge: Cambridge University Press, 1994), 894–914; and David Reynolds, "World War II and Modern Meanings," *Diplomatic History* 25 (July 2001): 457–472, 463, 470.

3. Mark Harris, *Five Came Back: A Story of Hollywood and the Second World War* (New York: Penguin, 2014); Harriet Hyman Alonso, *Robert E. Sherwood: The Playwright in Peace and War* (Amherst: University of Massachusetts Press, 2007). On Capra's insecurity, see Joseph McBride, *Frank Capra: The Catastrophe of Success* (New York: Simon and Schuster, 1992), 474. Capra may not have known it, but his homefront service was actually the experience of the majority of US personnel during World War II: see Aaron Hiltner, *Taking Leave, Taking Liberties: American Troops on the World War II Home Front* (Chicago: University of Chicago Press, 2020).

4. Grayson Kirk, "National Power and Foreign Policy," *Foreign Affairs* 23 (July 1945): 620–626, 626, 625.

5. Samuel Flagg Bemis, "The Shifting Strategy of American Defense and Diplomacy," *Virginia Quarterly Review* 24 (Summer 1948): 321–335, 331, 333.

6. Report to the President by the National Security Council, November 23, 1948, *Foreign Relations of the United States* (hereafter *FRUS*), 1948, vol. 1, Part 2: *General; The United Nations* (Washington, DC: GPO, 1976), 663, 665–666.

7. *General Marshall's Report: The Winning of the War in Europe and the Pacific* (Washington, DC, 1945), 1.

8. Kirk, "National Power," 620.

9. Franklin D. Roosevelt, Radio Address from Puget Sound Navy Yard, August 12, 1944, *APP,* https://www.presidency.ucsb.edu/node/209747.

10. Paul Kennedy, *The Rise and Fall of the Great Powers: Economic Change and Military Conflict from 1500 to 2000* (New York: Random House, 1987), 357–372, quoted at 357. See also Michael Mandelbaum, *The Fate of Nations: The Search for National Security in the Nineteenth and Twentieth Centuries* (New York: Cambridge University Press, 1988), 129–132; Melvyn P. Leffler, *A Preponderance of Power: National Security, the Truman Administration, and the Cold War* (Stanford: Stanford University Press, 1992), 1–6; and, for an arresting comparison of US and Soviet losses, Melvyn P. Leffler, "The Cold War: What Do 'We Now Know'?" *American Historical Review* 104 (April 1999): 501–524, 513.

11. Marshall to Brehon B. Somervell, April 14, 1943, enclosed in "Survey of Demobilization Planning," June 18, 1943, and Stimson to Robert P. Patterson, July 7, 1943, RG107, Entry 99, box 4, National Archives and Records Administration, College Park, MD.

12. "Army to Give Priority to Fathers, Overseas Veterans in Demobilizing," *New York Times*, September 6, 1944; "V-E Day to See Army Cut 250,000 Monthly," *New York Times*, February 28, 1945.

13. Vincent Davis, *Postwar Defense Policy and the United States Navy, 1943–1946* (Chapel Hill: University of North Carolina Press, 1966), 172–175.

14. Michael J. Hogan, *A Cross of Iron: Harry S. Truman and the Origins of the National Security State* (New York: Cambridge University Press, 2000), 46.

15. Bemis, "Shifting Strategy," 332, 334.

16. "Want Cost Details on Reconversion," *New York Times*, May 23, 1943; "Canceled Contracts," *Wall Street Journal*, August 7, 1943; "Delay in Industrial Conversion May Result in 12 Million Jobless After War," *Wall Street Journal*, August 21, 1943; Board of Governors of the Federal Reserve System (US), Federal Advisory Council, "Meeting documents, November 14–15, 1943," Minutes and Recommendations of the Federal Advisory Council, https://fraser.stlouisfed.org/title/minutes-recommendations-federal-advisory-council-1152/meeting-documents-november-14-15-1943-1873.

17. Douglas T. Stuart, *Creating the National Security State: A History of the Law That Transformed America* (Princeton: Princeton University Press, 2008), 151.

18. Glenn Altschuler and Stuart Blumin, *The G.I. Bill: A New Deal for Veterans* (New York: Oxford University Press, 2009).

19. Quoted in Frank T. Hines, "The Human Side of Demobilization," *Annals of the American Academy of Political and Social Science* 238 (March 1945): 1–8, 8.

20. "Provident Loan Net Off 28 Per Cent in '44," *New York Times*, February 28, 1945.

21. Nathaniel Peffer, *America's Place in the World* (New York: Viking, 1945), 74.

22. Kirk, "National Power," 620.

23. Paul Russell Anderson, "National Security in the Postwar World," *Annals of the American Academy of Political and Social Science* 241 (September 1945): 1–7, 3. For Willkie, see Samuel Zipp, *The Idealist: Wendell Willkie's Wartime Quest to Build One World* (Cambridge, MA: Harvard University Press, 2020). On the UN, see Townsend Hoopes and Douglas Brinkley, *FDR and the Creation of the U.N.* (New Haven: Yale University Press, 1997), 172, 179. In general, see Wesley T. Wooley, *Alternatives to Anarchy: American Supernationalism Since World War II* (Bloomington: Indiana University Press, 1988); Or Rosenboim, *The Emergence of Globalism: Visions of World Order in Britain and the United States, 1939–1950* (Princeton: Princeton University Press, 2017); and Petra Goedde, *The Politics of Peace: A Global Cold War History* (New York: Oxford University Press, 2019).

24. For analyses of UMT, see Michael S. Sherry, *Preparing for the Next War: American Plans for Postwar Defense, 1941–1945* (New Haven: Yale University Press, 1977); and Hogan, *Cross of Iron*, 119–158.

25. George C. Marshall, Speech to the Salvation Army, Kansas City, MO, November 18, 1945, *Papers of George Catlett Marshall*, vol. 5, ed. Larry I. Bland (Baltimore: Johns Hopkins University Press, 2003), 360.

26. George C. Marshall, Testimony before the Senate Foreign Relations Committee, February 14, 1947, *Papers of George Catlett Marshall*, vol. 6, ed. Larry I. Bland and Mark A. Stoler (Baltimore: Johns Hopkins University Press, 2013), 44.

27. Marshall to Truman, "Basis for a Post-War Army," May 5, 1945, *Papers of George Catlett Marshall*, vol. 5, 165–168.

28. Roy K. Davenport, "Implications of Military Selection and Classification in Relation to Universal Military Training," *Journal of Negro Education* 15 (Autumn 1946): 585–594.

29. Harry S Truman, Address Before a Joint Session of the Congress on Universal Military Training, October 23, 1945, *APP*, https://www.presidency.ucsb.edu/node/230966.

30. Myron W. Curzon, "The Nation's Military Security," *Scientific Monthly* 62 (January 1946): 66–70, 66; Legion quoted in Sherry, *Preparing*, 83. For other pro-UMT arguments on the specific grounds of national security, see Albert L. Cox, "Military Training," *Social Science* 20 (April 1945): 93–96; Thomas H. Evans, "Universal Military Training," *Military Engineer* 37 (June 1945): 211–213; Mary Earhart, "The Value of Universal Military Training in Maintaining Peace," *Annals of the American Academy of Political and Social Science* 241 (September 1945): 46–57; and Halford L. Hoskins, "Universal Military Training and American Foreign Policy," *Annals of the American Academy of Political and Social Science* 241 (September 1945): 58–66.

31. Marshall, Speech to the Salvation Army, 360.

32. Marshall, Speech to the Salvation Army, 362.

33. Sherry, *Preparing*, 191–193, 217; Davis, *Postwar Defense Policy*, 180–181, 213–215 (quoted on 216). Marc Gallicchio, *Unconditional: The Japanese Surrender in World War II* (New York: Oxford University Press, 2020), 14–16, 76–77, is good on the popular pressures for demobilization.

34. Jason Berger, *A New Deal for the World: Eleanor Roosevelt and American Foreign Policy* (New York: Columbia University Press, 1981); Elizabeth Borgwardt, *A New Deal for the World: America's Vision for Human Rights* (Cambridge, MA: Harvard University Press, 2005).

35. Hugh Rockoff, "Banking and Finance, 1789–1914," in *The Cambridge Economic History of the United States*, vol. 2: *The Long Nineteenth Century*, ed. Stanley L. Engerman and Robert E. Gallman (New York: Cambridge University Press, 2000), 665–675; Alfred D. Chandler Jr., *The Visible Hand: The Managerial Revolution in American Business* (Cambridge, MA: Harvard University Press, 1977).

36. Jacob Javits (D-NY) remarks, *Congressional Record-House* 93:6, June 20, 1947, 7511.

37. Truman, "Address . . . on Universal Military Training"; Marshall, Speech to the Salvation Army, 359.

38. Merze Tate, *The Disarmament Illusion: The Movement for a Limitation of Armaments to 1907* (New York: Macmillan, 1942), xi.

39. Quoted in Daniel Yergin, *Shattered Peace: The Origins of the Cold War and the National Security State* (Boston: Houghton Mifflin, 1977), 197.

40. Frederick Muhlenberg (R-OH) remarks, *Congressional Record-House* 93:2, March 6, 1947, 1721.

41. Franklin D. Roosevelt, Message to Congress on the Bretton Woods Agreements, February 12, 1945, *APP*, https://www.presidency.ucsb.edu/node/210026.

42. Franklin D. Roosevelt, Statement on the Dumbarton Oaks Conversations, October 9, 1944, *APP*, https://www.presidency.ucsb.edu/node/209901.

43. David L. Bosco, *Five to Rule Them All: The UN Security Council and the Making of the Modern World* (New York: Oxford University Press, 2009).

44. Franklin D. Roosevelt, Letter of the O.W.M.R. Advisory Board on the Postwar Economy, April 7, 1945, *APP*, https://www.presidency.ucsb.edu/node/210099.

45. Benn Steil, *The Battle of Bretton Woods: John Maynard Keynes, Harry Dexter White, and the Making of a New World Order* (Princeton: Princeton University Press, 2013).

46. Quoted in Benn Steil, *The Marshall Plan: Dawn of the Cold War* (New York: Simon and Schuster, 2018), 192, 216.

47. George Malone (R-NV) remarks, *Congressional Record-Senate* 93:2, March 25, 1947, 2531.

48. Michael J. Hogan, *The Marshall Plan: America, Britain and the Reconstruction of Western Europe, 1947–1952* (New York: Cambridge University Press, 1987), 22. In fact, the Marshall Plan resulted in US dollars underwriting comprehensive European welfare states that went far beyond the New Deal: John Lewis Gaddis, *We Now Know: Rethinking Cold War History* (New York: Oxford University Press, 1997), 197.

49. Harry S Truman, Annual Message on the State of the Union, January 6, 1947, *APP*, https://www.presidency.ucsb.edu/node/232364.

50. See Aaron L. Friedberg, *In the Shadow of the Garrison State: America's Anti-Statism and Its Cold War Grand Strategy* (Princeton: Princeton University Press, 2000); Leffler, *Preponderance* (quoted on 163).

51. S.J. Res 54, *Congressional Record-Senate* 93:1, February 3, 1947, 732.

52. See, respectively, Frankfurter's dissent in *United States v. State of California* 332 US 19 § 38 (1947), https://www.law.cornell.edu/supremecourt/text/332/19; "Industry and Defense Cited for Seaway by Acheson, Olds and Army-Navy Chiefs," *New York Times*, February 19, 1946; George Aiken (R-VT) remarks, *Congressional Record-Senate* 93:6, June 18, 1947, 7189; Lansdale Sasscer (D-MD) remarks, *Congressional Record-House* 93:6, June 25, 1947, 7666; Stephen Pace (D-GA) remarks, *Congressional Record-House* 93:2, March 10, 1947, 1902.

53. As Leffler points out, ideological difference with the Soviet Union, which had existed since 1917, wasn't alone sufficient to make it seem like a threat: Melvyn P. Leffler, *The Specter of Communism: The United States and the Origins of the Cold War, 1917–1953* (New York: Hill and Wang, 1994), 3–32.

54. George Fielding Eliot, *The Strength We Need: A Military Program for America Pending Peace* (New York: Viking, 1946), 9–10, 15, 14. For Niebuhrian Christian realism, see Reinhold Niebuhr, *The Children of Light and the Children of Darkness: A Vindication of Democracy and a Critique of Its Traditional Defence* (New York: C. Scribner's Sons, 1944); and Niebuhr, *The Irony of American History* (New York: Scribner, 1952). On Dulles and the founding of the UN, see Andrew Preston, *Sword of the Spirit, Shield of Faith: Religion in American War and Diplomacy* (New York: Alfred A. Knopf, 2012), 384–409.

55. Federal Council of Churches of Christ in America, Commission on a Just and Durable Peace, *Six Pillars of Peace: A Study Guide Based on "A Statement of Political Propositions"* (New York: Federal Council of Churches of Christ in America, 1943). For different contexts of "convergence," see John Lewis Gaddis, *The United States and the Origins of the Cold War, 1941–1947* (New York: Columbia University Press, 1972), 41; Warren Kimball, *The Juggler: Franklin Roosevelt as Wartime Statesman* (Princeton: Princeton University Press, 1991), 198–199; and Preston, *Sword of the Spirit*, 357–360. More broadly, see David C. Engerman, *Modernization from the Other Shore: American Intellectuals and the Romance of Russian Development* (Cambridge, MA: Harvard University Press, 2003).

56. On totalitarianism, see Thomas G. Paterson, *Meeting the Communist Threat: Truman to Reagan* (New York: Oxford University Press, 1988), 3–17; Abbott Gleason, *Totalitarianism: The Inner History of the Cold War* (New York: Oxford University Press, 1995); Benjamin L. Alpers, *Dictators, Democracy, and American Public Culture: Envisioning the Totalitarian Enemy, 1920s–1950s* (Chapel Hill: University of North Carolina Press, 2003). On monolithic, see Marc J. Selverstone, *Constructing the Monolith: The United States,*

Great Britain, and International Communism, 1945–1950 (Cambridge, MA: Harvard University Press, 2009).

57. Arnold Wolfers, Notes for Lecture 25, "National Objectives and the Pressure to Attain Them," draft syllabus for "Foundations of National Power," Yale University, Fall Term 1944–1945, Wolfers papers, box 17, folder 207, Manuscripts and Archives, Sterling Memorial Library, Yale University (hereafter Wolfers papers).

58. David A. Baldwin, *Power and International Relations: A Conceptual Approach* (Princeton: Princeton University Press, 2016), 94.

59. Leffler, *Preponderance*, 11.

60. Arnold Wolfers, "Objectives of State Policy," lecture and discussion at the National War College, October 3, 1946, Wolfers papers, box 18, folder 229.

61. George F. Kennan, *American Diplomacy, 1900–1950* (Chicago: University of Chicago Press, 1951), 95.

62. George F. Kennan, "The Sources of Soviet Conduct," *Foreign Affairs* 25 (July 1947), 582. On Kennan's policy formulations, see John Lewis Gaddis, *Strategies of Containment: A Critical Appraisal of Postwar American National Security Policy* (New York: Oxford University Press, 1982), 25–88. On his religion, see Preston, *Sword of the Spirit*, 422–427.

63. Edward Mead Earle, *Against This Torrent* (Princeton: Princeton University Press, 1941), 17; Edward Mead Earle, ed., *Makers of Modern Strategy: Military Thought from Machiavelli to Hitler* (Princeton: Princeton University Press, 1943). On Kennan and Earle, see Anders Stephanson, *Kennan and the Art of Foreign Policy* (Cambridge, MA: Harvard University Press, 1989), 332n36; and John Lewis Gaddis, *George F. Kennan: An American Life* (New York: Penguin, 2011), 233–234.

64. Chamber of Commerce of the United States, *A Program for Community Anti-Communist Action* (Washington, DC, 1948), 9. For the general trend, see Schrecker, *Many Are the Crimes*, 144.

65. Kennan to James F. Byrnes, February 22, 1946, *FRUS, 1946*, vol. 6: *Eastern Europe, the Soviet Union* (Washington, DC: GPO, 1969), 709.

66. Leffler, *Preponderance*, 97.

67. Quoted in Gaddis, *Strategies*, 39.

68. Gary Gerstle, *Liberty and Coercion: The Paradox of American Government from the Founding to the Present* (Princeton: Princeton University Press, 2015), 251–270.

69. Sherry, *Preparing*, ix; Stuart, *Creating the National Security State*, 274; Hogan, *Cross of Iron*, 23.

70. Quoted in Stuart, *Creating the National Security State*, 92.

71. See esp. Stuart, *Creating the National Security State*. But see also Alfred D. Sander, "Truman and the National Security Council, 1945–1947," *Journal of American History* 59 (September 1972): 369–388; Hogan, *Cross of Iron*, 23–68; and Amy Zegart, *Flawed by Design: The Evolution of the CIA, JCS, and NSC* (Stanford: Stanford University Press, 1999).

72. Quoted in Hogan, *Cross of Iron*, 26.

73. Harry S. Truman, "Our Armed Forces Must Be Unified," *Collier's*, August 26, 1944, 16, 64.

74. Harry S Truman, Special Message to the Congress Recommending the Establishment of a Department of National Defense, December 19, 1945, *APP*, https://www.presidency.ucsb.edu/node/229834.

75. White's most important books were Leonard Dupee White, *Introduction to the Study of Public Administration* (New York: Macmillan, 1926), which was later revised and expanded; White, *Trends in Public Administration* (New York: McGraw-Hill, 1933); White, *Government Career Service* (Chicago: University of Chicago Press, 1935); and White, "The Meaning of Principles in Public Administration," in John M. Gaus, Marshall E. Dimock, and Leonard D. White,

The Frontiers of Public Administration (Chicago: University of Chicago Press, 1936), 13–25. On War Department usage of his work, see Stuart, *Creating the National Security State*, 77–78. On White and Merriam, see Leonard D. White, ed., *The Future of Government in the United States: Essays in Honor of Charles E. Merriam* (Chicago: University of Chicago Press, 1942).

76. Stuart, *Creating the National Security State*, 78, 84. On Navy objections, see Davis, *Postwar Defense Policy*.

77. Edward Robertson (R-WY) remarks, *Congressional Record-Senate* 93:4, May 14, 1947, 5247.

78. George Aiken (R-VT) remarks, *Congressional Record-Senate* 93:2, March 3, 1947, 1600.

79. Hogan, *Cross of Iron*, 24.

80. Eliot, *Strength We Need*, 142.

81. Hogan, *Cross of Iron*; and Rebecca U. Thorpe, *The American Warfare State: The Domestic Politics of Military Spending* (Chicago: University of Chicago Press, 2014).

EPILOGUE: SECURITY NATION

1. Franklin D. Roosevelt, Annual Message to Congress, January 4, 1939, American Presidency Project (hereafter *APP*), https://www.presidency.ucsb.edu/node/209128; Eisenhower quoted in Robert R. Bowie and Richard H. Immerman, *Waging Peace: How Eisenhower Shaped an Enduring Cold War Strategy* (New York: Oxford University Oress, 1998), 45.

2. Franklin D. Roosevelt, Radio Address at a Dinner of the Foreign Policy Association, October 21, 1944, *APP*, https://www.presidency.ucsb.edu/node/210407; military officials quoted in Melvyn P. Leffler, "The American Conception of National Security and the Beginnings of the Cold War, 1945–1948," *American Historical Review* 89 (April 1984): 346–381, 350.

3. Ernest R. May, "The Nature of Foreign Policy: The Calculated versus the Axiomatic," *Daedalus* 91 (Fall 1962): 653–667.

4. Robert J. McMahon, "Credibility and World Power: Exploring the Psychological Dimension in Postwar American Diplomacy," *Diplomatic History* 15 (Fall 1991): 455–471.

5. Dwight D. Eisenhower, News Conference, April 7, 1954, *APP*, https://www.presidency.ucsb.edu/node/233655.

6. On the domino theory before Eisenhower, see Frank Ninkovich, *Modernity and Power: A History of the Domino Theory in the Twentieth Century* (Chicago: University of Chicago Press, 1994), esp. 99–132 for Roosevelt. On the argument over Dong Dang, and by extension over national security itself, see Andrew Preston, "From Dong Dang to Da Nang: The Past, Present, and Future of America's Thirty Years War for Asia," *Diplomatic History* 46 (January 2022): 1–34. For a thoughtful assessment of Eisenhower's interpretation of his own theory, see William I. Hitchcock, *The Age of Eisenhower: America and the World in the 1950s* (New York: Simon and Schuster, 2018), 105–106.

7. James A. Michener, *The Bridges at Toko-Ri* (New York: Random House, 1953), 43–44. A year later, Michener's novel was turned into a successful Hollywood movie starring William Holden and Grace Kelly. This dialogue remained in the film.

8. Dulles Statement, May 5, 1953, *Mutual Security Act of 1953: Hearings before the Committee on Foreign Relations, United States Senate* (Washington, DC: GPO, 1953), 3. On the emergence of the idea that communism was an undifferentiated mass, see Marc J. Selverstone, *Constructing the Monolith: The United States, Great Britain, and International Communism, 1945–1950* (Cambridge, MA: Harvard University Press, 2009).

9. Richard H. Immerman, *Empire for Liberty: A History of American Imperialism from Benjamin Franklin to Paul Wolfowitz* (Princeton: Princeton University Press, 2010), 175.

10. Campbell Craig and Fredrik Logevall, *America's Cold War: The Politics of Insecurity* (Cambridge, MA: Harvard University Press, 2009), provides a detailed, compelling account.

11. Harry S Truman, News Conference, May 24, 1951, *APP,* https://www.presidency.ucsb.edu/node/231112.

12. Quoted in Max Hastings, *Abyss: The Cuban Missile Crisis 1962* (London: William Collins, 2022), 85.

13. Laura McEnaney, *Civil Defense Begins at Home: Militarization Meets Everyday Life in the Fifties* (Princeton: Princeton University Press, 2000); David Monteyne, *Fallout Shelter: Designing for Civil Defense in the Cold War* (Minneapolis: University of Minnesota Press, 2011); Thomas Bishop, "'The Struggle to Sell Survival': Family Fallout Shelters and the Limits of Consumer Citizenship," *Modern American History* 2 (July 2019): 117–138.

14. Quoted in John Lewis Gaddis, *Strategies of Containment: A Critical Appraisal of Postwar American National Security Policy* (New York: Oxford University Press, 1982), 202. Rostow remained unrepentant: see W. W. Rostow, *The Diffusion of Power: An Essay in Recent History* (New York: Macmillan, 1972), 605–607; and W. W. Rostow, "Vietnam and Asia," *Diplomatic History* 20 (July 1996): 467–471. For more on Rostow, see the brilliant analysis in David Milne, *America's Rasputin: Walt Rostow and the Vietnam War* (New York: Hill and Wang, 2008).

15. Franklin D. Roosevelt, Message to Congress on Appropriations for National Defense, May 16, 1940, *APP,* https://www.presidency.ucsb.edu/node/209636.

16. Quoted in Gaddis, *Strategies of Containment,* 240–241.

17. Dean Rusk, News Conference of May 4, 1961, *Department of State Bulletin,* May 22, 1961, 763.

18. Quoted in Donald W. White, *The American Century: The Rise and Decline of the United States as a World Power* (New Haven: Yale University Press, 1996), 297.

19. For a more detailed explanation of this dynamic, see Andrew Preston, "Munich and the Unexpected Rise of American Power," in *The Munich Crisis, Politics and the People: International, Transnational and Comparative Perspectives,* ed. Julie Gottlieb, Daniel Hucker, and Richard Toye (Manchester: Manchester University Press, 2020), 133–152; Preston, "America's Global Imperium," in *The Oxford World History of Empire,* ed. Peter Fibiger Bang, C. A. Bayly, and Walter Scheidel (Oxford: Oxford University Press, 2021), 1217–1248; and Preston, "The Fearful Giant: National Insecurity and U.S. Foreign Policy," in *Ideology in U.S. Foreign Relations: New Histories,* ed. Christopher McKnight Nichols and David Milne (New York: Columbia University Press, 2022), 169–184.

20. Andrew Preston, "John F. Kennedy and Lyndon B. Johnson," in *Mental Maps in the Early Cold War Era, 1945–1968,* ed. Steven Casey and Jonathan Wright (New York: Palgrave Macmillan, 2011), 261–280.

21. Report of Southeast Asia Tour, n.d. [May 1961], *The Pentagon Papers: The Defense Department History of United States Decisionmaking on Vietnam,* Senator Gravel Edition, vol. 2 (Boston: Beacon Press, 1972), 57–58.

22. Lyndon B. Johnson, telephone conversation with McGeorge Bundy, May 27, 1964, Michael R. Beschloss, ed., *Taking Charge: The Johnson White House Tapes, 1963–1964* (New York: Simon and Schuster, 1997), 370.

23. Lyndon B. Johnson, Remarks to American and Korean Servicemen at Camp Stanley, Korea, November 1, 1966, *APP,* https://www.presidency.ucsb.edu/node/237717.

24. Quoted in Doris Kearns Goodwin, *Lyndon Johnson and the American Dream* (New York: Harper and Row, 1976), 313, 329.

25. Fredrik Logevall, *Choosing War: The Lost Chance for Peace and the Escalation of War in Vietnam* (Berkeley: University of California Press, 1999), 289, 380–381.

26. Michael Herr, *Dispatches* (New York: Alfred A. Knopf, 1977), 60. Emphasis in original.

27. Quoted in Stein Tonnesson, "Hanoi's Long Century," in *A Companion to the Vietnam War,* ed. Marilyn Young and Robert Buzzanco (Malden, MA: Blackwell, 2002), 13.

28. Lyndon B. Johnson, Remarks at Ohio University, May 7,1964, *APP,* https://www.presidency.ucsb.edu/node/238876.

29. Lyndon B. Johnson, Remarks in Peoria at the Convention of the Illinois State Federation of Labor, October 7,1964, *APP,* https://www.presidency.ucsb.edu/node/242461.

30. Lyndon B. Johnson, Remarks at Chicago Stadium, October 30,1964, *APP,* https://www.presidency.ucsb.edu/node/241725.

31. Dwight D. Eisenhower, News Conference, December 15,1954, *APP,* https://www.presidency.ucsb.edu/node/233470.

32. Quoted in H. W. Brands, "The Idea of the National Interest," *Diplomatic History* 23 (April 1999): 239–261, 249.

33. Mary L. Dudziak, *Cold War Civil Rights: Race and the Image of American Democracy* (Princeton: Princeton University Press, 2000).

34. Lyndon B. Johnson, Special Message to the Congress on Law Enforcement, March 8,1965, *APP,* https://www.presidency.ucsb.edu/node/242223.

35. Elizabeth Hinton, *From the War on Poverty to the War on Crime: The Making of Mass Incarceration in America* (Cambridge, MA: Harvard University Press, 2016), quoted on 87. On the New Deal's racial compromises, see Ira Katznelson, *When Affirmative Action Was White: An Untold History of Racial Inequality in Twentieth-Century America* (New York: W. W. Norton, 2005); and Ira Katznelson, *Fear Itself: The New Deal and the Origins of Our Time* (New York, 2013). On the New Deal's incipient carceral state, see Anthony Gregory, *New Deal Law and Order: How the War on Crime Built the Modern Liberal State* (Cambridge, MA: Harvard University Press, 2024). On the internal wars, see Elizabeth Hinton, *America on Fire: The Untold History of Police Violence and Black Rebellion Since the 1960s* (New York: Liveright, 2021); and Tom Wells, *The War Within: America's Battle over Vietnam* (Berkeley: University of California Press, 1994). For the confluence of these two conflicts, see Simon Hall, *Peace and Freedom: The Civil Rights and Antiwar Movements in the 1960s* (Philadelphia: University of Pennsylvania Press, 2004).

36. Martin Luther King, Jr., "A Time to Break Silence," Riverside Church, New York, April 4,1967, *America in the World: A History in Documents since 1898,* ed. Jeffrey A. Engel, Mark Atwood Lawrence, and Andrew Preston (Princeton: Princeton University Press, 2023), 272–274.

37. Jimmy Carter, State of the Union Address Delivered Before a Joint Session of the Congress, January 23,1980, *APP,* https://www.presidency.ucsb.edu/node/249681.

38. George W. Bush, Inaugural Address, January 20,2005, *APP,* https://www.presidency.ucsb.edu/node/214048.

39. Michael S. Sherry, *In the Shadow of War: The United States since the 1930s* (New Haven: Yale University Press, 1995), 206–207.

40. See Rebecca U. Thorpe, *The American Warfare State: The Domestic Politics of Military Spending* (Chicago: University of Chicago Press, 2014); Linda Weiss, *America Inc.? Innovation and Enterprise in the National Security State* (Ithaca, NY: Cornell University Press, 2014); Christopher J. Fuller, *See It/Shoot It: The Secret History of the CIA's Lethal Drone Program* (New Haven: Yale University Press, 2017); Michael Brenes, *For Might and Right: Cold War Defense Spending and the Remaking of American Democracy* (Amherst: University of Massachusetts Press, 2020); and Jennifer Mittelstadt and Mark R. Wilson, eds., *The Military and the Market* (Philadelphia: University of Pennsylvania Press, 2022). The military-industrial complex had deeper roots, however: see, for example, Katherine C. Epstein,

Torpedo: Inventing the Military-Industrial Complex in the United States and Great Britain (Cambridge, MA: Harvard University Press, 2014); and Mark R. Wilson, *Destructive Creation: American Business and the Winning of World War II* (Philadelphia: University of Pennsylvania Press, 2016).

41. Dwight D. Eisenhower, Farewell Radio and Television Address to the American People, January 17, 1961, *APP*, https://www.presidency.ucsb.edu/node/234856. For context, see Aaron L. Friedberg, *In the Shadow of the Garrison State: America's Anti-Statism and Its Cold War Grand Strategy* (Princeton: Princeton University Press, 2000).

42. Alain C. Enthoven and K. Wayne Smith, *How Much Is Enough? Shaping the Defense Program, 1961–1969* (New York: Harper and Row, 1971); Adam Yarmolinsky, *The Military Establishment: Its Impacts on American Society* (New York: Harper and Row, 1971), 93–94, 110–133, 237–282.

43. Arthur M. Schlesinger Jr., *The Imperial Presidency,* with a new epilogue (Boston: Houghton Mifflin, 1989), 457. Schlesinger's book was originally published in 1973 in response to the excesses of Richard Nixon. For context, see Andrew Preston, "The Emperor Is Dead—Long Live the Empire: The Enduring Legacy of the Imperial Presidency," *Modern American History* 6 (July 2023): 259–264. On prerogative in American law and war, see Clement Fatovic, *Outside the Law: Emergency and Executive Power* (Baltimore: Johns Hopkins University Press, 2009).

44. Mary L. Dudziak, *War Time: An Idea, Its History, Its Consequences* (New York: Oxford University Press, 2012).

45. For example, see Harold Hongju Koh, *The National Security Constitution: Sharing Power after the Iran-Contra Affair* (New Haven: Yale University Press, 1990); David C. Unger, *The Emergency State: America's Pursuit of Absolute Security at All Costs* (New York: Penguin, 2012); and Mariah Zeisberg, *War Powers: The Politics of Constitutional Authority* (Princeton: Princeton University Press, 2013). Even admirers dated the origins of this development to Roosevelt's policies: for example, see Schlesinger, *Imperial Presidency.*

46. For superb overviews, see Sherry, *In the Shadow of War;* Andrew J. Bacevich, *The New American Militarism: How Americans are Seduced by War,* rev. ed. (New York: Oxford University Press, 2013); David Kieran and Edwin A. Martini, eds., *At War: The Military and American Culture in the Twentieth Century and Beyond* (New Brunswick, NJ: Rutgers University Press, 2018); David Fitzgerald, *Militarization and the American Century: War, the United States and the World since 1941* (London: Bloomsbury Academic, 2021); and Mark Philip Bradley and Mary L. Dudziak, eds., *Making the Forever War: Marilyn B. Young on the Culture and Politics of American Militarism* (Amherst: University of Massachusetts Press, 2021).

47. Harold D. Lasswell, *National Security and Individual Freedom* (New York: McGraw-Hill, 1950), 126–127, 156–157, 161–162.

48. In addition to Hinton, *From the War on Poverty,* see Heather Ann Thompson, "Why Mass Incarceration Matters: Rethinking Crisis, Decline, and Transformation in Postwar American History," *Journal of American History* 97 (December 2010): 703–734; Amy Kaplan, *Our American Israel: The Story of an Entangled Alliance* (Cambridge, MA: Harvard University Press, 2018), 261–269; and Stuart Schrader, *Badges without Borders: How Global Counterinsurgency Transformed American Policing* (Berkeley: University of California Press, 2019).

49. See, respectively, Elaine Tyler May, *Fortress America: How We Embraced Fear and Abandoned Democracy* (New York: Basic Books, 2017); and Matthew D. Lassiter, *The Suburban Crisis: White America and the War on Drugs* (Princeton: Princeton University Press, 2023).

50. See, for example, David Cunningham, *There's Something Happening Here: The New Left, the Klan, and FBI Counterintelligence* (Berkeley: University of California Press, 2004); Donna T. Haverty-Stacke, *Trotskyists on Trial: Free Speech and Political Persecution Since the Age of FDR* (New York: New York University Press, 2015); Ellen D. Wu, "It's Time To Center War in U.S. Immigration History," *Modern American History* 2 (July 2019): 215–235; Joseph Darda, *Empire of Defense: Race and the Cultural Politics of Permanent War* (Chicago: University of Chicago Press, 2019); and Beverly Gage, *G-Man: J. Edgar Hoover and the Making of the American Century* (New York: Viking, 2023).

51. On the growth of secrecy, see Kathryn S. Olmsted, *Challenging the Secret Government: The Post-Watergate Investigations of the CIA and FBI* (Chapel Hill: University of North Carolina Press, 1996); Louis Fisher, *In the Name of National Security: Unchecked Presidential Power and the Reynolds Case* (Lawrence: University Press of Kansas, 2006); Matthew Connelly, *The Declassification Engine: What History Reveals About America's Top Secrets* (New York: Pantheon, 2023); and Sam Lebovic, *State of Silence: The Espionage Act and the Rise of America's Secrecy Regime* (New York: Basic Books, 2023). For the government losing track, see Matthew Connelly, "Why Do Documents Marked Secret Keep Showing Up in Strange Places?" *New York Times,* January 14, 2023. On whistleblowing, see Kaeten Mistry, "A Transnational Protest against the National Security State: Whistle-Blowing, Philip Agee, and Networks of Dissent," *Journal of American History* 106 (September 2019): 362–389; and Kaeten Mistry and Hannah Gurman, eds., *Whistleblowing Nation: The History of National Security Disclosures and the Cult of State Secrecy* (New York: Columbia University Press, 2020).

52. Quoted in Schlesinger, *Imperial Presidency,* 457.

53. On the wait-and-see, trial-and-error approach to risk, see Aaron Wildavsky, *Searching for Safety* (New Brunswick, NJ: Transaction, 1988).

54. Edward Mead Earle, "A Half-Century of American Foreign Policy: Our Stake in Europe, 1898–1948," *Political Science Quarterly* 64 (June 1949): 168–188, 183.

55. Quoted in Melvyn P. Leffler, *Safeguarding Democratic Capitalism: U.S. Foreign Policy and National Security, 1920–2015* (Princeton: Princeton University Press, 2017), 254.

56. Ron Suskind, *The One Percent Doctrine: Deep Inside America's Pursuit of Its Enemies Since 9/11* (New York: Simon and Schuster, 2006). For a trenchant analysis of this logic in the context of the Iraq War, see Corey Robin, *The Reactionary Mind: Conservatism from Edmund Burke to Sarah Palin* (New York: Oxford University Press, 2011), 189–190.

57. Douglas J. Feith, *War and Decision: Inside the Pentagon at the Dawn of the War on Terrorism* (New York: HarperCollins, 2008), 295.

58. See Melvyn P. Leffler, *Confronting Saddam Hussein: George W. Bush and the Invasion of Iraq* (New York: Oxford University Press, 2022).

59. Walter Lippmann, *U.S. Foreign Policy: Shield of the Republic* (Boston: Little, Brown, 1943), 88; Henry R. Luce, "The American Century," *Life,* February 17, 1941, 62.

60. Alvin O'Konski (R-WI) remarks, *Congressional Record-House* 93:3, April 23, 1947, 3893; "Communists in U.S. Are Put at 55,000," *Washington Post,* May 3, 1950.

61. For the first utterance, the only one before 9/11, see George W. Bush, Remarks to National Guard Personnel and Reservists in Charleston, February 14, 2001, *APP,* https://www.presidency.ucsb.edu/node/215292.

62. George W. Bush, letter to the American people, July 16, 2002, in Office of Homeland Security, *National Strategy for Homeland Security,* July 2002, https://www.dhs.gov/sites/default/files/publications/nat-strat-hls-2002.pdf. There were, of course, many precursors to the concept in the world wars and the Cold War: for one, see Matthew Dallek, *Defenseless Under the Night: The Roosevelt Years, Civil Defense, and the Origins of Homeland Security* (New York: Oxford University Press, 2016).

63. Office of Homeland Security, *National Strategy,* 1–2.

64. Amy Kaplan, "Homeland Insecurities: Transformations of Language and Space," in *September 11 in History: A Watershed Moment?* ed. Mary L. Dudziak (Durham, NC: Duke University Press, 2003), 55–69; Kaplan, *Our American Israel,* 240–241, 255–259.

65. "Homeland Security Goes Abroad," *New York Times,* December 26, 2017.

66. Megan Black, *The Global Interior: Mineral Frontiers and American Power* (Cambridge, MA: Harvard University Press, 2018), esp. 51–116.

67. Quoted in Kaplan, *Our American Israel,* 258.

68. Dusty Johnson (R-SD) quoted in "What Will the Next Farm Bill Look Like?" *Agweek,* February 18, 2023, https://www.agweek.com/news/policy/what-will-the-next-farm-bill -look-like-we-asked-some-lawmakers-who-plan-to-play-a-part-in-crafting-the-bill; "S.3089— Food Security is National Security Act of 2021," October 27, 2021, https://www.congress .gov/bill/117th-congress/senate-bill/3089.

69. Glenn S. Gerstell, "The National-Security Case for Fixing Social Media," *New Yorker,* November 13, 2020.

70. Neta C. Crawford, *The Pentagon, Climate Change, and War: Charting the Rise and Fall of U.S. Military Emissions* (Cambridge, MA: Harvard University Press, 2022).

71. Jessica Tuchman Mathews, "Redefining Security," *Foreign Affairs* 68 (Spring 1989): 162–177, 163, 169, 172, 174–175, 162, emphasis in original. The most relevant Barbara W. Tuchman books here are Tuchman, *The Guns of August* (New York: Macmillan, 1962); Tuchman, *The Proud Tower: A Portrait of the World before the War, 1890–1914* (New York: Macmillan, 1966); and Tuchman, *The March of Folly: From Troy to Vietnam* (New York: Alfred A. Knopf, 1984). Mathews was the first in a new wave of scholarship on the insecurity caused by environmental collapse. See Thomas F. Homer-Dixon, "On the Threshold: Environmental Changes as Causes of Acute Conflict," *International Security* 16 (Fall 1991): 76–116; Thomas F. Homer-Dixon, Jeffrey H. Boutwell and George W. Rathjens, "Environmental Change and Violent Conflict," *Scientific American* 268 (February 1993): 38–45; Joseph J. Romm, *Defining National Security: The Nonmilitary Aspects* (New York: Council on Foreign Relations Press, 1993); and Robert D. Kaplan, *The Ends of the Earth: From Togo to Turkmenistan, from Iran to Cambodia, a Journey to the Frontiers of Anarchy* (New York: Random House, 1995).

72. Jessica T. Mathews, "Power Shift," *Foreign Affairs* 76 (January–February 1997): 50–66, 51. For a good example of applied human security, see UNESCO, *Human Security: Approaches and Challenges* (Paris: UNESCO, 2008), https://unesdoc.unesco.org/ark: /48223/pf0000159307. For a canonical theoretical statement, see Mary Kaldor, *Human Security: Reflections on Globalization and Intervention* (Cambridge: Polity, 2007).

73. "Introduction and Overview," in *Rethinking America's Security: Beyond Cold War to New World Order,* ed. Graham Allison and Gregory F. Treverton (New York: W. W. Norton, 1992), 17. Emphasis in original.

74. Stephen E. Flynn, "America the Vulnerable," *Foreign Affairs* 81 (January–February 2002): 60–74, 68; Philip Zelikow, "The Transformation of National Security: Five Redefinitions," *National Interest* 71 (Spring 2003): 17–28.

75. Melvyn P. Leffler, "Defeating Today's Top Threats Requires Rethinking Our Idea of National Security," *Washington Post,* January 26, 2021.

76. Paul O'Neill, ed., *Securing the State and Its Citizens: National Security Councils from Around the World* (London: Bloomsbury, 2022).

77. Joel Wuthnow, "China's New 'Black Box': Problems and Prospects for the Central National Security Commission," *China Quarterly* 232 (December 2017): 886–903; Jude Blanchette, "Ideological Security as National Security," *CSIS Reports,* December 2, 2020, https://www.csis.org/analysis/ideological-security-national-security; Sheena Chestnut Greitens,

"Xi Jinping's Quest for Order: Security at Home, Influence Abroad," *Foreign Affairs,* October 3, 2022; Sheena Chestnut Greitens, "Xi's Security Obsession," *Foreign Affairs,* July 28, 2023. China's Ministry of State Security quoted in "No Laughing Matter," *The Economist,* January 13, 2024, 55. It's possible, though, that Chinese officials have deliberately chosen to mistranslate the phrase "state security" to "national security" to have it resonate with foreign observers: Steve Tsang and Olivia Cheung, *The Political Thought of Xi Jinping* (Oxford: Oxford University Press, 2024), 34, 218n67.

78. Susan B. Glasser, "What Does National Security Even Mean Anymore, After January 6th and the Pandemic?" *New Yorker,* March 4, 2021.

79. Michael McCaul (R-TX) quoted in House Foreign Affairs Committee press release, January 1, 2023, https://foreignaffairs.house.gov/press-release/mccaul-applauds-creation-of -house-select-committee-on-china/; "China Select Committee Hearing Highlights Partisan Divide on Beijing-Countering Strategy," *Politico,* March 1, 2023, https://www.politico.com /news/2023/03/01/china-select-committee-hearing-00084926.

80. "U.S. Pulling Troops from Northern Syria Posts," *CBS News,* October 7, 2019, https://www.cbsnews.com/news/syria-withdrawal-lindsey-graham-blasts-us-withdrawing -troops-northern-syria-posts-2019-10-07/.

81. "Taiwan is Readying Citizens for a Chinese Invasion," *Washington Post,* August 3, 2024, https://www.washingtonpost.com/world/2024/08/03/taiwan-china-war-invasion-mili tary-preparedness/.

82. Lisa Mascaro, Seung Min Kim, and Aamer Madhani, "Biden Brings Congressional Leaders to White House at Pivotal Time for Ukraine Aid and US Border Deal," Associated Press, January 18, 2024, https://apnews.com/article/biden-speaker-johnson-border-security -ukraine-government-shutdown-fa505e84f1ffd1767eb01a250a161393.

83. "The DeSantis Foreign Policy," *New York Times,* March 22, 2023.

84. "Transcript of J. D. Vance's Convention Speech," *New York Times,* July 18, 2024, https://www.nytimes.com/2024/07/17/us/politics/read-the-transcript-of-jd-vances -convention-speech.html

85. "The Biden Administration's International Economic Agenda: A Conversation with National Security Advisor Jake Sullivan," Brookings Institution, April 27, 2023, https://www .brookings.edu/wp-content/uploads/2023/04/es_20230427_sullivan_intl_economic_agenda _transcript.pdf. See also "Remarks by National Security Advisor Jake Sullivan on the Biden-Harris Administration's National Security Strategy," October 12, 2022, https://www.whitehouse .gov/briefing-room/speeches-remarks/2022/10/13/remarks-by-national-security-advisor-jake -sullivan-on-the-biden-harris-administrations-national-security-strategy/; and Jake Sullivan, "The Sources of American Power: A Foreign Policy for a Changed World," *Foreign Affairs* 102 (November/December 2023), 8–29.

86. Joseph R. Biden, NSM-2, Memorandum on Renewing the National Security Council System, February 4, 2021, *APP,* https://www.presidency.ucsb.edu/node/347949; Biden, NSM-3, Memorandum on Revitalizing America's Foreign Policy and National Security Workforce, Institutions, and Partnerships, February 4, 2021, *APP,* https://www.presidency.ucsb .edu/node/347942.

87. Joseph R. Biden, Message to the Congress on Continuation of the National Emergency with Respect to Ukraine, March 2, 2022, *APP,* https://www.presidency.ucsb.edu/node /354713.

88. Joseph R. Biden, Remarks in a Meeting with Senior Military Leaders, October 26, 2022, *APP,* https://www.presidency.ucsb.edu/node/358551; National Security Strategy, October 2022, https://nssarchive.us/wp-content/uploads/2022/10/Biden-Harris-Administra tions-National-Security-Strategy-10.2022.pdf. See also National Intelligence Estimate NIC-NIE-2021-10030-A, "Climate Change and International Responses Increasing Challenges to US

National Security Through 2040," October 2021, https://www.dni.gov/files/ODNI/doc uments/assessments/NIE_Climate_Change_and_National_Security.pdf; Department of Defense, Report to the National Security Council, "Climate Risk Analysis," October 2021, in Engel, Lawrence, and Preston, *America in the World,* 430–432.

89. Robert McNamara, Address to the American Society of Newspaper Editors, Montreal, March 18,1966, Robert S. McNamara, *The Essence of Security: Reflections in Office* (New York: Harper and Row, 1968), 142.

90. Robert S. McNamara, *In Retrospect: The Tragedy and Lessons of Vietnam* (New York: Times Books, 1995), xvi.

ACKNOWLEDGMENTS

Writing this book proved to be a greater challenge than I first anticipated, and so it took a longer time than planned. My debts are correspondingly numerous.

Brooke Blower, Jeff Engel, Kate Epstein, Daniel Immerwahr, Ryan Irwin, Emma Mackinnon, and Daniel Sargent read the entire manuscript and offered encouragement, advice, and sometimes unsparing but always constructive criticism. For their detailed comments on drafts of individual chapters, I'm grateful to Jeremy Adelman, Angus Burgin, Brian DeLay, Aaron Friedberg, Bev Gage, Tony Hopkins, and Joel Isaac.

I benefited from the hospitality of several institutions that generously invited me to speak or that held workshops about my book-in-progress, and I'm grateful for all the comments I received. Pre-circulated drafts of Chapter 1 received feedback from audiences at Berkeley, Cornell, and Princeton; Chapter 3 from colleagues and students at Yale; and Chapter 4 from audiences at Manchester and Sciences Po. For their interest in and comments about the project overall, I'd also like to thank audiences at Boston University, the Engelsberg Seminar in Sweden, the Graduate Institute of International and Development Studies in Geneva, King's College London, the London School of Economics, Oxford University (All Souls College, Jesus College, and Pembroke College), Peking University, Southern Methodist University, Washington State University, and the universities of Bristol, Oslo, Sheffield, Texas at Austin, and Toronto, as well as colleagues at various annual meetings of the American Historical Association, the Organization of American Historians, and especially my home away from home, the Society for Historians of American Foreign Relations. My real home for over twenty years was Cambridge University, where colleagues and students have heard me talk about this book on many occasions, not least at the venerable American History Seminar (which heard early versions of Chapters 1 and 4 as well as an overview of the entire project) and Clare College.

I have been extremely fortunate to discuss this book with many friends over many years. For advice, for an invitation to speak, for insightful questions and comments during a session, or for just humoring me as I try out new ideas and knowing exactly when to spur me on and when to rein me in, I thank Alvita Akiboh, Andrew Arsan, Tony Badger, Beth Bailey, Duncan Bell, Lauren Benton, Megan Black, Tim Borstelmann, Bob Brigham, Paul Chamberlin, Kuan-jen Chen, Chris Clark, Patricia Clavin, Greg Daddis, Gareth Davies, Mario Del Pero, Darren Dochuk, Saul Dubow, Susan Ferber, Zach Fredman, Gary Gerstle, Anthony Gregory, Nancy Hewitt, Fabian Hilfrich, Elizabeth Hinton, Will Hitchcock, David Hollinger, Richard Immerman, Will Inboden, Lizzie Ingleson, Julia Irwin, Margaret Jacobs, Bill Janeway, Matthew Jones, Ira Katznelson, Kevin Kruse, Barak Kushner, Charlie Laderman, Dan Larsen, Steven Lawson, Elisabeth Leake, Sam Lebovic, Erika Lee, Mel Leffler, Fred Logevall, Peter Mandler, David Milne, Kaeten Mistry, Hang Nguyen, Chris Nichols, Sarah Pearsall, Mark Peterson, Sarah Phillips, David Reynolds, Doug Rossinow, Andy Rotter, Dom Sandbrook, Jayita Sarkar, Bruce Schulman, Sarah Snyder, Matt Sutton, Heather Thompson, Helen Thompson, Hans van de Ven, Penny Von Eschen, and Arne Westad.

At Harvard University Press, I first began working with Kathleen McDermott two decades ago. As she did then, when I was starting out, she showed faith in this book from the very beginning—and then proved just how deep that faith was as I tested it with more words, and more time, than she'd bargained for. My other editor at Harvard, Joseph Pomp, gave what I thought was a finished manuscript a much-needed final workout, spotting hidden traps and helping me safely spring them all. Julia Kirby then copyedited the manuscript expertly and efficiently. But none of this would've happened without my agent, Andrew Wylie, first doing what he does best.

A lot happened while I wrote this book, including the loss of my beloved younger brother Kevin, who is much missed. Getting through it all was possible thanks to the love and support I have at home. Fran, Rosie, Lizzie, Olive: couldn't have done it without you.

This book is dedicated to John A. Thompson, who introduced me to the national security problematic when I first came to Cambridge to be his PhD student more than a quarter-century ago. John taught me many things, but the most important was to be skeptical of received wisdom and canonical, timeless, seemingly objective terms. He was a pioneer in first identifying, and then solving, the national security puzzle, and it's fair to say I wouldn't have even had the idea to write this book had it not been for him. He and Dorothy aren't just intellectual role models; they're treasured friends. John doesn't agree with everything in this book—I know for certain, because he's told me many times over pints and meals at a Red Bull Seminar in Newnham—but it's just as much a certainty that whatever merits it has are due in no small measure to him.

INDEX